NO SHINING ARMOR

MODERN
WAR
STUDIES

Theodore A. Wilson, *General Editor*

Raymond A. Callahan

J. Garry Clifford

Jacob W. Kipp

Jay Luvaas

Allan R. Millett

Series Editors

NO SHINING ARMOR

THE

MARINES

AT WAR IN

VIETNAM

AN ORAL HISTORY

OTTO J. LEHRACK

University Press of Kansas

Published by the University Press of Kansas (Lawrence, Kansas 66049), which was organized by the Kansas Board of Regents and is operated and funded by Emporia State University, Fort Hays State University, Kansas State University, Pittsburg State University, the University of Kansas, and Wichita State University

The paper used in this publication meets the minimum requirements of the American National Standard for Permanence of Paper for Printed Library Materials z39.48-1984.

Library of Congress Cataloging-in-Publication Data

No shining armor : the Marines at war in Vietnam: an oral history / [edited by] Otto J. Lehrack
  p. cm. — (Modern war studies)
  Includes bibliographical references and index.
  ISBN 0-7006-0533-9 (alk. paper). —
  ISBN 0-7006-0534-7 (pbk. : alk. paper)
  1. Vietnamese Conflict, 1961–1975—Regimental histories—United States.
  2. United States Marine Corps. Division, 3rd. Battalion, 3rd—History. I. Lehrack, Otto J. II. Series.
DS558.4.N6 1992
959.704'3373—dc20 91-39414

Printed in the United States of America
10 9 8 7 6 5

FOR KAREN—

wife, lover, editor, and best friend

GRUNTS

Beasts of burden sloppily loaded
with personal belongings and tools
of modern mayhem, walk, head down,
bodies scarred and eroded
by overwork, lack of sleep and
exposure to nature's cruel edges.
Banded together by cramps,
cuts, sores, sweat, and the everpresent threat
of death so pervasive that it
can only be coped with by deriding it.
No shining armor a flak vest.
No bright colors or plumes, but leaf patterns.
No rest, no wine, no end
to gripping the ground and
waiting for the round.

> April 1969
> *Major General Richard C. Schulze, USMC,*
> *who commanded the 3d Battalion, 3d*
> *Marines, in Vietnam in 1969*

CONTENTS

• • • • • • • • • • • • • •

PART ONE

Countering the Viet Cong: War against Guerrillas, 1965–1966

MAPS AND ILLUSTRATIONS

· · · · · · · · · · · ·

PREFACE

· · · · · · · · · · · · · · · ·

At the time I decided to do this book, I was collecting material for another work. The collection effort brought me in contact with T. J. Kelly, a former Marine with whom I had served in Vietnam. Kelly had begun searching for some of his former comrades from Vietnam and had found several hundred men who had been there with the 3d Battalion, 3d Marines, our battalion. He was kind enough to share his list with me and to keep me updated on new additions.

After talking to just a few of these men I realized that no one had adequately told what it was like to be a grunt in Vietnam. At this point I put my original project aside and began a five-year task of contacting the Marines and sailors of the 3d Battalion, 3d Marines (3/3),* and asking them to record their impressions of the war.

Some welcomed the opportunity. For others, the experiences of Vietnam, and the years after, were so traumatic that even twenty years later, it was still

---

*Marine infantry and artillery battalions are most commonly designated by a numeral representing the battalion number, a slash, and a numeral representing the regiment; thus, the 3d Battalion, 3d Marines, is usually written 3/3 and pronounced "three three."

too emotional an issue for them to talk about. Some wept as they recounted their tales.

This work is a product of their collective memories. It is an oral history. The vast majority of the material herein originated in oral tapes that were recorded specifically at my request for this project between 1986 and 1990, in most cases more than twenty years after these men had left the war. A few were recorded during the war and survived until the present. Most were done by individuals, but some were recorded in pairs or small groups. The taped material is supplemented in a very few cases with thoughts from letters and telephone calls. As with any history project, the raw material greatly exceeded what remains in the final product. The nearly three thousand pages of data I received from individual contributors were heavily edited and distilled. My objective in this process has always been to present a coherent and accurate account of what the infantry experience was really like in the eyes of the men who lived it. If, through the editing process, I strayed from that goal or the intentions of any participant, it was not purposeful, but I accept full responsibility.

To provide a framework for the personal material, I used 3/3's official Command Chronologies, which were declassified in 1988. Finally, I supplemented this work with information provided by other scholars. I tried to provide additional information only in those instances where it was necessary for an understanding of what was happening at the small-unit level.

These men chose me, rather than the other way around. I contacted every member of the battalion that I could find during these five years and asked them to participate. Every one who agreed to do so is here. The more articulate and introspective are obviously overrepresented in terms of volume. But, again, my intent was to help them all relay their most important thoughts about the war to the world. All ranks are represented, and all the larger minority groups.

Although the words on these pages came from the members of a single Marine infantry battalion, they are representative of the experiences of all those who served in infantry battalions in Vietnam. I chose this battalion for the best of reasons. It was the unit in which I served, first as S-4 (logistics officer) and later as the commanding officer of India Company, in my first Vietnam tour in 1967–68. Therefore, some of the men of 3/3 had known me in Vietnam, others knew of me, and the rest learned that I had served in combat with their battalion. This led them to trust me to organize their experiences in such a way that outsiders might begin to understand.

This reason aside, the 3d Battalion, 3d Marines, is an ideal representative of the infantry experience of the Vietnam War. Neither the first battalion to land nor the last to leave, it fought in every section of I Corps in its more than four years of service there. Landing on the beaches of Chu Lai in 1965, it provided security for the construction of the airstrip. It lost its innocence in the first big operation of the war, STARLITE, where one of its members, Robert O'Malley, became the first Marine to be awarded the Medal of Honor in Vietnam.

The 3d Battalion, 3d Marines, went on to Hill 55, west of Danang, where its commander, Lieutenant Colonel Joseph Muir, was the first battalion commanding officer (CO) that the Corps lost in Vietnam. It participated in the pacification effort by building churches and schools and providing medical care to Vietnamese civilians. In Danang in 1966 the battalion witnessed the Buddhist protests and the divisive splits in the South Vietnamese Army.

Moving later that year to Northern I Corps, it contested control of the Demilitarized Zone with North Vietnamese regulars, a sophisticated, well-trained foe often supported by heavy artillery. Finally, in late 1969, as part of the Vietnamization of the war under President Nixon, it was withdrawn.

I have tried to present the stories of these men in such a way as to mirror their experiences, to interfere as little as possible with their accounts, and to attempt to give the reader a sense of how it felt to serve with the Corps in Vietnam. If the events sometimes seem confusing to the reader, they were often equally mystifying to the men of the 3d Battalion, 3d Marines, as they were experiencing them.

With the exception of the Marines who landed in 1965, most who went to Vietnam went singly, in replacement groups, and were assigned to a unit upon arrival. This constant flow of BNGs (brand new guys) reached Vietnam and experienced a number of unexpected shocks. The new arrivals were lonely, and their loneliness was intensified by what they felt was cold treatment from the old salts. After a while they began to realize that the veterans had formed incredibly close bonds with other Marines who had been proven and accepted as members of the unit, only to have them shattered by combat loss or rotation. For some of these men the avoidance of friendships with the newcomers was a defense mechanism, a sort of emotional scar tissue built up to avoid further trauma. For others, it was a "wait and see" attitude that was usually overcome by shared hardship and danger. When the newcomers eventually won acceptance and became bonded with their fellow Marines, they "developed relationships where you would do anything to protect the next guy; whether you knew him or not; whether you knew his name; whether he was a southerner or northerner, or a black or a white . . . you protected each other" (PFC Vito Lavacca).

Their ranks thinned by the war, Marines finished their thirteen months, said good-bye to their comrades, and rotated home to a world filled with indifference and hostility.

In other wars, Marines returned to a grateful country. In World War II, for example, it was almost universally agreed that the enemy they fought was evil and needed to be defeated. The United States and its allies won that war, and its fighting men came home to find the values they had fought for not only preserved but enhanced by their sacrifices. There was tangible gain for the country in return for their losses.

Marines who served in Vietnam made sacrifices and endured hardships as great as any in our nation's history. Yet they returned alone to a population that seemed not to care about them. For twenty years many of them felt cast out of the American mainstream because of their participation in the war.

I was drawn to the experiences of these men by my personal observation of their exemplary human qualities and sacrifices, both during and after Vietnam. Their stories, singly and in combination, are a powerful account of what it was like to serve there. In order to preserve this power, I have for the most part elected to let them speak for themselves.

A book of this type is possible only through the contributions of the men who provided the material. For many it was a difficult task to put aside their apprehensions and talk about an event that so shaped their lives. I will always be grateful for the courage that they demonstrated in dredging up old memories and recording them. Two of the participants deserve special mention. T. J. Kelly's dedication in collecting names and addresses of our old comrades in arms was invaluable. So was John Mick's effort in putting together a reunion in Florida in 1988.

In addition to the participants, many others made this book possible. An interview with my former boss, Lieutenant General Charles G. Cooper, USMC (Retired), provided inspiration for the direction of this project. Colonel John K. Hyatt, Jr., USMC (Retired), spent a week of his life copying official records of the war for my use. The entire project might have failed had it not been for encouragement early on from Benis Frank, then the oral historian of the Marine Corps Historical Center, and Henry Shaw, at that time the chief historian. Helpful, too, was Ed Nicholls, who shared some valuable information on Operation STARLITE with me. Others who were supportive in spirit although their words did not make it onto these pages are Carlton Armstrong, Peter Burgoon, and Joe Thompson. Numerous people read early editions of the manuscript and provided much valuable advice on its final form. They include Dr. Keith Fleming, Dr. Alexander Cochran, Major General Edward J. Megarr, USMC (Retired), my close friend Jon Marshall, Lieutenant Colonel John Rybczyk,

USAF (Retired), my editor, Michael Briggs, and my friend and fellow historian Massey Goto.

Special thanks to Mrs. Sally Schulze for use of the poem "Grunts," which was written by her late husband Richard C. Schulze at the time he commanded the unit described here.

Finally, and most importantly, I would like to acknowledge the sacrifice of those whose names adorn the Vietnam Memorial in Washington. Many of those names also honor this book.

DRAMATIS PERSONAE

. . . .

In Order of First Appearance

Ranks throughout the book are those held by the individual at the time.

During the Vietnam War, Marine infantry battalions had four rifle companies. Those in 3d Battalion were officially designated Companies I, K, L, and M, but they were almost always referred to as India, Kilo, Lima, and Mike companies.

Corporal Vito J. Lavacca, Squad Leader, Mike Company

Lieutenant Commander (Chaplain's Corps) Robert W. Bedingfield, Battalion Chaplain

PFC William H. Brocksieker, Rifleman, Mike Company

Sergeant David L. Horne, Squad Leader, India Company

Gunnery Sergeant Eugene Breeze, Company Gunnery Sergeant, India Company

Sergeant Richard G. Kidwell, Platoon Guide, Lima Company

Captain David A. Ramsey, Battalion Assistant Operations Officer

Sergeant Patrick Finton, Engineer Attachment

PFC Gary W. Hammett, Rifleman, India Company

PFC H. Tyrone Belanger, Rifleman, Mike Company

PFC Howard G. Miller, Machine Gunner, India Company

PFC Charles "Chuck" Fink, Rifleman, India Company

First Sergeant Arthur Petty, First Sergeant, India Company

Corporal Kenneth G. Ransbottom, Fire Team Leader, Mike Company

Lieutenant (Chaplain's Corps) "Father Guy" I. McPartland, Battalion
    Chaplain

Sergeant James Austin, Flamethrower Squad Leader, H and S Company

PFC Rod W. Consalvo, Rifleman, India Company

PFC Thomas C. Mosher, Rifleman, India Company

Lance Corporal John W. Norman, Jr., Rifleman, Kilo Company

Captain John W. Ripley, Commanding Officer, Lima Company

Lieutenant Daniel F. Ryan, Platoon Commander, India Company

Lieutenant William R. Masciangelo, Platoon Commander, India Company

Corporal Joseph J. Davis, Fire Team Leader, Lima Company

Lieutenant Lee Ashburn, Platoon Commander, Lima Company

PFC James P. Finn, Mortarman, H and S Company

Lance Corporal Stanley E. Kerlin, Rifleman, Lima Company

Captain Roger Zensen, Battalion Operations Officer

Captain Raymond F. Findlay, Mike Company Commander

Major Michael H. Harrington, Battalion Executive Officer

Lieutenant Jack Wright, Platoon Commander, Lima Company

PFC Thomas F. Ryan, Rifleman, India Company

Lance Corporal Gary D. Conner, Artillery Forward Observer, Kilo Company

Captain Otto J. Lehrack, Battalion Logistics Officer

PFC John A. Mick, Rifleman, Mike Company

PFC Richard V. Sherwood, Rifleman, Lima Company

PFC Kevin T. Sweeney, Rifleman, Mike Company

PFC Michael Velasquez, Rifleman, Lima Company

Lieutenant Robert Montgomery, Artillery Forward Observer, Kilo Company

PFC Joe D. "Reb" Turner, Rifleman, Mike Company

PFC James K. Yost, Rifleman, India Company

PFC Robert L. "Lex" Payne, Rifleman, Mike Company

PFC Craig Pyles, Machine Gunner, India Company

Lieutenant William D. Kenerly, Platoon Commander, Mike Company

PFC Thomas J. "T. J." Kelly, Radio Operator, Tactical Air Control Party

Gunnery Sergeant Jimmie C. Clark, Company Gunnery Sergeant, Kilo
    Company

PFC William W. Clough, Jr., Mortar Forward Observer, H and S Company

Hospital Corpsman 3d Class Alan B. "Doc" Sams, Kilo Company

Corporal Carl E. "Tank" Elliott, Squad Leader, Mike Company

PFC Edwin Seretti, Rifleman, Kilo Company

PFC Thomas Evanoff, Rifleman, Mike Company

Sergeant Major Neal D. King, Battalion Sergeant Major

PFC Bobby Jefferson, Rifleman, Mike Company

PFC William Frantz, Rifleman, Lima Company

Corporal William W. Sessions, 3.5-in Rocketman, Mike Company

PFC Anthony Stanisci, Rifleman, Lima Company

PFC Jack W. "Pops" Wandell, Rifleman, Mike Company

PFC Kenneth K. George, Rifleman, Mike Company

PFC James D. Howe, Rifleman, Mike Company

PFC Peter A. Tramonte, Rifleman, Mike Company

Lance Corporal Vincent C. Morrison, Alpha Battery, 1/12, Artillery Support

Hospital Corpsman 3d Class Douglas D. "Doc" Stone, India Company

Hospital Corpsman 2d Class Jeffrey B. "Doc" Bussiere, Mike Company

PFC Ray K. Wilmer, Rifleman, Lima Company

Captain Paul B. Goodwin, Commanding Officer, Kilo Company

Lieutenant Richmond D. O'Neill, Platoon Commander, Kilo Company

Lieutenant Colonel Robert C. Needham, Battalion Commander

Hospital Corpsman 3d Class John A. "Doc" Combs, Alpha Battery, 1/12, Artillery Support

PFC James W. "Birdman" Byrd III, Rifleman, Kilo Company

PROLOGUE

· · · · · · · · · · · · · · · ·

Vietnam Homecoming

Corporal Vito J. Lavacca

I managed to survive Vietnam and got back to New York. . . . The change
was just shocking. It was totally devastating. Clothes had changed. People's attitudes had changed. Close friends that you had that had been clean-cut, athletic
types when you last saw them now had hair down to their shoulders. They were
wearin' big medallions around their necks. And . . . beards. Christ . . . earrings.
And bell-bottomed pants and high heel boots. And . . . givin' peace signs.

Vietnam wasn't a war where all the veterans came home together. We kind of
straggled home by ourselves and you had no one to share your experiences with.
You couldn't share them with your family and friends, because, first of all, they
didn't understand. And you were still trying to figure them out. They all looked
so strange. You were tryin' to figure out what the hell happened to everybody.

It was very, very . . . depressing. You didn't recognize anything. You didn't
recognize the sense of values. . . . And the things you were anticipating that you
were gonna come home to just weren't there anymore. And I think I, like a lot

of other guys, just kind of withdrew. Maybe we make more of an issue of it than it actually is . . . but everybody's got a story to tell.

Lieutenant Commander (Chaplain's Corps) Robert W. Bedingfield

After I left Vietnam . . . we landed in California. I was in a Marine uniform. I had reservations for Durham, North Carolina, where my family was. In order to get to Durham, I had to fly to O'Hare Airport in Chicago. Put down in O'Hare and sat on a bench waiting for the flight to go. And while I sat on the bench, reading a magazine, looking around, being just amazed to be back in the world I'd left just twelve months before, a man came by, a very well-dressed man. And as I recall, he looked at me just once and spat on me. And he kept going.

I was really too shocked to do anything. There is no way I could respond to him. No way that I would have if I could have. And I thought, and have thought ever since . . . what a different world it was for us out there.

What a different world . . .

• • • • • • • • • • • • • •

PART ONE

COUNTERING THE VIET CONG

WAR AGAINST GUERRILLAS,

1965–1966

1

· · · · · · · · · · · · · · · · ·

THE BEGINNING:
CAMP PENDLETON, CALIFORNIA

Before the Vietnam War began, infantry Marines generally spent one year out of each five or six on an unaccompanied tour in Okinawa. They would join an infantry battalion at Camp Pendleton, California, and "lock-on" to a period of about fifteen months. The first two months of this time were spent in California, forming the unit, preparing equipment, enduring readiness and tactical inspections, and training intensively as a team. The idea was that a battalion would become a cohesive, well-trained unit that would be ready to deploy and fight anywhere in the Far East, if the need arose, from its home base on Okinawa.

Upon completion of the lock-on period, the Marines said good-bye to their families and embarked for the western Pacific. The battalions left California as members of a 1st Marine Division regiment, the 1st, 5th, or 7th Marines. When they arrived in Okinawa, they were redesignated to become part of either the 3d or 9th Marines, which were regiments of the 3d Marine Division.

By 1964, more than a decade had passed since the guns of the Korean War had been 5 silenced. Although the Marines in Okinawa were a "Force in Readiness," designed to police the western Pacific, recent history seemed to indicate that they would spend their tours at peace. Few among them were seriously worried by the Johnson administration's increasing involvement in Vietnam. They knew that Marines had gone ashore in Lebanon in 1958 and had stood by to land in Laos and Cuba in 1962. Almost to a man, they expected to serve their thirteen months overseas without incident and then return to California where discharge, or orders to a new duty station, awaited them. Those whose accounts open this chronicle shared that assumption. The 3d Battalion, 3d Marines, was one of the last units to lock-on, train, and rotate under the old transplacement system.

OCTOBER 1964

PFC William H. Brocksieker

I was in Mike Company, 3d Battalion, 3d Marines. Four of us from Hancock County in Ohio . . . we joined the Marine Corps at the same time. We all ended up going through boot camp together at Parris Island, South Carolina. We were all together through ITR [Infantry Training Regiment] right after boot camp. The instructors there for the first time informed us that we'd probably end up in Vietnam. I guess I was ready to go. I sure was glad I was a Marine. The only regret I ever had was getting out.

Sergeant David L. Horne

There were eight sergeants who all left Quantico, Virginia, together, went out to the West Coast, and joined the 2d Battalion, 1st Marines, which eventually was going to be the 3d Battalion, 3d Marines.

Gunnery Sergeant* Eugene Breeze

There were something like twenty-one former staff NCO [noncommissioned officer] drill instructors who brought their leadership into the battalion. [Drill instructors are chosen from the best Marines the Corps has to offer. Having this concentration of them in any unit is remarkable.]

Sergeant Dave Horne

Of those eight sergeants that left Quantico, six of them were killed during their first tour. One died from wounds later on and then I stepped on a land

---

*A gunnery sergeant is both a rank and a position—that of the operations NCO of a rifle company.

Corporal Bill Brocksieker, who may have been the only Marine to serve two tours with 3/3 in Vietnam, is shown here on his second tour. (Courtesy Bill Brocksieker)

mine. So, it really took a toll of our group. It was . . . We did what we had to do. I don't feel awfully bad about it.

Gunnery Sergeant Gene Breeze

I think that [the experience of these NCOs] added significantly to the small unit leadership. We had a working relation with the newly commissioned lieu-tenants, the ones right out of OCS [Officer Candidate School]. They handled the tactics, we handled the troops and supplies and so forth, and we tried to stay out of each other's hair.

Sergeant Dave Horne

Vietnam had not started back in '64 when I joined them in October. So we had a unique experience, we NCOs. We got to know families, the girlfriends . . . . It was like that old movie *Battle Cry*, so to speak. We got to know the peacetime Marine and his history.

Sergeant Richard G. Kidwell

Definitely, because every fire team leader knew all his men. They knew the family problems, the weaknesses, the strongnesses.

Sergeant Dave Horne

And then we all went to combat together.

Sergeant Richard Kidwell

I think we were one of the last battalions to do this.

PFC Bill Brocksieker

We all trained together there in California and loved it. We went down to San Diego Bay and got on several different ships and went out for the weekend and we had wet-net training. We'd go climb down the nets and get in landing craft and steam around a little bit and then come back and climb back up on the ship.

Sergeant Dave Horne

We had this one fellow . . . "the Greek." He was later killed. His name was Tchakarides and he was one of these fellows that you could let fall in a mud hole and he'd come out looking like he just came out of the laundry. He was immaculate. He looked like Clark Gable. He always had a handlebar mustache. Although we wasn't supposed to have them, they let him get away with it.

The Greek was . . . from the old school. He didn't have any qualms about slapping people around if he thought it came to that. One day . . . he was marching the company and just as he went by the Quonset huts there, he gave the company a 'column left' and this one fellow did a brig step right in front of the company commander. And the old Greek, he just yelled, "Maaark tiiime," and he reached out and he started choking this guy. Well, the company commander had to go run and hide so he wouldn't see this. But this was the Greek's way of doing things and nobody seemed to question him . . . . And he was quite a controversial character, but a fine, fine Marine.

Gunnery Sergeant Gene Breeze

Late one afternoon a staff sergeant friend of mine said, "I want you to look across the parade deck. That young fellow over there is the only lance corporal in the battalion at this time who is a squad leader." Well, everybody else had shoved off for liberty and this young Marine had his squad out behind the barracks for a rifle inspection, which spoke highly of him.

It wasn't too many weeks later that there was a promotion board and the battalion executive officer headed up the board. There was a couple of lieutenants, a couple of company gunnies. I sat on that board and we were calling these young men in for promotion to corporal. We were working on the five-point system.

We'd ask them five or six or ten questions and we'd give them anywhere from three, three-and-a-half, four-and-a-half points, whatever, with a max of five.

One particular young man came in, a sharp-looking young Marine. I thought he looked familiar. It turned out that he was the one that had been inspecting his squad that afternoon. Anyway, we asked him several questions. He executed a smart about-face and left the area. We voted and I gave him something like a 4.8 out of a possible 5. One of the lieutenants gave him a 2.2. When I asked why he said, "I just don't like his looks." Well, Gunny Sergeant Bob Cotton and I both said almost in unison, "If looks had anything to do with it, we'd still both be privates."

Anyhow, the young man did get promoted. I thought it was very ironic that he received the first Medal of Honor in Vietnam. It was Corporal [Robert E.] O'Malley [see Appendix B].

2

. . . .

TO OKINAWA

PFC Bill Brocksieker

On January the 6th, 1965, we all went down to San Diego and we got on the USNS *Sultan*, a MSTS ship—Military Sea Transport Service or whatever. The bow of the ship had about 1,000 dependents on it and we weren't allowed to be up there. We were back in the stern of the ship.

It was like an ocean liner, but we had berths and everything. We had about five mess halls there and we played liar's poker and slept up on the deck and watched the flying fish. When we'd get bored, we'd go back to the fantail of the ship and watch the sailors throw out the garbage and the egg trays and the coffee grinds, or help them do it, even, just to pass the time of day.

We steamed for about three days and we got to Pearl Harbor and we got a day and a night liberty. We went to Hotel Street and Pearl Harbor and went out and seen the *Arizona* and the shopping center in Waikiki. We had us a good time. The next day we got back on the ship to sail for Okinawa.

We stopped eight or nine days later in Yokohama, Japan, and we got a day and part of the night liberty there. We had to change our money into yen and went down to what they called Chinatown. I suppose every port has a Chinatown. You know what usually goes on there. They gave us like $50 at one table and at the next table we had to change it into yen. Boy, I had a big wad in my pocket. You got a lot of yen for the dollar at that time. I went out to a club and I ordered a drink and, man, they wanted about half my wad right there. The prices were so expensive. The girls, they drank the tea in a whiskey glass that looked like whiskey and was tea, we found out later.

Anyway, we got back on the *Sultan* and went on down to Okinawa. We landed at Naha and from Naha we trucked on up to Camp Schwab.

Sergeant Dave Horne

We spent, oh . . . from January until April . . . in Okinawa. It was pack up and unpack. Pack up and unpack. Nobody seemed to know when the actual gun was going to be fired, and this loading of ships was going on. There was a lot of unsureness where we were going to be from one day to the next.

The uncertainty among Marines in Okinawa reflected events in Vietnam. By late 1964 the government controlled less than half of the country as the Communist forces continued to gain strength. Hanoi began upgrading the weaponry of some Viet Cong (VC) units, outfitting a few of them, for example, with the AK47, a weapon that was a vast improvement over the surplus and obsolescent weapons they had used earlier. Also at this time, the first VC unit of division size, the *9th Viet Cong Division*, was formed and began operating north of Saigon. More ominous still, the first regular North Vietnamese Army (NVA) regiment left its home base for South Vietnam in September. Two others followed by year's end.

PFC Bill Brocksieker

We stayed on Okinawa . . . had training at NTA [Northern Training Area] and classes, mock Vietnamese towns that we had to go to, and jungle training. The idea was that we would stay on Okinawa and then we would come back to the States in thirteen months. They would send us to cold-weather training at Camp Fuji in Japan and they'd send some of us to Hong Kong and some of us would go down to the Philippines, train around there. But our base of operations would be out of Camp Schwab, Okinawa.

Gunnery Sergeant Gene Breeze

On Okinawa, Staff Sergeant Melton and I, we used to go down to the Army Topper Club every Tuesday night. It was Country and Western Night and being southern boys and liking country and western music, we could have a night for about $4. It was an 80-cent cab ride and it cost you $1.25 for a steak and I think a mixed drink was 20 cents. Anyhow, we had to leave all that behind when we went to Vietnam.

Sergeant Dave Horne

We had a fellow, old Charlie . . . When we were stationed there in Okinawa, he was the next company up from me, just two or three doors. And I would get up in the morning and I would go up and check on those folks.

Charlie had false teeth . . . and he had this dog called Skosh. Well . . . we'd get up in the morning and Charlie would go to the head and wake people up, and what have you, and he'd lay his false teeth there on this wooden desk between the bunks there in the NCO rooms at the end of the squad bay. While he was gone, every morning for over two months we'd take that dog and let him lap Charlie's teeth off and then we'd lay them on that table. Charlie'd come back and put his teeth in . . .

We never told him at the time. This went on for two months and he finally . . . took that dog over with him to Vietnam and the dog died of distemper but Charlie made it, so we used to have a lot of fun with him.

In February 1965, U.S. Army Lieutenant General Bruce Palmer visited all four corps into which South Vietnam was divided. He found that the Viet Cong controlled or had cut railroads, highways, and other lines of communication in various parts of the country, and threatened normal social and economic life. The country seemed on the brink of disaster. Danang, the major population center in I Corps, had received a visit from Westmoreland's deputy, General John Throckmorton, who pronounced it in grave danger.

In order to protect the vital airfield against possible air attack from North Vietnam, Westmoreland requested a Hawk missile unit and received the Marine Corps' 1st Light Antiaircraft Missile (LAAM) Battalion. This was quickly followed by two Marine infantry battalions, 3/9 and 1/3, which landed on 8 March. Marine battalions were chosen to defend Danang because one of their LAAM battalions was already there, and General Westmoreland decided that this would preclude interservice confusion. (General William C. Westmoreland was commander, U.S. Military Assistance Command, Vietnam [COMUSMACV]. Sometimes both he and his command were referred to as MACV, pronounced "Mack-Vee.") Their mission was to occupy and defend critical terrain features and certain facilities to secure the airfield. In no uncertain terms, they were instructed to "not, repeat not," engage in day-to-day actions against the VC. The landing of the Marines at this point was regarded by the Johnson administration as a one-time affair, to fulfill a specific requirement.

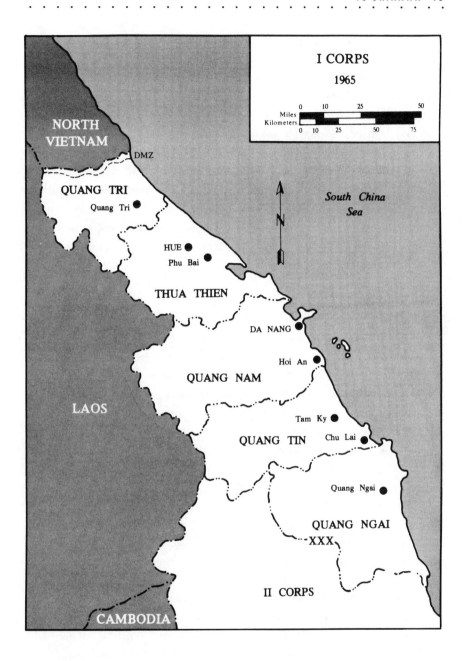

Army Chief of Staff Harold K. Johnson, who was in Vietnam during the landings of the two battalions, returned to Washington with the recommendation for deployment of a U.S. division. Not yet ready for such a large increase, President Lyndon Johnson authorized two additional Marine battalions in National Security Action Memorandum 328, issued on 1 April. This document also authorized a "change of mission for all Marine battalions deployed in Vietnam to permit their more active use."

The makeshift quality of the Johnson administration's policies on Vietnam was already showing through. Within a few short weeks, the United States had already shifted from an effort to protect an airfield to an "enclave strategy" whose most visible proponent was General Maxwell Taylor, at this time American ambassador to South Vietnam. "Enclave strategy" meant that U.S. forces would deploy in enclaves around major bases, from which they would be permitted to conduct offensive operations within a fifty-mile radius. This strategy would also have a short life.

PFC Bill Brocksieker

All through March and April, they kept telling us, "We're going to mount out [pack up and move] and go to Vietnam." Then they told us that we were going to go to Camp Fuji, Japan, for cold-weather training. We were issued cold-weather gear and we got on the *Whitfield County* and we steamed four hours away from Okinawa and they turned the ship around and brought us right back. I think that was about the time the VC blew up this restaurant along the Saigon River. Several hundred people and some Americans were killed.

Then they took all our cold-weather equipment away from us and they started to send to Japan for ammunition and for different equipment that we would need down in Vietnam. There were about 19,000 Marines on Okinawa—the 9th Marines at Camp Hansen and the 3d Marines were at Camp Schwab. The 4th Marines were in Hawaii. [These are the regiments that make up the 3d Marine Division.]

Around April 15th, we were told to get our laundry out of the shops and to take our combat boots to the base cobblers for better soles and heels as we would need them in Vietnam. We were also issued mimeographed copies of Vietnamese words and phrases. Our seabags were packed and unpacked all this time through March and April. I believe that we started to mount out like eight times, three times for cold-weather training and five times for Vietnam. We also had our rifles checked at the armory, our M14s; and our record books were gone over real good at the office and dependents' insurance updated, and we stored extra dress uniforms and civilian clothes that we didn't want to take along. We were also issued mosquito netting and insect repellent.

On May the 5th we had a farewell beer party before leaving for Vietnam. We left Okinawa on the *Iwo Jima*, LPH-2 [helicopter carrier], on May the 8th.

The battalion was headed for a newly approved airfield site south of Danang.

3

• • • • • • • • • • • • • • •

PROTECTING THE AIRFIELD:
CHU LAI, REPUBLIC OF VIETNAM

Chu Lai is not a Vietnamese name. Marine Lieutenant General Victor Krulak, the Commanding General, Fleet Marine Force, Pacific (the parent command for all combat Marine Corps forces from the Mississippi River to India), had visited the site several times to look for an appropriate location for the airfield. An old China hand from before World War II, Krulak had learned the Chinese characters for his name. "Chu lai" was how the Vietnamese pronounced these characters.

Captain David A. Ramsey

We arrived in Vietnam on the 12th of May, Lieutenant Colonel W. D. Hall commanding. I was the 3A [assistant operations officer]. Bruce Webb, later to be killed in action and also to receive posthumously the Navy Cross, was commanding India Company. Captain J. A. Doub was commanding Kilo Company. Captain Paul Fuetterer was commanding Lima and Captain Cal Morris was commanding Mike Company.

Aerial view of Chu Lai at the beginning of construction of the airfield.
(Courtesy Department of Defense)

When we landed, we landed at Chu Lai and we were at the south of the perimeter. Our left flank was on the South China Sea and our right flank was tied in with Lieutenant Colonel [Joseph R.] "Bull" Fisher's 2d Battalion, 4th Marines. Another battalion of the 4th Marines was up on the northern part the perimeter, so we had three battalions in the Chu Lai area. The construction people had come in and set up a rock crusher and some other types of construction equipment out there and set up an expeditionary airfield.

The 3d Battalion, 3d Marines, was assigned to the operational control of the 4th Marines while at Chu Lai. Because of the fluid nature of the war, it became common practice to assign battalions to other than their parent regiment. All Marines in Vietnam became part of the III Marine Amphibious Force (III MAF), which had been activated on 6 May as the III Marine Expeditionary Force. The change in designation was made the following day when it was pointed out that the word *expeditionary* might create unfavorable comparison with the French Expeditionary Corps, which had lost an earlier war to the Vietnamese. Initially commanded by Major General William R. Collins, III MAF was taken over by Lieutenant General Lewis W. Walt on 30 May.

By the time 3/3 landed, the mission of the Marines in Vietnam had become: 1) to establish defensive bases; 2) to conduct deep reconnaissance patrols of the enemy's avenues of approach; 3) to conduct offensive action as a reaction force in coordination with the South Vietnamese; and 4) to intensify offensive operations to fix and destroy the Viet Cong. In accordance with the first of these, their initial task was to assist in securing the Chu Lai area for the construction of an airfield.

PFC Bill Brocksieker

When we came off the ship, we got on helicopters and we landed and nobody really told us anything and we thought there was a gook behind every tree and a land mine every three feet. We landed and we looked ahead of us and there were the Seabees working on the airstrip. They got us off the helicopters and we went about 200 feet from where we landed and we just sat down. We stayed there that night and then the next day we found out we had been behind the lines that night.

Captain Dave Ramsey

We did have an expeditionary airfield with an arresting gear and JATO (jet-assisted take off) bottles on the aircraft. A-4s [attack aircraft] and then C-130s [cargo planes] would come in every once in a while. When it rained, the red clay, the laterite, that was underneath it would wash away and they'd have to rebuild it. And it was just a big pain in the ass all the time, that airfield. I don't know if it was really all that worth it or not.

We had very, very few supplies. We requisitioned foot powder. One can per man. And the battalion got four cans. That's four of these little, little tiny cans of foot powder that you issue to one man to carry in his jungle kit. Well, we got four. That's all that they had.

One time most of the helicopters were inactive. We had the H-34s which was the workhorse as far as troop carrying was concerned. Most of them, 70 to 75 percent of them, were down because we didn't have any tail rotors and the sand there on the beach would eat away at these tail rotors whenever they'd land and we didn't have any to replace them.

The first sandbags that we got, we poured sand in them and it went right out the other end. They were totally unserviceable. We couldn't get barbed wire for the longest time. We'd go in with requisitions for all kinds of barbed wire so we could set up a perimeter and we'd get maybe one roll of concertina. That's for a battalion perimeter. It was really disgusting. Somebody, somewhere, had not been doing their job in maintaining these war stocks.

PFC Bill Brocksieker

We had the M14 rifle [semiautomatic with a twenty-round magazine] and we were out on an outpost the week after we got there. One of the guys was sleeping or about half-awake and a little kid came up and grabbed his rifle and took off with it. When we landed in Vietnam we could have a magazine in a rifle, but we couldn't have a round in the chamber.

The next night that kid came back and he had one round left in the chamber. He came back to the same place and I suppose he came back to get more ammunition. He stuck that M14 over the top of the parapet, the sandbags that this guy had built up, and the guy grabbed the barrel of the rifle and it went off and shot the guy . . . the same guy that had his rifle stolen the night before . . . went through his arm. They medevaced him [medical evacuation]. It was a clean wound . . . he was back in a few weeks.

And I suppose the kid . . . or the Viet Cong had fired at Marines all day with those twenty rounds. He had one round left and came back to the same place where he got the rifle. But the Marine got his rifle back, so he didn't get into too much trouble.

Sergeant Patrick Finton

We were a bastard engineer outfit attached to 3/3. We got there in May of '65. And there really wasn't much of anything there, except for some tentage.

Our primary purpose at the time was to support the battalion and other units there. And they were attempting to build an airfield fairly close to the beach. One of their problems that they had at that time was to stabilize the sand to make it useful as an airfield. We helped, somewhat, with the limited amount of equipment that we had. And as always, equipment kept breaking down, especially in Vietnam. It seemed to wait until it got there to break down.

First couple of three weeks we were there, we helped put a causeway together. Charlie Med [Charlie Company, 3d Medical Battalion], our detachment, was there. And we worked putting in . . . makin' their hospital tents a little more habitable for them.

Captain Dave Ramsey

The rules of engagement when we first got down there were ridiculous. We weren't allowed to shoot at anybody unless they shot at us first. It didn't make any difference if they were armed or not. Needless to say, there was a lot of bending of these rules of engagement, but I'm just reciting them for you . . . to show you how ridiculous some of the constraints were. We couldn't fire outside of our TAOR [tactical area of responsibility] and we were put on the perimeter, so technically we couldn't fire in front of our own positions with mortars and artillery without getting the [Vietnamese] district chief's permission. And that, of course, was always very, very slow in coming and sometimes not even the same day that we asked for it.

Rules of engagement bedeviled Marines for the entire war. The guidelines were part of an attempt to find a balance between allowing the force necessary for Marines to accomplish their mission and minimizing the number of casualties inflicted on noncombatants. As part of an after-action report, then classified *Secret* and dated 12 June 1965, 3/3's battalion commander advised:

> It is felt that authority to call for supporting arms should be delegated to the commander on the scene as he is in the best position to judge what is necessary to reduce the enemy. By the time an officer reaches the grade of captain he has received a good deal of training and experience and anything less than complete faith in his judgement seems a violation of special trust and confidence. It is understood that we are attempting to fight a compassionate war but when a commander sees his men fall as a result of enemy small-arms fire it does not seem proper to deny him what supporting arms he feels he needs simply because we do not want to inflict casualties upon the population that allows the enemy to live among them. It is respectfully submitted that the company commander at the scene of the action be allowed to call the supporting arms he needs and if the FSCCs [Fire Support Coordination Centers] along this chain remain silent, the supporting fires be delivered without delay.

Sergeant Pat Finton

One day they brought some villagers and it was the first time that I really saw something that was . . . related to war. Kids arms hangin' by muscles . . . and uh, women, pretty bad cuts all over, from our own artillery. They were in an area they weren't supposed to be in. This happened quite a bit over there. And they got hit and hit pretty hard. Made you realize that you were there and somebody got hurt.

Captain Dave Ramsey

One more thing, too. We couldn't get naval gunfire support so we'd put a tank on a Mike boat [landing craft medium] and have it offshore and call tank fire in from the Mike boat. Well, of course, that was a very, very popular mission . . . being the coxswain of that Mike boat. . . . They really ate it up. Once the word got out that we were doing this, then of course DDs [destroyers] showed up, Christ, by the half dozen practically. And then the politics of the situation were such that we *had* to find targets for them. Even if we didn't have anything, you know . . . we'd say, "Yeah, right. Suspected assembly area." And we'd direct their fire in on the Van Tuong Peninsula which was across the Tra Bong River and then we'd have to give them some battle damage assessment.

Sergeant Dave Horne

We began running operations. It was more like a desert area than it was jungle.

Gently rolling sand dunes, broken up with small pines, rice paddies, and huts, characterize the terrain at Chu Lai in the vicinity of the airfield. A mile or so inland the soil turns from sand to clay and the terrain becomes hilly. Temperatures averaged 94 in midafternoon and rainfall was relatively scarce in May.

We were taking sniper fire and not very much heavy activity. It was great because we could learn combat a little bit slower. We didn't jump right into a major confrontation. On patrols we learned . . . some night activities and the basics of doing things in combat versus in peacetime. It's not like you go to the field in peacetime and they want to get everything done in twenty-four hours. We got a little bit more time to get our thoughts together.

Sergeant Pat Finton

We set up a shower point and soon after we got there, a LAAM battalion came in from [Marine Corps Base] 29 Palms, California, and set up the Hawk missiles, in and around Chu Lai. They came down to take showers every night. . . . And one evening these guys got out of the truck, oh, probably about twenty of them. And they went over to the portable showers, and they took their showers and left.

All of a sudden I heard an explosion. What had happened is, these guys being new . . . one of them took a hand grenade and hung it, by the pin, on the throttle of the truck. And he'd been carrying a hand grenade that way for some time.

Anyway, when he started up . . . to take the group of people back . . . the pin had finally pulled itself out. . . . Of course, the grenade dropped to the bottom of the cab. The driver picked up the hand grenade, tried to heave it through the back window where all the troops were at, just after they got out of the showers. Well, he got his hand hung up in the canvas somehow and the hand grenade dropped between the back of the truck and a five-gallon gasoline can, which was sitting in the back of the truck. And then the grenade went off and acted just like a Claymore [a directional antipersonnel mine] to those kids in the back of the truck. It pretty much wiped them out. That was the first time I'd seen somebody that had got hit. Our own people.

PFC Gary W. Hammett

It was very scary when we first got there, but after a while we got kind of used to it. We had a lot of patrols. I think we started our patrols about the end of May or the first of June and when we got there we had the old uniforms. The old utilities, the old leather boots and all this stuff you humped through the rice paddies and everything else and it wasn't too good, especially when rainy season came and you got wet, and wet, and wet, and never dried out.

Stateside uniforms of heavy sateen material and all-leather boots were unsatisfactory for the terrain and weather of Vietnam. Neither dried very well in Vietnam's climate. The Marines call their field uniform "utilities"; in the Army the same uniform is called "fatigues."

First patrol we were on, we were choppered in and we had to walk back to the battalion area. We were sweeping this one village and received like two sniper shots. Nobody got hit that day. We had these Vietnamese troops with us, teaching us what to look for and how to work with the people and etc. A couple of these guys got ahold of these prisoners and they did some pretty rough stuff to these people. And I guess mainly because these Vietnamese troops knew that they were VC sympathizers.

But as of yet we really hadn't gotten into it with the Viet Cong. So we just mostly stood around and watched the people and kept them back while the Vietnamese troops did all the work. That was about all we did for a couple of months. Just patrolled here and patrolled there and began night patrols and we did some night ambushes and stuff like that.

Sergeant Richard Kidwell

I took one of the first recon [reconnaissance] patrols out and lost half my patrol by . . . not sticking together. It was late at night and going through one of the vills we lost communications and half of our squad. I had another rally point and we picked them up but it scared the hell out of me.

PFC Bill Brocksieker

Our first casualty was Roy Lynwood Murphy. I went through Parris Island with him and went through ITR with him. It was the first real attack by the VC on the Chu Lai combat base there. He got shot on the 29th of May 1965 and he died.

My platoon sent an outpost overlooking Highway 1, which was about a mile in front of the airstrip. We checked civilians by the day that came up and down Highway 1 there and we stayed on the hill at night. We worked with a platoon of ARVN [Army of the Republic of Vietnam] soldiers. We were there sixteen days when we were attacked by VC and three ARVNs were killed. [The term ARVN (pronounced to rhyme with "Marvin") was commonly used to refer to individual soldiers as well as the South Vietnamese army itself.]

Then the ARVNs found a VC bearing his rifle—I believe it was a 1903 Springfield [the standard U.S. weapon in World War I]—and they worked him over pretty bad. Then they took him up over a hill and shot him.

The first four weeks in Vietnam, there was no hot chow, no post office, no free stamps, no showers, no beer, very little mail, and also we didn't get no combat pay. They hadn't passed it [the law authorizing combat pay] yet. We didn't have no jungle boots or no utilities. Everybody, we drank a lot of water. We were dehydrated easy trying to get adjusted to the heat, a lot of people fainting, a lot of confusion that first thirty days or so.

The Marines were learning lessons about Vietnam that would be valuable during the four and a half years the battalion spent there. Each patrol leader filled out detailed reports sharing their discoveries—that two canteens per man were not enough; that the Stateside boots they wore had a disconcerting squeak when worn wet; that more time needed to be allowed for nighttime patrols. They began to realize that barking dogs would signal their activity near villages. Signs of deep footprints were recognized as the marks of people (VC?) carrying heavy loads (weapons?). A patrol, during these early months, uncovered a store of empty shell casings and gunpowder in one of the villages. Through an interpreter, the villagers claimed that the shell casings were used by the children as toys and the gunpowder was part of a special diet that they fed their pigs to keep them from various diseases. One hopes that this story was not believed.

Sergeant Richard Kidwell

I got this listening post ready to go out. It was about four men. I briefed the leader and then I inspected them prior to sending them out. General Krulak, when I was on the drill field, did away with polishing your boots because they wouldn't breathe and he had us use black saddle soap. Well, I happened to have a can of black saddle soap, and of course we couldn't get any supplies and didn't have any camouflage grease paint. I had these men rub this saddle soap on their face. They looked good. I inspected them. No rattles, they knew what they were doing. They got out there and they were out there about a half hour.

I was in my bunker and over the phone Corporal Davis says, "We need some help." I said, "What's the matter?" And he said, "We can't see." I says, "Why?" He says, "Our eyes are burning from the sweat and that saddle soap." And they were all temporarily blinded.

So here I am. I didn't want anybody to know about this, so I crawled out there myself and brought them back in. I thought I was doing the right thing and as it turned out I almost got my troops killed.

PFC Bill Brocksieker

Our company, on June 5th or 6th, was sent out by helo [helicopter] six to eight miles ahead of the lines to check out a village for VC. We stayed out several days, probably the first time we went out on any kind of a company operation. There was no VC, but the people were pretty hostile to us. I guess it was VC area. There weren't any young men in that village and there were only old people, women, and children. We were sent back. It was too risky to set up any kind of permanent position out there.

Sergeant Pat Finton

Until the beginning of June we worked in and around Chu Lai with the hospital and with command units building this and that. Chairs built, desks built . . . shelves, strongback tents. Par for the course in the Marine Corps, we never did have much material. The Seabees came in and they had everything that we could ever have hoped for. And a wish list. We were using ball peen hammers and oversize sledge hammers to pound eightpenny nails. Stuff that should have been checked out over the years to make sure it was up to date never was. We opened these mount-out boxes and you'd pick up canvas that would fall apart. Some tools would be the same way. And what we had to work with was in limited quantities and people had a tendency to lose it. And in the Chu Lai sand, you never did find it again.

From the beginning, the Marines used much of their precious material to relieve the suffering of the extremely poor Vietnamese population. School rooms were built and furnished in the villages. Each month, hundreds of people were inoculated, most for the first time in their lives, against cholera and other diseases. Food, soap, books, salt, building materials, candy and toys for the children, and many other commodities were donated. Some of this came directly from military sources, other material was raised indirectly, from the Marines' relatives and church and civic organizations in the United States. A great deal of publicity was generated regarding the quantities of goods furnished the Vietnamese. Unfortunately, this was not accompanied by an objective method of evaluating whether this effort really contributed to the pacification of the population.

Sergeant Pat Finton

Raymond-Morrison-Knutsen [RMK] came in, which was a civilian world-wide heavy construction outfit, to augment the Seabees in building this airstrip there in Chu Lai. They came in in sixty-foot American-made house trailers with hot and cold women in there to take care of *all* their needs. It's a funny thing. They could drive all up and down Route 1 there in Chu Lai and never get shot at. But by golly, you take a military vehicle out of the limits of our perimeter, we'd get nailed every time. But RMK never did get shot at. With them and the Seabees, they finally did stabilize the soil.

By late 1965 this firm had become RMK-BRJ, for Raymond, Morrison, Knudsen–Brown, Root and Jones. They signed a contract with the U.S. government to construct facilities at the rate of $40 million per month for a year.

PFC H. Tyrone Belanger

We never used trails unless absolutely necessary. We used to use the paddies, the bush, anything, to stay away from the mines, as the Viet Cong knew that the American fighting men were very lazy and did not want to get their feet wet and go anywhere out of their way.

One time we were going out and it got so thick, we had to get onto a trail. When I broke through the bush onto the trail, I probably moved maybe fifteen or twenty yards up the trail when all hell broke loose as far as I was concerned. The next thing I know, I was face to face with a water buffalo charging right down the trail. Being scared out of my wits, the first thing I did is open fire, hoping to knock him off the trail before he knocked me off. While firing, I was able to get off the trail and give this water buffalo a chance to go by.

But afterwards, the lieutenant got on the radio and wanted to know what the hell was going on. And I explained to him the situation. I can recall him telling me that I'd better damn well bring some steak with me when we came back.

As the Marines in Chu Lai learned to fight a new type of war, most were unaware of major developments in enemy troop deployments to South Vietnam. The North Vietnamese began to react to the air attacks on their home country and to the introduction of American troops into South Vietnam. Contrary to the hopes and expectations of the Johnson administration, their response was to send more troops south. By June 1965, intelligence had determined that elements of the *325th NVA Division* were already in country, and there was evidence that the *308th* was on the way. Westmoreland asked for the speedy deployment of additional forces, and on 22 June he was told that forty-four combat battalions would be sent as soon as possible.

At approximately the same time, the enclave strategy became a dead issue, overcome by the "war of attrition" that would characterize American efforts for most of the conflict. Marked by the first search-and-destroy operation conducted by U.S. Army units near Saigon later that month, this strategy was designed to find the enemy and to eliminate him, his base camps, and his logistics installations. Although much criticized, the war of attrition approach was one of Westmoreland's few remaining options, once the administration ruled out invasion of, or even the use of full military force against, North Vietnam.

4

A MAJOR OPERATION

Sergeant Pat Finton

The latter part of June 1965, 3/3 mounted an operation, the first major operation that they utilized three companies. They had two companies come in shore in LVTs [landing vehicle tracked, also referred to as amphibious tractors, amtracs, and tracks] and one company making an envelopment, in helicopters, far enough in to catch the enemy sleeping, and then we would come together and capture the enemy. That's the way it was suppose to work on paper. But it didn't. This was the 29th of June of '65. It was the first one where I really saw a lot of . . . terrible things. The battalion commander was relieved because of what happened.

Captain Dave Ramsey

The battalion commander, Colonel Hall, had a task force . . . over across the Tra Bong River on the Van Tuong Peninsula and they'd gotten into a scrap. They were in such a scrap that they felt they were unable to break contact. It was getting dark and I was taking all the heat from regiment.

Marines of K Company cross a field in search of Viet Cong near Chu Lai, South Vietnam.

The regimental commander was screaming at me to tell the battalion commander to get his ass back across the river and I, of course, I . . . gave it to Colonel Hall in exactly those words on the radio. So they came back in very bad order. They had broken contact, yes, but they had taken casualties.

Sergeant Pat Finton

For our small part in it . . . I was attached to one of the line companies with an engineer platoon that come in by LVT. And we landed and we went in quite a ways. And really didn't hit any opposition or nothing at all.

But somebody had got word that there was a stash of weapons or something that the intelligence community could use back in this village that we had went through. The lieutenant and eighteen to twenty people were in the group that went back to this village to try to find the cave that supposedly had arms and some intelligence information inside. We went back in two LVTs.

We got back there and we got out of the LVTs and walked down one side of the village, which was split in half by a pretty good size rice paddy. And we walked down this village on one side and all we could see was women and children. No men.

We got to the end of the village and then we traversed back on the other side of the rice paddy, on the other side of the village. And we eventually found a cave . . . and I went inside and looked around and found nothing at all. Then as we came out of the cave, we were going back to the LVTs and we got ambushed. There was a black Marine right ahead of me and he got nailed first. He was the point.

The lieutenant had got ahead of us and was bringing the LVT up to where we were at. The LVT come rollin' up and he yelled that . . . he'd give us covering fire while we moved to the LVT and the rice paddy. Which he did. After all of us had got in and the ramp was about ready to be brought back up, we realized that this Marine was still out there that was shot. So I told two guys to go back and pick up the Marine and bring him in. I followed them out to give them covering fire close in. They drug the Marine in and they put him on the deck of the LVT and we raised the ramp. And then we started to catch all kinds of hell from the village.

They must have known we were coming even before we got there because this was the first time that we ran into a large contingent of VC. The other LVT was gone and we were it. We started to head back towards the battalion CP [command post] from whence we left, and we got in the middle of the rice paddy and we threw a track on the LVT.

We were at the mercy of the VC and they were in the . . . village, surrounding this rice paddy on both sides, and we started catching an awful lot of incoming fire. We were trying to return fire and this Marine says, "I'm gonna shoot." And he raised himself up above the LVT to shoot and he got nailed right between the running lights. The round went right through the middle of his helmet and seemed to go all the way around the top of his head, just like a can opener, and lifted the top of his head right off inside his helmet. I didn't realize this until I came down from shooting and said, "What happened?" And his helmet fell off his head and he was dead.

The lieutenant had asked for volunteers to go back and get us some support, because apparently we had no radio communications with anybody and we were on our own. So I said, "I'll go." I got back to the CP and the colonel said, "Do you think you can get back there?" And I said, "Yes." So I took a relief party back. We got the Marines out of the disabled track, got 'em inside this other amtrac, and then I set some charges on the amtrac and blew it up.

Captain Dave Ramsey

They destroyed an amtrac. And this was back in the days when you couldn't do that sort of thing. You had to account for everything. They also destroyed a couple of mechanical mules. They came back in quite a bit of disorder. I sound like a military historian, but that's what it was.

Well, the next day General Walt came down. He was commanding the division . . . a damn fine Marine. He came humming into camp that morning and he had "axe" written all over him. He and his colonel, his 3. They conducted their investigation, and at the end of the day, Colonel Hall had been relieved for cause.

Relief of commanding officers through the battalion level was not unusual in Vietnam. Frequency depended on branch of service, the period during which they served in Vietnam, and other variables. In some units more than 30 percent of these men were relieved.

Sergeant Pat Finton

It was the first time that a lot of people had got shot at and everybody acted different when they got shot at.

Captain Dave Ramsey

We lost our first officer, a lieutenant by the name of Doug Wauchope, who was killed during this firefight.

Each death and most wounded were noted individually and in detail in the battalion's battle reports in these early days. In the engagement just described, three Marines were killed in action (KIA): Lieutenant Wauchope, PFC Lee, and Hospital Corpsman 2d Class Stiles, the first of many outstanding medical corpsmen who died with 3/3. With a disregard for his own personal safety that has typified our "Docs" in every war, Stiles was shot while attending the wounded. In all, five Marines were wounded in action.

As the war escalated and casualties mounted, the personal approach gave way to reporting numbers only. There is ample evidence that casualty reporting in the after-action reports for the entire war suffered from inaccuracies. For example, the total number of killed and wounded listed in the administrative section of the unit's Command Chronology rarely matched the number reported in the operational summary of the same document.

JULY 1965

Captain Dave Ramsey

I became the 3 and Lieutenant Colonel Joe Muir, a little redheaded guy, came down to take over the battalion. He was a dynamic personality and one of the finest Marines that I had the pleasure to serve with. Joe Muir moved around an awful lot. Just he and I and a couple of radios and I was always safer when I was a company commander than I ever was as the 3 with Joe Muir. We wound up in wild spots. "The Grasshopper" is what we affectionately called him. He would go anywhere. Just didn't care at all for his personal safety which was a matter of concern to all of us.

Gunnery Sergeant Gene Breeze

For some reason, I don't know why, after we were down there a couple of months Staff Sergeant Melton and I were sent back to Okinawa on the same set of orders. I think it was a mix up in some gear or a shipment or something. We were on official orders and we landed at Kadena Air Base about eleven o'clock on Saturday night. We had scrounged around H and S [Headquarters and Service] Company CP down on the beach and found some old mildewed civilian clothes. Of course, we didn't have any shoes and we had lost so much weight due to the heat and the shortage of chow.

We got off that airplane at Kadena and we jumped into those civilian clothes. Sergeant Melton had a pair of black trousers on that had green mildew all over them. He didn't have a belt, so his trousers were held up with a guy line from a shelter half.

I don't remember exactly what I had on, probably one of those red and white shirts that looked like a tablecloth and a pair of army combat boots, the type with the buckles on the side, and the buckles were broken and they were flapping in the breeze.

We hadn't had a cold beer or a steak for many, many weeks, so the first place that we went was to that fabulous Army Topper Club. We approached the door and we were stopped by a duty master sergeant, whatever the Army had, with his cutaway, his cummerbund, spit-shined shoes, and his well-manicured hands, and he wanted to know who we were.

We informed him that we had just come from down south [a Marine euphemism for Vietnam] and of course he wanted to know where down south was. He would not let us in the club. He turned us away. We had to go out in town and find someplace that was open and we had a couple of beers. We went there for about three days and we brooded on how we were treated by this Army master sergeant. So we went to a print shop and we had 500 handbills printed that said "Monday night" (which was the night that we were leaving) "at 7 o'clock, it is Free Night at the Topper Club. Everything free. Everybody welcome." And we got in a cab at Camp Schwab and went the full length of Okinawa, hit every bar, and passed out these 500 handbills. We don't know what happened on that Monday night, but we figured if everybody showed up at that club with one of those handbills, we had our revenge.

5

• • • • • • • • • • • • • • •

THE FIRST BIG ONE:
OPERATION STARLITE

By the summer of 1965, the Marines were beginning to show frustration with fighting a guerrilla war. Expressions of hope in some contemporary intelligence reports that the VC would tire of running and stand and fight revealed an ignorance of unconventional warfare strategy.

Operation STARLITE was supposed to have been named Operation SATELLITE. The mistake was made because of a failure of the generator that supplied power to the bunker occupied by the operations clerks who were typing the order. By the time the mistake was noticed the order had already been issued and STARLITE was adopted as the official name. In some accounts, including 3/3's after-action report, it has been misspelled as Starlight.

PFC Bill Brocksieker

All through July and August we patrolled the Van Tuong Peninsula. We kept having more and more opposition every time we went out there. A platoon would

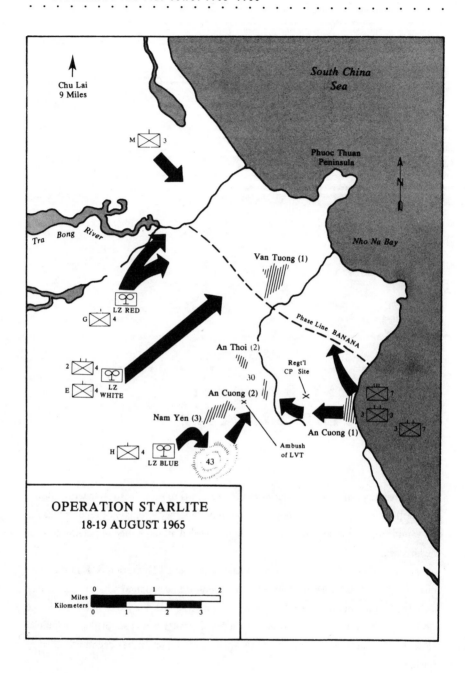

Chu Lai
9 Miles

M ⊠ 3

South China
Sea

Phuoc Thuan
Peninsula

Tra Bong River

Nho Na Bay

Van Tuong (1)

LZ RED

G ⊠ 4

Phase Line BANANA

An Thoi (2)

2 ⊠ 4

LZ
WHITE

E ⊠ 4

.30

Regt'l
CP Site

An Cuong (2)

Nam Yen (3)

An Cuong (1)

⊠ 7

3 ⊠ 3

3 ⊠ 7

H ⊠ 4

LZ BLUE

43

Ambush
of LVT

OPERATION STARLITE
18-19 AUGUST 1965

Miles
Kilometers

0   1   2

0   1   2   3

go out . . . and then companies would go out. And companies would get more opposition so we wouldn't send too many companies out . . . so the whole battalion would go out at a time. And there were so many booby traps out there. The Viet Cong . . . had been in there for years and the people were hostile to us and there was a lot of barbed wire.

When we were out there on this roadblock, every day there would be people walk through with bales of barbed wire. We thought . . . we had only been there a week or so . . . we thought that they were taking it down to fortify their village. I think what they really did with it is . . . they fortified their villages. But it wasn't against the Viet Cong. It was against us.

Many of the villages and hamlets in the Van Tuong Peninsula area were fortified with barbed wire that was often festooned with anti-American signs. One discovered in the STARLITE operations area had an encircling trenchline, a double-apron barbed wire fence, numerous punji pits, and spider traps.

PFC Bill Brocksieker

This big peninsula was about five miles from our combat base at Chu Lai. . . . They had fortified every village out there and every time we would go out there we would take casualties after casualties after casualties. Wounded and dead. Wounded and dead. So, eventually, it was hard to get out there without any kind of trouble. Then during August, 3/3 operations were switched from in front of the airbase to tactical responsibility for the Van Tuong Peninsula, which was due east from Chu Lai and was divided from Chu Lai by the Tra Bong River.

Allied intelligence was certain it had located the *1st VC Regiment* on the Van Tuong Peninsula. Consisting of the *60th* and *80th VC Battalions* and reinforced by the *52d VC Company* and part of the *45th Weapons Battalion,* this force numbered about 1,500 men.

PFC Bill Brocksieker

The information we received after the 15th of August was that the *1st Viet Cong Regiment,* including a lot of NVA regulars mixed in, were working their way toward Van Tuong for a sneak attack on the airbase . . . to drive us into the sea. General Lew Walt, the head of all Marines in Vietnam, got an okay from LBJ and Westmoreland to make an offensive drive on the VC before we were attacked by them.

It was decided to send three battalions of Marines, making a full regiment, with support. This was called RLT-7 [Regimental Landing Team 7].

Captain Dave Ramsey

We were the amphibious battalion and "Bull" Fisher (2/4) was the heli-lifted battalion. And then we had 3d Battalion, 7th Marines, offshore as the floating reserve. Lieutenant Colonel Bodley commanded that battalion. They put Colonel [and later Major General Oscar] Peatross' RLT-7 headquarters in charge of the whole operation. And we went ashore on Operation STARLITE.

PFC Howard G. Miller

We were briefed on Operation STARLITE as being a hammer and anvil operation, with the hammer being I Company, K Company, and L Company, and the anvil being M Company. [In such an operation, units on the move would play the part of the hammer, driving the enemy in a desired direction. The anvil was a blocking force that would cut off the enemy's escape, thereby trapping him.]

PFC Bill Brocksieker

Mike Company went to sleep real early on the night of August 17th and about 10:30 P.M. we were woken up and we walked about four or five miles out to the Tra Bong River. The only way we could get out there was to hold on to the person in front of you's back . . . backpack so we wouldn't get lost. We went single file, the whole company.

Our job was to set up a blocking force and then they would run them into us. About two-thirty we got out to the Tra Bong River. We were put on amtracs and we were taken across, ferried over to the peninsula on its western side.

Sergeant Richard Kidwell

They put the rest of us on LSTs [Navy landing ships]. They didn't tell us where we were going to go. That was a well-kept secret from everybody. That was General Walt's baby. We had no indication where we were going until we got there.

The Navy had been informed of the operation on 16 August, and one ship on its way to Hong Kong just made it back for D-day. To further safeguard security, Vietnamese allies were informed of the operation only at the highest level. Just two Vietnamese generals were told, and they were cautioned to hold the information until the battle actually began.

The operation plan called for 3/3 to land India and Kilo companies abreast on Green Beach at 0630 on 18 August. Lima Company was to land in trace as battalion reserve. Mike Company was to be already positioned on a ridgeline four miles northwest of the landing area, ready to act as blocking force. Lieutenant Colonel Bull Fisher's 2/4 was to come into three separate landing zones by helicopter, linking up with 3/3 and driving through the Van Tuong village complexes.

Sergeant Dave Horne

The next morning was a bright sunny day and we took off to make an assault on the beach. We hadn't made any major amphibious assaults, and the amtrac drivers also had not at that time, and when we hit that beach we were hub to hub. If they'd had a machine gun, I believe they could have gotten half of us.

PFC Charles (Chuck) Fink

I was on the first tractor that hit the beach. When we loaded on the tractor I thought I was being smart. I got up and went forward because I'm thinking, "Hey, man, when we hit the beach, that little opening in the back will open and everybody will run off. I'll be the last guy off the tractor." I didn't realize that the tractor opened in the front until we got to the beach and the light cracked around the door and I thought, "Oh, Jesus!" I knew I'd screwed up big time. But I thought, "You can't go back now." The ramp dropped and they ran us up on the beach. It was real narrow . . . there wasn't fifty feet from the shoreline to the woods.

1st Sergeant Arthur Petty

We rushed out on a beach of sand about 200 or 300 yards in length. The beach suddenly became crowded and I wanted to get the Marines in off the beach, but Captain Webb [the India Company commander] realized that we had landed a little out of our sector and was moving the troops down the beach a short ways.

PFC Chuck Fink

The first thing I saw was this old man in high-boogie, beating his feet down this trail away from us. I was doing my best to be John Wayne, but those boots were too big. The old man had a cane, it was obviously a cane, but they'd said it was a free fire zone. "If it moves and it's not in Marine Corps green, shoot it." I thought about killing him and I thought, "God damn, not only is he an old man, but you're going to be shooting him in the back," and I couldn't do it.

Sergeant Dave Horne

When we landed there was a loud explosion just in front of the tractor that I was on. The VC had set up a command-detonated explosion, but they prematurely let it go, so nobody got hurt.

1st Sergeant Art Petty

Gunnery Sergeant Martin traced the wire from the point of explosion to a trench where a battery had been used to set off the charge. This was at the edge of a village and there were a number of civilians cowering in the trenches and holes but no known Viet Cong.

Sergeant Dave Horne

Well, we got off the amtracs and we moved inland and the day starts to get mixed up . . . . The sniper fire was heavy and started to escalate as we moved in closer on the objective.

PFC Gary Hammett

We swept through the first village without any contact, but later we received some fire from this village. It was pretty intense so we called in air support. With the air support we received our first casualty, Corporal Walker, who was hit by a piece of fragmentation from the bomb and was medevaced out.

Sergeant Pat Finton

We found a tunnel complex. And the VC had made a false bottom and I found the false bottom and we ended up takin' out seventy-five women and children. We got the ARVN interpreter over and asked if there was any VC in there that wanted to come out. 'Course they didn't so we went in and set up explosives. We put 480 pounds of C4 [plastic explosive] in that tunnel complex and then we blew that booger up. Aannd . . . it blew two armed VC, one of them completely out and of course he was dead. The other one wasn't dead. Part of his body was caught inside after the explosion and his head and shoulders were outside. This lieutenant from the S-2 [intelligence] section of 3/3 come over and said, "Shoot him, Sergeant Finton." I just looked at the lieutenant and walked away. The guy, the VC, was dying but . . . hell, I didn't have the stomach for shooting him.

Sergeant Dave Horne

The amtracs picked us up . . . and we moved to this one assembly area and another amtrac came alongside and several of the guys got off this one amtrac and got on this other one and I talked to Lieutenant Coursey and I said, "I don't know about this, Lieutenant, I'm going to get off the top of this thing and get inside it."

I got inside it and just as they closed the ramp, a B40 rocket [shoulder-fired, antitank rocket used by VC and NVA troops] went across and it hit one of the other amtracs. We went about another quarter of a mile and then all of a sudden we had intense mortar fire, and the amtrac stopped. I was on the inside and I told them to drop the ramp. The driver was killed. He slid down inside the amtrac and the ramp went down about halfway and the lieutenant, for some reason, said, "Close it." We closed it up and just as that thing got almost closed, a mortar went off right in front of it and probably would have landed right on top of us. They just got it closed. When they opened the ramp again and when we came out, several mortars had gone off, and there was nothing but Marines all over the place . . . bodies. In my platoon we lost nine killed right at that spot. And numerous wounded.

Captain Dave Ramsey

Our India Company and Bull Fisher's Hotel Company were the two link-up units. And, of course, as luck would have it, they were trying to link up right in the face of the heaviest concentration of enemy.

Hotel Company 2/4 landed, by chance, right on top of the *60th VC Battalion*. In a tactic that became familiar during the course of the war, the VC permitted the first wave to land without interference and then opened up as the others came in. The idea was to pin down a small, manageable American force and then chew up the inevitable reinforcements piecemeal during the very vulnerable time in which they were attempting to land.

1st Sergeant Art Petty

Immediately, heavy fire could be heard from Company H's area, and it became obvious to Captain Webb that Company H was in trouble. Captain Webb asked permission to go out of his zone of action at this point and help Company H out with their problem. Permission was granted and Company I made a pivot and swung to the left and it advanced very rapidly taking an ever-increasing amount of small-arms fire.

PFC Bill Brocksieker

Colonel Muir called in naval gunfire from the USS *Galveston* and the USS *Ticonderoga*. This relieved pressure off 2/4 and the pincer movement was started again.

Sergeant Dave Horne

Of course, we had air and air was doing a job on them as they were trying to get out. So it was a pretty exciting day and when they came in with the choppers to get us out, every time a chopper would land, they [the VC] would open up with everything they had and I sort of felt sorry for those chopper pilots. They'd have to set there while we were loading people up, but they didn't seem to be many of them that got knocked down.

I had one fellow in my platoon that got killed that day. His name was R. F. Batson. He was always concerned about his family. He had two little girls and . . . He wasn't afraid or anything, he was just overly concerned because of his family and I recommended we put him back in the company supply.

Well, we got him back there and he was doing a super job. On this day they knocked out the amtrac he was in, and they were carrying C-rations. All the C-rations were thrown against his weapon [pinning it] and he came out with a K-Bar knife and they cut him down. Sort of one of those odd things that happen. You think you are safe and all of a sudden you find that you aren't.

Sergeant Pat Finton

We were catching sniper fire from a hill, where the battalion CP had just set up. And we had a flame tank [a tank whose main weapon is a large flamethrower] and Colonel Muir called that flame tank in and leveled that whole damn hill. And no more sniper fire. Beautiful!

Another thing that we didn't know either . . . that they had 60-mm mortars. And we started to hear those mortars go *plunk*, and I told the platoon sergeant, I said, "Sergeant Williams, they're mortaring us." He said, "No, they're not." And I said, "Yes, they are. Look." And there was a 60-mm round that had just impacted about four feet behind me, but it didn't go off. It landed in the rice paddy. You could see the fins below the water and where the splash had occurred on the ripples, and he said, "Bullshit," and we both made a dive into this irrigation ditch.

1st Sergeant Art Petty

At this time Company H had requested air support and was being supported by a bombing run. We were very close to the Viet Cong and we were taking them under fire and could see them breaking and running. The shrapnel from the bombs made us hold up momentarily. Pieces of the shrapnel were landing among us and some of the Marines were juggling the hot metal around their hands. The VC would just lay with his eyes and his mouth clamped shut tight as some of them do. He laid stiff as a board. We either had to kill him or carry him, so one of our big Marines carried him like a log on his shoulder and we put him on a helicopter and flew him out.

Sergeant Pat Finton

The company commander called in an airstrike on the village. And it was kind of funny because the airstrike would come in and shoot their cannons and machine guns and drop a bomb or two. And they would go around for another pass and . . . when they would do that, it would force the VC out of the village into the open. And there are 200 Marines, 150 or 200 yards away, who opened up with small-arms fire. We've always been told that the Marines are the best shots in the world. Well, here's 200 Marines shooting, M14s, and I didn't see one VC drop. By that time that A-4 would come around and make another pass and the VC would head on into their holes or whatever cover they had there in the village. After the pass the VC would come back out again and . . . try to get out of the village and when they would, here's 200 Marines opening up again.

1st Sergeant Art Petty

Captain Webb moved the 1st Platoon out and across the semidry river bed in and over a Viet Cong trench and into an area occupied by the Viet Cong. He was determined to not let the Viet Cong escape with their wounded and weapons. Too many times in the past they had fired on us and escaped.

The captain moved his command post out right behind Staff Sergeant Wright's 1st Platoon. Too close, I believe. There was a lot of action—exploding grenades, the tanks were firing, machine guns, mortar rounds were landing, and a lot of small-arms rifle fire, carbine fire, and so forth.

PFC Gary Hammett

Corporal Thomas was hit, but he wouldn't go back because he said he wasn't hit so bad that he couldn't stay to help. So he stayed. Our platoon moved on a couple of more hours. After a while there wasn't really too much action; it had kind of simmered down.

Before we stopped for chow, Captain Webb and them were coming up from behind. There were about six of them in the captain's little group there. This one staff sergeant was shooting these dead VC in the head. The captain told him to stop doing it because it was inhumane. Well, right after that, three or four minutes later, this VC, who was supposed to have been dead and wasn't, had a grenade and when he rolled over, the pin was already pulled.

PFC Chuck Fink

Captain Webb came up. He was like the fifth man in line. I was thinking, "My God, what is he doing up here? He's the company commander." The closest he should have been was behind the point squad or point platoon and here he was behind the point fire team.

Staff Sergeant Jean Pinguet, who was my platoon sergeant, fought in the French Resistance in World War II and he was hard as nails. He was walking through shooting the VC that were laying there. Captain Webb told him not to do that. He said, "That's inhumane, don't shoot them." Not two minutes after that one of them rolled over that wasn't dead and chucked a grenade at him and got him and the radio operator.

PFC Gary Hammett

We lost our captain. We lost our radioman and we lost a private. The XO [executive officer], a staff sergeant, and another one were wounded. If there hadn't been for the captain telling the staff sergeant to quit what he was doing, Captain Webb might not be dead today. Captain Webb was a good man. Captain Webb wouldn't tell you to do anything that he wouldn't do. So that was the end of Captain Webb.

1st Sergeant Art Petty

I was shocked by knowing the captain was hit. However, I directed a helicopter into the closest open spot that I could find and I went back with the aid of two more Marines and I carried the captain and put him on the first helicopter. In all, it took three helicopters to carry the wounded out because they had to be carried in a prone position because of their wounds.

At this time a Huey [HU1E], an armed helicopter, came in and landed. He had had his fuel line shot up and was forced to land. Lieutenant Purnell, the executive officer, took command and we started to move out. However, we were directed by higher authority to leave ten Marines for security around the Huey which we did.

PFC Chuck Fink

We immediately formed a perimeter around him and he unhooked the rocket pods. He took off and left the rocket pods there. So rather than leave them for the VC to get, we were waiting for the engineers to come up to blow the pods because we didn't have anything but grenades with us.

PFC Howard Miller

It seemed like the operation was not so much one large attack but of a bunch of smaller firefights, all taking place at the same time. The Viet Cong would come out of their bunkers and they would be in the middle of us, behind us, in front of us, and we had to react to each separate little thing, therefore causing a great deal of movement and confusion as to the actual lines of combat. I was a machine gunner assigned to the weapons platoon of I Company, 3/3. Fairly early in the day as we were crossing an open field under fire, the other members of my team were all killed.

PFC Chuck Fink

We were going across this dry paddy area. I'm looking around and I'm seeing these holes in these low mounds. They were like a hundred yards long. I couldn't figure out what they were, so I went over and looked in one of them and here was a cotton-picking rocket for an RPG [rocket-propelled grenade]. These things were ventilation shafts; this was a bunker complex in there.

So I called over to Sergeant Emereck who was my squad leader and I says, "Hey, there's a rocket in here." "No, leave it alone, let's go." Well, as quick as we moved away from that, those suckers came blowing out of there and they shot us like crazy from the rear. We had tanks with us and the tanks were getting knocked out right and left. There was a slight hill to the right that was heavily wooded. This VC was up there with a rocket launcher and he was knocking out all these tanks.

So myself and this man named Jemison, he was our grenadier, went back to see what was going on, why we were getting all this fire from the rear. We went down this hedgerow and then to an "L" and stopped and we rolled out behind this rice paddy dike. There were these VC . . . they had helmets, khaki uniforms, and they had underbrush strapped on their backs. They had an automatic weapon that was shooting at the tanks and the main body of the rest of my unit.

Jemison didn't see them. They were fifty yards from us. There was our rice paddy dike (the one we were behind), a dry paddy, and then another dike fifty yards away, and they were behind that, shooting over our heads. They weren't looking close in, so they didn't see us sitting there. I'm saying, "Jemison, Jemison, there they are, right there!" And he just couldn't see them. So I said to him, "I'm going to shoot a tracer round," and I thought, "Well, hell, at fifty yards he ain't going to see a tracer round where it goes anyway." So I thought, "I'll shoot under the gun so it makes the dirt fly up and maybe he'll see that." So I told him, "Shoot low. Right over where this hits is where the gun is."

So I shot, he saw the dirt, and the first round out of his M79 [a shoulder-fired, 40-mm grenade launcher], the first round he ever fired in combat, landed right on that gook gunner's head. I mean right smack dab on his helmet. I said,

"God, what a shot, Jamie!" So he rolled over on his side and put another round in and flipped back over and as quick as he did that, another gook jumped on that gun. They saw us then when the M79 went off.

The gook fired off a burst and two of the rounds hit Jemison. I was scared to death. When Jemison got killed, we were shoulder to shoulder. He was dead instantly. When I rolled over, I felt him jump and I looked at him and I knew what had happened. I just finished out everything I had in my magazine on that gun and I flipped over, put a new magazine in. Evidently one of my rounds hit that gun or they left, because it didn't shoot anymore.

This VC that was up on the hill with a rocket launcher must have thought we were a sniper or something. He fired a rocket at me and it hit the dike right in front of where I was laying, and the explosion caught me in the arm, the side of my face, and flipped me up over on my back. My helmet was turned around backwards, my glasses were cocked up on the side of my head, and I had blood squirting out of my arm and all that mess.

I grabbed my arm, rolled back over, and I was looking for some movement. I saw something moving out of the corner of my eye. That was his last rocket and he was crouched over and had the rocket launcher in his hand and he was running. There were pieces of shrapnel all in the stock of my rifle which kept me from catching that whole thing in the face. I figured that was the sucker that got me and the rifle looked like it would shoot, so I killed him.

My hand got tight and it wouldn't function anymore, so Corporal Jones came over and he rolled me over and patched me up. We had one tank that was working and we were trying to get some of the guys that were really bad wounded up on the thing. They were shooting the men that were already wounded, the VC were. We were lifting this one guy up on the tank and a bullet hole appears right in his side, and I thought, "Man, you slimy bastards!"

That was when my whole attitude started to change. I went from being scared to death to being madder than hell, and I got worse as I stayed over there. There were a lot of periods where I did some things that I personally feel like I was ashamed of in that maybe I didn't do it like John Wayne would do it. But it was really funny what happened when the adrenaline took over and the anger came in.

1st Sergeant Art Petty

We moved out against light sniper fire. We had killed and captured a number of Viet Cong in the area where the captain was killed, and we had also captured and were carrying some weapons that had belonged to Viet Cong. We had eight or nine prisoners, Russian rifles, American carbines, M14 rifles, a M79 grenade launcher, several Viet Cong packs full of 40-mm M79 rounds.

I was placed in charge of the rear command group and had two guards on the prisoners. We met Lieutenant Colonel Muir and his battalion headquarters group coming up the hill. Colonel Muir turned over an amphibious tractor and several Ontos to our company. [Ontos, which means "the thing" in Greek, was a lightly armored, tracked vehicle that sported six 106-mm recoilless rifles.] There was not enough room for everyone on the amphibious tractor and the Ontos, so I was left with the rocket squad and prisoners with the headquarters group. The company moved out and went down the hill. Being crowded, some of the troops were off-loaded and reloaded on the other amtrac, and they moved out and to the right a short distance and came under fire of the Viet Cong. The Viet Cong were using 57-mm recoilless rifles with which they scored a hit on a tank, and the tank was sprayed with .50-caliber machine-gun rounds and other small-arms fire.

A gas can was shot up and the gas was burning. The tankers came out of the escape hatch on the bottom of the tank and were in turn picked up by one of the amphibious tractors. The company moved on a few hundred yards and ran into the area where two other amphibious tractors were bogged down and one had been hit. This was supply column twenty-one. This name came from the supply call sign on the radio which is "two one."

The company tried to disembark from their amphibious tractors when the Viet Cong hit them with 57-mm recoilless rifles, 81-mm mortars, .50-caliber machine guns, and all types of small arms. The 81-mm mortars did the most damage as the Viet Cong did not waste a round. The first round hit an amphibious tractor and cleared the top of it of its personnel.

The Viet Cong put a couple more rounds of 81-mm mortar in among the wounded and dead as the company reorganized and pushed out into a nearby trenchline.

Most communist bloc forces were armed with 82-mm mortar, but the Viet Cong had some 81s captured from allied units or left over from World War II and the war with the French. For Marine infantry battalions, 81-mm mortar was organic. Eight 81-mm mortars, with their crews of nearly sixty mortarmen, were collectively known as 81s and supported the four rifle companies.

Captain Dave Ramsey

This supply convoy was amtracs, maybe six of them . . . had a tank on the front and a tank on the back. And they were coming up the road and they came under extremely heavy RPG fire and recoilless rifle fire [both of which have armor-piercing capability]. They knocked out the lead tank and the rear tank almost immediately. The tracks were so close together that they couldn't let the ramps down.

This . . . went on into the night. They were fouling up the battalion radio net. The people inside the amtracs, of course, were panicking. And they were screaming for somebody to get down there and save them. Apparently the Viet Cong were up on top of the amtracs and we had some real scared Marines in that convoy. We lost . . . our amtrac platoon commander. . . . [He] was half in and half out of an amphibian tractor and a mortar round landed on the vehicle just to the rear of him. And that did him in.

Adding to the confusion, the radio operator of one of the amtracs panicked. Depressing his call button for nearly an hour while he pled for help, he effectively prevented the battalion from obtaining essential information regarding the convoy's situation and location.

PFC Gary Hammett

After the . . . mortar rounds had stopped . . . it felt like a lifetime, but it only lasted three or four minutes at the most . . . the automatic weapons stopped. Everything. It just became calm, quiet. So I went back through the bushes to the amtrac, where I first jumped off, to see if I could help. No more than fifteen feet from me was Private Brand. Dead.

After I passed him, I walked out to the center where the mortar rounds had hit and there were people laying all over the place. Arms missin', legs missin', their rear ends missin'. And the ones that we couldn't really help, we put them aside and tried to help the wounded. One of the wounded was my squad leader, Corporal Thomas. Me and Corporal Reynolds was helping him. Corporal Reynolds was giving him water and I was holding him and he looked up at us, put a little smile on his face, closed his eyes, and passed away. That will be in my memory forever. Having that man die in my arms.

Sergeant Richard Kidwell

We were just sweeping to the end of the beach there on the perimeter. I moved out and I was about twenty-five yards away and, *boom*! I looked back, and there

A MAG-16 helicopter evacuates STARLITE *casualties while a Marine M-48 tank stands guard.*

one kid who was carrying some mortar rounds was laying in a trench, no arms, no legs, no blood. He was still alive. Chuck Rightus was there first and he said, "Kidwell, grab him." And I remember, I was like in shock and I says, "Grab him where?" because he didn't have any arms or legs. So he jumped down in there and pulled him up, I grabbed his head, and we put him on a stretcher.

I had a young sergeant attached to me. Taglione was his name and he was married. He was a machine gunner and he got hit. He just got one hole in him. We put him on a stretcher. We called in a helicopter for a medevac and they called back and we could see the helicopter right there. The helicopter said, "We can't land. There's too much fire. You're under fire." I got so pissed off I took my M14 and I opened up on the helicopter. Thank God I didn't hit him. It was emotional for me because Taglione was such a great guy.

Finally they came. We threw a poncho over him and as we were carrying him to the helicopter his hand fell down. He used to talk about his wife all the time and I can still remember seeing his wedding ring. That's the only time I cried. The kid died on the helicopter on the way to the hospital.

Sergeant Robert E. O'Malley, the first Marine to win the Medal of Honor in Vietnam. (Courtesy Department of Defense)

PFC Bill Brocksieker

Corporal Robert E. O'Malley of I/3/3, from Woodside, New York, became the first Marine in Vietnam to win the Medal of Honor when he ran across an open area and eliminated eight of the enemy in a trenchline. Then he medevaced his entire squad, who were all wounded and one dead, before he allowed himself to be medevaced, after being wounded himself.

1st Sergeant Art Petty

It was not until the next day that I found out what had happened. Once the company had gotten their wounded out, they had advanced around and over another hill to my right. A squad had jumped a VC company and had worked them over until the VC company organized and tried to outflank the squad.

Corporal O'Malley and Corporal Buchs took turns jumping into a trench full of VC and killed quite a few—twenty-seven, I'm told. O'Malley was wounded in the action and evacuated. Corporal Buchs won a Silver Star. This wound that O'Malley received was his third for the day.

Captain Dave Ramsey

I wrote the citation for his Medal of Honor. It certainly was the first Medal of Honor citation I ever wrote and it flew [see Appendix B]. With very little polishing. So I was kind of proud of that. Sergeant O'Malley was one fine NCO. And he certainly earned that Medal of Honor. Out there carrying on almost a one-man battle, against a trenchline full of VC. But India Company was particularly badly chewed up. . . .

That evening, we were reinforced by at least a company of 3/7. They came into a hot zone and started taking casualties right away. These folks had not been acclimated at all and they were taking heat casualties at night. As a matter of fact, the company commander evacuated himself at ten o'clock at night. He walked to the helicopter and climbed aboard and went back to the ship. Left the company under the command of his executive officer, who was a hell of a fine lieutenant. Staff Sergeant Bill Wright, who was in India Company, went out and got that company and brought it back into the perimeter.

The next morning when that guy . . . that company commander came back out . . . when he got off the helicopter, I was going to throttle him. But Joe Muir gave me a direct order to leave him alone. But he told the captain that he wasn't fit to march with our battalion after that display that he put on the previous evening, leaving the scene of the battle.

PFC Chuck Fink

They finally got us down to the LZ [landing zone], myself and several of the other guys. Little Joe Foster, from Waycross, Georgia, had a piece of shrapnel stuck right in his temple. It didn't go into the skull, but it was right underneath the skin. It was sticking out like about that far [one or two inches]. You couldn't see the shrapnel, all you could see was the entry hole and this bulge on the side of his head. It was right there in his temple. And he was sitting there saying, "God, I've got a headache." I often wondered whatever happened to him.

I got medevaced out to the *Iwo Jima* and the medical care I received was out-standing. I wasn't real bad, my arm just didn't work. They cleaned me up and since I wasn't real bad, they said, "Are you hungry?" And I said, "Yeah." They had ice cream. I'd been eating C-rations and I couldn't believe it. The guy says, "You want something to eat? We got steak, whatever you want." I said, "I want some of that ice cream." I ate the ice cream. They didn't keep us on there very long. They got us off of there and into the medical area back in the rear.

Sergeant Dave Horne

Later that day I went out to the USS *Iwo Jima* and that's where O'Malley was. That was the last time I saw him. In fact, I got him some food. He was wounded pretty bad. He jumped into a trenchline and killed several of them. It was quite an exciting day.

PFC Chuck Fink

They medevaced me to Yokosuka, Japan. They didn't know if I had nerve damage or bone damage or anything like that, so they needed to get me some-where where they could find out.

I called my parents that first night when I got to Yokosuka. My mom got on the phone and as soon as she heard my voice, she got real upset. She'd seen the thing about STARLITE on the news. She said, "Are you okay? Have you been shot in the head?" And I said, "No, why?" And she says, "Because I saw the thing on STARLITE. I know you were in it because they mentioned your unit. I saw a picture of somebody that looked just like you with a bandage around their head." I says, "No, it wasn't me. I got hit in the arm but I'm okay. I've got little pieces of shrapnel in my face but nothing big."

The point of that was that people that were back in the States would see some-thing like that and the trauma that it would cause them thinking that they had seen somebody that they knew, a son or something like that. Of course, them not knowing, their mind is going to work overtime. I could see where that could really create some problems. I remember my mom's reaction. I didn't think it was fair to them is what it boils down to.

PFC Howard Miller

After that we were transported back aboard ship, the USS *Paul Revere*. I was one of the first men to climb back up over the net, and as my foot hit the deck, over the PA system of the ship they began to play the Marine Corps hymn [that is, "The Marine's Hymn"]. We were all tired and worn out and we just sat any-where we could find a place to sit down. It was amazing that the Navy personnel actually brought meals around to us wherever we were at. We never had to go to the mess hall or anything. After we had a chance to rest up a little, most of us went downstairs to the compartments and cleaned up.

PFC Bill Brocksieker

This was the first amphibious landing under fire since the landing at Inchon in Korea.

PFC Howard Miller

The one picture that sticks in my mind more than anything else is on Operation STARLITE. A little after sunset a couple of us were sent back to try to get water for the rest of us. As we got back to where the water supply was, I seen all of the packs and all of the weapons of the dead and wounded all lined up real neat, and I seen many of the dead in body bags all lined up real neat as if they were there for inspection. And even though these were not the first dead Marines I'd seen, the number of casualties, the wounded and the dead, and the manner in which everything was laid out was just something unbelievable.

India Company was hit the hardest of any 3/3 unit, with 15 killed, including their captain and a corpsman, and 52 wounded. The Marine casualty count for STARLITE—45 dead and 203 wounded—represented more killed and wounded than the total for the rest of 1965. STARLITE was a rite of passage for the battalion. At a memorial service held on the beach several days later, muffled sobs were heard as the names of the fallen were read. Neither 3/3 nor the war was ever the same thereafter. The unit had been blooded, and for a long time, until the battalion began going up against NVA regulars in 1967, STARLITE was the operation against which all others were compared.

The operation resulted in 614 VC KIA, by actual body count; enemy losses were possibly much higher. Nine prisoners, 42 VC suspects, and 109 assorted weapons were captured.

First Sergeant Art Petty

Three of the fifty-two wounded [in India Company] disobeyed orders from their doctors when the doctors ordered them to go to Danang. Instead, they checked out new rifles when they got to the rear area and hooked a ride on a helicopter back and rejoined the company in this action.

The Marines were learning that the VC gave top priority to removing weapons belonging to their casualties from the battlefield for reuse. Second priority was to remove as many bodies of their dead as possible. This was intended to lower allied estimates of their success.

A joint honor guard of the 1st and 3d Marine Divisions passes in review at a ceremony at Danang, marking the arrival of the 1st Marine Division in Vietnam.

PFC Howard Miller

For twenty-four hours it was continuous nonstop combat. Actually, it was not one large assault but just constantly fighting trying to find out who was behind you and who was in front of you. How anyone ever made any sense of the situation, I'll never understand.

PFC Bill Brocksieker

We went back to Chu Lai and we rested up and didn't do a whole lot for three or four days, and then we started patrolling the peninsula. The Viet Cong started acting up on the other side of the combat base now and we started sending patrols out there.

The battalion's sector of Chu Lai was renamed Camp Bruce D. Webb, in honor of the fallen India Company commander.

6

· · · · · · · · · · · · · · · · · ·

OPERATION GOLDEN FLEECE

Captain Dave Ramsey

Operation GOLDEN FLEECE was an operation up in the Danang area to protect the farmers, and that was the operation that Colonel Joe Muir was killed on. They flew us up to Danang, and we got off the plane in Danang and we were racing for the helicopters, [C]H-34s, which were all revving up. We were going to Hill 55, a large hill just south of Danang. And Colonel Muir says, "Dave, get out and just hold the hill. I'll be right behind you."

With the dispatch for which Marines have become known as the "First to Fight" in several wars, 3/3 picked up and moved to the Danang area rapidly by fixed-wing aircraft and helicopters. Orders came at 1140 on 10 September. Movement commenced at 1231, and the first units became airborne at 1325. The entire battalion was in place in its assigned position by 1800 the same day.

An hour and five minutes later, a Marine from Lima Company was killed when he stepped on a 155-mm howitzer shell rigged as a mine. The United States inadvertently supplied such weapons to the enemy. The dud rate for artillery fired was 2 percent and

5 percent for bombs dropped from aircraft, providing the enemy with hundreds of tons of explosives monthly.

PFC Bill Brocksieker

This [Operation GOLDEN FLEECE] was so the South Vietnamese could harvest their rice. We were to give them some security so they could get out to these contested areas and get their rice in. We had no real threat from the VC at this time, but we did take some casualties, mostly from booby traps and punji stakes.

Captain Dave Ramsey

Right. So off we went. And . . . we got there and landed on Hill 55 and got all settled in and got our perimeters set up and everything and on the topographical crest of the hill there was a little . . . kind of walkway of white rocks. Maybe . . . fifteen to twenty white rocks on either side of what appeared to be a trail. So my gunnery sergeant and I, Gunnery Sergeant Versimato, we avoid walking in that trail. We went around to the side of it every time that we were up around there, and we were up there frequently. Hell, we issued C-rats that evening to the troops from there. We drove a mechanical mule around up there and everything. I'm saying all this because there was a mine up there. And it's what Joe Muir stepped on.

That evening, I guess it was about midnight, Joe Muir came up there to where I was. And we sat there. It was a bright moonlit night and we sat there and we looked out. We could see all the surrounding countryside, the moon was so bright. And we were talking about what we were going to do the next day, where he wanted me to send my patrols and that routine, to deny the Viet Cong the freedom of movement in the area. It was just starting to get light and he says, "Well, I'm going to go back down to the CP," to do something, to have some breakfast or something. Well, my gunnery sergeant and 1st Sergeant Petty . . . we were standing there watching him go. And he hadn't gone fifty yards when he stepped on this damn thing.

It turned out to be a 155 artillery shell, buried with an antipersonnel fuse on the nose. Those little half-dollar-size fuses. And I don't know how my gunnery sergeant and I missed it. We were sure walking around all over that area. Anyway, parts of the colonel splashed over the three of us. I ran over there to see what had happened and the colonel had been killed. Both of his legs were gone, most of both arms . . . actually, he was gone from about the rib cage down. And there was absolutely no possibility of him being alive. One other man was killed. He was a radioman. Jay Doub, who at this time was the 3, had been badly wounded and lost one of his eyes. There was a lot of bleeding and he was in bad shape.

Another radioman . . . I remember him because he was a tall, good-looking guy with a good personality. He had been my radioman at one time or another. And I liked the guy. And here, all of one leg, part of another leg, his genitals, part of an arm were gone. He also had a bad laceration across his forehead, which . . . was producing a lot of blood, running down into his eyes. But he thought that was his only wound and he was asking the corpsman, he said, "Will it leave a scar?" He was good-lookin' and he knew it. But he wasn't aware of the way he'd been mutilated. There were two guys of the six in the colonel's party who got off without a scratch.

PFC Bill Brocksieker

The colonel's body was pretty well shredded and the bottom part was gone. They stuck his remains in a willie peter [waterproof] bag.

Sergeant Pat Finton

I found the bottom part of his .45. Either his or the radio operator's .45 holster. I found his burned dungarees or the radio operator's burned dungarees. I found a belt buckle but no belt.

PFC Bill Brocksieker

The helicopter came in and they hauled the willie peter bag over there, and the crew chief on the chopper flagged us away, saying that they weren't taking any personal equipment, they were just taking casualties. And the guy told him, "Hey, this is our battalion commander." And they loaded him up and took him away. He was a good man. He was the kind of guy who would come around and talk to you. He was a good officer.

Sergeant Richard Kidwell

The whole hill cried.

Sergeant Pat Finton

So we ended up trying to clear out the mines. We did find quite a few. We found a 500-pound bomb that they had rigged up. And some other small stuff and a hell of a lot of punji . . . stakes. They seemed to know the LZ or the exact spot that we were gonna sit down at. It was like somebody had mapped everything out for them. Thinking back, I'm sure somebody did.

After only four months in country, the battalion commander was replaced for the second time. The original executive officer, the operations officer, and all of the other company commanders had changed. Captains Dave Ramsey and Cal Morris were the only two officers in a company commander billet or higher who had landed with 3/3 in May and were still with the battalion in September.

SEPTEMBER–OCTOBER 1965

PFC Howard Miller

Sam was a mongrel dog that the engineers attached to our outfit on Hill 55 managed to save from the cooking pot. Evidently, his Vietnamese owner was going to use Sam for food. I understand that Sam had tried to attack the owner several times, probably because Sam had been severely beaten, and the information I received from the engineers was that he did not like Orientals in any way, shape, or form. Sam was also hard of hearing, possibly as a result of artillery fire.

The amazing thing about Sam was, he would accompany us on patrols and through his other senses he always seemed to know when we were about to be hit, either by rifle fire or by artillery fire, and he would immediately start to growl and then look for cover. Sam had other bad habits besides not liking Orientals. He could not stop himself from attacking their livestock, such as chickens, ducks, small pigs, things of that nature.

After a period of time, a new lieutenant was transferred into the company. His name was Roger Okamoto, of Japanese descent. Naturally him and Sam had an immediate dislike and hatred for each other. Lieutenant Okamoto informed us that if Sam was to kill any more livestock, he would kill Sam. One day going through a village, Sam attacked a farmer's livestock—his chicken, ducks—and Lieutenant Okamoto went over and shot Sam. Naturally everybody felt bad about it, and quite a few of us said, "Well, someday the lieutenant will get his," and called him some uncomplimentary names. Well, the bad part about it is, it wasn't too long after that that on one of the patrols we were on, on the hill near Hill 55, Lieutenant Okamoto stepped on a booby-trapped artillery round and was killed. Naturally everybody then felt bad about what they said, but I guess that's war.

Hill 55 area was a very bad area—not that we had large fights, but almost every day we would become engaged with squad-sized Viet Cong units. It's amazing how much damage six to ten men can do with automatic weapons and how hard and how expensive it is to eliminate those men. Not enough to really call in air support or artillery barrages, but yet the cost of human lives that they could extract would be tremendous. Every day and every night it seemed like we had some small contact, almost every patrol. There were usually always snipers in the area that would take potshots at you on the hill.

.

PFC Bill Brocksieker

That was Operation GOLDEN FLEECE. We were sent back to Chu Lai after the operation [on 14 September]. Also, at the beginning of September 1965, we were allowed to write "Free" for the first time on our mail sent out of Vietnam.

.

Sergeant Richard Kidwell

We were on a patrol one time with Captain McDavid one night. You know how it gets pitch-black. Of course, no smoking. The captain hollers down the line, "Put out that cigarette." Well, it wasn't a cigarette. There was lightning bugs out there. So the word come back, "Well, kill them."

.

Captain Dave Ramsey

Bill Lanagan took over the battalion and he was just a great guy. He had come to us from the 1st Battalion, 3d Marines. First Battalion, 3d Marines, was leaving country and rotating back to Okinawa and he came down and took our battalion.

And there was lots of guys that asked for battalions. Lots and lots of guys were always screaming about how badly they wanted a battalion. But they did their screaming to the bartender back in Marble Mountain or 3d Division head-quarters or something. Because when battalions became available because commanding officers had been killed, then, of course, a lot of people all of a sudden just decided, well, you know, some logistics S-4 work would be professionally rewarding. And you don't have them all screaming out there, volunteering.

But guys like Lanagan, Muir, these guys were true Marines. Lanagan, for chrissakes, had two battalions and he was a good battalion commander.

Morley Safer was with us about then. I think he was with [Captain Cal] Morris's company. But we had a lot of newspaper people with us. And we had good newspaper people and we had lousy newspaper people. I class Ed Adams as one of the good ones. Keyes Beech as a good one. Jimmy Breslin, a good one. Guys like Morley Safer and Peter Arnett were losers in my book. Morley Safer, the one that did the article on the burning of Cam Ne, the cigarette lighter bit, for one of the news magazines.

Cam Ne was a hamlet where three Marines from a rifle company had been killed in action. On 3 August the company swept through the same area with orders to destroy the enemy and his positions. In the ensuing firefight four Marines were wounded. Safer's film crew recorded Marines setting fire to huts, claimed the burning of 120–150 houses, and painted a picture of wanton destruction. He did not refer to the earlier action in which Marines had died, or to the trenches, mines, and booby traps, or to the hostile fire encountered in the village. Moreover, the Marines' after-action report noted that there had only been 51 structures in the village at the beginning of the operation.

Most Marines in Vietnam learned not to like the media very much. As early as STAR-LITE, there were numerous official complaints of newsmen hampering operations. The most common sin in the early years of the war was the last-minute appearance of a journalist who wanted to accompany troops into combat. Since the helicopters used in those days had very limited lift capability, Marine formations were sometimes compromised in order to accommodate these people. This, and the failure of many media representatives to share the hardships of the average grunt, often severely strained relationships.

Captain Dave Ramsey

Keyes Beech was a journalist over there and he spent some time with I/3/3, on more than one occasion. I remember one time when . . . somebody, one of the guys was bringing in some prisoners. Had about four or five of them. And he had them all wound together with det cord [a high explosive in the form of a cord that is detonated like dynamite] around their necks, which I thought was pretty innovative. It put the prisoners under immediate control. It only took him to control it. He had the whole thing wired up. Blasting cap, hell box [the mechanism that sends an electrical charge to the firing device]. And, uh, I thought that was pretty good thinkin' on his part. Well, there was more than one journalist with us. And Keyes came over to me and he said, "Skipper, you see that guy over there?" And he nodded his head toward a man with a camera. And he says, "If he gets that . . . picture of those guys with the det cord around their neck, it'll get to Saigon and you're gonna get in some trouble." So I told the gunny, "Get the guy and the prisoners with the det cord and get them out of the area. Take them somewhere."

Keyes was a Marine in WW2. And in Korea, he was a journalist. So this was his third war. He wasn't any spring chicken. But he would still stay out with us and he'd eat the same chow as the troops ate, and if there wasn't any coffee to be had, he went without coffee. He didn't require any of the niceties that some of those journalists did. You almost had to set up a special area for some of those pukes. But Keyes Beech was a Marine's correspondent.

October . . . we had some sappers get in behind our lines. My company, India

Company, was stretched out around the Chu Lai airfield. Jimmy Breslin was with us there a little while, and he went back and wrote a real nice story about the company. And my gunnery sergeant was from Brooklyn and my first sergeant was from Flatbush, so both of them hit it off right away with Jimmy Breslin.

But in any event, Lima Company, which by that time was commanded by Pat DeMartino, had been airlifted out of there to supplement the forces around Da-nang. Now, Pat and I had had the perimeter around the Chu Lai airfield. When he left, I had to stretch out to cover the entire perimeter which was previously occupied by two rifle companies. To further aggravate it . . . I had a platoon out at this rock crusher that we had to guard for the construction company. And so, really, what we had was just a little bit better than a reinforced platoon holding an area that had been occupied by two rifle companies.

We had a standing regulation—no rifle firing where we were because of the proximity of the friendly troops around the area. We had amtracs, we had Sea-bees, we had artillery. All sorts of people . . . plus we had the air group. M79 grenade launchers and hand grenades and that was about it. We weren't allowed to use rifles and pistols.

Well, about eighteen sappers got in . . . no telling where they came through. They could have come through in any one of a dozen places as spread out as I was. They got in and they had these little, kind of homemade satchel charges, made of bamboo or wicker-type casing and I don't know what the hell kind of explosive it was. We had . . . our A-4s parked nose to tail, just one alongside another one in a nice straight line and nice and close together.

They put the satchel charges under every other airplane. They were badly made, flawed, somehow only a couple went off. So only one plane was damaged. And then they tried to get out. We ran 'em down and we killed eighteen. I don't think there was any more than that.

And we had them layin' out to dry the next morning when General Westmore-land came hummin' in there on a helicopter . . . all brand-new starched uniform and lookin' real sharp and smellin' nice. And we'd been up all night long, and so when he wanted to know how they got in, I told him that I could take him around the perimeter. My jeep wasn't workin' but if he wanted to ride on a mechanical mule, I'd be happy to take him around the perimeter and show him exactly how I was spread out. He thought that my answer was a little sharp, and he started to cloud up and rain all over me. General Walt was there, and he stepped in and he said to General Westmoreland, he says, "General, if you've got any problem with the Marine dispositions here, you've got the problem with me." And he told Colonel Lanagan, "Bill, you and Captain Ramsey are excused."

So General Walt, I'm sure, saved me from doing something incredibly stupid.

But I was tired and we'd been up all night long and I had been clipped. I don't know who got me, whether it was a VC that was kind of crossing my path there when he opened up with a Thompson submachine gun, or whether it was one of our air wing. Because when he opened up with that submachine gun, I think the air group opened up with their FPL [final protective line], and we were between the FPL and the enemy. So, it's a wonder that more of my people weren't at least hit, if not killed.

7

THE FIRST MOVE NORTH: DANANG

Captain Dave Ramsey

On Operation BLUE MARLIN II, that was in November [1965], right around the Birthday, 10 November [the anniversary of the founding of the United States Marine Corps], we left Chu Lai and moved to Danang, and a battalion of the 7th Marines moved from Danang down into Chu Lai. I think that we were finally reunited with our parent regiment. We hadn't been under 3d Marines' control since we landed. . . .

Colonel Lanagan got dengue fever and he was evacuated. And a colonel by the name of Dorsey took over.

The November move was the first of a series of northward migrations that would culminate in the battalion's fighting along the Demilitarized Zone (DMZ) for nearly three years. During November, the unit also had its first experience of the monsoon, with its heavy rainfall, overcast skies, and relative cold. The weather's side effects included a rise in diseases from sanitation problems associated with the dampness and difficulty of maintaining personal hygiene.

Marines from 3/3 cross a beach in the second phase of BLUE MARLIN. *Vietnamese fishing boats are in the background.*

Captain Dave Ramsey

We were down on a hill called Hill 22. It was a cemetery and during the rainy season, the only place that was out of the water was cemeteries and villages. Moving into a village was out of the question, so we moved onto this Hill 22. We were tied in with a battalion of the 1st Marines. We were on this little hill and we ran patrols, set up ambushes . . . and just general interdiction operations.

One time up on Hill 22, it was raining like hell; it was miserable. One of the men got a bright idea to write a letter to the University of Texas and inform them that Company I, 3d Battalion, 3d Marines, was holding a beauty contest. And we wanted to see pictures of all the girls that would like to enter this beauty contest and we would send them a suitable award. The winner would be crowned the "Queen of I/3/3."

They laid out restrictions and whatnot on how the photographs should be taken and whether they should be color or black and white. I don't know all the details, but all the photographs were all done essentially the same way. They looked like they'd been done with professional photographers, too. Some of those girls took this real seriously. As I'm sure some of the troops did.

Wellll, it was an amazingly successful game. We were flooded with pictures,

Marines of L Company cross a river to make a sweep on a village during the second phase of Operation BLUE MARLIN.

many of which were wet because the mail got wet. And we had 'em hanging up in the same tent that we put up for socks to dry. And I mean there were some good-lookin' honeys that sent their pictures out to us. So the men held the contest and had a little voting and all of that routine and came up with a winner and sent her a bottle of perfume that somebody had gotten from Hong Kong and got one of these warm-up jackets with the map of Vietnam on the back and had it embroidered "The Queen of I/3/3." Everybody just loved it. I thought it was an amazing example of Marine ingenuity. He brightened up an otherwise somewhat dismal landscape with his little idea to get all these photographs of these beautiful girls.

In early December, part of the battalion became engaged in their sharpest firefight since STARLITE when they participated in Operation HARVEST MOON. The command group of 3/3 and Lima Company became part of Task Force Delta, and the battalion assumed command of companies E and G of 2/9.

HARVEST MOON was a spoiling attack designed to prevent the VC from capturing the

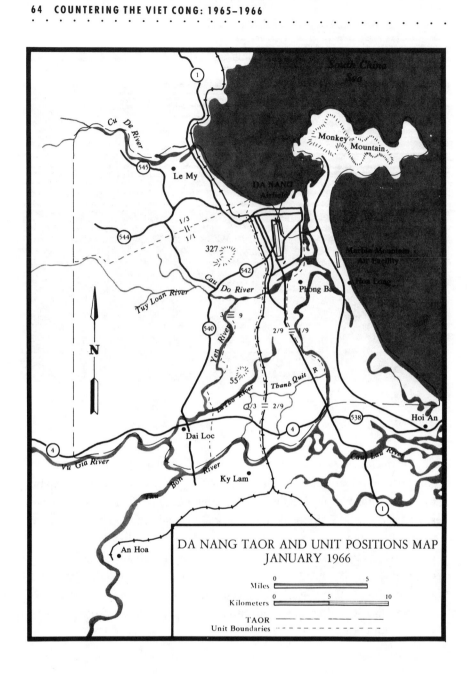

DA NANG TAOR AND UNIT POSITIONS MAP
JANUARY 1966

Marines move through a village in Operation HARVEST MOON. *Each of the riflemen is carrying two 60mm mortar rounds in addition to his own weapon and ammunition.*

city of Que Son, their announced objective. A B-52 strike immediately preceding the operation apparently caught the enemy off balance, as the Marines discovered twenty-five VC bodies, most of which were missing limbs from the violence of the bombs, in the objective area. The enemy was 3/3's old foe from STARLITE, the *1st VC Regiment*.

The operation was characterized by several sharp firefights, and the Marines lost 11 dead and 51 wounded. Enemy casualties were 101 KIA by body count and evidence of another 120 dead. Over 90 tons of foodstuffs and a wide assortment of enemy material were captured. Among the items were 500 VC uniforms and materials for many more, including 15,000 buttons and 7 sewing machines. Four hundred tubes of toothpaste, 2,000 ball-point pens, 9 bicycles, 150 bicycle tire tubes, and 1,200 cubic feet of blank paper also were taken. Captured weapons were almost all World War II vintage.

Captain Dave Ramsey

On Christmas Day our CP was in an abandoned schoolhouse in Cam Ne II. There was supposed to have been a truce, and Gunnery Sergeant Versimato . . . had gotten a "care" package from home, and he was from Brooklyn and there

Marines of L Company huddle behind a machine gun as they watch Marine artillery preparatory fire chew up the valley in front of them during Operation HARVEST MOON.

were some steamed clams in there. We had missed Christmas dinner that had been set out by battalion and it was all raining and sloppy anyway. It was just pouring rain. And so the gunny said, "Hey skipper, I got these steamed clams." So we heated those up. The schoolhouse in which we had our CP had no roof. It had been bombed out or burned out or something, just had a little overhang of roof around the main room there. So Gunny Versimato and I were hunkered up against the side of the wall trying to get out of the rain and eating these clams. And Ed Adams, the correspondent, who was just a great guy . . . started laughing all of a sudden, and he took a picture of the gunnery sergeant and I and he said, "There's two duty stations in the Marine Corps, Conus [acronym for continental United States] and Anus." He says, "And you know where you are." So we all had a big laugh about that and offered him some clams and that was our Christmas dinner in 1965.

For their first Christmas in country, the battalion chaplain managed to obtain and distribute presents for all members of the battalion and also had Christmas music played in the mess area. The Marines also had a Christmas Eve party for the children of the village of An Trach and gave them 250 pounds of candy and toys. Not all was peaceful, however.

Although a cease-fire was in effect, a post along the river manned by India Company got into a little firefight around noon on Christmas Day when they were fired upon by four VC. Observers saw one VC fall and be carried off by another.

Captain Dave Ramsey

One of the things that I never could get over was the sheer guts of those . . . those Viet Cong. You know, when we were over there, it was right at the beginning of the war, and we hadn't run into any big main-force units. Yet. Our encounters were with little . . . the little guy, in his black pajamas, World War II carbine. And here is an entire rifle company, perhaps more, advancing across a rice paddy, two platoons up, one back, tanks, all of this firepower, and here old Nguyen breaks out the carbine and takes a shot at somebody. It was just . . . incredible, the bravery of some of those little guys.

There were always certain places where we knew we were gonna get into trouble. You could . . . as soon as you got into the vill . . . you could sense it. All the animals were tethered, for instance, so they wouldn't start runnin' around when the firing started. Perhaps all the women and children were in the main house in the center of the vill and there aren't any young men around. It just made your skin crawl. You know that there is going to be a scrap before you get out of that vill, it's just a matter of when do they open up. Such was a little town called Bic Bac . . . down near Hill 55. Every time we went to Bic Bac we'd get somebody . . . shot. You know, you'd get one of your men gut shot . . . . It was just terribly, terribly irritating. And so we used to take some extraordinary measures. We took a line-charge down there one time, an LTVE 1, and fired a line-charge into that vill. And, uh, from then on, we didn't get a helluva lot of grief from that particular area.

Of course, if the command had found out that we were doing this sort of thing . . . we would probably get into a lot of trouble. For instance, whenever we set ambushes up, the rules were such that all killing had to be visual. When I was down in the Hill 22 area, we used to set up ambushes with bangalore torpedoes and det cord and sensor. And, of course, there were people that got killed when those bangalore torpedoes were set off. I'd set them up fence-post style and then put the det cord around the top and wire them all together and then hook up a blasting cap at the end . . . and have a plunger and sensors. And as soon as you'd get a reading on your first sensor and then your second sensor and as soon as you got all three or all four needles, depending upon how many sensors you got out there, crank that rascal off. Aannd, there were people that got tangled up in it. We killed an awful lot of animals, too.

I think General Walt knew what was going on because he'd come out the next morning and he'd want to know what happened. "Uh, a little ambush set down there, General." And, he'd look at me and he'd say, "You're not doing anything illegal, are you, Ramsey?" "Oh, no sir."

We would have snipers in the tree lines and whatnot. I found one of the most effective ways with dealing with persistent snipers is massive retaliation. We had this one area south of Hill 22 that invariably we'd get . . . just a few rounds. But, you know, it just upset everything. And pesky was I guess the best way to describe it. I had an Ontos set up there. Had him zeroed in on that area that the fire normally came from. And one night when the sniper opened up, I said, "Six 106 rounds, right straight into the spot where he fired from." Well, we never heard from him again. And I don't know whether we got him or whether he just decided to take up another line of work or what.

But very often, that was extremely effective. Massive, massive firepower. And sometimes if you don't kill them, they just get discouraged. They figure it's not worth it.

·

The New Year and the new location brought about some changes for the battalion. The Danang area—headquarters for III MAF, the huge airfield complex, manned by both the Marines and Air Force, and the sprawling logistics support system—was an enticing target for the enemy.

Viet Cong activity in 3/3's new home increased both in number of events and in intensity. Sniper incidents now often meant being on the receiving end of several hundred rounds of small arms by a small group rather than a random shot from an individual. However, if there was ever a period in Vietnam when it could be said that the battalion had a relatively easy time, the first nine months of 1966 would probably fit the bill. Marines still fought and died, but their operations were generally minor affairs conducted against Viet Cong guerrillas who were organized in small units and armed with outmoded weaponry. From January to August, the battalion was in the relatively civilized area west and south of Danang. It had some access to such amenities as showers, tents, recreational opportunities, and prepared food. For a few months in early 1966, the battalion even had a limited liberty policy in the Danang area. During daylight hours, several groups of carefully supervised Marines could go to some of the shopping areas and make purchases. Limited as it was, it was one of the few times that the average Marine ever had any "normal" contact whatsoever with Vietnamese civilians.

By February 1966, all but a few of the original members of the battalion had departed or were about to. Their thirteen-month tours were over. All of the men of 3/3 from this point would be replacements who reported to Vietnam in ones and twos and were assigned to the unit upon arrival. No more would most of the men in the unit spend much

Lieutenant Colonel Joshua W. Dorsey III, commanding officer, 3/3, confers with Brigadier General Jonas M. Platt, commanding officer, Task Force Delta. Dorsey's battalion is about to enter the Phuoc Ha Valley, a known VC main base area.

of the tour together. When a new man arrived, he found himself surrounded by some Marines who were about to finish their tours, others who had been in country only a few days, and the rest who were in between.

As this narrative continues, that absence of a common experience will occasionally strip a measure of objectivity from some events and obscure certain facts. Whenever things seem confusing, the reader should consider that they were often equally unclear to many of the participants.

8

. . . .

PACIFICATION

General Westmoreland was critical of the mode of operation that the Corps brought with it to Vietnam. Perhaps because of their experience in the pre–World War II campaigns in Nicaragua, Haiti, and the Dominican Republic, the Marines stressed the importance of population control and pacification. General Walt discovered soon after he assumed command of III MAF that there were 150,000 civilians within 81-mm mortar range of the Danang airstrip. Thus, he declared, "The Marines are in the pacification business." His views were shared by the commandant of the Marine Corps, General Wallace M. Greene, Jr.

Westmoreland did not agree, believing that the emphasis on population control around the established beachheads left the Viet Cong free to expand their main force operations and move in the hills with impunity. This led to a great difference of opinion over how the war should be fought. Although III MAF was under Westmoreland's operational control and bound by his instructions, Marines continued their attempts to win over the Vietnamese people.

A schoolhouse built by Marines for Vietnamese children, one of whom later burned it to the ground. (Courtesy Pat Finton)

Staff Sergeant Pat Finton

We built a schoolhouse. And we felt that we were doin' something positive . . . for the kids. I really felt sorry for the kids over there. If we could win one or two of them over to our way of thinkin' and show them that we weren't the bad guys that the Viet Cong kept tellin' them that we were, that was a point for us.

We got the villagers to help us build the schoolhouse. They built the . . . thatched roof and all that. I scrounged a bunch of material in Danang to build benches and school desks. We had just dedicated it and the ARVN had sent out a teacher for the kids in the village . . . and that school hadn't been in operation more than a week. It was sitting right in the middle of our village which the Marine perimeter was around, but there was Viet Cong sympathizers in there and one morning about four o'clock we looked over and that . . . that school was on fire. All our benches and everything went up in smoke. And that was inside the village that the Marines were protecting, so you kind of begin to wonder what a crazy place it was over here.

The schoolhouse was set on fire by a ten-year-old boy. He had been given 100 piasters by the VC, less than one American dollar, to set the blaze and had been promised another 900 piasters upon completion of the job. He was sent to the Vietnamese district head-quarters after he was caught and questioned. His fate, and whether he ever collected the rest of the bounty, is unknown. The school, which served forty-four children, was rebuilt by the Marines some months later, when materials once more became available.

Staff Sergeant Pat Finton

I did snuff. Copenhagen. I dipped snuff and Copenhagen was hard to come by in Vietnam. And my mother and my wife, which wanted me to quit over the many years, they'd keep sendin' it to me. We'd make the search-and-clear operations and I would always have Copenhagen in my mouth. We would come into some of these villages and these old ladies and old men, but primarily old ladies, would be chewing betel nut, and their lips would be all red and their teeth, part of them would be gone . . . and so here I was chewing and dipping snuff. They'd look at my lips and they'd look at what I was doin' and they thought I was chewin' betel nut when it was only Copenhagen. I'd spit and they'd spit and then they'd laugh with their red lips. They thought I was doin' their betel nut kick there, I guess. . . .

In 1966, 3/3 also began "County Fair" operations. Described by the Marines as the "seeds of population control," these were cordon and search tactics designed to separate the guerrillas from their population bases. As officially described, County Fairs were to "convince the people that the GVN (Government of Vietnam) was an effective government that was interested in the welfare of the people and that a GVN victory against the VC was inevitable."

Typically lasting for a day or two, the operations began by sealing off one or more hamlets with troops. The population would then be herded through a tent where identification cards would be checked against the census of those who lived in the village. Those who could not properly identify themselves were moved off to one side for questioning. To minimize the potential for resentment, the verified population would be examined by the battalion doctors and corpsmen for illnesses and, when possible, receive treatment on the spot. (In fact, by late spring, 3/3's medical people were treating more than 6,000 Vietnamese civilians around Danang each month for hookworm, diarrhea, and more serious diseases.) They were also usually treated to food and drink and sometimes entertainment. General Westmoreland grew to like the County Fairs and in his memoir states that he pressed for countrywide adoption of the program.

Staff Sergeant Pat Finton

The company commander had a Coleman stove. And I would go into Danang and get cornmeal and hot dogs and flour and we'd make a batter and we'd make these hot dogs with dough around them and deep fry 'em. We did this about once a week. All the kids in the village were walkin' around with these hot dogs on sticks that we'd fried in deep batter. They'd never had anything like it. And to see the smiles on their faces. That was worth it all, I think.

We did a lot for the village . . . and you know . . . I left in March '66 . . . and I heard that the village was overran in May of '66. A lot of Marines were killed, and a lot of the Vietnamese that lived in the village that were friendly to us got killed.

Before STARLITE, Marine reports were mentioning the progress they were making in pacifying the civilian population on the Van Tuong Peninsula. Whether this was true or wishful thinking will probably never be known. A great deal of publicity was generated regarding the quantity of materials supplied by the Marines to the Vietnamese, as well as goods contributed by American church and civic organizations. However, this was not accompanied by an objective method of evaluating whether this effort really secured the allegiance of the population. The very nature of the war made relations with the Vietnamese civilians uncertain at best. Members of the same family would take different sides; combatants included women and children; and the lack of boundary lines made most areas suspect to the Marines in the field.

9

· · · · · · · · · · · · · · ·

RELOCATION

Pacification of the population was an important concept that suffered in execution. Although U.S. troops were reluctant to open fire in populated areas, the Viet Cong and NVA often fortified villages and fired on Americans from them. The resulting damage done to Vietnamese society by allied military operations made it difficult to convince villagers that Americans had come as liberators and not oppressors.

An often-used type of pacification that the Vietnamese found particularly unpalatable was relocation. Whether for their own protection or for the creation of free fire zones that would neutralize specified areas, allied forces sometimes uprooted peasants and moved them to another location. The peasants were reluctant to leave their villages, where they had established homes of relative comfort by their own standards and where they had honored the spirits of their ancestors for generations. A relocation operation was not pleasant under the best of circumstances. Under the worst, it could be tragic.

Corporal Kenneth G. Ransbottom

I was a corporal, a fire team leader in M Company in 3/3, and we were located west of Danang in an area called An Trach. It was a series of villages. This had to be early in 1966 . . . February or March. Our objective on this particular operation was to go in and clear this village and get all the civilians out . . . they were going to be relocated.

We were given very good instructions on how to move these people, how to execute movements in the village. It seems as though everything was very well defined, it was very well detailed, it was all cut and dried. We knew what we were going to do, but evidently the villagers didn't know what we were going to do.

There were a lot of people. They were moving some out in amtracs. They were moving some out in helicopters. It seemed like we had everything we needed to do the job. I heard loudspeakers with South Vietnamese officials talking.

This village was real spread out, though. It was groups of two or three hooches, banana trees, little pineapple patches, little gardens, sweet potato gardens where the mounds were built up to three or four feet off the deck. Immaculately kept. It was like many little villages hooked into one big village.

I felt like I was swallowed up by that village. Contact with other people was mostly by shouting. You couldn't see a skirmish line, you couldn't see a line that was clear. It was so thick that you couldn't really keep eye contact with much that was going on around you.

Well into the clearing of the village . . . well into the operation of clearing the place out, it seemed to turn into chaos. The people and their unwillingness to cooperate seemed to generate aggression. Being just a fire team leader, seemingly having small tasks to perform, it didn't seem like much to me. But as more and more people were being pulled through that village, they'd get a small group of people together and they would be moving towards the area that they were to be herded up into. In the middle of moving, after it seemed like they had accepted the fact that they were leaving . . . right in the middle they would change their mind. Some would seem to want to break and go back to their hooch or house or area.

The South Vietnamese were getting louder, trying to be more convincing, and then we started hearing some shooting. It was nothing to be particularly alarmed about. To my fire team it was no particular threat. If anybody had gotten hit, it would have been a random shot that could have also hit one of the civilians that we were among. For some reason I wasn't even concerned about the shots. They sounded high and seemed so wide that it didn't even bother me. But it did add to the confusion amongst the civilians. At some point, the people accumulated around my team, and it was like they were going to have a little sit-in or something.

There were engineers blowing bomb shelters and underground storage . . .

Sergeant Ken Ransbottom, who was to earn a Bronze Star Medal for heroic action in the first battle of Khe Sanh. (Courtesy Ken Ransbottom)

that was very well marked. There was nothing that seemed like a sneaky hiding place. Nonetheless, the engineers were behind me and my platoon sergeant . . . occasionally I would get eye contact with him. . . . He was coaxing me to move on and somewhat directing me, which seemed at the time like it was the only link that I had with any . . . leadership of what I was doing.

I got to a spot where I had a lot of civilians . . . a group of maybe twenty-five. And I had a very large bomb shelter. There were mostly women and children, with us showing no aggression, only being stern in our pointing and coaxing. I was becoming really uneasy. We could get a few of them to move who were scared, but others were so scared that they wouldn't move. This bomb shelter had a really unique opening to it. It was probably only about twenty-four inches wide and maybe thirty-six inches high—the opening—but it was lined with real heavy material, and it went in maybe two or three feet and then turned so you couldn't see inside of it. As I was down on my knees trying to look in, the civilians behind me . . . the momentum of their jabber and uneasiness . . . told me something was wrong. I could tell that they didn't want me messing with that bomb shelter.

I was on my knees with my head in the bomb shelter; I could hear very faint human noises. I could feel people in there. But I had not yet made it far enough in there to peer around the corner. I knew . . . I knew there were women and children. . . . Nothing could have convinced me then that there wasn't totally innocent people in there. Now, I knew what else, what could have been in there. I knew that they could have been held hostage . . . voluntarily been in there with VC . . . armed, uh, I don't know. I know that with all of my senses . . . I know that there were people in there. I think the reason that I backed out of there was the screaming . . . and attitude of the civilians that we had herded up near there.

I felt so compelled to help. I felt so much like a liberator, finding a bunch of people that needed help and I was the answer to safety for them. I hesitated and moved and hesitated and moved, trying to decide whether to go in there or not. The tempo increased . . . and suddenly, engineers were almost on my back. "Is it clear? Is it clear? Come on, move out, move out. We got to blow these things." By the same token my platoon sergeant was screaming for me to "move it up, move it up. Come on, let's clear this village. Come on, move it up. Come on, get those people up here."

With, uh, this, I became . . . more . . . became . . . irritated but I kept hoping that my squad leader or my platoon sergeant would come and see . . . the dilemma I was in. The crescendo of everybody, especially those civilians . . . they were almost screaming . . . and the engineers were trying to outscream the civilians. I think there were two of them, and they wanted me to move those people so they could blow that bomb shelter. My fire team was just like . . . they were just like tin soldiers. They were just there, doing exactly what they had to do.

I wasn't told about this kind of a situation. The engineers were being pushed and pushing me and my platoon sergeant was screaming at me and I think that the civilians saw the dilemma I was in and added to it. I think they saw, without knowing what was being said to me . . . just the tone of voice and the attitude . . . I think they saw that they might be able to crack me and let them go and move away from that bomb shelter and be gone. I think that attitude was their way of . . . getting me to do what they wanted.

I tried to ignore everything that was going on around me. I got down on my knees again and got near the bunker. And . . . so . . . humbly spoke, "*Chao ba, chao ong, chao co*" [Vietnamese greetings], over and over as though I knew they were there. I didn't want to scare them. I . . . could feel them. I knew they were there and I repeated . . . several times. I was pouring my heart out . . . the thing that I had to do, since they couldn't see me or look into my eyes and let me convince them that I was just trying to help. I poured it out of my heart as Vietnamese as I could, as pleading as I could. I could hear cloth being brushed as though maybe somebody moved their arm or their leg and the clothing brushed against . . . one leg against the other. But it was very hushed, it was very secretive. . . . What was I gonna do?

As I cleared the entrance of the bunker with my head, back out into the screaming, the babies . . . the babies were just going nuts. The women, the old men, some were down on their knees like they were praying to Buddha. Hands clasped together, thumbs on their forehead, bowing and screaming. I think everybody knew from the look on my face . . . the engineers, my people . . . I think everybody knew . . . how torn apart I was getting and really . . . what was at stake. I looked around and nobody, seemingly nobody, was on my side. It seemed like everything was against me. With a Marine staff sergeant telling me to move it out, I had to revert to my basic training . . . I had to keep that foremost in my mind.

Then a man . . . I won't say an old man . . . but he was . . . I'd hate to guess his age. I don't know. But he was hardy . . . he wasn't all hunched over. I noticed his legs. . . . The calf muscles weren't great big but very long and stringy-looking and tough.

He walked right to me. He knew. He knew without hesitation what was going on. I felt like it was Moses walking toward me. This guy, to me, this guy represented my answer . . . how I could get out of this thing gracefully. I needed help.

He walked right straight up to me, since I was so close to the bomb shelter. . . . And the crowd quieted down. The kids were still crying. But it seemed like it peaked out . . . the commotion, the chaos. It seemed like it peaked out and I had a chance because I had help. I felt like this guy was liberating me from this fiasco.

I put my hand on his shoulder. I didn't have a helmet on at the time. He could see my face, he could see my eyes. I pleaded with him to get the women and children and babies out of there. This guy, to me, was my "exit stage left." I was so relieved because I was so open with him and the way I talked. And my eyes. I knew . . . I knew this guy was going to help me. He knew, he knew exactly where I stood. I mean there was friction between us . . . there was an electricity or signals or sensing or whatever you might call it. He knew that I was a good person.

I, again down on my knees near the bunker, "*Chao ba, chao ong, chao co.*" Motioning to him to do the same. I stood back up and I put my hand on his shoulder, and he gave me the, "*Khong biet, khong biet,* khong biet" [meaning "I don't understand," which Ransbottom interpreted as an insulting refusal].

It was a heartbeat. For me, I knew I lost. For me, I knew nothing mattered. It didn't make any difference about anything. I was still on the end of the plank and somebody was sawing the goddamned thing in half. I was stuck. Everybody, everybody started in screaming again then. I grabbed him by the back of the neck with my right hand. And I took my right leg and kicked him in the shins and ankles tripping him forward, and he hit the deck like a wad of wet dough smacking on top of a cutting board. He got up on all fours and he grabbed for my weapon, but he grabbed my leg. It was a powerful, deadly grasp. All his strength was in his fingers. I took my right leg and I drove my boot, my foot, into his exposed left side and I caught him midway up his rib cage, probably in the middle of his ribs. It felt like I kicked a pile of wet brush and it broke. I straightened up and I don't think I heard a whisper. I know they were still screaming, but I didn't hear anything. I could see the grimace on faces. I looked back down at this guy and he was up on all fours, and he either coughed or snorted and sprayed blood out of his nose and mouth, all over the ground. I was so angry that I just kicked him again. But this time, I buried my foot as far into his chest as it would go. He collapsed. I assume he was dead. I got a lot of things to think about right there. I think I just tried to get more aggressive than anything that was aggressing me.

I wished many things right then. I felt like I was at the bottom of a toilet for the world and the only thing I could do was somehow turn it off, get it done, and get the hell out of there. But there were so many things that I can't just easily say right now. Things that I thought about when I was starting to stick my head into that bomb shelter. Things that I thought about when I was bringing my head out of it.

I don't think any of the civilians quieted down any. I think that my people just moved them out and I mean those guys did some pushing. They got them out of there. I grabbed that guy's collar and waistband and slid him over to the opening of the bomb shelter and shoved him in there. I just looked at the engineers and said, "Blow it. I'm tired of this shit."

Then I heard my engineers give a "Fire in the hole," and that baby went. One of them wouldn't even walk up there. The other one, I think he looked as he went by. 'Cause he knew. I walked over and looked. It looked like a huge beef potpie. I was left standing there by myself. I just turned and walked away. I don't know how I acted. I don't even remember what happened after that incident and the rest of the day I was stunned. Hardly anyone would even talk to me. Eye contact was very . . . emotional . . . between me and the people that knew what went on. I just tried to maintain what we were doing. I tried to maintain safety. I tried to maintain discipline. But it was like . . . phony. It was like the word got passed around very quietly and quickly what happened. There was nothing more said about it. Nobody said anything. And I felt it in the looks. I felt it in the air. . . .

I had a lot of afterthoughts. I groped for something just to keep me going. I thought that if there is a way to do something good, that will help change what . . . I've just seen and been a part of. . . . I thought maybe somehow . . . I can get in the position to help somebody. My chance came the next day. The next day we moved into another village complex. It was like one huge rice paddy with little islands in it that contained these small units of civilian houses and . . . we moved along these little peninsulas. You'd come out of one and it would narrow down and you'd be in a rice paddy moving across into another little village. And . . . shooting broke out occasionally.

We were trying to fight and trying to help at the same time . . . but it seemed like it was a funny way to help people. I saw a man . . . he wasn't old. He looked like he was in his thirties . . . a villager. And with him was a young boy, maybe eleven, twelve years old. Tall and skinny. And they were holding hands. To me they appeared to be father and son. I could see it, I could feel it. For some reason as he moved toward our column—we were halted—for some reason he came straight to me . . . . He moved right toward me as though he knew something. There was shooting going on, not in my vicinity but from farther up the column, where evidently they had something spotted.

This man and boy moved quickly toward me, and I felt as though this was an answer . . . this is what I was looking for . . . somebody I could help. The man pointed to an area behind me. A small village that we had just come out of. I could still see it. Separated by maybe a hundred yards . . . a hundred and fifty yards of rice paddy. I could sense . . . this boy was terrified. This boy was so shaken and he was so dependent on his dad. He stood there. He would have taken anything as long as he could hold onto his father's arm. And I thought that if there is anything that comes out of this day, I'm going to help these two people. Whether they were good or bad, I don't know. Everything boiled down to the basics. I passed the word around me—"Let these people go. All they want to do is get back to that village."

I got close to this man for the brief minute or two we stood there and . . . he had one arm behind the boy's head, across his shoulders and with the other hand had the boy by the arm. . . . They were standing side by side and he was hugging him . . . comforting him . . . expressing to the boy some hope . . . expressing all that feeling. It was like helping somebody that sincerely needed it. Sincerely needed help.

When I passed the word to let these two people go through the lines, that they were okay, I heard the word get passed down behind me as though it had been passed down by command. I didn't care. I didn't know what we were going to do with them anyway. I had no order. I had no . . . nothing. I didn't know. But I knew one thing. I was going to help them. By helping them I was helping myself. 'Cause I felt bad. I felt terrible. Reflections of that bomb shelter were really getting to me.

The tempo of the exchange of fire really started to increase. . . . In a kneeling position, facing this man and his son, I pointed toward this little peninsula that we had come from. And he shook his head yes as though, "That's where I want to go." Now there were no more Marines out in the paddy. Everybody had crossed the paddy.

I could see some change, I could feel it, in this man's attitude. I mean if you could ever see sincerity or detect it . . . I was picking it up like radar. I could see the relief when I pointed toward that little village, that little peninsula, and he understood that I knew that is where he wanted to go. I motioned to him, I put my hand on the boy's shoulder and patted him. And I pointed in that direction and they moved off. Quickly.

I glanced back a couple of times as they were moving across the paddy, and I heard a gunship cross over to what seemed like the front of the column. He peeled off and went in for a run on the two people crossing the paddy. I knew what the gunship was going to do . . . I knew it. I almost went into a puddle. I almost just melted into a puddle. I could see the people in the gunship. I could see where they were looking. They weren't fifty meters off the deck. They were angled just right. They must have . . . they must have . . . come around there and spotted that and just kind of straightened the ship out, and they unloaded on them.

I just . . . I was just . . . oh, my God . . . I just don't know . . . I was just so . . . shaken. I just couldn't understand it. I couldn't figure it out. I just . . . they just piled it on them. Now . . . what am I thinking? What can I make out of this? I could do no good. Somehow I reached in and I said, "I am going to survive. I am here to survive. I am just going to watch my people. I am just going to watch my ass. And I'm gonna just hang the hell in here. But I can't make heads or tails out of this. This is just beyond me." I wonder . . . I wonder what that man thought when that gunship peeled over on him. And started that run. I bet you he thought, "You son of a bitch. You sent me out here and sicced them on me." Oh boy, I bet he thought I really trick-fucked him. I hope they died in an instant. I hope they didn't have time to think that.

·

Preoccupied by mostly small actions through the first quarter of 1966, the Marines none-theless continued to learn from their experiences. They discovered that a rifle sling could be used to effectively bind the arms of a VC suspect while he was being moved; that scout dogs became too distracted in populated areas to be of any real value; that the VC fre-quently used sugarcane stalks as aiming stakes for their 60-mm mortars; that flashlights were needed for searching tunnels and bunkers; and that their old family of radios was very unreliable.

They also began to experience manpower and equipment shortages. At the end of March 1966, for example, the battalion was twenty-four infantry officers, eighty enlisted, and ten corpsmen short of manning level. The firefights continued.

Corporal Ken Ransbottom
There was a particular firefight in which I was the point team of the point squad of the point platoon on a movement of some kind and we were in a high area. There were like . . . little cliffs. It was a real eroded area with splashes of thick, dense cover.

One of my team, Juan . . . I think his name was Juan Trevino, got shot in the chest and stomach on almost the opening burst. We got pushed back. It was get-ting dark. His sidekick—Whaley? Wiley? Whaley? I don't know. The nicknames confused me. Some guys, I didn't even know what their name was, it was just a nickname. To me just a nickname. And a ghost now.

But Whaley was Trevino's sidekick. They were as close as two people could

Marines of K Company guard a street while their buddies move out into the open from a village during a sweep-and-clear mission south of Danang.

get. When we pulled back . . . when we got pushed back . . . they had us cold. I got up close to where Trevino had laid. But the flies had covered Trevino. When I first saw him it looked like a blanket had covered him. He'd been opened in the stomach. I heard it before I smelled it. But I felt it before I heard it. It is hard to know which came first. But the sound of those flies . . . I could hear from a distance.

The [machine] gun ammo ran short real quick. They were pushing us again. My platoon sergeant . . . a staff sergeant . . . hollered for extra gun ammo. He had come up to direct activity before we got hit. There was no more gun ammo to be had, and I took it upon myself to move toward the rear and get gun ammo to move forward. As I was moving forward, this little fighter plane, the Skyhawk, the little jet plane . . . they looked like green-winged teal coming into a pond . . . a bunch of teal. Just fast, darting, maneuverable. They were coming in and I saw a bomb fall from this one plane and I saw it hit the side of this little hill, on a rock. And the bomb bounced probably fifty meters and it went off right where I had left my platoon sergeant and Whaley. And it killed both of them. Whaley was within three feet of Trevino. It was ironic that they died side by side. Less than a day apart.

But somehow that was not traumatic for me. Other things were. The flies. The smell. The feeling. To me that was traumatic. And to see the little pictures they had in their helmets of their girlfriend or their wife or mother or brother. Those kind of things eat me up. They just eat me up. I accepted the . . . unfortunate . . . accidents . . . that bomb not going off where it should have and bouncing. . . . I accepted those things. But to go through gear. Little pictures, letters, unopened mail, the reality of the loss . . .

The flies just keep plaguing me and to this day . . . a fly in my kitchen or my living room . . . I go out of my way . . . I go extremely out of my way to kill a fly. I don't know what that fly is on when I go for it. It doesn't make any difference. I'll get a fly with a chair, a shoe, a book, a flyswatter, my hand. They just get to me. I'll tear a screen out to kill a fly. And I feel so . . . so terrible after going through a routine like that. I can't stop it. And sometimes I don't even realize that I've done it until after it is done. I'll find a screen bent or something broken, a fly on my windshield. I'll just give it my personal best. . . . I think that I would wreck a car and sacrifice safety to kill a fly.

That sound . . . later around the DMZ. I mean the next year and the year after that . . . in '67, '68, the flies in the DMZ, I could hear that from a long way away. It was easy to find bodies. I'm sure I'm not alone on that. There are a lot of guys that would know that sound.

·

PFC Chuck Fink

May 1st they pulled us off Hill 55 and brought us back to the airstrip. We thought we'd died and gone to heaven when we got back here to the airstrip because we had strongbacks [tents], we had cots. This was the only time that we had anything that was remotely close to human living facilities. We thought we'd died and gone somewhere.

10

· · · · · · · · · · · · · · · ·

A TROUBLED ALLIANCE

The spring of 1966 brought trouble for our Vietnamese allies. Buddhist leaders dissatisfied with the Saigon government organized heated antigovernment demonstrations that revealed a country on the brink of civil war. They were particularly militant in Danang after Premier Nguyen Cao Ky dismissed General Nguyen Chan Thi, a Buddhist favorite and the Vietnamese commander of the military region that composed I Corps. Although the Marines attempted to stay clear of the dispute, they were drawn into it by a series of incidents. Numerous ARVN units sided with the dissidents, and on 18 May the most dramatic of the confrontations took place. The rebel "Struggle Forces" seized the Danang River bridge and rigged it with demolitions. Without this bridge, III MAF headquarters and the Marine helicopter facility at Marble Mountain would be cut off from the rest of Danang. Lieutenant General Lewis Walt, the senior Marine in Vietnam, went to the scene personally to take charge.

Corporal Ken Ransbottom

This was around May sometime . . . 1966. There was some kind of shin-
dig going on in Danang where the army was fighting the government or the

government was . . . I don't even know what was going on. We got loaded up in six-bys and went to Danang and crossed this river on this bridge and there were ARVNs? Mongolians? I don't even know what the hell they were. They had charges set on the bridge and they had the detonators. The kind with the handles that you pull up and there was like a handle on top and you had to take both hands and push it down.

I don't know if they were on both ends of the bridge, but I had to run past this soldier, this ARVN or whatever it was, and there was a Marine standing there with a shotgun to his head. And there were troops that had a perimeter around each entrance to the bridge. I ran past the Vietnamese guy with the detonator . . . and his troops had a perimeter set up and we just, man to man, joined their perimeter.

And I just sat down next to this ARVN or South Vietnamese troop of some kind, and he had an M1 and he took the safety off and put the muzzle in my face and he had a smile on his face, so I just unlocked my M14 and pointed it in his face. And we sat there and . . . there was a general . . . I think General Walt . . . that went walking up to the guy that was in charge of the man that was on the detonator.

The dissident-force representative on the bridge was a Vietnamese warrant officer. Refusing to be intimidated by General Walt, who said he was going to call for the Marines to take over the bridge, the Vietnamese officer raised his hand, said, "General, we will die together," and brought his hand sharply to his side in a signal to blow the bridge. Fortunately, as General Walt was keeping the Vietnamese officer occupied, a Marine engineer crept along the underpinnings of the bridge and cut the demolition wires.

The rebellion effectively ended when Premier Ky sent 1,000 South Vietnamese marines to help with the suppression effort.

Corporal Ken Ransbottom

It is kind of strange. I don't remember the details. I was more impressed with the M1 pointed at my nose. It looked like a 106. I wasn't scared. I just didn't have any idea what was going on.

They defused the detonator and the general walked away and we took security on that bridge for a while . . . a day or two. It was kind of nice to be out of the bush and away from the patrol routine and to be within somewhat of a clean environment . . . and such a great change that I didn't even care about it. If I had a book about it, I don't think I would even read it.

I still had this pretty heavy weight on my chest. I didn't want anything to do with any civilians. I just wanted to steer clear of them. I thought about it a lot. I tried to keep my mind busy with anything. Humor . . . and not getting bogged down with anything. Like when that ARVN had his rifle pointed in my face, to me that was nothing. It bothered me less than some of my thoughts. I just couldn't handle trivial bullshit like that ARVN pointing his rifle in my face. I was more intrigued at the smile on his face than I was the rifle in mine. I didn't like his smile but . . . I took it as . . . somehow I took it as one of his relatives had gotten killed in a bomb shelter. Or . . . one of his relatives got gunned down by a Huey gunship.

11

•　•　•　•　•　•　•　•　•　•　•　•　•　•

A CHAPLAIN GOES TO WAR

Rather than record a tape for this project, Father Guy McPartland preferred to lend me over three hundred letters he wrote to his family while he was in Vietnam. Most of these were addressed to his mother. His comments herein are in every case excerpts from them.

Lieutenant (Chaplain's Corps) "Father Guy" I. McPartland (Brand New Guy)
20 June 1966, Vietnam
Hello again! Hope that all is well at home. I arrived here in Danang yesterday (Sunday) at 4:00 P.M. Vietnam time. When I stepped off the plane, the heat hit me like the exhaust from a Turkish bath.

I won't be going up to the forward area for at least a week and possibly two. They require all newcomers to stay back for a brief indoctrination course. I'll be going to the 3d Battalion of the 3d Marine regiment which in turn is one of the regiments of the 3d Marine Division. It just happens to be all 3s, so it should make it pretty easy to remember what outfit I belong to. I'll be the battalion chaplain, a battalion consisting of about 1,000 men. They're located just a

Father Guy McPartland holding mass in the field near the Rockpile in March 1967. (Courtesy Department of Defense)

few miles from here, on the other side of a big hill. War may be hell, but it sure is boring in between the hell parts. It should pick up once I get with my own battalion.

3 July 1966

I arrived at my new post today with the 3d Battalion, 3d Marines. Our camp is pretty well protected. We've got twenty-six bunkers surrounding us on the outer perimeter. Each bunker has two men on guard all night and armed "to the teeth." They've got machine guns, grenades, and flares. Plus there's a triple layer of barbed wire all around.

I said three masses for the men today. I spread them out over a lot of territory. I couldn't begin to reach them all on Sunday, but I'll get to the other units during the week. My third mass today was offered for two young Marines who were killed yesterday while on patrol. Remember them in your prayers.

11 July 1966

We dropped by chopper into VC territory not too many miles from here and spent the next three days on the slopes of the mountains. The heat was unbelievable. By 10:00 A.M. the sun is already high and scorching. You have to drink water constantly to avoid dehydrating. Every so far we managed to find a stream or an irrigation ditch for the rice paddies. We'd fill our canteens and drop in a couple of these special iodine pills (they give us) into the canteens and in twenty minutes it's fit to drink. It tastes terrible but at least it won't give you scurvy.

After a few nights of sleeping on the ground, digging my own little "head" in the morning (not even the luxury of a four-holer) and subsisting off of C-rations, I began to adjust to the conditions. Every day I'd go from one end of our line to the other, sometimes up to my knees in those crusty rice paddies. When we'd get to a stream of any size, we'd just plop in and relax for a few minutes. The water was about the same temperatures as the atmosphere (that is, hot) but it still helps to revive the body a little. By the time the operation was over, I was really "ripe." It felt good to take a shower for the first time in six days; also to drink something real cold. No hard liquor in the forward area but at least soda and beer.

By the way, that boy who lost all his limbs and eyesight did die back at the hospital in Danang. Remember him in your masses. I thought they'd save him. He must have had a very strong and stout heart.

Tuesday, 19 July 1966

As I've mentioned in previous letters, the people here are extremely poor. We've been trying to do as much as we can to improve their living conditions, etc. For instance, introducing them to soap and toothbrushes and paste. They've all got the rottenest teeth you've ever seen. What ones haven't rotted already and fallen out are as black as coal. I think the blackness is caused by something they chew, called "beetle [betel] nut." Seven out of every ten of their babies die at birth. Many that survive contract TB and are dead before they're twenty-five. Just a few dollars goes a long way over here. The average workman (hard laborer) draws anywhere from 50 cents to $1.00 per day. And they work pretty hard, even by American standards.

What I'm leading up to is this: If any of your groups at home (bingo, CFM, Opus Dei get-togethers) would like to do a real work of charity and at the same time help to win this war, they could have a little "bash" at somebody's house, take up a little collection, and send it to me via a money order. I could then convert it into piasters and put it to immediate use. For each donation I'd give you a written report of what I've used the money for and maybe even have a few pictures taken of the people that were helped. I don't have in mind anything big. I wouldn't have the time or apparatus to administer anything like a big project. A $10.00 or $15.00 or $20.00 would do wonders for a child, a sick mother or father, etc.

The people who would be helped by anything sent would be not only Catholics but Buddhists and Protestants as well. It would be used to help destitute people and not religious as such. In the final analysis, just to help these people

A Marine from 3/3 uses a flamethrower to clear obstacles near Hill 55, south of Danang.

get on their feet so that they can help themselves. And they really want to help themselves.

Remember, "he who does it for the least of my brothers, does it for Me!"

Saturday, 20 August 1966

Hello again! How's everything and everybody at home? Received your letters of 15 and 16 August bringing me up-to-date on all the doings and activities of the family. Yes, I've received all the donations you've sent for the poor Vietnamese; a total of $23.00. I've only spent $7.00 of it so far. I bought enough soap to give a bar to about 350 school kids. I went to two schools located in our area and all the kids ran out with their eyes popping in anticipation. Not used to getting any kind of a "present," they were really thrilled to line up in single file and come up for their "own" bar of soap!

To a kid back in the States it wouldn't mean a thing, but to these kids it's a real big deal. Maybe their fathers (or some of them, at least) will use the soap to trade for some bamboo to fix up the leaks in their crusty and dinky little hut! But they'll all be better off, no matter.

You asked about our food over here. There are three types of meals. A-rations, B-rations, and C-rations. A-rations are fresh meats and vegetables cooked in quantity and are best tasting and, because of being prepared in quantity, the least expensive. B-rations are canned foods but cooked and canned in large quantities. They're the second best tasting and a little more expensive than A-rations. C-rations are individually canned units of food and are precooked; all you have to do is heat them up. Actually you can just open the can and eat them cold, as most do. An individual C-ration is a complete meal for one person. It may have, for instance, a can of franks and beans, all precooked, a can of crackers and cheese spread, a small can of peaches and a plastic bag containing four cigarettes, matches, two Chiclets, a small wad of toilet paper, a small package of instant coffee (about a teaspoonful), sugar and powdered cream for one cup of coffee, and some salt. All this is in a little cardboard box about 3 inches by 8 inches and 5 inches high. If you're out where they can't provide either A- or B-rations, you are given three individual units of C-rations per day, one for each meal.

It's so hard to find anything for the boys. I've got a "chicom" grenade that failed to go off. I thought I'd bring it back as a souvenir for little Iggy. It's been fully deactivated by our engineers, so it's totally harmless but it's still perfectly intact. It's called "chicom" because it's made by the Chinese Communists and given to the VC for use in the war. It's pronounced as if the "chi" rhymed with "sky" and then add "com." I can't send it through the mail as all packages leaving this country are subject to U.S. Custom's inspection and I doubt they'd let it go through. I'll have to bring it back with me. Maybe I'll get other souvenirs for the rest of the boys. I still have plenty of time to do so.

JULY–SEPTEMBER 1966

Sergeant James Austin (Brand New Guy)

I left California the 16th of July, landed in Danang, got assigned to 3/3. At that time 3/3 was still in Danang, southwest of the airstrip. The first little operation I was on in Vietnam in Danang when I got there, we come across this little hamlet. I saw stuff on TV that said once you got in Vietnam, you really don't believe you're there. And you don't. A guy had a .30-caliber carbine he was shooting at us out of this hooch, it was a 400-yard shot across the dikes, the bullets would go *zoop, zoop,* you could almost see 'em. It might be sick, but it was the greatest thrill I had in my life.

In August, the battalion became the Special Landing Force (SLF) and went to Okinawa for a few weeks to refit. During most of the Vietnam War, there were two Special Landing Forces, each consisting of a reinforced battalion. Although they were under the direct operational control of the commander-in-chief Pacific (CINCPAC) for use as strategic reserve anywhere in Asia, they were most commonly utilized in Vietnam. MACV was required to request permission for their use from CINCPAC. Pending their assignment to a specific mission, they were generally held aboard ship or on Okinawa.

The 20th of August we packed up, we was on the SLF. We got on the ships, rotated to Okinawa to get all our gear squared away. Our colonel was Lieutenant Colonel Earl DeLong who was our 6 [commanding officer]. Major Stoss Warwzyniak [a famous Marine, winner of two Navy Crosses in Korea] was the 5 [executive officer]. I was assigned as the major's bodyguard and driver. He was some kind of character, that Stoss Warwzyniak. He was a mustanger. [A mustang is a former enlisted man who has won a commission.] Earl DeLong was a disciplinarian. He knew that the politicians would not let us fight the war. He hated to lose anybody. The helmet and flak jacket rule was strictly enforced while he was in command. When he did go on operations before I arrived there, he had air strikes, artillery pulverization to soften them up, then he went in. Because he really didn't think that place was worth losing an American body to, where we were going.

While in Okinawa, new men were assigned to replace combat losses and normal rotations. By the time they boarded ship to return to Vietnam, the battalion had a total strength of 1,250 officers and men, including their Navy corpsmen, doctors, and chaplain. Of this total, 715 were replacements.

Lieutenant Colonel Earl "Pappy" DeLong, commanding officer of 3/3 for parts of 1966 and 1967. Ribbons represent three Silver Star Medals for gallantry in action, a Legion of Merit Medal, and two Purple Heart Medals. As was the custom during the Vietnam era, Colonel DeLong is wearing only his personal decorations. (Courtesy Department of Defense)

PFC Rod W. Consalvo (Brand New Guy)

I joined India Company 3/3 in Okinawa. They came back to regroup of September of '66. We spent three weeks there in Okinawa at the Northern Training Area at Camp Schwab. And we trained in NTA for two weeks durin' some real rough monsoon weather. It was pretty good training. It's where I really learned how to become miserable without really trying. And then we got orders . . . outpost to 'Nam. And we left Camp Schwab and went down to the docks and boarded the LPH, USS *Iwo Jima*.

Father Guy McPartland

Okinawa, 30 September 1966

Well, Mom, this is going to be another short letter. The reason is beyond my control this time. As I told you when we came here back on the 6th of September, we were supposed to stay on Okinawa for six to eight weeks and return to Vietnam sometime during the last week of October. Well, that was all changed today.

At 10:30 A.M. today we got the word we'll be moving out tomorrow! That's not much notice and we have all our gear to repack and get ready to be shipped. We'll be going aboard a helicopter carrier (LPH), the *Iwo Jima*, and heading south. By Thursday or Friday of next week we'll be off the coast of Vietnam, up around the 17th parallel and the DMZ area.

Then we'll be flown inland by helicopters. Seems like the North Vietnamese are building up quite a force there and preparing to step up their operation with the coming of the monsoon rains in about twenty days from now.

. . . .

PART TWO

FIGHTING THE NORTH

VIETNAMESE

WAR AGAINST PROFESSIONALS,

1966–1968

12

● ● ● ● ● ● ● ● ● ● ● ● ● ● ●
THE ROCKPILE

The 3d Battalion, 3d Marines, left Okinawa earlier than planned to assist in dealing with the escalated infiltration of North Vietnamese Army units across the DMZ and into South Vietnam. The NVA perceived that U.S. forces were succeeding in destroying the Viet Cong infrastructure in the south and were winning the population of South Vietnam over to the allied cause. In order to reverse this trend, the NVA decided to move additional forces south. In February 1966 they sent two NVA divisions, the *324b* and the *341*, across the DMZ into Quang Tri Province. At the same time, large units were transferred from Laos across the border into Thua Thien Province, the region just below Quang Tri.

These two provinces were already separated from the rest of South Vietnam by a mountain range that stretches from Laos to the sea, which made the potential for their forced isolation a real threat. If Hanoi's strategy was to draw Marine forces away from the pacification effort near the population centers, it was largely a success. Most of the Marine battalions had to abandon or at least sharply reduce their pacification programs in order to meet what was becoming the invasion of one country by another. The response was Operation HASTINGS, mounted in mid-1966, out of which developed the first **99** large-scale battle of Marines versus NVA. Nearly 900 NVA were killed, but their losses did not break Hanoi's determination to subdue South Vietnam with armed force. The dispatch of new troops across the DMZ was escalated even further toward the end of the year.

Westmoreland responded to this with a general shifting of forces northward. Before long, all major Marine commands were north of the old Chu Lai region, and the I Corps region was supplemented by a substantial number of U.S. Army units. American forces also began constructing all-weather ports along the shores of the two northern provinces.

The Marines, then, were forced to give up pacification as the centerpiece of their plan. With little exception, the officers and men of the 3d Battalion, 3d Marines, would fight along a narrow strip of Northern I Corps for three years. Regardless of the name of the operation, its exact location, or official purpose, 3/3 was to spend the rest of the war engaged in the ageless activity of the infantryman, "to locate, close with, and destroy the enemy."

No more would 3/3 fight guerrillas who used outmoded weaponry. The North Vietnamese Army was tough, seasoned, and equipped with modern arms, including supporting artillery and tanks. Captain Paul Goodwin, who fought the Viet Cong in his first tour in 1965, likened that experience to "cops and robbers" compared to his later tour in the DMZ region against the NVA. In this author's opinion, man for man and unit for unit, NVA troops were the equal of the Americans. The latter, however, could call upon a far more capable system of supporting arms. It was the Americans' use of combined arms that gave U.S. units the edge in the DMZ fighting.

The war against professionals had its price. The bulk of the war was to be fought in I Corps. Comprising only five of South Vietnam's thirty-five provinces, I Corps accounted for 28 percent of friendly combat deaths for the remainder of the war. Of this number, nearly one third occurred in Quang Tri Province which bordered the DMZ.*

Despite the professional abilities of the NVA, the war remained a war without frontlines or permanent objectives. The average Marine, therefore, set his own objective—to finish his thirteen-month tour in one piece and go back to "the world." What prevented this from being a free-for-all was the essence of the Corps—the glue that held men together in the worst of times and on the most aimless of missions. This adhesive, in the best tradition of the Corps, was the camaraderie among Marines. For a Marine, the worst that could be said about another human being was that "he wasn't there when we needed him."

---

*Thomas C. Thayer, "Patterns of the French and American Experiences in Vietnam," in *The Lessons of Vietnam*, ed. W. Scott Thompson and Donaldson D. Frizzell (New York: Crane, Russak, 1977).

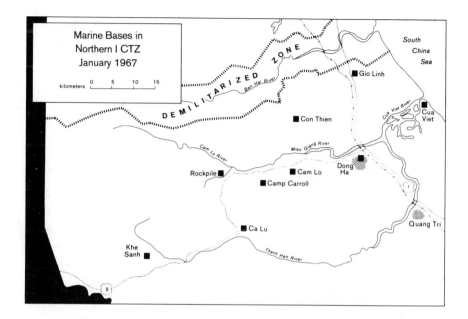

Marine Bases in Northern I CTZ January 1967

kilometers 0 5 10 15

DEMILITARIZED ZONE

Ben Hai River

South China Sea

■ Gio Linh

Cua Viet River

■ Cua Viet

■ Con Thien

Cam Lo River

Mieu Giang River

■ Rockpile

■ Cam Lo

Dong Ha ▨

■ Camp Carroll

■ Ca Lu

Quang Tri ▨

Khe Sanh ■

Thach Han River

9

Father Guy McPartland

10 October 1966

We arrived off the coast of Vietnam on the afternoon of the 5th, but due to some change in the situation up north they never set us ashore. We're still waiting for the word to go. Right now it looks like we'll be flown into the area west of Cam Lo, the area they call the "Rockpile," in the next few days.

I'd recommend you hold off sending money for the poor Vietnamese children. If we go into the DMZ area, we won't be doing much social work among the people there. The situation up there is a little different than it is further south.

PFC Thomas C. Mosher

We were on the *Iwo Jima* and we thought, "Well, this is it. We're going back over there." And they told us about going in the jungle and the DMZ. This went on for about a week. We still hadn't landed and we were out there for another week. They said, "Well, we're just going to float. We're going to be a floating unit for a while."

So, sure enough, about two or three weeks out, we needed resupply. As anybody that's been on a ship can imagine, when there's all kinds of Marines around, they're the working parties. We were told to get up on the hangar deck and form big lines and the stuff would be passed over from the supply ship to us, and then we'd take it off the nets and manhandle it down into the storage areas.

As this stuff was coming through, I'm looking and I says, "Hmm. A case of tunafish. I could probably use some of this when I get back ashore." So that case of tunafish disappeared. Here came another case. It was marked "hams." Well, we didn't need hams. They needed to be refrigerated, so we didn't want that. Along came a big case of peanut butter and nobody really wanted that because that just stopped up your system. But along came this big old case of sardines. Sardines don't seem like a fun thing to have, but we knew that we were going to be living on C-rations and stuff, so I just kind of pushed that off to the side and we divvied that up.

The ship life was pretty good. We used to have a movie every night. We were able to go to the Geedunk [any place that has ice cream, candy, and the like] and all that stuff. We were kind of sorry we had to get off the ship.

PFC Rod Consalvo

When we got off of the *Iwo Jima*, we flew in in the old 34 helicopters. Felt like a shake and bake. Each chopper carried about seven or eight people with their gear and we were flying probably at about 5,000 feet over the water to Dong Ha. And when we got to Dong Ha, we set up a perimeter . . . and there was no wire, no bunkers, no nothing.

My first night on guard duty in "enemy territory," I was the automatic rifleman and I had my M14 and I had my bipods down [two-legged weapons mount], and when it started gettin' dark I started gettin' scared . . . so I put my bayonet on my rifle. I didn't know how much good that would have done me but . . . at least it *looked* awfully tough. And the first couple of nights weren't too bad, but it was hard to get used to the sleeping arrangements. Our battalion always thought that we'd either get hit in the morning or get hit in the evening. So the standing orders were, from seven o'clock until nine o'clock, everybody was on 100 percent hole watch. You were in your hole. Your weapons were locked and loaded. You had your flak jackets and your helmets on. Then at nine o'clock you went to 50 percent and one of you would go to sleep. Two hours later the other one . . . you'd get up and you'd watch from eleven to one, go to sleep from one to three, three to five would be your turn, and then from five o'clock to seven o'clock you'd again be on 100 percent hole watch.

So we were lookin' at four hours of sleep a night and that was broken sleep. I think that was the hardest thing to adjust to. I didn't think that would continue for the entire thirteen months, but it did.

We spent a couple of more days standing perimeter watch out there at Dong Ha. And then the next thing I knew, we were packin' up all our gear, puttin' on our transport packs, and gettin' on 34s again. And that's when I really got to see Vietnam as it is. We headed west flyin' at about three or four thousand feet. It

PFC Rod Consalvo at the Rockpile. (Courtesy Rod Consalvo)

A Marine helicopter makes a one-wheeled landing on top of the Rockpile in the DMZ sector.

was the first time I saw the Rockpile—750-foot, jagged piece of rock, sittin' in this little valley, with mountains all around it and a couple of rivers goin' by it.

The Rockpile is a cone-shaped hill, located ten clicks [kilometers] south of the DMZ. It rises some 240 meters out of a river bottom to sit astride several major infiltration routes from North Vietnam and Laos. It dominates part of Route 9, the Vietnamese highway that parallels the DMZ and runs from Dong Ha past the Rockpile and on through Khe Sanh before it becomes a dirt track that reaches into Laos.

Impressive as it is in its immediate vicinity, the Rockpile is overshadowed by other, higher hills within a few miles in nearly every direction. To the northwest is Dong Ke Soc mountain, 685 meters high. Due north is Nui Cay Tri, known in Marine lore as Mutter's Ridge after the radio call sign of the 3d Battalion, 4th Marines, the first battalion to be blooded there. The northeast is shaded by Dong Ha mountain, another landmark to achieve notoriety in the annals of 3/3.

Sergeant James Austin

We were there from two days after we left Dong Ha [2 November 1966] until about January 12th, 1967. I think we lost probably forty-five guys in that time. We had five confirmed NVA kills.

Some guys in Mike Company went out and met the NVA coming down a trail. Our guys pulled off and set up an ambush. Five NVA walked into it. We got them all. The guys tied them on sticks like deer and brought them in.

Everybody was rejoicing. The doctor field-trained his medics with them and cut them open showing the corpsmen the different organs and all that good stuff and what to do. So at the conclusion of that, Major Warwzyniak pressed a bulldozer into service. He dug a revetment in our LZ and we throwed these five NVA soldiers in. The bulldozer covered them up, and when resupply choppers come in, the major told the pilots, "You just landed on the bodies of five dead NVA." That got back to the 3d Marine regiment chaplain. He gets Colonel DeLong on the horn. Major Warwzyniak comes to get me and our CP group, we get the bulldozer back, we dig 'em up. The guys been in the ground thirty-six hours, maggots have taken over, what a stench. So what we had to do was get 'em up, put 'em on our mechanical mule. They dug some graves down at the ammo dump. We had to rebury them and put grave markers on them.

PFC Rod Consalvo

And we started diggin' our bunkers. We put up our shelter halves on stilts and we looked like a Montagnard village. Our fighting holes would be right in front of us. We were there about four or five days when we realized what else is involved in fighting a war. We had to start goin' out and pullin' patrols and ambushes.

It was sunny, too, but the monsoon was setting in. And we began to be always wet and that was a hard thing to live with, always being wet. And the grayness of it was awful depressing. 'Cause you'd look out at that jungle, knowin' there was somebody out there . . . not knowing where. . . . And the grayness . . . It was hard to keep motivated, just setting there and waiting for something to happen. The patrols would break the monotony. And we were doin' a patrol every other day and an ambush every other night.

The thing I hated most, I think, was the ambushes. Especially if it was raining. I hated going out at six o'clock in the evening as the sun was going down, and if it was raining, just going out there with a poncho, finding a spot in the jungle, pushin' back the leaves and the wet, and then just layin' down in it.

One night we were settin' up, gettin' ready for hole watch. It was about seven-thirty; all of a sudden word came down the line, "Squad saddle up." I said, "What the hell is goin' on?" They said some company was in trouble and they needed help carryin' back some of the wounded. And it was one of those typical Vietnam nights. Light drizzle and a light breeze blowing. Well, they saddled us up at about seven-thirty and we went out and we didn't find these guys until one o'clock in the morning and found out what we hadda do.

We weren't carrying back any wounded. They had six dead men. They were exhausted from their hump and they couldn't handle it anymore and they needed help. So . . . we carried back six men, wrapped in ponchos. Me and another guy carried this Marine back for five hours. Never knew the guy's name. Never knew who he was. That was a little bit of a shock.

As we were goin' out . . . me and my buddy . . . Homer B. Cassada . . . I remember how we passed the time. We were talkin' what we're gonna do when we get back to the States. We both decided we were gonna transfer to the Navy. Make sure . . . that we would always have clean sheets and a hot meal. We'da killed for clean sheets and a hot meal at this time. I think that's what kept our sanity for that trip. Fantasizing what we would do.

·

Sergeant James Austin

On November 9th, the day before the Marine Corps Birthday '66, we got out of water. It was raining, but we sucked up all our water and had a nice little downpour coming and we were really humping. I hope I never get hungry enough to have to eat anybody, but if I get as hungry as I did thirsty that day, somebody would be in trouble.

It was raining and we just sucked our lips right around them tree barks, sucked up the water as it was coming down the trees. Everybody had leeches on their mouths, looked like Christmas tree decorations. We'd take cigarettes, burn them out. Some of the biggest leeches I ever saw. All kind of lice, insects, and animal life, which a lot of that stuff was new to me. What I saw in high school biology—the specimens we had wasn't as big as what I saw. I was in California, I seen four- and five-inch scorpions. In Vietnam I seen fourteen-inch scorpions, I seen tarantulas, three-inch leeches, tigers, miniature deer, rock apes that throw rocks at you . . . it was pretty confusing.

·

Lance Corporal John W. Norman, Jr.

We got in a new platoon guide. I was a squad leader then, and three-fourths of my tour was through. I was sitting on my bunker in my only pair of utility trousers. We hadn't been resupplied in a while and they were ripped in the crotch. The new guide, he gets off the chopper, he's coming around checking the lines. He stopped in front of me and he said, "Marine, those trousers are unserviceable." I said, "Yeah, sarge, I know they are." He said, "Well, get them

Three Marines from 3/3 relax for a moment in November 1966 during Operation PRAIRIE *and attempt to keep dry.*

off." And I tried to explain to him that these were the only trousers I had. But he didn't want to hear that shit because he still had starchies on. So I said, "Okay," and I took them off and threw them in the bunker.

And the captain, he came out and he looked down over the hill and he saw me sitting there in just a pair of Ho Chi Minh sandals and my soft cover [cloth cap], and he hollered down, "Norman, what the fuck is wrong with you? What are you doing?" So I explained to him what happened, and he run on down the line and got that new guide and brought him back and just chewed him a new asshole. And if the dude didn't understand, then later on he found out what it was like to be a grunt.

Political interference with the way the war was run excepted, it was the supply problem that irritated Marines more than any other during the entire war. The author knows from personal experience that units in the rear areas generally had three hot prepared meals per day, access to movies, liquor, PXs [post exchanges], USO shows, and so forth. Most rear-area people slept in real bunks with a roof over their heads and had showers and means to do their laundry.

Lance Corporal John W. Norman with an M14 rifle in early 1967.
(Courtesy John W. Norman)

On the other hand, the grunt, particularly after late 1966, was faced with a shortage of just about everything. As many in this narrative relate, one of the biggest shocks for a BNG was the life of severe deprivation in which he suddenly found himself, just a few days after leaving the richest country in the world. It was as if the casualties, the dirt, the humping of monstrous loads, the heat and monsoon weather were not enough. These men had to deal with severe shortages of the basic necessities of life as well. His home was the hole he dug himself, wet weather or dry. All his possessions were carried on his back. Rations, potable water, clothing, ammunition, critical items of equipment—all showed up on the shortage list. By this time, 3d Battalion, 3d Marines, was in need of helmets, flak jackets, boots, and jungle utility uniforms. Before long, the Marines began to take the helmets and flak jackets, and even the boots, off their dead and wounded in order to supply the living.

13

. . . .

WINTER ACTION

In November, five members of the battalion died in action and another twenty-three were wounded. In December, this climbed to twenty-six dead and ninety wounded. In the type of tragedy that was to haunt 3/3 for the rest of the war, Mike Company was mistakenly bombed by U.S. aircraft in December, resulting in seventeen of the KIAs that month.

By this time, after-action and intelligence reports began increasingly to mention North Vietnamese Army regulars instead of Viet Cong guerrillas. It became clear that 3/3 now had to learn to fight a well-trained, better-armed, and more determined foe.

PFC Rod Consalvo

One time the helicopters picked us up and we got turned around, shit, we had no idea where we were at. This was the first week in December of '66. We were goin' on our first operation. We hit some flat land and they set us down by some villages and we were just goin' through the bush. Search and destroy. 'Course, we didn't find anything to destroy. And we went through this one village durin' the day and came back through the village that night, probably around five or six o'clock.

We set up about three or four hundred yards away from this village and put up our perimeter and did our hole watch. We were told we were gonna get up at three o'clock in the morning and become a blocking force. So at three o'clock in the morning, I ended up takin' off as point man. And . . . goin' through this village. Me and my buddy Homer. He was right behind me. We got to the village. Right at the trail leading into the village, I lost my bearings, so I said, "Homer, do you remember your way through the village? I can't remember what the hell . . . which way I was goin'." And he says, "Yeah, I remember." So, he took off on point and I was right behind him. And we start diddy-bopping up this trail. And all of a sudden, both Homer and I heard voices. And we stopped the platoon. And then we saw some flickering of a campfire. And we got the squad leader and the machine gunner. Both came up with us and we saw this one hooch with lights. And it's still pitch-black.

Well, the squad leader walked up on this gook that was brushin' his teeth by the tree at four in the morning. And the gook looked up at 'em, saw he had a rifle, put his head back down, and continued brushing his teeth.

I was tryin' to sneak up on the hooch and I stepped on a twig, and I said, "Shit," under my breath. The next thing I know is, the . . . machine gunner— and we couldn't see shit—he said, "They're goin' for their guns," and he started cuttin' loose. And I emptied two magazines into the hooch. Homer was changin' magazines and some gook came flyin' out the back, through the back of the hooch, and he dropped him. The machine gunner unloaded about eighty rounds and the squad leader threw the gook that was brushin' his teeth to the ground, stepped on him, and started firing into the hooch. That gook was the only one that lived.

The platoon heard all this shit goin' on and it sounded like a major firefight. And then total silence. Then we heard some moaning from the hooch. The lieutenant came up and brought another squad with him and he's askin' us what the hell's happening. "What's goin' on?" The adrenaline is pumpin' so hard, we didn't know what the shit is going on. All we know is we started poppin' rounds into this hooch.

It ended up there was five dead NVA in the hooch. We captured the one and there were fully loaded NVA packs. What was great about it was three of them were a sniper team. They had nailed a couple of Marines in one of the other platoons the day before. The other dude that was in there turned out to be an NVA pay officer that was paying the local VC villagers in the area. We made a real good kill on that one. The adrenaline was pumping so high, but the lieutenant made us go out and set up a perimeter. Boy, I didn't want to go out and set up on the perimeter. I wanted to stay there where we killed those guys. We were pretty much jazzed up at the time and we wanted to stay with what we had done, but he made us go out and set up a perimeter.

·

Sergeant James Austin

One of the silliest things I ever saw was Christmas of '66. We go out on a routine patrol. We were allowed to have a magazine in our weapon, but we wasn't allowed to have a round chambered. We had F-4 Phantoms flying around that wasn't carrying any bombs. The rules of the war.

Christmas Day was spent uneventfully in the lull of a truce. The only action was the sighting by a listening post which reported twenty civilians moving along Route 9. There is a possibility that they were enemy on the move.

JANUARY 1967

As the new year began, the Marines intensified efforts to counter increased NVA activity across the DMZ. In order to keep communications over this major infiltration corridor open, the command decided to try to control Route 9. In January 1967 three major combat bases were positioned along its fifty-kilometer length. Dong Ha sat on its eastern terminus where it connected with Route 1. Near the Laotian border, Khe Sanh guarded its western end. Camp Carroll sat in between on an artillery plateau named for a fallen Marine company commander.

The bulk of 3/3's efforts for the entire year were directed at trying to keep this vital land route open. From January to April, most units fought in the vicinity of the Rockpile while others operated along Highway 561, a loose-surfaced spur of Route 9 that connected Cam Lo with Con Thien.

Nineteen sixty-seven was a year of change in Vietnam. It is the year that public opinion in the United States began to turn against the war, and North Vietnam's leaders, confronted by the fact that they were losing the war in the field, had to move decisively in new directions. Meanwhile, the individual Marine, uninformed for the most part on military objectives above the platoon level, did not ask for much more than competent leadership and a fighting chance to return home in one piece.

Lance Corporal John Norman

We were right on the river, the Ca Lu River by Route 9, between the Rockpile and Khe Sanh. And then most of our firefights were up on Mutter's Ridge. We'd go up it and come down it, go up it and come down it. We used to send out corporals, sometimes even lance corporals, in charge of the patrols. They would grab their maps, read the maps, find out where they were going on patrols. They would go out sometimes 2,000, 3,000 meters from the CP area on their patrols and, of course, come back. Most of the time there was no enemy encounter, or even if they encountered enemy, they would get away from them, fight them off, whatever they had to do, and then they would make their way back to the CP.

.

Captain John W. Ripley

I took Lima Company. This was about the 2d or 3d of January '67. They were living in a place called the Punch Bowl near the Rockpile, terribly unlovely place, in conditions I could best describe as squalor. Mud up to your knees. No one concerned themselves with their welfare because they frankly saw it as impossible. What can you do?

Well, there's a lot you can do. The first thing I did was I called to the rear and I said, "Send me my cook out here and bring the burners." Each company had two burners and at least one cook and I said, "I want him out here. I don't know what the hell he's doing in the rear, but I want him with me out on this hill." And they sent him out. The S-4 raised Cain about it, but they sent him out. "What do you want him for? You can't cook hot chow." I said, "I'll deal with him. You just get him out here." So he came and I took these burners and I would heat water so the men could shave, and most importantly I heated some kind of beverage . . . hot coffee was like liquid gold . . . to have something for those ambushes and patrols when they came back.

And that did wonders for morale. And then the "Cookie" caught on. He found out how loved he was. He started making sheet cakes and soup. My God! They built his bunker for him. He was the most protected man in the company. Little things like that had such a huge pay-off in morale.

.

Sergeant James Austin

We were on the west side of the Rockpile at ground level. The engineers built a water filtration plant down there and we had showers. That was the first shower that we had since we got off the *Iwo Jima* the end of September. That

Marines of 3/3 prepare to board a helicopter during a sweep on Operation PRAIRIE *near the DMZ.*

was one of the worst things about being over there besides the insects, is the inability to stay clean. The monsoons were there, all your spare clothes was wet and greasy with body scum. You couldn't lay down on the ground. You had to elevate yourself up. The leeches would get you anyhow, but you had less leech attacks if you was on your "rubber lady" air mattress. Sleeping with wet clothes on a Marine Corps-issue rubber lady didn't give you too much relaxing sleep when you got a chance.

The "rubber lady"—also called less delicately a "rubber bitch" but known officially as a "mattress, pneumatic"—was always in limited supply. For several months running, the battalion S-4 reported a shortage of 650. Most Marines just learned to curl up in their hole or bunker and sleep on the ground.

Father Guy McPartland
[Excerpts from letters to his mother, January 1967.]
26 January 1967
Tomorrow we'll have completed 3 months on the line. Usually they don't keep

the same Battalion up front this long. They seem to be having a little difficulty finding an available Battalion to replace us. I haven't had my sweatshirt off in over a month . . . it's really dirty and as you can imagine it's about ready to "walk away." I think it's getting warm enough now to take it off and get it washed in the river.

14

. . . .

TWO NEW LIEUTENANTS

Lieutenant Daniel F. Ryan (Brand New Guy)

We wind up in Danang and a warrant officer there says, "Ah, a bunch of lieu-tenants." So he says, "Alright, you're going to the 3d Marine Division. You're goin' north." I said, "Alright," so I go catch a plane and I wind up in Phu Bai. And another old salt says, "Okay, you're goin' to the 3d Marine Division, you're goin' north." And I said, "Isn't this 3d Marine Division?" He says, "Yeah, but you're goin' further north."

So I catch another plane, continuing north. And I'm thinkin' I'm already in Hanoi anyway. I wind up in Dong Ha and a guy says . . . this is after we crash-land . . . at least it seemed like it. We pull in and I get to meet the first sergeant and he says, "Well, we're in the rear right now. You're goin' out in the next couple of days." Anyway, me and Billy Masciangelo who were schoolmates in PLCs [platoon leader's class] and Basic School wind up out at the Rockpile.

Landings at Dong Ha were not reassuring to newcomers who were used to the smoother

practices of commercial airliners. For one thing, the runway at Dong Ha was short, and upon touching down, the C-130 pilots would reverse the props and hit the brakes in order to stop quickly. For another, Dong Ha was within artillery range of North Vietnam. As a result, the pilots would drop the ramp while the aircraft was still in motion, and everyone would grab their gear and head for one of the trenches that bordered the airfield.

Lieutenant William R. Masciangelo (Brand New Guy)

I felt very prepared for my job, my assignment as a platoon commander. I felt fortunate when I reported to Vietnam that I was assigned to the 3d Battalion, 3d Marines, because my entire experience with them was very positive. They had very strong leadership.

Lieutenant Dan Ryan

The guy that did impress me was the CO of the unit, Lieutenant Colonel Earl "Call me Pappy" DeLong. And his XO, Stanley Warwzyniak. DeLong, I'm told, has a Ph.D. in Russian and I meet the guy and right away he calls me "Dan." And I liked this. He says, "Welcome to 3/3. You probably heard it's a horseshit outfit and it's true, but we do pretty good here."

Warwzyniak I knew from Basic School. Last time I saw him he was spitting tobacco and falling out of a tree on the end of a rope, testing new equipment. Warwzyniak was DeLong's foil. He was the foulest, most outspoken Marine I've ever met in my life. Some of the platoon commanders . . . you had these mustangs like a guy named Jerry Chase who had 2d Platoon, India, and Ed McCourt who had the weapons platoon.

The guy I replaced was a guy named Bob Schrader, who had 3d Platoon. Another mustang. So just walkin' in was a pretty hard act to follow. All these old-timers. You know . . . the old men of the 'Nam. And there was a guy over in Lima Company . . . John Ripley, who I really, really liked. Got close to and respected him. He was squared away. . . . I said, "Ah, this is a Marine captain. This is what they look like." Anyway, they drag me down to the 3d Platoon, India Company, and that's where I met this staff sergeant named Bill Roach.

Of the guys that I spoke of, Warwzyniak took a shine to me, and we'd be on an operation and he'd say, "Come here, kid, I want to show you somethin'." He was an old recon guy. He'd touch a flower or . . . a bush or something and he'd say, "Now watch this," and the thing would close up. He says, "If someone came by here a few minutes before, this would be closed, and it opens in such and such a time." Quite a guy. During several barrages, I used to see him counting rounds and walkin' around. The guy thought he was actually bulletproof. And he was.

Oh, I forgot to mention the chaplain. It was Father Guy McPartland. Order of Carmelites. An old Irishman. Beetle-browed and just a fine, fine man. A New Yawker. And full of blarney as a Christmas turkey. The only chaplain, I might add, that I've seen on operations, walkin' around with the troops.

Lieutenant Bill Masciangelo

I remember Colonel DeLong and Stanley Warwzyniak and a company commander by the name of Stumpf. I was very fortunate to be with good leaders, who put emphasis on personal hygiene, sanitation, those type of things, which required the basic principles of being a Marine. We saw, later on, a lot of units that did not have that same self-discipline, did not take care of their personal hygiene and make sure their helmets were buttoned and make sure their flak jackets were zipped up and snapped.

Those types of things, I think, left a very strong impression on me. 'Cause these were the things I expected from leaders and I expected to do with my men. Everything from changing the socks so they didn't get immersion foot . . . those little attentions to details. Fortunately, I was involved with a unit that had that type of leadership and I think that served us in good stead through our entire time in Vietnam.

Lieutenant Dan Ryan

Staff Sergeant Bill Roach was an NCO who had come off the drill field at Parris Island. A great guy. We bunked together. My first exposure to his techniques were . . . one of the brothers came into the bunker and he started referring to one of the 'dudes.' About this time Roach jumped up and smacked him right in the chops, and he said, "These ain't a fucking 'dude,' they're United States Marines and that's all they are. You motherfucker, get your heels together, you're speaking to a Marine Corps officer." So I said, "This isn't too bad. I don't have to do a thing. This guy just goes around killing people for me."

Any situation that popped up, Roach would handle. He was a hell of a troop leader and he ran the platoon very tight. He would con these guys . . . uh, if he couldn't con the squad leaders, he would threaten them. I never had any sense of Roach going to be fragged or me . . . or anybody was going to get hurt other than from the gooks. The squad leaders were outstanding. Because of the tightness, the discipline in dealing with troops, and also a great amount of care and attention, a lot of the troops went home alive. Most of the Marines I had were drafted. They were very courageous, they worked together. I don't remember particularly any racial problems and definitely didn't have any drug problems that I was aware of. We were so isolated from civilization, being at the Rockpile and concerned with daily living, that these things were not really important.

Lieutenant Bill Masciangelo

I always hated to hear the phone ring in my bunker. That particular shrill, the way it would whine. It always came after midnight and it always was an emergency and a problem, and invariably it required us to mount out. It almost seems like on a regular basis, somebody from the 9th Marines would be in a world of trouble, have the shit kicked out of them. . . . They would call up at one o'clock, two o'clock in the morning. "Mount up." They'd send the trucks in from Dong Ha. We'd hop in the trucks, drive back to Ca Lu, or maybe Cam Lo.

By then you could see the eerie flares being dropped in the night, about two or three clicks to the north, and you'd be hiking, walking from Route 9 there . . . and by the time you got there it was morning and you'd find Marines wounded and dead bodies all over the place. And then we'd spend a week running around these whole grid squares up there seeing nothing or very little of anything. And then they'd take us back to the Rockpile.

I think I did that more than three or four times. And there was very little . . . operational success other than a walk in the sun. Other than an occasional sniper or very minor skirmishes or an ambush or something like that. But nothing, ever, of major consequence. It always happened to the 9th Marines. I think that we know now that the NVA was certainly looking for the 9th Marines and continually harassed them and really socked it to them on every occasion they had. I even found leaflets that were specifically addressed to the 9th Marines. More so than anybody else. So the sound of a phone. The landline phone ringing, for a long time, drove me crazy, because it always meant something significant was happening.

The 9th Marine regiment, and in particular the 1st Battalion, 9th Marines, was tagged as a hard-luck unit in Vietnam. It was not until after its superb performance in Operation DEWEY CANYON under Colonel Robert H. Barrow (later general and commandant) that this reputation was eradicated once and for all.

Lieutenant Dan Ryan

So it was kind of slow and we went on a couple of ops [operations] with the battalion, and I remember having my platoon in reserve and seeing my first dead Marine come back through the lines, in a poncho, swimmin' in his blood . . . really an eye-opener.

Lieutenant Bill Masciangelo

It was the quietest two months I ever experienced in my entire Vietnam operation. The point of this was that you began to get soft mentally. Not constantly in any kind of danger, you began to lull into a false sense of security. I know when the battalion finally picked up and moved and went back to Dong Ha, we started getting sent up in the C2 area and those places. I mean the whole tenor of the ballgame changed. From . . . the junior varsity to the Super Bowl. Almost overnight.

FEBRUARY 1967

Father Guy McPartland

3 February 1967

Will leave from here for Dong Ha by truck after my masses on Ash Wednesday. Am going into Dong Ha tomorrow to pick up a container of blessed ashes for distribution to my men on Ash Wednesday. Have to get my ashes from the local Catholic church in Dong Ha. They have a thriving little parish there with a Vietnamese priest as pastor and a French priest as assistant. They used to have a French pastor, but the VC killed him about six months ago. They killed his two little altar boys at the same time! All three are buried right in front of the church. I'll try to get a picture of the church the next time I go into Dong Ha.

·

Sergeant James Austin

At that time they started dropping Agent Orange from our position to Khe Sanh to the northwest and to Con Thien and Gio Linh to the northeast. The vegetation, in two weeks, just disappeared. Guys were sitting around talking, wondering why the water tastes funny even though we put halizone pills in it and everything. We ended up putting Kool Aid in there because you could never get the water right. At that time we didn't know what Agent Orange was.

15

. . . .

RIPLEY AND HIS RAIDERS

The small group of Marines in 3/3 who proudly refer to themselves as Ripley's Raiders got that name for their actions on 2 March 1967.

Captain John Ripley

We began the morning of the 2d of March having had an action the previous day in an effort to take the pressure off of 2/3 which had been overrun. Their entire CP group was to a man killed or wounded, to include Colonel Vic Ohanesian and Sergeant Major Wayne N. Hayes. The only survivor out of that whole action was Major Bob Sheridan, the S-3 who crawled under a tank along with a couple of radio operators and survived the night, badly wounded, and made it out.

Another interesting aspect of that was that PFC Anderson won the Medal of Honor in the action which his colonel was killed, by scooping up a grenade and absorbing the blast. And although that is not in and of itself unusual, what is unusual about it is he was the very first black Marine to win the Medal of Honor. That was on the night of 28 February.

So we began the morning of 2 March having fought the day before a couple of moderate actions, less than 10 KIA, WIA [wounded in action], and then we moved out that morning in the attack as the lead element to proceed down a trail, generally west, with instructions to arrive at a trail junction and to hold at that position while the battalion closed.

We began and followed a trail which we soon named "Bloody Rice," the trail having been marked by simultaneous trails of blood and rice mixed together, something grotesque but very clearly identified. It wasn't long after we jumped off that morning, about 0700, that we had our first encounter with a sniper and dealt with that pretty quickly, continued to move and finally arrived at the trail junction of Bloody Rice, which was due south of the location given for the contact later on.

It was there in a cleared area that we popped out of the jungle. My instructions from battalion were to set out security strong points in the fashion of an ambush and hold the position. The northernmost strong point was a squad commanded by Corporal Hobbs, and they began moving up the northern trail to establish their position. While they moved out, we moved around this clearing and found several fresh graves which we disinterred and found recent enemy dead, confirming the action of the previous day. When Hobbs moved out, he had not gone too far along, maybe a click, when he spotted to his north and west a position that looked suspicious. So he went into his stealthy-cat approach and found a sentry facing away from him and sitting on the edge of a hole with his feet in the hole. Hobbs motioned the rest of the squad to move into a secure attack position while he crept forward. In so doing he moved quite literally right up behind this sentry who was wearing a headset and a knee key for a very sophisticated radio, a Chinese radio. Hobbs was able to move right up on him because the man was wearing the headset and couldn't hear his approach. He reached down and got him in a headlock and yanked him out of the hole silently and subdued him as a POW, and then the rest of the squad moved up and quickly recovered the gear. We knew we were onto something big when we saw the radio. He called back to me, immediately told me what it was and I moved forward with the platoon to investigate. On arrival I immediately recognized in a nearby tree a double rhombic antenna, which indicated that this was not your standard unit but had to be certainly a battalion-level unit to have such a sophisticated radio. A knee key meaning he was sending his messages CW [Morse or International code] and not in voice, lots and lots of it. When I got to the position, I indicated that I wanted a second platoon to come up and one platoon to remain there as a reserve.

My numerical 3d Platoon remained in reserve at the position to await the battalion while I was with my 1st platoon; and the 2d Platoon, then unemployed, moved forward to my location, which I radioed back to battalion and told them the significance of the find. They told me to go ahead and investigate, which I began doing when my 2d Platoon arrived.

So with the 1st platoon on the right and the 2d Platoon on the left, I began a sweep of the area. We immediately entered what was an extensive base camp, indicated by a number of fighting holes which were connected with a landline [communications wire] and lots and lots of packs which had been left there. We had obviously surprised a large unit and they had decided to leave their gear. We moved on line two platoons abreast and began systematically moving forward into this base camp with the hopes that we would turn up even more. We started through this camp, and I suppose we had not moved more than twenty-five meters when all hell broke loose. On a front from left to right we were taken under fire, very heavy fire. Automatic weapons, small arms, grenades, mortars, the works. This unit had obviously backed off through the camp itself, gone to the other side, and awaited our movement.

We were stuck. We had fire completely along our front. It was murderous. We could not take cover, so we did the only thing we could. We fixed bayonets and moved into the attack rapidly. We were armed at the time with the M14 and not the M16 rifle. We had two platoons engaged. My 3d Platoon, you will recall, still remained back at the clearing area to await the battalion. As our movement progressed I found that the fire was just overwhelming, convincing me that I had to continue to move or we would have never left our tracks.

Lieutenant Terry Heekin commanded the first platoon. Lieutenant Forest (or "Butch") Goodwin commanded the 2d Platoon and was on the left when we went into the attack. As we began the attack, casualties appeared immediately but we pressed on, hoping to by speed overwhelm the defenders.

The 1st platoon managed to turn the enemy enough so that he fell back on our right. On my left the 2nd platoon ran into two machine guns which were the wheel variety, where the gunner sat on a little seat just aft of the receiver. As 2nd platoon broke into the clearing, the gunner of the machine gun in the center fired a volley right smack into the attacking platoon commander, Lieutenant Goodwin, which killed the lieutenant and, beside him, Corporal Strahl. Strahl was on his next to the last day in the field when he was killed—a super Marine. The platoon sergeant, Pete New, immediately picked up the platoon. Francis McGowin, the guide, became the platoon sergeant and the platoon was as well handled as it ever had been. It was an extremely good platoon. We moved into the open, overwhelmed the enemy; but the enemy, still in his retreat, managed to pour fire into us, so we returned fire and consolidated on their objective there.

Battalion had been listening while we were in the attack and knew that we were into some kind of fix. I began calling in covering fire and suppressive fire on the mortars, which was delivered initially in the form of artillery from the 12th Marines at Camp Carroll. As we were still taking fire, we received fixed-wing support as well.

We were very heavily engaged. I had a number of casualties which we collected and moved back to a small clearing, requested medevacs to get them out. As we broke into the open, we were feeling very good about ourselves because we had managed to stop the enemy there, and we felt that we had overwhelmed him and chased him off this objective. But what we hadn't appreciated was that he still had fight left and more people and it wasn't the end of the day at all.

He pulled back out of our immediate visibility and held his fire and then began mortaring us and the mortars came soon—but not before the assistant division commander, Brigadier General Ryan, who had been listening to this action, came out to have a look around and in so doing landed his helicopter smack on the objective, jumped out asking for a quick report.

In the process of reporting to him, I showed him around and showed him the mounds of equipment all over the place. One sight I remember particularly was one of the machine guns I mentioned earlier, the heavy machine guns which were on wheels and a little seat that the gunner sat on. The gunner had been hit with white phosphorus and was burning as he sat on his machine gun there— a gruesome but indescribable sight. General Ryan walked by and was shaking his head. He remained there maybe fifteen minutes or so, could see the extent of our wounded and the high number of casualties, and moved back to his helicopter and flew away.

In the meantime my battalion commander was trying to get in touch with me and talking constantly and saying, "Where are you?" and so forth, and I told him and he had said he didn't want me to engage. Well, I had had no choice in the matter. Once I started moving, they engaged me and it wasn't a matter of me being able to control the action, that is, to turn it off, to stop it. After the general left I began consolidating, checking with my men, redistributing ammunition, reassuring them that the casualties were being looked after, and indeed the casualty evacs had already started. I could tell that they were pretty shaken by this thing because the whole company had been very heavily engaged, and certainly on a man-for-man basis, they had seen a heck of a lot of combat in that one short span of time. It was easy to see that a number of the new joinees were excited to the point of almost coming apart.

We then began making preparations for medevacs, consolidating, redistributing ammunition, moving crew-served weapons in the appropriate positions, and frankly expecting what would almost assuredly be an enemy counterattack. When this was going on I began to hear helicopter blades. I looked up and the same helicopter which had been previously there to deliver the assistant division commander, General Ryan, was proceeding back. The pilot began to flare—that is, to raise his nose a little bit and then rock it back and forward without actually touching down. I could see these big boxes inside the helicopter. General Ryan had gone back to Delta Med and gathered up all the life-sustaining medical supplies he could get his hands on and sent them out to us because he knew we were in such bad shape. He dropped in trach tubes, blood volume expander, plasma, all sorts of things.

As these boxes were being pushed out of the helicopter, which was in a hover, in came the mortars. I was running to the helicopter trying to wave him off to get him out of there because I knew that the situation was just going to be intolerable very soon and that he would not survive it. One of those mortars, I'm convinced, went right through his rotor blades, because a box of medical supplies landed underneath the helicopter and the mortar actually hit the box of medical supplies, detonated, and the shrapnel from it flew over in all directions. I happened to be on one end and it hit me, threw me through the air, and it hit my radio operator, Price, and threw him through the air, straight upside down.

I'll never forget the sensation of being blown through the air and looking over at my operator, Corporal Price, and Price was 180 degrees inverted. His feet were straight up. His head was straight down. He still held the handset to his ear. It looked as if someone had taken him and turned him upside down and stuck him on his antenna. An amazing sight! The same mortar blew me a considerable distance down. On impact, rather than landing on my back or front, I landed on my side, and worse was I was wearing my battle dress open. When it blew me through the air my pistol inverted and the muzzle was sticking up. The mortar round that hit me had also hit me on the left side, penetrated the handle of my K-Bar, and then imbedded in me a piece of hot shrapnel. In the process I landed on the muzzle of my pistol and I continued to fall smashing into the ground. I immediately had an enormous pain where my pistol muzzle had broken some ribs. And I had this pain on my left which is where the mortar hit me. I literally thought that I had taken a round and it had gone right straight through me, and I was scared to death to look because I knew it would confirm that I didn't have much time. When the helicopter pilot saw this action, he popped out of there as quickly as he could. I never saw him again.

The mortars continued to come, along with some small-arms fire. It suddenly occurred to me that the big success we had been enjoying earlier was fleeting. We had thought we achieved a great victory by pushing the enemy off this hill when in fact he had fallen back to another position and mortared us and began firing from that other position, with jungle separating him from us so we couldn't directly observe him.

The situation looked frankly rotten at this point. I knew I had a number of casualties. I was now hit. Like as not, whenever you're hit you try to be positive about it, but you expect the worst. The other radio operator . . . came running up and saw the mess that was lying there. Price was covered in blood and looked horrible. In my case I was just tossed about. Unthinkingly he reported open [uncoded] over the net to battalion, "The skipper's hit. The skipper's hit." This report was monitored back at the division headquarters where the G3, in fact the whole COC [Combat Operation Center], was listening to the action. In the COC they heard that comment, "The skipper's hit. The skipper's hit." They made an immediate little yellow message-pad comment, took it straight into the CG [commanding general] who was at that time talking to the acting G3 (who happened to be my brother, George Ripley) and handed it to the CG who in turn showed it to my brother. That's another story in itself, and of course they knew we were still without help. There was nobody there to give us a hand and it appeared that we were surrounded, certainly outnumbered, so you can imagine the trauma involved in brother knowing brother is beyond help and wounded and not knowing how badly wounded.

In any case we began consolidating what we had. Elements of the first platoon ran over and began helping myself and Price back on our feet. Surprisingly, both Price and myself continued to function. Price looked terrible, but he seemed to be able to get around. Corpsmen came up and patched us up a bit and then we kept moving. We didn't have anywhere to go. We just sought cover elsewhere.

The same barrage which had hit me and Price and a number of other Marines killed my first platoon commander, Lieutenant Terry Heekin, and very severely wounded his platoon sergeant, Sergeant Wakowsky. This led to a very interesting series of events I'll talk about. The platoon guide was a corporal who was off doing other things, and Lieutenant Heekin's radio operator was a lance corporal, Chuck Goggin, who was one of several drafted Marines we had. These fellows were quite an anomaly at the time. You never saw a drafted Marine and yet these one or two of them were. Well, Goggin was damned good stock. He'd been in the minor leagues fighting to get into the majors when his draft notice came, went into the Marine Corps, and happily I got him in Lima Company. He was just a super lad and very switched on, knew precisely what was going on, what the situation was, what needed attention, paid attention, something a radio operator had to do.

He reported to me the situation. I said, "Goggin, you're in charge. Take charge of what's remaining. Keep the attack oriented on your front and produce as much fire as you can." Well, the first platoon was in good hands. I immediately promoted him to corporal, although I probably didn't have the authority, I did it. In five days the commanding general came out and promoted him to sergeant, which was wonderful. He kept that platoon until a lieutenant could come, and that was considerably later.

The situation was now approaching late afternoon. We still hadn't received any reinforcements. The battalion was sending a platoon from India Company to try to close the distance and give us some help, but they were not there yet. Frankly, things looked very grim. I knew I couldn't abandon the position because the enemy was around me and would very much like to get back on that position and gain all the stuff that they'd left—their equipment, their rucksacks, radios, and so forth. So we held. The mortar barrages continued. I was getting all the artillery and air support I could handle, which did a real job on the enemy as well. The mortaring stopped at that point. We carried on, went back to where the casualties were, and were trying to make them comfortable in preparation for getting them out of there.

By this time the small arms had stopped but the devastation was incredible. As I looked around me I had numerous wounded Marines; the ones who were ambulatory still manned positions and were in the process of returning fire although wounded. There was one in particular I recall who was lying in a hole next to his dead buddy whose face had been blown off. He was lying there sort of caressing, rubbing his shoulders and his chest, and sort of talking to him, reassuring him that everything was okay and they were going to make it out. Of course, his buddy was quite dead.

With the arrival of the first medevac bird, the first thing off the bird were correspondents, both television correspondents and radio correspondents. They gathered around me and were running around the rest of the Marines there. Of course, they landed right where the wounded were and they were trying to talk to the wounded, which infuriated me. We were in the process of getting the wounded on the aircraft and trying to get them out of there, which we did and then away went the helicopters.

We had two separate teams of correspondents, one of them filming and another one just walking around with a microphone and a tape recorder. They were talking to anyone they could talk to. They tried not to distract the business at hand, which was returning fire. They did make some tapes, unbeknownst to me as I had other things to do than pay attention to them. These same tapes were how my father and my wife saw this action of 2 March. They saw it on television and on one very celebrated incident. One of my casualties was being carried in a poncho while these fellows were filming it, and a mortar came in and they sought rapid cover and dropped the poncho, and the face of this casualty was filmed and his parents saw that. They knew it was him. It was a CBS film team. They were greatly chastised. They were sanctioned or something or other by their company for doing that, and that marked the beginning of some kind of control by the major networks over what was being shown.

I participated in loading casualties, and one of the film crews, as the helicopter was leaving, ran over and threw his camera and equipment in the back of this CH-46; the ramp was up, he threw it in and grabbed the ramp and began struggling to get into the helicopter. He was so anxious to get out of there that he threw all of this equipment on the casualties which were in the helicopter. One of my Marines almost shot him. In any case he did not get out.

Corporal Joseph J. Davis

My platoon, commanded by Lieutenant Osborne, was a reserve platoon. My most vivid recollection was when we were linking up with India Company. We almost shot the one squad that linked up with us. Myself and the other members of my fire team were alerted by sounds of someone crashing through the brush. Knowing that India Company was going to be linking up with us, we took the chance and called out to them hoping we'd get a positive response, and that's who they were.

Captain John Ripley

About 1700 or 1800, getting toward the end of light and happily, almost in movie fashion, the cavalry arrives and it was the platoon from India Company, commanded by a gunnery sergeant whose name was Mack, a tremendous guy. Boy, were we glad to see him! He brought some surprising news. He said we are "to leave this position, abandon it, and you are to move back with me," to the place we had started that morning, which was the clearing where the battalion was to be located.

I was more than just a little surprised that we had to do that since I'd spent the whole day defending this position having wrested it from the enemy at great expense to my company. Now we were told to abandon it along with all the equipment and to move back and consolidate with the battalion. I would have thought that they'd have come up and joined me to defend what we'd gained, but that was not the case and we were ordered back, and there was utterly no way we could carry all the equipment that we'd captured with us. So I was told to make an attempt to destroy it. Even that was a tall order which we couldn't do. We just simply could not destroy everything—to include, for example, large metal ammunition cans that were lead-sealed and you had to use an E-tool [small folding shovel] to chop into them. I simply didn't have enough time to do all that.

Corporal Joe Davis

As we moved away from the area, all along the trail were gook bodies, and one of the bodies that was on the trail was over six feet tall. That's when I realized that the North Vietnamese were being advised by the Chinese.

Captain John Ripley

We moved back and then found the battalion there. My column was pathetically thin, no more than thirty Marines, if that. We moved into the battalion position where we rejoined my second platoon, which had been there the entire day defending that location while we were just up north of them.

I met the battalion commander there and he was a bit upset because his instructions to me were not to engage and I had to convince him that there was no way I could avoid engagement. I was in effect locked on. It was like flying into flypaper and trying to disengage. I was in the enemy's grasp and the only thing I could do was to engage and push him out and then defend what I had. General Ryan was very pleased with that day's activity by Lima Company, had been directly involved flying in and so forth, and I think his comments to my battalion commander convinced him that Lima Company was well acquitted that day and did a tremendous job in smashing the enemy, wresting from him a very important position at certain expense to ourselves. In keeping with what we were trying to do, it took the pressure off of 2/3 which had been hit so badly.

It appeared that this NVA regiment had been very thoroughly engaged along a wide front, so we had apparently run right into their regimental headquarters, which intelligence later proved to be the case. We literally wrecked this headquarters and a good portion of the enemy which had been defending it there. I was constantly assailed by radio reports asking me, "How many confirmed? How many confirmed?" In other words, how many enemy dead do you have there? I wasn't paying a lot of attention. They were dead enemy around us. I had suffered so many casualties, they wanted some kind of equity here, and they were demanding some accounting, but I never could get them. I could only see what was around me and I sure wasn't going to go searching for them. That seemed to be a big concern of division's the whole time.

Corporal Lindy R. Hall, K Company, sets fire to a Vietnamese hut on Operation PRAIRIE.

The next day the proof of our efforts was really laid out when, just after first light, a bird dog [a light observation aircraft] was up with a friend of mine and he told me that while he was flying he was directed over our sector to try to establish what the enemy was doing. He saw a great column of the enemy moving out of the position we had fought him in, making no serious effort to hide themselves and carrying as many wounded as they could out of the area. Of course, they left their dead.

So ended the effort to stop what had been a very large-scale enemy assault due south across the DMZ into the area south of Con Thien and north of Cam Lo, and it had been their intention to go right through Cam Lo all the way to Route 9 and from there to begin a larger-scale attack around Dong Ha and so forth.

We stopped them north of the river in a continuous attack, pushed them all the way back to the DMZ. But the price was tremendous. I lost every single squad leader, my two lieutenants killed in action. Of the 200-odd Marines, including all the attachments, scout dogs, engineer teams, correspondents, all the other things that go with you, when we finally got back to that road, there were only 15 men in my company who hadn't suffered a wound or been killed in action during that whole period, and I wasn't one of them either.

To show the contrast between the intensity of daily experience to participants and what appeared in official records, the action Captain Ripley described above was condensed to about a page of double-spaced text in the battalion's Command Chronology.

16

A TURBULENT EASTER

Father Guy McPartland

12 March 1967, Passion Sunday

You know that cross (crucifix) I put on the grave of those five NVA soldiers we killed up at our old position. Well, that territory is now in the hands of the NVA since we moved a little further south last January. But our patrols sweep through that area periodically and they tell me that the grave marker and crucifix haven't been touched! I guess the NVA thought we did a real fine job of burying their dead. Usually, anything we leave behind they rip apart. But they must of appreciated our giving their soldiers a decent burial.

I'm beginning to think I don't want any souvenirs from dead NVA. In fact, I don't want any "souvenirs" of this war at all. Hope the kids won't be disappointed if I don't bring anything home.

.

Members of K Company cross a stream on March 19, 1967, as the battalion conducts a seven-day search west of Cam Lo early in Operation PRAIRIE.

17 March 1967, St. Patrick's Day

Hello again and how are you? The "top of the morning" to you, and a very Happy St. Patrick's Day to you and all the folks at home.

It's now 11:15 A.M. and we'll be moving out on an operation in about one hour! Just wanted to drop you a line before I left. They say it'll only be a three- or four-day jaunt, but they've said that before in the past and we've been out for a week or ten days! Here's hoping they're more accurate this time and we will be back in three or four days.

We'll be going back into the same area we were in on the last operation. That is, the area northeast of our position here at the Rockpile (more east than north). Please God, the rain will continue to hold off so we can get some sleep at night.

Lieutenant Dan Ryan

I guess it must have been about March 20th . . . we were cut loose. The NVA, the *324 . . . b* [NVA Division], I think, were in Leatherneck Square [the area bounded by Dong Ha, Gio Linh, Con Thien, and Cam Lo] lookin' for fights. So we decided . . . good Marine tactics . . . let's send a company in and see if they make contact. And if they do, then we know where they are. So, we're walkin' and shootin' and takin' some sniper fire and this and that. Well, anyway, on March 25th, Good Friday, I had a squad leader, James Raymond Kelly III. Good, good guy. A real ass-kicker. The only reason he was still in the Marine Corps, he was serving bad time. He was an A-J-Squared-Away guy. But he liked to fight and fuck around and that's show biz. Well, anyway, we're out walkin' around and this resupply chopper comes in and there was . . . we were shorthanded from gettin' whacked a few times. And heat stroke and what have you.

And Kelly said, "Lieutenant, I'm short [nearly at the end of his tour]. I got a couple of weeks or whatever, can I take this R and R?" He was one of my most capable squad leaders. I turned him down. I said, "I'm sorry, Bud, I can't spare you." That was about noon. At about three-thirty we walked into a . . . an encampment of gooks. They had the fighting holes, the whole works. They were just waitin' on us. The shit started flyin'. A bunch of people got killed. I got wounded. I had the point, so I'm trying to hold these guys while 2d Platoon maneuvers in their classic flank envelopment. Here comes Gunny Pichon. I understand later that he was havin' a lot of family problems and basically said, "Fuck it." He comes on with his .45 and his hand grenade, and he says, "Come on fellas, let's go get 'em." And . . . you know, the school solution is you get your guys on line, lay a base of fire, and get your maneuver element around one of your flanks to stop the assholes from takin' you. So I told him, "Gunny, get the fuck out of here, this is my outfit." And he says, "Ahh," and away he goes and just charges right into 'em. And of course they ate him up. I carried his body out with a couple of other guys, another swimmer in the poncho.

After that, the gooks figured they had some fresh meat and started movin' in on us, and they came down this one trenchline on our flank . . . about ten of them. Kelly spotted 'em, jumps up with his M14. "Hey, motherfuckers . . ." *bup-bup-bup-bup-bup-bup*, and starts firin' and stopped 'em. He caught everybody's attention and of course the gooks, uh . . . let Kelly have it.

The crazy thing about war . . . the crazy thing about the mind . . . how it turns off . . . I went over to Kelly. I saw him lyin' under a tree. I went over to him and I was convinced that he was asleep. And I went over and I kicked him. I says, "Get up, you son of a bitch. You're sleepin'." And I knew it was him from the corporal's stripes on his helmet. 'Course there was a hole in the helmet. Tough time. I remember him well. I guess that's some of the guilt that I carry: Would he be alive today if I'd let him go? He had a pregnant wife and another kid. The usual sad story.

The next day, the 26th, we're up in this village, southwest of Con Thien. And in the morning we went in there and destroyed a bunch of hooches and trenches and shit and burned a bunch of stuff down. It was durin' the afternoon. We thought we had 'em all. . . . India was to the south and Lima or Mike was to the north with the command group and had the 81s [mortars] with them. We're doin' this parallel sweep and all of a sudden we're gettin' incoming. Mortars. So everybody is cowering in their holes and tryin' not to get hit by mortar fragments.

The weapons platoon was under Gunnery Sergeant Chester Pavey, who was just a fine, fine guy. An old barbershop singer and certainly a good mortar man. He jumps up with his crew. And you know, when the shit starts flyin' and you're in artillery or mortars, you gotta be on your feet doin' your thing. Otherwise they're gonna eat ya. The 03s [riflemen] can say, "Well, okay, I'm just a grunt, I can stay in my hole."

Anyway, more mortars came in; I went over and got Pavey and he got one right through the chest. He was dead as a mackerel. Uh . . . very sad. But the saddest part was . . . we were doing some crater analysis and we were lookin' at some of these tail fins. They were 81s. What had happened, we figure, is that the gooks were in between us and would jump out of their spider hole or whatever . . . pop a few 60s over at us . . . and few over to the north . . . toward the 81 section and Lima Company. And what they did, they got us involved in a duel . . . between Marines. So much for fire coordination.

During that time we knew we were really in the shit. So, as always, we continued to walk and walk and walk. And the next day was Easter Sunday. What a lovely day. Bright and cheerful. And everyone is lookin' around and wonderin' who is gonna die tonight. Or today. That night we holed in . . . I think it was right next to a graveyard. There was an old gook church. A Catholic church. I remember there was a waterfall. It was a very peaceful pastoral scene.

We were settin' our night positions and I never did like to dig holes anyway, so I'm goin' around and gettin' the guys set in and makin' sure they're diggin' holes and everything else. And all of a sudden . . . Charlie Chan starts throwin' shit at us again. Only this time it's good stuff 'cause, as I recall, we were just south of the southern portion of the Z [DMZ]. I don't know what kind of range they had, but they were right on it.

So here I am without a hole. I go to jump in a hole and there's three Marines in it. They say, "Sorry, Lieutenant." Here I am crouched down behind a rock

During Operation PRAIRIE, *Marines of I Company patrol a hill near the Rockpile.*

wondering when the rock is going to explode and I'm gonna meet the Lord. What they were doin' was firin' their 120s. And you could hear 'em comin'. That *swi-swi-swi-swi*. That whispering. You know. They say if you can hear it, it's not gonna get ya. Well, I don't know about that. They kept us there all, all night. It was . . . it was a terrible, terrible time. Several people got killed.

Father Guy McPartland
29 March 1967

Hello again and how are you? Well, thank God, we returned from the "operation" last night. Hope you'll forgive my not writing last night, but I was so very tired and exhausted.

As I wrote in my last letter, we left on St. Patrick's Day, the 17th. It was only supposed to take about three or four days for the sweep, but as it turned out it lasted twelve days. And it was the longest and most terrifying twelve days I've ever lived through. We were hit continually, day in and day out! We suffered heavy casualties, unfortunately. But God was good in providing that I could get to most of the KIAs. You can't imagine how much these kids appreciate having me with them at that awful moment!

I've had many different jobs during the course of my priesthood, but none will equal in importance the work I'm doing right now. If, like Pop always said, God performed a miracle through the intercession of St. Theresa, to save my life when I had polio as a kid, perhaps this was the reason I was spared. Maybe He foresaw that thirty-five years later some kids would need the ministrations of a priest on the battlefield of Vietnam. That may sound melodramatic to some, but not to me.

Momma, I'm writing like this, realizing that some of the things I mention may worry you. But I think I ought to write about them for a number of reasons. Small talk is alright, but I do enough of that in my letters. During the last twelve days I wrote this letter many times in my mind.

Day after day, as I lay in my hole, and the mortar shells were hitting all around me, rattling my teeth as the deadly shrapnel particles were barely whizzing past my body, I prayed with all my heart for God and His Blessed Mother to spare me to write this letter. You can hear every round coming in and you can tell by the loudness of the "whistle" how close they're going to be to your own hole. When the "whistle" is very loud and distinct, you know it's coming right down into your immediate area, maybe even right down on top of you.

I must have said the Memorare 500 times during the last twelve days. I prayed out loud (and I came to find out most of the men do the same). A few times I could hear that very loud and distinct "whistle" sound; and I knew this could be it! I braced myself, gritted my teeth (which was kind of pointless because it wouldn't make any difference if it came down on top of you), and just before it hit I broke off Memorare and said out loud, "Momma, I love you"! The shell hit about 12 to 18 inches from the edge of my hole and the hole is only about 4 feet long, 2 feet wide, and 2 feet deep, just enough room to curl your body up and stay below the surface of the ground. Funny that these words should come so instinctively to my mind at a moment like that. I vowed to Almighty God that if I should live through these twelve days I would write and tell you how much I really mean those words. I guess I felt deeply guilty of not expressing myself and my love for you over the years.

I'm not really interested in analyzing the reasons why, all I know is that I didn't want to die before I had an opportunity (at least one more opportunity) of telling you that I love you with all my heart and I'm deeply sorry for all the many sorrows and aggravations I've caused you during my life. Momma, of all the women and mothers in the world, you are the finest! God has been so good to me in giving me such a wonderful woman for my mother. I know I always knew that, but I guess it took a war to make me really appreciate it. God spared me to say this and I pray that I will never forget it even after the memory of the past twelve days has faded.

3 April 1967

Heard from the division chaplain (my boss) today. He says my replacement will arrive up in this area to relieve me a week from tomorrow, Tuesday, 11 April.

Most officers of Father McPartland's rank rotated out of a line unit after about six months, but Father Guy served nine months in the field with his Marines. He was awarded the Bronze Star medal and the Vietnamese Gallantry Cross for his service.

MARCH 1967

Sergeant James Austin

At the end of March of '67 they took away our M14s and issued us M16s. A lot of guys up on Hill 861 got sent home in body bags because our M16s didn't function. A lot of guys told me they jammed up and they was up there throwing rocks.

So Congress heard about it and they sent a team up. After their team came and they got the answers that they wanted to hear, they passed down a division order to make 1,000 rounds per man available for fam firing. I don't know what the purpose was, to familiarize ourself with that or file down the rough parts to those Matty-Mattel-mother-fucking guns. Anyway, we went out every day shooting until you shot off your 1,000 rounds.

The M16 was first used in large numbers in Vietnam by the U.S. Army in the Ia Drang Valley battle where it was credited with a major role in the victory against the NVA. By early 1967, the Marines began the transition from the older semiautomatic M14 to this newer weapon. The rifle was lighter, used much lighter ammunition, and could be fired on full as well as semiautomatic. As Sergeant Austin points out, the Marines had problems with the M16, and many lost confidence in it when some of their fellows died with jammed weapons in their hands. The Marines' official history states, "The earlier [M16] weapons—even when cleaned to usual standards (not always possible in any sustained combat)—still developed microscopic 'pits' in the chamber. . . . The [rifles] would then fail to extract, usually at an awkward time." In order to alleviate the problem, the Marines retrofitted a chrome-coated chamber assembly and a modified buffer group to the weapon. The controversy continued in spite of the changes. Over a year later, 3/3's after-action report for a major battle near Cua Viet stated, "A critical problem was experienced when a combination of rain and sand reduced the majority of M16 rifles to an inoperative state." PFC William Frantz describes this incident on page 280.

·

Lieutenant Dan Ryan

There was an incident around this time where Roach was still the platoon sergeant. We were out holdin' some little post, somewhere on a sweep, and we had a guy up on a listening post and it was foggy. Nobody could raise him on the radio, so we thought we'd lost him. We sent some Marines back out to get him, and the guy was asleep. They brought him back in. His name was Mallet. He was a French Canadian and the goofy son of a bitch joined the U.S. Marine Corps. Mallet was as big and as strong as a horse. I'm about ready to kill the guy and I say to Roach, I says, "Sergeant Roach, will you straighten that son of a bitch out?" And he says, "You bet, Lieutenant." He goes over and hits Mallet right in the face with his .45. Drops him like he was shot. Ooh boy, that was a bit much.

Mallet is the same guy that you'd bet him that he couldn't carry a case of beer and ice up the Razorback while we were up there. "Oh yeah, watch this." And off he went. So pistol whipping him in the face probably just . . . you know, made him blink a little bit. I don't think it got to his brain-housing group much.

·

Lieutenant Bill Masciangelo

The company commander was very particular about Marines staying alert when they were on watch. And the company commander and the gunny would walk around, every evening, to check lines. And as platoon commanders we dreaded the next morning's company commander's meeting when he would chew one of us out, invariably, because he found people sleeping on the lines. And of course it went downhill from there to the platoon sergeants and to the squad leaders and, you know . . .

As lieutenants we were constantly trying to make sure this didn't happen and we did everything we could to motivate our squad leaders. Specifically, I can remember asking a new Marine, who was sitting in his hole during maybe his first week . . . and I said, "Hey, Marine, did the company commander come around last night?" He said, "No, sir." And this was with a very straight face. "Just the gunny and some guy named Skipper."

17

. . . .
THE FIRST BATTLE OF KHE SANH

Sergeant James Austin

The *324 Bravo* [NVA Division] come back in March, the end of March. We had operations around Hills 881, north and south, and 861. The first guys that went out didn't come back.

Hills 881 North, 881 South, and 861 dominate the Khe Sanh plateau from the northwest and major infiltration routes from Laos and North Vietnam. In what has been called the "First Battle of Khe Sanh," to distinguish it from the famous siege of 1968 (in which 3/3 did not participate), Marines fought for these hills in order to protect the Khe Sanh Combat Base, originally a Special Forces outpost and now essential to countering infiltration from the western DMZ area.

General Westmoreland, in the autumn of 1966, ordered the Marines to establish a presence at Khe Sanh with a reinforced battalion. According to his memoir, he hoped eventually to launch a corps-sized operation into Laos in order to interdict the Ho Chi Minh Trail and to destroy NVA sanctuaries there. Khe Sanh was to be the staging area for this operation. The Marines objected, largely on the grounds that a battalion at this

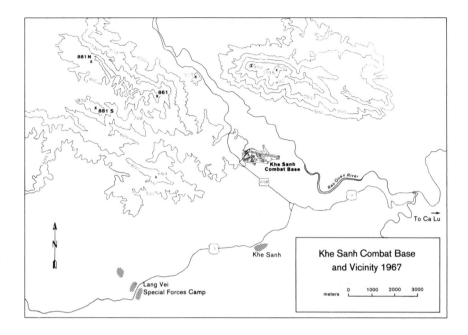

Khe Sanh Combat Base
and Vicinity 1967

then-remote outpost would be one less for their pacification program. Lieutenant General Krulak, in particular, felt that Khe Sanh was a tactical albatross. He read the move
as part of Westmoreland's strategy of attrition, a strategy to which he did not subscribe.

Throughout late 1966 and early 1967, the frequency of enemy contact with Marine
units increased in these hills. On 23 April a company from 1/3 found itself heavily
engaged on Hill 861 and noted considerable enemy activity on Hills 881 North and
South. Kilo 3/3 and the battalion command group were sent to assist. When this help
failed to carry the hill, Mike 3/3 and Mike 3/9 were added to the force. This gave
Colonel Wilder, 3/3's CO, command of a makeshift unit of companies from three separate battalions.

Upon securing Hill 861, the hybrid battalion was diverted to 881 South, and 2/3 was
brought in to attack Hill 881 North. On the evening of April 29, thirty-three aircraft
sorties pounded 881 South with more than 250 2,000-pound bombs. Thirteen hundred
rounds of artillery also pockmarked the position during the night. At first light 3/3 assaulted behind the last of the preparatory fires. Despite their best efforts, the attack was
thrown back by midafternoon. Forty-three Marines died in the assault and 109 were
wounded. Mike Company 3/3 ceased to function as a fighting unit because of its high
number of casualties, and the survivors were sent back to Dong Ha via Khe Sanh that
evening.

Ken Ransbottom, who had served with 3/3 a year earlier in the Danang area, was
back in action, voluntarily, with 2/3. He kept extending his tour and served twenty-seven

continuous months in the field in Vietnam, possibly as long as anyone in the entire war. Lieutenant Colonel Earl "Pappy" DeLong was back in the fight too. The former 3/3 commander had taken over 2/3 when their CO, Lieutenant Colonel Victor Ohanesian, was killed in March. Ransbottom saw the remnants of 3/3 come off Hill 881 South.

Sergeant Ken Ransbottom

We moved out of Khe Sanh, up towards the hills where 3/3 made contact. I had the feel for what was coming, although I didn't know how bad it was going to be, but I knew that I had an edge and my squad had an edge and that we could make it through. All we had to do was use our heads.

Then I saw remnants and I do mean stragglers. I saw one Marine all by himself with no weapon, with a soft cover on, just walking back down a trail. Here we were with flankers out, everybody kind of on edge waiting for something to happen, moving, and it was like something you'd see on television. Just some guy walking, just bopping down the trail. He didn't look enthusiastic. He looked like he had seen a ghost. I knew what those ghosts were. Those ghosts were another part of me. I could feel it.

I was exuberant, I was thrilled, I was exhilarated just seeing this guy and then seeing bodies. Now, I wasn't *happy*. It was as though I was a tank with eight goddamned guns on it coming up to help. But in reality I knew that I was just me and my squad and we were going to learn some things real quick.

Now we saw columns, like maybe twenty-five guys in a column, moving out, moving off of the hills. They were part of 3/3. They too looked like they got their ass kicked. By the same token there was a sparkle there like, "Okay, you guys go up there and give them a little payback for us." A unit that's had their ass kicked, there wasn't too many eyes sparkling because there wasn't too many people thinking about retribution.

After regrouping, reinforcement by Company F 2/3, and another night's pounding by artillery and air, the hill was finally captured. The Marines found 250 heavily fortified bunkers tied in with communications wire. They were carefully positioned to provide interlocking fields of fire. Some of the larger bunkers had as many as eight layers of logs and four feet of dirt on top. By 4 May, Colonel DeLong's 2/3 had captured Hill 881 North, which was similarly fortified. Hundreds of NVA were killed, many in close combat. Sergeant Ken Ransbottom won a Bronze Star medal for heroic action during the attack.

18

. . . .

ROUGH RIDERS ON ROUTE NINE

Route 9, the major east-west artery, runs the width of Vietnam just south of the DMZ and the major bases. With the route in friendly hands, it was possible to supply Gio Linh, Cam Lo, Alpha 3, Con Thien, the Rockpile, and Khe Sanh by road. Whenever the enemy controlled it, supply of all these bases depended on a helicopter lifeline that became very tenuous in the seasonal monsoon. The Marine supply convoys that attempted to travel the roads in Vietnam were known as "Rough Riders."

Captain John Ripley

During the early period of 1967 in March, April, the 3d Marine Division was outposted all along the DMZ from Dong Ha to Khe Sanh. Khe Sanh was not in very great strength, never much more than a battalion. One of our jobs was to protect the road, Route 9, which was the only ground access to Khe Sanh.

In April after some very heavy fighting in the Con Thien area between Cam Lo and Con Thien and the Rockpile area, my company was pulled out of activity there and sent to Ca Lu, which was one of the small locations on the road, on Route 9 to Khe Sanh. We were sent there for outpost duty as sort of an R and R   143 [rest and recuperation] after having been pretty severely bled in previous combat operations.

Corporal Joe Davis

Ca Lu was a respite. We had a lot of fun out there. In spite of all the death and destruction around us and in our midst, Vietnam was still a beautiful country. We didn't let our guard down, but we did take the time to sit back and think and reflect about how beautiful that place was.

Captain John Ripley

We arrived at Ca Lu and began establishing our base, patrolling, etc., in the area. Not long after arriving there we were required to perform convoy security for those Rough Riders, carrying provisions, ammunition, etc., to Khe Sanh. The Rough Rider would come from Dong Ha with light security and then to the Rockpile, and then from the Rockpile on Route 9 to Ca Lu. There my company would board with a considerable amount of weapons—generally a heavy section of tanks and security—and then we would proceed from there out to Khe Sanh.

It was a major operation, to say the least. The condition of Route 9 from Ca Lu to Khe Sanh was incredibly bad. It had been an old French road that was grown over with jungle. The surface was barely recognizable. There were a huge number of bridges and culverts, but the only ones that were serviceable were the bridges en route to Ca Lu. The ones beyond that could still be crossed, but the surface of the bridges was virtually gone. The trucks would be driving across the bridge on stringers, which are the longitudinal I-beams of which the bridge is constructed. You could look down through the surface and see the river beneath you. Planking was placed across these to keep the vehicles from falling through. The road was cut out of the cliffside. The river on the south side of the road was very far below the road. There were no guard rails. It was an absolute tactical nightmare because of the jungle preventing anyone from seeing anything.

It was impossible to secure from ambush. In an effort to build this road up, we received an engineer platoon from 3d Division which set about building culverts, reestablishing the washouts, and trying to make the road serviceable so that convoy operations could begin on a continuous basis out to Khe Sanh. Of course, the enemy was well established in the area and these engineers required security in order to go to and from.

On one particular occasion on the 24th of April in '67, the 12th Engineers Platoon was en route to several bridges out beyond Bong Kho. On the way there they passed what we called "the Elbow," which was a severe turn in the road that came back on itself past 90 degrees. They were hit at that elbow in an L-type ambush. All the vehicles were destroyed. The security which went along with them, which included a Duster (which is a [twin] 40-mm gun on a small tank) and an Ontos, were both destroyed. There were ten killed in action and twenty-four wounded in action in the platoon itself. Virtually every Marine involved was killed or wounded. It was a 100 percent ambush.

My company was notified of this ambush when one wounded Marine managed to make his way back to our perimeter, very bloodied but still living, and notified us of the condition of the rest of the engineer platoon. At this point we launched a recovery force to go down and try to give them some assistance. Once we had recovered and evacuated the casualties at the Elbow ambush site, we then moved back to Ca Lu, and in the days following there was a larger effort to complete the road, secure the bridges, rebuild those bridges and culverts, and eventually link with Khe Sanh by surface. When the road was sufficiently repaired and useful and was at the point where we could hazard moving on it, the Rough Rider convoys began coming out in earnest.

The procedure of the Rough Rider was to depart from my position at Ca Lu. The previous day, however, before the Rough Rider arrived there, we would send a platoon of security with the bridge platoon from the 12th Engineer Battalion. They would proceed out to the hairpin [another severe turn on the route to Khe Sanh] and build and secure the bridge there overnight. It was an extremely hazardous undertaking because, with only a platoon of infantry Marines and a smaller platoon of bridge personnel, they were sitting ducks out there trying to build and protect the bridge.

Lieutenant Lee Ashburn

When you drew the assignment of going out with the bridge platoon the day before the Rough Riders came through, you had an almost impossible task. There were several avenues of approach into this area and you had only your platoon and a bridge platoon. Once you got there, your men provided security for the bridge platoon while they got the bridge set up. Then you moved away from the bridge to the high ground and defend yourself for the night.

Captain John Ripley

It took such precision and such organization, split-second timing, everything! To watch these Marines do what they had to do—no second-guessing, no delays, no nothing, just *wham, wham, wham*, there were people driving pins in. They were building a whole bridge that you could take tanks across.

The bridge would remain there overnight, and the next day the remainder of the company would leave Ca Lu with the Rough Rider. The point vehicles would be armored vehicles or a quad 50 with a tank following. The quad 50 was [four power-operated] machine guns in the bed of a six-by which would be the point security and had enormous firepower. It would defoliate a jungle in front of it just by sustained fire. We would fire into likely ambush spots the whole way out, as well as using hand whizzers [hand-activated pyrotechnic devices] to catch the grass on fire and indeed caused enormous fires which, although it didn't do much for the environment, sure protected us.

Following the point there would be the security commander, which was me, and I always rode with the bridge platoon which had embarked [loaded aboard] a spare bridge in case something happened to the one we already put up. I put my CP in a dump truck because a dump truck has got good armor on it and we'd put machine guns on the forward end of the bed there. Following us was the main body. We would move with the understanding that the column would constantly move. If for one reason a vehicle was mined, the plan was to push the vehicle out of the way, which meant over the side of the road and down into the river valley far below us, but under no circumstances would the column stop. We would prep fire with our quad 50 and other automatic weapons, to include the tank's 90-mm, at likely ambush spots; for example, the Elbow where the engineer platoon had been previously ambushed. We would move through those spots, and finally we got to the hairpin where the Marines had been from the previous night. They cheered madly when we arrived there, with the sense that the whole operation would soon be over.

Lieutenant Lee Ashburn

After they passed through that position [the hairpin] going to Khe Sanh, you remained there and were very uneasy until they returned.

Captain John Ripley

Passing through the hairpin, we then moved uphill for approximately two miles to what was called the Coffee Plantation at the intersection of Route 9 and the access road on into Khe Sanh. We turned there into the access road and here we saw an amazing and a very memorable sight. There was a French planter there and a small—very small, I would say three to four years old—blond child, which obviously was Caucasian and belonged to the planter's family. Well, my Marines went absolutely nuts with this little girl standing there waving as we went by. They would unload everything they had of any value to a child. All the candy from C-rations, everything. That little child was buried in everything we could give her. I have to say in all candor that there were some tears and bitter feelings seeing her standing there and relating our own memories to our own children and sisters, etc., who were at home. It was very poignant passing that little child each time.

Lieutenant Lee Ashburn

It was one of the only children that you saw for months that looked like your children. She became a good-luck charm, and we looked forward to going through the plantation and catching a glimpse of her.

Captain John Ripley

We would proceed from that point on into Khe Sanh base where the convoy arrived after a rough three to four hours of movement, and we would rush down and begin dumping all items from the Rough Rider. Generally the ammunition would go straight to the dumps and the chow obviously would go to the various stowage areas. On one trip out there, in the trucks were three pallets of de-hydrated cabbage. I couldn't help thinking, "Here I am risking my life to protect dried cabbage which nobody is going to want to eat and somebody's getting rid of it in a cushy spot like Danang while they're having proper food and we're protecting this crap to take it to Khe Sanh."

Lieutenant Lee Ashburn

Probably the roughest part was when you were in the staging area at Khe Sanh. Words can hardly describe, if you've never been there, the smell of war, the smell of death, the constant fear of knowing that you were zeroed in. You can't wait to get these trucks loaded and get on them and start moving again. Even though you've still got a good rough ride ahead of you, and a very danger-ous ride, it's not as bad as sitting there in Khe Sanh knowing that they can hit you any time they want.

Captain John Ripley

Having unloaded all the equipment, the convoy would reassemble and just as rapidly turn about, and at a high port gallop [moving out rapidly with weapons at ready], we would move back out over the same ground hoping that the enemy had not had time to set up a return ambush or mine the road.

When we got back to the hairpin bridge, the convoy would stop for the first time and the engineers, after the last vehicle had crossed, would rip the bridge up, reload it onto their trucks, which were positioned there at the end of the convoy, and having done so, load [the Marines].

Lieutenant Lee Ashburn

It took about forty minutes to pull the bridge up.

Captain John Ripley

The security would load and then the entire Rough Rider would move back to Ca Lu. There were always in excess of twenty-five to thirty trucks involved in these Rough Riders. On virtually every case we saw enemy action, but happily it was handled by the point or the rear point or the security en route.

The whole 26th Marines went out to Khe Sanh under our protection, a whole regiment. We took them out there. We escorted them out.

Lieutenant Lee Ashburn

Once when I had bridge security, I lost my bunker at Ca Lu to a cobra. When the convoy came through the hairpin, they were telling me that they found a cobra in my bunker and had thrown tear gas in there with him. I turned that bunker over to the snake and never went back in.

The NVA, the weather, our own weaponry, and the shortage of supplies were not the only enemies Marines faced along the DMZ. One of the more bizarre episodes of the war involved wildlife and 3/3. In April 1967, Corporal David Schwirian, a squad leader from Captain Ripley's Lima Company, was manning an ambush site north of Route 9 in the middle of the night when a large tiger pounced on him. The big cat pinned the corporal's weapon hand to the ground by standing on it and began tearing big chunks of flesh from his other arm and shoulder. Schwirian lost nearly his entire bicep and suffered a great loss of blood. It took three hours for his men to carry him back to the company position where he was emergency medevaced. The wound was serious enough to end Corporal Schwirian's tour in Vietnam. The tiger escaped and it, or one like it, claimed another victim about a year later, when a Marine from another battalion was killed by a tiger within a few hundred meters of the spot where Corporal Schwirian had been attacked. See John Ripley's article "Tiger Tale" in the *Marine Corps Gazette*, June 1977.

MAY–JULY 1967

Lieutenant Bill Masciangelo

I think I am the only Marine who went to Vietnam who actually gained weight. I didn't smoke, and even to this day, when I get nervous . . . I have a high metabolism . . . I will eat, continuously. It's almost an obsession, like I'd never seen food before. Yet I have not gained any weight, particularly. I'm in good shape. But I ate . . . it was an obsession to have all this food always available. I carried more food with me on operations and ended up bringing food back. Marines, those who smoked, would trade for cigarettes, so I carried cigarettes and guys would trade this stuff . . . it was crazy. I also really got a thing for instant oatmeal . . . and had it delivered. Everybody I ever wrote to, I asked them to send me oatmeal. I got enough oatmeal to feed the battalion for one meal. But I carried instant oatmeal with me and ate it continually. Because it was hot . . . it was filling . . . didn't take a lot of water . . . it was good. And it was easy and, most of all, it was lightweight. So, I think I'm the only one who gained weight during the entire time.

·

Lieutenant Dan Ryan

There was another guy, his name was Corporal Dage. His trademark was when you go on an operation and he'd take very little chow; he'd take a knapsack full of hand grenades and this guy could throw them like Joe Namath. I'll never forget seein' him in action where we'd be pinned down or whatever and he'd get up and start whippin' these hand grenades. He'd pull the pin and his cry was, "One time, Chan," and he'd let these hand grenades go. I think the gooks ran away. Maybe that's why we won.

Lieutenant Bill Masciangelo

The problem with Sam Dage, like a lot of Marines, I think was that he was a combat Marine and not a garrison Marine. When I say garrison, I mean even within our perimeter he was bad news. This kid was . . . a troublemaker, who constantly had problems with everybody. Yet put him in actual combat . . . take him outside the perimeter and the guy was fantastic.

·

Sergeant James Austin

We didn't have any big morale problems. Everybody done what they was supposed to do, but towards the end of my rotation in '67, I saw my first marijuana heads. I had these two birds, one was a black corporal, one white. Every time I looked around they was back behind some bushes smoking marijuana and giggling. That's the first incident that I personally saw of narcotics usage. Most of the abuse that I saw over there was just abuse of beer. It was hard enough fighting the elements, the animals, insects, inferior weaponry. We sure didn't need nothing over there screwing around with your brains.

·

Lieutenant Bill Masciangelo

On one of those occasions where we had to go out and rescue the 9th Marines, we were going through a village that had been burned up, and we got involved in a firefight that day and came under a mortar attack. It was one of those short and intense, thirty-minute type things. First time I'd ever been mortared. And that will get your attention real quick. And then we pulled back that evening, after we'd evacuated the casualties and what have you.

We found our first POW that I'd ever seen. And this guy was shot up bad, but my platoon found the guy and I had his wallet and looked through his wallet. And there was a picture of him in his uniform, standing with his parents and his wife in the backyard of his home. Wherever he came from. And that reminded me so much . . . the backyard looked just like my grandparents' yard, where I, too, several months before, stood in the backyard and had my picture taken in uniform. And that day . . . really brought back that . . . you know . . . that we had similar feelings and . . . fears . . . it brought the human element of this whole thing down to the basic elements of human beings . . . similar feelings and de-sires and expectations and pride of who we are and what we're doing and that it came down to that. It could have been me and yet it was him.

•

As spring became summer, a serious problem arose with malaria. Between June and September, when the battalion moved to Cam Lo, 206 of its members contracted the disease. Many others came down with FUO, fever of unknown origin. There were times when this and other diseases removed more Marines from the ranks of the able-bodied than did the enemy.

•

PFC James P. Finn (Brand New Guy)

It was in July of 1967. I touched down at Danang Airport upon an Eastern Airlines jet from Okinawa. I thought all the way in as we were approaching that the minute I got on the tarmac that I was going to be shot at. Because there was a war raging down there, and didn't John Wayne get shot at the minute he hit the beaches? We arrived at about four-thirty in the morning and the sun was just starting to come up, and I thought at any minute that we were going to take incoming rounds all over the place. Little did I know that I was at the second or third or fourth busiest airport in the world in those days. And probably as secure as anything in New York was at that time.

My first impression of Vietnam was that I thought I was in Dodge City, seeing guys walking around and everybody had guns. Everybody was carrying weapons.

And with the totally free, chaotic kinds of things that were going on, there didn't seem to be any leadership. Guys were wandering around and people were doing whatever they wanted to do.

I had gotten to 'Nam with a young man who was on his second tour and he knew his way around. He took me under his wing and he told me not to report to the battalion right away. He said, "Don't worry. They won't even miss you. They probably even don't know you're coming." And he was right. So we hung around Danang for a couple, three days and we went up to the PX up on top of the hill there, to the beer gardens. And we had a great time drinking beer and meeting other guys and listening to war stories. I walked into the beer garden and on the wall they had the biggest arsenal that I had ever seen in my life. Every kind of weapon that we were carrying in those days. M14s, .45s, .38s, you name it. They were there hanging on the wall. I thought I was in the movie set of some picture someplace in California, not in Vietnam.

I eventually got tired of doing all that craziness and flew into Dong Ha. It was a total change. Tent cities everywhere and incoming rounds at different points all over the base. Those days are still fascinating to me. The total freeness with which we could move. And nobody asked questions. You just kind of wandered around. You could do just about anything you wanted to do. And it was wild, it was wild.

·

Lieutenant Bill Masciangelo

I went to Danang for the very first time when I was going on R and R and spending the night down there and just could not believe people lived as luxuriously as they did . . . and they looked at you 'cause you were dirty and your boots weren't shined. And it seemed like everybody had a vehicle and there was an officer's club and there was bands and there was Americans running around . . . Red Cross girls . . . That was almost just like culture shock because I got to the point that a little old villager with betel nut started lookin' good.

·

Lance Corporal Stanley E. Kerlin (Brand New Guy)

After several days in Vietnam we got on a resupply convoy and headed out to the Rockpile area where I joined with L/3/3. I was assigned to 3d Platoon. I spent the first few days getting adjusted to the climate and the area. Probably spent a lot a time filling sandbags, since that is something that we did a lot. We were always trying to improve our bunkers, filling those sandbags.

It was several days or a week before I actually was able to get a complete pair of jungle utilities and jungle boots. I had to use Stateside utilities and the regular leather boots for a while till I was finally able to get a pair of jungle boots that fit me. Because I wore such a common size I ended up getting them off a guy that got wounded. Either that or he was dead.

19

. . . .

CA LU

In the action described below, Mike Company was providing security for an engineer unit operating on Route 9 when an ambush was discovered. They engaged in a lengthy firefight with an estimated NVA battalion. Mike Company suffered nine dead in the action; all told, fourteen Marine and Army personnel were killed and forty-two wounded. Enemy casualties were not reported in the after-action report. After this engagement, no convoy was to make it through to the Khe Sanh Combat Base until the following spring, when Operation PEGASUS reopened Route 9 after the so-called seige.

Captain John Ripley

The whole time there was an inescapable feeling that large-scale action was inevitable. Toward the end of July, the enemy had moved into the area from the Rockpile to Ca Lu, all along Route 9 and certainly around Khe Sanh in very heavy forces. They had prepared an ambush approximately a mile-and-a-half outside of Ca Lu all the way down to Bong Kho, a distance of five miles.

Lieutenant Bill Masciangelo

The story came back about the very alert Marine who noticed some move-ment, saw an NVA taking a leak, and before any of the trucks or vehicles got into the killing zone, they blew the whole thing apart.

If that convoy had gotten into this killing zone . . . and it was one hellacious killing zone—the fighting positions, the mortar concentrations along the road, the minefields and booby traps along one side . . . so that Marines that jumped off, they would have really been in hurt city. But fortunately that thing did not happen. I've used that in many illustrative examples of how to set up a good ambush, except the bad part of it was, of course, was that some NVA ding-a-ling blew the whole thing by being observed and that blew all the preparations. But thank goodness, for us . . .

Captain Roger Zensen

As I think back and wonder if that NVA soldier hadn't been taking a leak along the side of the road that evening and that rifleman hadn't seen him and shot at him and started that firefight, we probably would have gone zipping through there the next day with 240 trucks.

Lieutenant Lee Ashburn

Maybe one of the big heroes of that war is the gook that was out taking a leak. The troops riding that convoy had no place to go but to the low side of the truck and on that side were hundreds of hand grenades with trip wires, booby-trapped. If they let the entire convoy get into the kill zone before they opened fire, almost all of the troops would have evacuated the vehicles on the low side, away from the ambush. It would have been like jumping in the middle of a minefield. God bless that gook and thank God he had small kidneys.

Captain Raymond F. Findlay (Brand New Guy)

That ambush was when I first came to the company. The first day I arrived in Mike Company I saw a lot of bodies in the LZ when I jumped out of the helicopter; you know, I was smelling them. It was amazing to be confronted with that the very first second.

·

Lieutenant Bill Masciangelo

Ray Findlay, company commander of Mike Company, had been a Basic School instructor. And after all the training we received, people would say, "You don't do it this way by the book. You don't do this, you don't this. We don't do it that way in Vietnam." And he came over there and was doing things by the book and was running a very successful company.

Captain Ray Findlay

Everybody said, "This doesn't apply to Vietnam." That's because people didn't know what the basics were to start with or they knew at one time and they forgot. What we were teaching in the Basic School was absolutely 100 percent good stuff. The problem was we couldn't retrain the lieutenant colonels before they went.

Major Michael H. Harrington

Mike Company had fallen into a routine, having been in Ca Lu some six months by this time, in that they would send out a daily squad-sized patrol into some very small villages south of Ca Lu. Everyone thought it was very strange that there were old men and women, children, and many young women in the twenty- to thirty-year range with small babies, never any men in the twenty-, thirty-, forty-year range.

Mike Company's patrol would normally leave at 0800 and return at 1600 and report no significant events. Ray decided to change the routine. The squad went out as normal, but two other squads accompanied by the company commander followed in trace at an interval of some 200 meters, moved into an ambush position. The regular squad patrol continued its normal search of the village, came back, and about 1700 or 1800, a group of twenty to thirty Viet Cong returned down the path to their loved ones.

Captain Ray Findlay

We were taking a squad at a time out and using a Basic School checklist which I brought with me on scouting and patrolling, and some folks thought we were nuts that we were teaching classes out there. But if you're sitting in Ca Lu by yourself, you've got a lot of time to train. So I started taking these folks out on these weird patrols and we kept going a little bit further, a little bit further. We were doing everything the way we did in Basic School. One night we went up to the objective rally point and I said, "Now we'll go down to recon the killing zone." I was using Basic School terms.

I took the squad leader and a sniper and a couple of people down there, and this guy came running back to me and says, "Captain, there's really gooks out there." He says, "Now what are we going to do?" And the first thing that hit me was, "It beats the hell out of me. I'm a brand new guy here, too." Unfortunately, from time to time, we'd call the good guys *and* the bad guys "gooks," so

I said, "Which kind are they?" And I said, "Don't shoot at them. They may be villagers." And the guy came back and said, "Is it legal if they carry weapons?" And I said, "Blow them away," and we did. There were four of us crawled up over this little berm and all sighted in on one.

We engaged a group of NVA down there on the road. We don't know how many we got because we had to get out of there and it took us that night and a part of the next morning to get out, but we came out with all fifteen Marines, none wounded, and dropped at least eight or ten NVA on the road.

When I came to Ca Lu I moved up on this old French fort. Much to Joe Cialone's [the Mike Company XO] disagreement. On this ambush I'd told Joe, "You stay up on position." So he stayed up there because you could see down the whole valley. And there was an old minefield all the way around that fort. I wanted them to put up a sign, "Just take one step more." We did put a sign up there that said, "Ho Chi Minh sucks running dogs." When Joe was up there and we were down the road, somebody put a recoilless rifle round through that sign. When we came back, Cialone said, "That sign isn't going back up, Captain." I said, "I agree, we won't put it back up." So the next morning I had another sign up that said, "A lucky shot!"

20

· · · · · · · · · · · · · · ·

AMBUSH ON ROUTE NINE

Major Mike Harrington

On the 21st of August, I had arranged for our direct support battery at Camp Carroll to fire in our defensive targets around the main position at the Rockpile. We had just received three or four young second lieutenants right out of Fort Sill [the artillery school], and I joined them on the hill just to the southeast of Highway 9 overlooking the main CP area.

We proceeded for a couple of hours. Everything was going smoothly. The young lieutenants were acting professionally. We were finally getting our defensive firepower in play. I was sitting there scanning the hills to the west, really just looking at the beautiful scenery, when I saw masses of NVA troops moving over the hills north to south at a range of about 5,000 meters from where we were, in plain sight.

At about the time I spotted them, their point hit a small resupply convoy we were sending to Ca Lu. At first I couldn't believe my eyes since we already had the arty firing. I grabbed the radio, told them who I was, gave them a bold shift about 2,000 meters left, and 2,000 to 3,000 troops in the open, "Fire for effect" [the command given to artillery to tell them that their spotting rounds are on target and that no other adjustment is necessary]. No one ever questioned it. We got a Battery One [one round from each of the six guns in a battery] right in the middle [of the enemy]. I gave them a "repeat fire for effect," and we got everything at Camp Carroll the next time. I took off down to the CP area since I was the S-3, not a forward observer. Lima Company had already moved south to try to relieve the ambush on the convoy.

Captain John Ripley

For some reason I was over in the 3 bunker and in the background you hear the hum of all the radios. On one radio I heard erratic patterns, not even a pattern of traffic, but something different. And you key on these differences. So I began turning my attention to that. It turned out to be a Marine in a very hushed tone, whispering for help. "Please help me. Please help me. We've got to have help. They're attacking."*

So I went over and said, "What's going on?" to the operator, and he said, "Sir, I don't know. That's just somebody who's on our battalion net, which is unusual." So I said, "Well, what are you doing?" "Sir, I don't know. I'm just listening." I said, "Well, for Christ's sake, we've got to do something. Things are in a bad way." I presumed it was this convoy that had just passed through the Rockpile on its way to Ca Lu. I'd been down to Ca Lu myself for a couple of months and I knew this area. Every time we sent a convoy down there, it met with some kind of interesting problems.

I went running over to the company area, saddled up the company, and told them to get on the road as quick as they could. I would lead with my CP group, the intent of which was to get there, hopefully to provide some kind of fire support, to sort out whatever problems they had, and then my company would follow in trace as rapidly as they could.

As it turned out, one platoon was on the road already. So we started humping down the road, literally on the run. As we were running along, the 3 managed to get some support together, which turned out to be two Dusters and an ammunition vehicle . . . the company Duster's truck. And it caught up with me. I was 1,000 meters or so already past the south bridge by the time this thing caught up. I decided to put my CP group aboard a Duster, to get there rapidly and to try to sort out the situation and give them whatever help was possible. Because the way this Marine was talking, obviously what few security people he had weren't functioning. There were seven of us including myself, the company

---

*The Marine was Lance Corporal Leonard R. Budd, who spent six years as a prisoner of war.

gunny, two radio operators, the company net, the battalion net, radio operator for the arty FO, and the FO [forward observer] himself.

Lance Corporal Stan Kerlin

We got involved in my first real firefight when the captain, Ripley, had gone with the company gunny and a couple of his radio operators to an ambush two miles or so from the Rockpile. In very short order we started forming up on the road to take off on foot. We took off out there and we were moving real fast and at one time it seemed like we were too close together. I passed the word up to the squad leader that I thought we should spread out. He hollered back, "Just shut the fuck up and keep your eyes open." I guess that since I was the new guy I was learning that I shouldn't be making suggestions to somebody who had eight or nine or ten months in country. We kept on going . . .

Lieutenant Jack Wright

We moved at a full run towards the sounds of firing down the road. We all knew that we were probably going to run into a secondary ambush, but we also knew that our people were being clobbered. We had no choice but to hope that we could catch the NVA with a fast assault.

Captain John Ripley

Aboard the lead Duster we were moving quickly. As you go down that road you're in a very deep valley that later becomes Vandergrift firebase. But before you got to that part of the valley, the ridgeline came right to the road itself and it was heavily grown there, jungle growth right up to the road and hanging over the road.

At that point they had set up their first ambush. And as we were approaching that point, we were taken under fire by machine guns. One was a heavy, a 12.7 [millimeter]. And as I looked over, as they were firing, I saw an RPG, a rocket, coming straight at us. This was the first straight-on shot I'd ever seen. I'd seen them fired past me, but this thing was coming right down the throat. I saw the fins standing out and it slowly spinning as it was coming straight at us. Boy, I mean to tell you, that really got my attention. I made an immediate decision that we had to get off the vehicle. I knew the vehicle was going to get hit. I grabbed the machine gun which was positioned right on the side of the gun tub. It was right in front of me and nobody was using it, so I started firing back at this fire coming at us. I told my Marines to get off. This Duster was barreling down the road and we just bailed off and happily hit in the jungle instead of on the road. It still took the hide off of me, but it was the right decision, because the minute we got off the thing, it went maybe another 200 to 300 meters and hit this ambush, which was of course the secondary ambush, already prepared for whatever relief force was under way.

All three vehicles were hit. The first one was knocked out. The other two jammed up against him. The back Duster managed to back up quickly enough to spin around and extricate himself. He was the only one that made it out. The rest of them, these were all Army personnel, were systematically executed, shot through the mouth. I'd seen this a number of times before. [When Ripley later returned to the scene, he found that] they had gone along and taken all their propaganda, little cards [with] "Yankee go home" and the little messages on there, other little things they had, and they stuck them in the mouths of all the dead Army guys from the Dusters. They had chased them down and killed every one of them. But that one Duster managed to get away.

When we jumped off we immediately rolled up into a position behind one of the old, what we used to call "tombstones," the route markers that marked both Route 1 and Route 9, in this case Route 9. It looked literally like a rounded tombstone. We were all huddled up behind this thing and getting all kinds of fire. Of the seven of us, we just had one rifle. There was just one M16 that belonged to the FO's radio operator. I snatched it away from him and said, "I'm going to need this. You're too busy." So I grabbed his rifle and we had to move and move quick. They were on us and I knew there wasn't much time.

Major Mike Harrington

We quickly lost contact with John Ripley. I recommended to Colonel Needham that we take the command group and additional people from Kilo Company and move south to take command. Elements of Mike Company were moving north from Ca Lu.

Captain Ray Findlay

Mike Company had been down at Ca Lu doing counterambushes. We had a drill, if something happened on the road, we had a way were going to go do it. What else can you do when you're alone in a place called Ca Lu? We called ourselves the 398th Independent Rifle Company. [Mike Company would send in their situation reports from Ca Lu with "Remember the Alamo" playing on a little portable tape recorder in the background.]

Major Mike Harrington

Colonel Needham told me to take the command group and go, which I did. When I arrived at the ambush site, there were Marine casualties, ten or fifteen

NVA bodies, rice that was still warm. One of the Lima Company platoon commanders, Jack Wright, came running over to me and said that Captain Ripley, his gunnery sergeant, his radioman, were cut off and were in the elephant grass some 200 to 300 meters south. I told him to take off and managed to get the tanks firing. All this time the artillery was continuing to fire at these masses of troops which were breaking up and moving southwest at this time. The tanks were taking troops in the open with direct fire. I took my command group; the tanks were moving slow and we had a platoon of Lima Company in front of us and one platoon to the left cutting across to the elephant grass, and I proceeded to stride down Highway 9 as if I was walking down mainside Camp Pendleton.

Captain John Ripley

So I said, "All right. We're getting out of here. Follow me." I looked across a large sort of a meadow and knew I had to get to some cover and concealment which was across this field. I told them what we were doing and started running. My radio operator, Torres, was on my left and we ran across this field on a dead run. I mean I made Rafer Johnson look like a nun. I just blasted out of there. Well, they were all running behind me. I looked at Torres, and Torres suddenly—*bam!*—went down, just like somebody poleaxed him.

I thought, "Now I've got to stop and get Torres." I was mad at him for getting hit. So I stopped and I was going over to pick him up and try to drag him across the field when suddenly he got up and started running. When we got to the other side, he was missing his helmet. He had his helmet liner. We had airborne chin straps which connected to the helmet liner, and if you didn't weave your chin strap of your helmet through, then it wasn't actually connected. It stayed because of friction. Torres was hit on the side of the head with an AK47 round, and it went right through his helmet, blew his helmet off, and popped out the other side and took the helmet with it. Of course, it really rang his chimes. He was absolutely incoherent for about ten minutes. But we got to the other side.

Then we went into position there. As I got over there I looked around and, son of a gun, the FO and his operator did not follow me. Of course, it was hopeless now because there was no way I could get back and get him or he could follow my trace. Now we're separated into two and five. Wagons in a circle. They had seen us get to where we were, but they didn't have a good fix on us. We ended up under some cover and some concealment and were very close to the road, maybe at the very best ten to fifteen yards from it, lying flat and just trying to make sense of what was happening.

From left to right: Lance Corporal Chuck Goggin, a professional baseball player who became a platoon commander on March 2, 1967; Captain John Ripley, Lima Company commanding officer; and Corporal Jess Torres, Ripley's radio operator who had his helmet shot off his head on August 21, 1967. (Courtesy John Ripley)

Lieutenant Jack Wright

I was talking with Captain Ripley on the company tactical net. He whispered to me that they were surrounded and that if we didn't get there soon they would all be dead.

Lance Corporal Stan Kerlin

The word was being passed back that the captain was on the radio and was saying that if we didn't get out there in five minutes he was going to be overrun.

Captain John Ripley

I knew that at some point the enemy was going to come down there and police us up, or at least direct fire there. I didn't know what my next move was, but I started calling in artillery. The situation was so damned desperate! My second platoon, which was the lead platoon, was trying to close on us on foot. They were finally getting into position. As they approached, oh, I would say 1,000 meters separate from us, they got hit very hard and they took a number of casualties. They could advance no further. L. B. Johnson went down. He was the squad leader. Gunnery Sergeant Holt was the platoon commander and he was brand new. They had all they could handle just staying alive, so they couldn't close on me which was what they were trying to do. Frankly, they didn't even know where I was because I'd had to leap off this Duster. But they knew I was in trouble because they could monitor my radio traffic. They did everything they could to close, but it was out of the question.

Lieutenant Jack Wright

We got to within a few hundred meters of the ambush site when the NVA opened up with machine guns and automatic weapons. Our point man, PFC Benny DeJesus, went down in the initial volley of fire along with Corporal Hunter, my point squad leader.

Lance Corporal Stan Kerlin

The point guy, Benny, was hit in the neck. I couldn't actually see him because they were kind of around him. The point was probably fifty to seventy-five yards away and out of view. There was pretty heavy foliage and brush alongside the road. You really couldn't see off the road more than just a few feet. There were some open spots where you could see up on the hillside. You couldn't actually see where they were shooting from. After the first few rounds everybody dived for the ditches on the side of the road. The NVA were dug in on the other side of the road up on the hill on the right.

One of the corpsmen moved up and tried to get over to where Benny was. He jumped across the road and the machine gun opened up and stitched bullets up and down the road. Luckily he wasn't hit, but he wasn't able to get over to where Benny was. As it turned out, it would have been a waste of time anyway, because where he was hit was in the artery and he was pumping out so much blood that he was dead, probably within a few minutes.

We kept crawling forward, trying to get up to where the CO was. One of the guys in our squad had an M79 grenade launcher and he set it on the highest range, and whenever we could see a muzzle flash or smoke up on the hillside where we thought they were shooting from, he shot rounds up in that area. We kept moving forward and within a very few minutes we started having some artillery come down on the hillside. And there were some jets that came in and strafed the area, too. And some of our tanks came up. They started moving up the road beside us and the recoilless rounds were hitting them and not having any effect on them. I guess we had started to suppress the NVA fire 'cause we were up on our feet, on the road and moving forward. I was right beside one of the tanks when a round came and hit on the back of the tank.

One minute I was standing there and all of a sudden I was in a gray world that was filled with smoke and I couldn't hear anything and time seemed to just stand still. It seemed like there was a dead silence and the air was sucked out of the area by that round going off. Then all of a sudden, the air came crashing back in, and I was picked up and thrown back into the ditch. I kind of looked down at myself and one of my arms was covered with blood and I had blood on my other wrist and there was some running down my hand. I had quite a bit of pain in my right arm between the wrist and the elbow. One of the corpsmen came up and put some dressings on a couple of the holes I had in my arm. I slowly started working my way back to the rear.

Captain John Ripley

We stayed there for a period of probably three or four hours. The enemy knew where I was. They couldn't possibly not have known. They had followed my footsteps with fire right into that position. We were in a circle. Recall, I had the only rifle. I had a couple of grenades—we all did, and pistols. But we didn't have any really defensive means.

This was the only time I pulled a grenade out and bit the pins for rapid pull. I did that because a friend of mine at Con Thien about four months before that had been captured, and they skinned him alive and threw his skin back in the wire and I said, "That ain't happening to me." I knew if I really became disabled and couldn't fight, I was just going to pull that damned pin out and take the bastard with me.

So we lay there and in this process the supporting arms became very responsive. Boy, we had every single bit of direct support, general support, artillery available in the whole division at Camp Carroll. Everything was shooting for us. Not only that but A-4s flew in, a whole cluster of A-4s, under our control over FM. There was FAC [forward air controller] airborne who was talking to us and we were talking to him and they began firing. The fire support remained all afternoon long. At one point just after that . . . an NVA soldier came up; he was standing in the road. It almost seemed like we could shake his hand, he was that close to us. I know he knew where we were and he kind of squatted down, the way they would squat down. I could see his Ho Chi Minh Florsheims, those rubber-tire shoes. He'd squat down and he was looking right at us.

Well, we're lying down but he had to see us and I had the rifle pointed at him. I'm thinking at the time, "Do I squeeze this off and deal with him, or do I pretend that he doesn't see me and he pretends, etc.—a Mexican standoff and we just let things lie?" During that split second I said to myself, "Well, what the hell. If he comes back he's going to come with a gang, so why don't I go ahead and squeeze one off." And I did and it was a misfire. Here I had the only rifle and the bloody thing didn't fire. Then he stood up, and as he stood up one of the artillery rounds hit on the other side of the road from him and it just atomized this guy. We couldn't even find a fabric of cloth. He was just gone. Well, that was the end of that.

The rest of the day was calling artillery and trying to make the best of a bad situation, talking on the hook constantly with the battalion who was trying to get help out to us.

Lieutenant Jack Wright

For over a three-hour period we moved through the thick vegetation on the south side of Route 9. My platoon had taken heavy casualties and were fighting the NVA from very close range. We were heavily outnumbered but still moving. My troops were trying to protect the wounded and fight at the same time, and we were hoping that the rest of the company would link up with our rear and take some of the pressure off. I received some reinforcements from the weapons platoon and Staff Sergeant Chancy started putting out 60-mm mortar rounds at the NVA. At about this time Chancy was hit on the top of his helmet by an NVA mortar round. It turned out to be a dud and it knocked him cold, but other than a big knot and some blood, he was okay.

Captain Ray Findlay

We got from Ca Lu to where we were going to go. I got down there and it was a devastating sight because there were a bunch of Army folks dead on the road. I saw this truck on fire and there was a bunch of ammo burning in the truck. And there, like people will do in combat, I always wanted to do something heroic, so I jumped in the truck. When I got in it, half of the windshield was shot out and so I decided I was going to drive the truck off the road. I discovered then that I didn't know how to drive it. Talk about something ruining the perfect day! When I jumped out of the truck, I kept rolling on the side of the road, hoping that some people were watching me, but they weren't. Anyway, I rolled around and my face went into a water buffalo turd. Literally. And I was breathing hard and I breathed that in. You know the thought that went through my mind? "I want to get a color television set when I get home. I will never go through what I went through and live like this again without having some luxuries when I get home."

Captain John Ripley

Finally the battalion uncovered us as they came into position, and we went out to the road and I hooked up with the remainder of my company and went down to the ambush site and found this terrible mess, this execution.

Major Mike Harrington

About 150 meters down the road, Captain Ripley and his party come bursting out of the elephant grass and ran out to the road saying something to the effect that he was never so glad to see anybody in his life. I was really shocked. I said, "Where's the rest of your company?" And he said, "You're the first people we've seen in two to three hours." Fortunately, when I was acting as point, the NVA had withdrawn. The luck of the Irish, I guess.

We proceeded to pull back into the main perimeter of the Rockpile. By this time we had had multiple airstrikes, including napalm, on the NVA in a large draw heading southwest. I claimed over 400 kills for the day. I didn't spend the effort and perhaps the lives of our Marines trying to count the bodies. It was obvious the NVA had hauled their dead and wounded off during the night. But with the large amount of artillery, tank, and airstrikes, I still think 400 was a conservative estimate.

There were 109 enemy bodies found, but the evidence suggests a much larger number of enemy killed, especially out of the main area of the ambush where air and artillery were directed. The battalion estimated another 305 dead.

Captain John Ripley

The interesting thing is there was a culvert there, unbeknownst to anybody because the jungle hung over the road. You didn't even realize that this culvert was there; it was really a bridge. In our process of policing that area, I was looking over and I thought I saw one of our dead lying there. I went down and as I was walking down to this KIA, I suddenly realized that this road was no longer a road, it was a bridge. Underneath this thing was a masonry-constructed bridge, a big arch. Underneath this arch was an NVA barracks. They had gone in there with bamboo and erected scaffolding and put racks [bunks] in there. I counted on one side enough facilities there for about thirty men, and on the other side at least that, all living under that road the whole time we'd been using it and not even realizing it.

This voice I'd heard on the radio, this lone Marine, this guy was never found. No one ever saw him. He was a new Marine and didn't even have jungle utilities. He was declared missing in action. He was going out to join the unit.

Captain Ray Findlay

One of the things we did for a couple of days was—we went up into the hills and looked for that guy. We stayed up there until about midnight the night of that ambush looking for this guy and somebody in my company found his hat.

Captain John Ripley

Six years later when the prisoners of war came home from Hanoi, this lad [Lance Corporal Leonard R. Budd] gets off the airplane, the same kid. We didn't know they had him. I was watching television and here he gets off, now a staff sergeant. What a thrill it was to see him.

The FO and radio operator survived. They were uncovered first. Luckily, because there were only two of them, the enemy never really got past us. This first NVA was looking to see how much he had to deal with. Then he was going to go back to tell his platoon commander to come and get us when the artillery round got him. All seven of us survived. We were all hit. I had a hole through my heel. I had a hole through my webbing, a gunshot. Torres got his helmet shot off. Every one of us had a little hit somewhere, but nobody was hurt.

The next day we were still shook up. Of all the close calls I had, this was the predominant one. And that night I can remember just shaking, having been in this tension for so long, extraordinary tension, just trying to do the right thing and keep alert hoping it would come out okay. Well, the next day, totally unrelated, they flew out a trailer. What they used to do was, the dental contact teams would put all their toys in this trailer pulled behind a six-by truck with a dental chair and all the other things, and they'd sling-load under a CH-53 and drop into our position and hold dental call. I had time to go over there and I did and the doctor put me in his dental chair. It's now a day later and he's looking at me and he said, "Boy, everything in your mouth is bleeding. Have you been under any stress lately?"

Lance Corporal Stan Kerlin

We wounded finally moved back further and there was a truck there. We got on the back of that and headed back to the Rockpile, and from there we got picked up by one of the helicopters, which took us to Dong Ha where they had a med station. At that time they were bringing in quite a few helicopters because there was something going on somewhere else other than the firefight we were involved in, because they had a lot of wounded coming in.

It surprised me, the conditions under which the doctors were working. They were working in what seemed like a plywood building with bare walls and a concrete floor inside. They were doing surgery on guys who were just laying on a piece of plywood that was stretched across two sawhorses. The floor was just covered with blood. They gave us some morphine before we took off, so I wasn't really in any pain. They brought us in there and took a quick look at our wounds, but I don't think either one of us was bleeding that much . . . so they just had us wait.

They stuck us off to the side and we just watched for a while. They were doing surgery on people and they had buckets down below, and sometimes when someone had a bad wound and they had to cut a piece off or a part out, they would just throw it in this bucket. All they were really attempting to do was just stabilize people so they could put them on another plane and send them back to Danang, where they had a much more modern hospital. It really struck me as we were moving back, I know it wasn't the first dead body I'd seen. I'd probably seen a couple when I was younger, prior to going to Vietnam, but as we were moving back, we passed by Benny's body and I looked down at him and it struck me so much like when I shot my deer when I was about sixteen. I remembered seeing a scene so similar, the way the flies were gathering around him and he was laying there and he didn't look lifelike anymore. He looked like a manne-quin. There was so much blood. We got on a medevac chopper and went to Dong Ha and from Dong Ha they put us on another plane.

There isn't no such thing as a flesh wound from which you are just going to get up and keep walking and shooting. If you are doing that, it is because you have to. Anybody that gets shot anyplace with a rifle is not going to feel like get-ting up and continuing for the day with a Band-Aid on him acting like nothing has happened. That just isn't the case.

SEPTEMBER 1967

Major Mike Harrington

After the action on the 21st of August, we spent the next couple of weeks trying to improve our defensive positions and getting ready for the rainy period. We had a serious shortage of tools, saws, picks, shovels, etc., and almost no shoring material, lumber.

Lieutenant Dan Ryan

After all this battering and bloody experience, around September, they made me the S-4. 007: License to Steal. Transferred to H and S Company. I was workin' with a unit chief by the name of Staff Sergeant Pope, a little short

Lance Corporal Frank Isbell on left and Lieutenant Dan Ryan, Battalion S-4—007: License to Steal. (Courtesy Dan Ryan)

black guy. Built like Mr. T, only a foot shorter. A very nice, quiet, forceful guy. Enjoyed him very much. Very capable. It was Sergeant Pope's suggestion that, uh . . . I would make trips to the rear and coordinate with him and so on and so forth. That's how we got into Von Ryan's Express with all the convoys. That was a real trip. You knew that they were gonna get hit on the way out. And I would bring them out. I'd sit in the front seat and quietly say my rosary and expect something from China to go through the underneath of the truck.

·

Corporal Bill Brocksieker

Went into Danang and I ran into a guy I knew and he put me back up into 3/3. So I joined them up around Dong Ha and Quang Tri in September 1967. The whole thing of Vietnam changed from the first time I was there [in 1965]. The first time I was there, we fought mostly the guerrillas, the Viet Cong. They wore their own clothes as uniforms. You couldn't hardly tell them from the Popular Forces [South Vietnamese militia]. They had carbines. They had M1s. They had hardly any AK47s, mostly American weapons from WW2 and Korea.

But the second time we went over there, it was more conventional. They had an area that nobody was supposed to be in, free fire zones. We were fighting NVA this time. There was incoming all the time. Once in a while you'd get *mortared* the first time, but the second time, man, there was a lot of 122 rockets and the big guns on Mutter's Ridge . . . and in the DMZ, that would fire and hit clear back into Dong Ha and clear back into Quang Tri. Anyplace. You could be sitting anywhere and get blown away.

21

. . . .

DÉJÀ VU: AMBUSH ON
ROUTE NINE, SEPTEMBER 1967

In early September, at American urging, South Vietnam had a reasonably honest election and an inauguration free of VC influence. Eighty-three percent of approximately six million voters turned out. The communist artillery fire along the DMZ was one of their many responses to the process.

Captain John Ripley

At this time Mike Harrington was the 3. We happened to be augmenting security at Camp Carroll and it was election week. That was the week that all of the northern firebases were inundated with artillery. You could sit at Camp Carroll and watch these patterns of artillery working in Con Thien and Charlie 2, Cam Lo, Gio Linh, Charlie 1 [see p. 182], and they hit Dong Ha and blew up the ammunition depot that day. That was the day, the 7th of September, that I got back to the Rockpile. It was "back home," so to speak, relative term, to move into our bunkers. And we didn't even get back when the 3 called and said, "Get on the road quick. We've got another ambush."

Major Mike Harrington

On the 7th of September a convoy was set up to resupply Ca Lu. In little over a month's time we had gone from running three-vehicle convoys to where we had two tanks, a platoon from either Kilo or Lima Company, and about ten or twelve trucks, with engineers. A fairly formidable convoy for a relatively short distance moving through open country.

The convoy got about halfway to Ca Lu and they were hit. We almost immediately lost radio contact. I ordered the command group to be prepared to move out and recommended to Colonel Needham that we move the balance of Kilo and Lima Company south and whatever was available of Mike Company to move north out of Ca Lu. He agreed to this and I took the command group and headed south.

India Company was in the lead with a section of Dusters. I was particularly concerned with moving through the narrow pass on Highway 9, south of our main position where the ambush of the 21st of August had occurred. I dropped back and let India move forward, keeping my command group to the rear of India Company with Lima behind us. We were no sooner through the pass, maybe 300 to 400 meters south, when a large volume of small-arms fire opened up. I moved forward with my command group and to my amazement the India CO, his exec, and his company command group were standing in the middle of Highway 9 watching an NVA machine gun decimate one of his platoons. The people were in perfect parade-ground fashion, one long line, and the machine gun laid fire down the long axis of the platoon.

Lieutenant Lee Ashburn

You could hear it going off and you knew you were going to be in a fight and you knew they were using a .50-caliber machine gun. That's scary because there is no such thing as a flesh wound with a .50-caliber.

Lance Corporal Stan Kerlin

After I got back to the unit we got involved in another ambush on Route 9 headed toward Khe Sanh. Our company was sent out for support again.

PFC Thomas F. Ryan

Everybody piled on trucks, shot down till we got about a hundred feet from there. We had a new lieutenant, he was with us three days. He was a fellow from

Corporal Tom Ryan, who was to save a friend's life with a case of beer, filling his canteens at a stream. (Courtesy Tom Ryan)

Jamaica . . . mustang . . . up through the ranks. Showed up in a great big handle-bar mustache. *Big* handlebar mustache. Really looked distinguished. Of course, in 3/3 you weren't allowed a mustache. Not that *I* could grow one. Anyway, he shaved it off that night.

But when the shit hit the fan down the road, everybody jumped on trucks, like a posse getting together, and just shot down. We got all formed in an eche-lon and jumped on both sides of the roads and started sweeping down. As we reached this treeline, Dan LeBlanc, he heard a click like a safety flying off, in the trees. And he just turned and opened up on them. Sure enough, there they were, they were waiting for us. Then we swept back over into the trees to Knoll 70. Anybody that went up Knoll 70 got shot! If you *crawled* up you were alright. There the lieutenant was, standing up there. Everybody was telling him, "Get down, get down!" "I'm alright, I'm alright." He'd got his compass in one hand and a radioman laying on his back. Calling in air, calling in artillery, whatever the hell he was talking to, mortars. Everything started blowing up. They opened him up like a zipper. Man was in country three days and was dead. There must have been eight or nine guys dead, that quick. All the corpsmen were shot. My squad leader was hit. He was out behind a tree and we had to get him back in. You seemed to be alright if you did a low crawl. But if you got up on your knees or stood up, you got shot, it was as easy as that. So you just crawled around for a while. Mostly what we were doing was dragging people back from Knoll 70. That was a hell of an afternoon. Just woke up I/3/3 from a long sleep. Seemed like from then on in, we started moving from place to place.

Major Mike Harrington

The machine gun was only about 150 meters, or less, dug in behind a small stone bridge where there had been a Montagnard vill. The rest of India Company seemed mesmerized and were doing nothing. We still didn't know exactly where the convoy was, it couldn't have been more than 200 to 300 meters from there. I made the snap decision and said, "Charge." I had my command group, clerks, radio operators, and artillery liaison officer. We charged and overran the NVA position. All of a sudden I see our mortars falling right in front of us. I looked back. The 81 mortar platoon gunnery sergeant had come along with us with one section and was leading us down the road firing the mortars off the cartridge only.

We overran the position. There must have been twenty NVA in and around the machine gun. I can vividly remember kicking a few of the bodies to see if they were alive. A number of my command group were bayoneting the bodies. A couple were shooting. I stopped them, not necessarily for humanitarian purposes, but I was hoping to get some prisoners for some intelligence. We were trying to consolidate. India Company had taken a large number of casualties. I didn't know how many, but we had the bed of a six-by filled with them and I had already notified the CP that we were sending a large number of casualties back to be medevaced by helicopter.

Lieutenant Dan Ryan

I'm back at the Rockpile and I'm the S-4 and the word's comin' back that terrible things are happening on Route 9. Not to mention that everybody is pinned down and they are running out of ammo. So I get an ambulance from the battalion surgeon and we load it up with ammo, 60s and 7.62 [mortar and machine gun ammunition] and what have you. And off I go. There's no room for anybody else. I'm drivin' down Route 9 and I see smoke and shit flyin' around and some trucks are off the road. As usual, you don't see anybody. There's no gooks and no Marines. All you hear is some occasional shooting. I drive past this Duster and all of a sudden he lets loose with these 40 mike mikes [millimeters], right over my head. Little did I know that I had driven right into the killing zone. About this time, when they started openin' up, I said, "It's time for me to get the hell out of there." And I just bailed out of the jeep.

So here I am in the elephant grass and I still can't see anybody, but I know there's lots of bodies around me. And Uncle Dan's got his .45. And I'm thinking', "Here comes some son of a bitch. Well, am I gonna kill a Marine or kill a gook? Or am I gonna go to the POW camp?" At this point I says, "The better part of valor is to go back to the jeep with your ammo because that's what they need." So I got up and they open fire on the jeep again. Full of ammo. Me in it. I go to shift and here comes the gearshift off in my hand. It was like Loretta Young doing a show and finding the doorknob not on the door. I finally got the ammo out and we got a couple, three, four troops in the ambulance and away we went.

Major Mike Harrington

At this time, five or six minutes had passed since we overran the machine-gun position; it was about 1400, 1430 in the afternoon. It was extremely hot and I had been sick for a couple of days. I was very dehydrated. All of a sudden we were hit with a barrage of mortars coming from the west. Everybody dove for cover, including the truck driver that was to get our wounded out. Prior to that, I told my radioman, Lance Corporal Wilson, that he didn't need to follow me every time I jumped up and down and moved around. He just needed to stay close enough where he could get a message to me or I could holler to him. He just laughed and said, "Wherever you go, Major, I'll go. I'm telling you, the radio's important." I saw the truck driver jump out of his truck and the wounded in the back were unable to move. I jumped up on the road to get the driver back in and get those people out of there. One of the NVA had been playing possum. He threw a satchel charge between me and Lance Corporal Wilson. Fortunately I had a flak jacket on. I had just about taken it off, I was so dehydrated. It saved my life, but the satchel charge killed my radio operator.

Captain John Ripley

So it was the same routine all over again. This time I elected not to go in front of them. We moved down the road rapidly and I was getting briefed while on the move. This one sounded even more devastating than the previous one. We were in a route column, open file [marching for speed], and I could see smoke up ahead and hear all the firing. The company was doing just what they did so well. I didn't have to say a bloody thing. Suddenly we came around a bend where the bridge was and the secondary ambush was and I saw a PC, a little pick-up truck kind of thing. As we came around and I looked and there was a Marine in there and it turned out to be Mike Harrington. He was laying in there and his leg was all whacked to hell. This was the guy I'd just been talking to. He'd just briefed me.

Now India Company had been committed previously. They had been sent down to try to relieve the ambush. Things went from rotten to lousy. For some reason, India Company wasn't able to deal with it. As we first got to Harrington, he told me in no uncertain terms, "It's an unbelievable mess, unbelievable!" India Company was not very well held together. The company commander was just not capable of hanging on to it the way the previous commanders had. It's a pity because it had been a great company for such a long period of time and it lost a lot of direction, a lot of control. We became very negative [about India] because we lost Marines pulling their fat out of the fire and that became old quick. Harrington said, "Do what you can. Get there as quick as you can." And obviously we were already doing that. He was evacuated along with a couple of other casualties.

I got down to the position and there was a tank in front of me, dead square in the road, lots of firing, dead Marines in the road, which disturbed me. Nobody had even bothered to move them to cover. There was sporadic firing on both sides of the road and at this particular position, which I knew quite well having been there on the previous ambush.

As we moved up behind the tank and I could see him firing his machine gun and I leaned over as I passed a KIA and snatched his weapon. It was just lying there. Then I ran into the India Company XO, who was, I'll use the term, "addled." He just didn't seem to know what was happening. I finally grabbed him by the shoulders and said, "Where is your skipper?" And he said, "Sir, I think he's over here." So we walked over to the west side of the road and sure enough, he was sitting on the side of the road not even looking at the action. He was looking out into space. There was nobody but him there.

I walked up and slid down and I said, "What the hell's going on?" He looked at me and said, "Hey, you got any water?" He didn't even give me a briefing. I said, "Are you okay?" And he said, "Oh, I'm awful thirsty." I said, "Look, you're relieved. You get your people out of here, I'm taking over." He just kind of nodded. That was the last I saw of him. They got rid of him.

My men were already at work. The 1st Platoon deployed on the left and the 3d Platoon on the right, and the rest of them were in reserve and we were moving down the road. I went up and grabbed the tank infantry phone off the back of this tank. The tank platoon commander was in the turret at the time, and I was talking to him but I wasn't getting a response. The lieutenant stuck his head up and just yelled down, "Sir, I can hear you but I can't respond." I said, "Okay, just 'roger' by sticking your hand out of the hatch. Just indicate that you 'roger' what I'm telling you to do." "No sweat."

So we got things sorted out and off we go. I still had this M16 with me and off we were moving. I had Gunny Cox, a super, super guy, with me. Corporal Detora was to the right of him. Sergeant Jarvis was off to the right of him and then the radio operators and so forth and off we're moving.

Lieutenant Lee Ashburn

Ripley deployed my platoon, the 1st Platoon, to the left and told us to get on line and move over this hill. We did and I said, "Oh, my God! This is the way they did it on TV." We topped that hill and nothing happened and I thought, "This is great." We got about twenty yards over the crest of that hill and they opened up on us with everything. I went straight to the ground and a weed went straight up my nose and I spent the next few minutes pulling this weed out of my nose. I couldn't raise my head up because the bullets were flying right overhead. It was very intense fire. I forgot about the weed and about thirty minutes later I looked at my hands and I had blood all over me. I asked my radio operator, "Where am I hit?" He says, "You're not. Your nose is bleeding."

Corporal Joe Davis

Part of my platoon was directed to go around and do a flanking movement. We were taken over by the platoon sergeant, Sergeant Jarvis. We managed to low-crawl to the top of that hill. Unfortunately, Albert Larson got killed and so did Sergeant Jarvis. Sergeant Jarvis got hit and the NVA drug him off. They purged his body from all the jewelry he had on. As I recall they cut off his fingers to get his ring.

Captain John Ripley

As we get past this one spot, I looked over and there were about five or six enemy standing there as if they were in bleachers. They didn't even have their weapons at the ready. They were all standing there looking at us going by. All I could think to do was in an instantaneous response. I was carrying this weapon in my left hand and the tank infantry phone in my right hand and looking forward, and I looked over and saw this and I just went "*yyyyyeeeee*" and squeezed it and just sprayed over there and they all went down like duckpins. Just *boom, boom, boom, boom*, every one of them went down. And we just kept moving.

Detora, who was a big, good-looking lad, just a knockout Marine, threw his rifle up on his shoulder and started to fire. Then he took it back down again and looked at it, cleared it, and I thought it was a malfunction. He put it back up again and started to fire. Nothing. He pulled it back down and was banging it and he kept moving. At the end of the day, come to find out he'd been shot right here [the shoulder] and the round had gone through and through, right through his body, and it had cut whatever nerve it is that runs through your trigger finger. He thought the damned weapon was malfunctioning and didn't know his finger wasn't working. He didn't even realize it. No blood. A little tiny hole there and an exit hole but very little else.

As we were moving forward, we finally did break through the other side of the ambush and there was a wonderful action up on the left in the 1st Platoon area. There was a Marine who had just recently joined us named Lance Corporal Darden. There was another new Marine, even newer than Darden, named Wolfe. Wolfe looked like a mayonnaise body. He weighed about 400 pounds, solid white. Didn't even have a red neck yet. I don't know how in the world he managed to get through boot camp, ITR, and still come to us looking like a beached whale. But he was trying like hell to do the right thing and doing everything he could.

Somehow, Wolfe, in his exuberance or his unfamiliarity with how to deal with this, got out in front of the skirmish line. When he got out there an NVA jumped up and shot him, just *boom, wham,* down Wolfe goes. Darden saw this. Darden was an AR [automatic rifle] man. The squad leader was a guy named Davis, a black Marine, what a wonderful Marine he was, just wonderful. Well, they all go to ground immediately and Wolfe's lying out there, thirty meters maybe. That's a long way under fire.

Corporal Joe Davis

Wolfe looked like a big teddy bear. He was under fire from a Vietnamese in a spider trap. I called out to him and the next thing I knew, I had chicoms coming at me. For a while there, the gook and I were trading grenades back and forth.

Captain John Ripley

Darden went running out there and grabbed Wolfe, fireman's carry. He leaned over to grab him and Wolfe was a load. He had to grab him and pull him upright. He went down on his knee and he managed to get him over his shoulder and then shifted the load, and he was trying to get up.

In the meantime, the enemy are watching all this happen. Darden is struggling to get up on his feet with this heavy load. Wolfe was shot in the leg, so he couldn't move at all. He finally gets to his feet, this is spectacular, and this damned NVA comes back out with the same AK47 and shot Darden. It blew him backwards, but he kept to his feet, grabbed the muzzle of this weapon—and the AK47 has a raised sight. He grabbed the weapon, wrenched it away from him, with Wolfe on his shoulder, and beat that son of a bitch to death with the weapon with one hand. Swinging this thing and just knocked him into left field like a Louisville slugger, with his own weapon. And then he went down. Well, then Corporal Davis ran out with a couple of other Marines to pull them both back. All this takes place in like thirty seconds. A magnificent action. Both of them lived. They were both hospitalized and I recommended Darden for a decoration. He got the Silver Star which was certainly justified. I sent a copy of that to Wolfe's father. I said, "I want you to know what kind of Marine saved your son's life." I got a letter back from Wolfe's father. He said, "I want to know who this guy is. I want a picture of him. I want to know him for the rest of my life. He will never be in want of anything to the day he dies." It was great.

Well, to get on with the ambush. We finally punched through and by now it's literally the end of light. We had to police up what we had and get under cover. There was a great big draw on the right. The *804th NVA Regiment* occupied that draw and that's where a lot of their support was coming from. When we finally did this, they began to mortar us. There was nowhere to hide. This was one of the loneliest feelings I've ever had in my life. I was stuck in a place, mortars were falling, and I had nowhere to go. I just laid flat. It was one of these situations where you're laying there and you're trying to exhale to get your body lower. You don't know whether to turn on your side to get your helmet lower or to stick your head down. You want to hold your helmet, but that exposes your ribs so you want to put your hands down. So I'm looking down at the tank which is not very far away and I thought, "I'm going to run down to that damned tank. At least I've got the tank on one side and the hill on the other."

Just then, *boom*! A round hits right at my proposed location and just splattered. It didn't kill the tank or anything. It just splattered everything down there. The tank driver jumped out of the tank all of a sudden. He came up to me and said, "Sir, we've got to get out of here right now." I said, "I know it. Leave me alone. I'm dealing with this. You get back in your tank." And he said, "No, sir, you don't understand. My tank commander's been shot. I've got to get him out of here." That lieutenant I was telling you about who was sticking his hand up, he apparently couldn't hear me on one of these transmissions, and he stuck his body up out of the hatch and got a round right straight through the sternum, through and through, and fell back down inside the tank. And he lived.

Finally, at the end of the day we policed up what we had and got back to the Rockpile. I forget what the count was that day, but it was comparable to the previous ambush. It so impressed General [Creighton W.] Abrams that he sent a contact team, a couple of colonels, up there a week or so later to see what happened. [Abrams was Westmoreland's deputy at the time and would succeed him as commander of MACV the following year.] General Abrams wanted them to look at the ground and find out why we were so successful because our body count had been so high. And I was picked to take these guys back down the road. Well, we went down with a heavy-mech reinforced convoy loaded for bear. We didn't want the same thing to happen. We got down there and I stopped the convoy and these colonels, both of them said, "Get out of here. We'll believe whatever you tell us. Just get us out of here." We were all prepared to dismount and walk around. "For Christ's sake. We don't want to look at it *that* carefully. Get moving."

Lieutenant Dan Ryan

I got back to the LZ there at the Rockpile and saw several of my old troops and I felt a kinship . . . I felt bad not bein' there with them. On the other hand, I felt pretty good that I wasn't. I saw this one six-by pull in with wounded and bodies in it. Uh . . . there was a rise . . . there was a little hill or somethin' right there in the LZ. I remember as this truck pulled out there was blood runnin' from it like water. Somethin' you don't forget, I guess.

Lieutenant Bill Masciangelo

Corporal Sibilly had been wounded. It was one of those million-dollar wounds . . . you know . . . not bad enough to do him much damage . . . but good enough to get you home or out of the area for a while. I can remember putting him on a jeep and laughing and joking with him about going home and . . . saying how lucky he was and then the next day finding out that he died.

I found that so difficult to understand and comprehend and could not accept it. It was then that I realized the destructive power of shock. This young corporal had apparently died of shock. That's what I was told. His wounds, in and of themselves, didn't seem sufficient enough to kill him. But when I read the report the next day, that he had died, that to me was tragedy.

22

. . . .

WAR ALONG THE BARRIER

In the fall of 1967, U.S. forces in Vietnam undertook to reduce infiltration from the north by building a minefield, sensor, and barbed-wire barrier across the southern edge of the DMZ region. The Marines opposed the plan for numerous reasons, the most important of which was that it simply would not work. From the Great Wall of China to the Maginot Line, the history of warfare is replete with examples of the successful circumvention of barriers. Moreover, the Marines felt that a mobile defense would be more effective and less costly in terms of manpower than tying up large units in defense of this fortification. All of the Corps' generals went on record as saying so, as did Admiral U. S. Grant Sharp, Commander in Chief, Pacific. Nonetheless, at the insistence of the Department of Defense in Washington, D.C., and General Westmoreland in Saigon, it was begun.

Marine units and Seabees laid the groundwork by stripping a 600-meter belt, or "trace," of its vegetation, taking large numbers of casualties in the process. Originally, the barrier along the trace was to be supported by a series of combat outposts that would stretch from the South China Sea to Dong Ha mountain, an imposing peak some forty-five kilometers inland. Other barricades would be added later to halt infiltration across

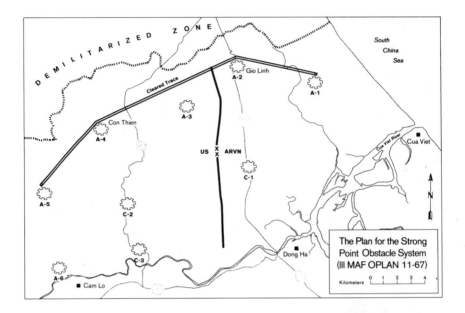

The Plan for the Strong Point Obstacle System (III MAF OPLAN 11-67)

the remainder of Vietnam and the Laotian panhandle. However, only four of the outposts were actually built, and the trace, though bulldozed, was never mined and wired as first envisioned. Code-named "Dye Marker," the barrier concept was abandoned later in the war, but from late 1967 until the following summer, 3/3 expended much energy in the barrier's construction and defense.

The outposts on the trace were given an A (or Alpha) designation. Alpha 1 near the South China Sea was to be occupied only by ARVN troops. Alpha 2, better known as Gio Linh, sat on Route 1 just south of where the road wound down the cliffs of the Ben Hai river basin and stretched into North Vietnam. Alpha 3 was known only by this name and was to figure prominently in 3/3's time along the DMZ. Alpha 4 achieved notoriety under its Vietnamese name, Con Thien.

Backing up these strong points were support bases that were located a few kilometers farther to the south and were given a C (or Charlie) designation. The ones built and manned by Marines were: C2, situated halfway between Cam Lo and Con Thien to support "Highway" 561, the dirt track that connects the two positions; C2-B (also known as C2 Bridge or "the Washout") which was not an original strong point but a hastily manned position north of C2, occupied to protect the bridge that was critical to keeping the land supply route to Con Thien open; and C3, or Cam Lo, anchoring this north-south line on Route 9. Three of the points of the strong-point system—Cam Lo, Con Thien, Gio Linh, and the Marine base at Dong Ha—formed the parameters of what has gone down in Marine Corps history as "Leatherneck Square."

Meanwhile, unknown to U.S. forces, the North Vietnamese were planning a new offensive that was to have far-reaching implications for the outcome of the war. The Politburo of North Vietnam, desperately looking for a way to tip the balance in their favor, had issued orders for a "General Offensive, General Uprising"—the Tet Offensive.

The plan was based on the beliefs that the South Vietnamese hated their American "oppressors" and that the ARVN was badly trained and not of a mind to defend the Saigon government. During Phase I, to begin in September 1967, the NVA would mount sizeable attacks around the frontiers of South Vietnam. This would draw U.S. forces away from the population centers, making it easier for the Viet Cong to infiltrate the major cities at the proper moment. In Phase II, the cities would be attacked and taken over, while U.S. bases and communication facilities would be assaulted. At this point it was expected that the South Vietnamese population would rise up in favor of expelling the Americans, who would be demoralized and isolated along the borders of the country and on their bases. Phase III called for the defeat and expulsion of U.S. troops.

In I Corps, Phase I began with attacks on the Marine outpost at Con Thien in September. Then, from Laos to the South China Sea the NVA began infiltrating additional units and supplies across the DMZ. Much of the action 3/3 was to see in late 1967 and early 1968 was a response to this plan.

Lance Corporal Gary D. Conner (Brand New Guy)

I got to Vietnam . . . and I had really not been prepared for what I saw. We went through a couple of vills in the back of this open six-by, watching these villagers walking from the fields. They were carrying those baskets on sticks with firewood on one side and pigs or chickens or tea leaves or whatever on the other side to balance off the load. Finally a realization hit me that I in fact was someplace very foreign, someplace that was totally different from anything I had ever seen.

There was one Marine sitting on the tailgate of the six-by and this guy looked like he had been in the field for a long time. He was cruddy dirty. His clothes were ripped. His flak jacket was filthy. He had a weapon, grenades hanging on him; a typical grunt. What I was to look like in a couple of months. He was kind of checking me out. We came to one spot and we stopped. A group of civilians, farmers, passed us there carrying whatever the heck they were carrying over their shoulders. This one woman looked up at me and at the time I thought she must be about forty-five or fifty.

I looked down at her and she smiled at me and all I could see was a black void when her lips parted. Her teeth were so rotted away or covered with that betel nut that it almost made me sick to my stomach. This grizzled Marine that was sitting on the tailgate looked up at me and I must have winced like, "Oh my God, I can't believe this." He rapped me on the leg and he says, "Hey, buddy.

In six months she's going to be looking real fine." I didn't say anything to him. I looked back. The vehicle started moving and I thought to myself, "God, I hope not. I really, really hope not."

•

The 2d Battalion, 4th Marines, was manning the C2 Bridge and had been in nearly constant contact with the enemy since moving north out of Camp Evans on 11 September. Combat losses had drained the unit's manpower until it was less than half-strength. On the night of 14 October, attacking under barrages of artillery, rockets, and mortars, the NVA severely mauled 2/4. The company commander of G Company was killed as were three of his platoon commanders, two of whom had just arrived in Vietnam that day. A replacement company commander was killed before he could reach the company. Moving to within grenade range of the battalion CP, the enemy killed or wounded the battalion's entire forward air-control team, killed the battalion medical chief, and wounded the fire support coordinator, the headquarters commandant, and the sergeant major. The 3/3 was sent to help.

Lieutenant Dan Ryan

So we haul out there and as soon as we jump off the six-by, at the C2 Bridge, they hit us with rockets and mortars. I'm in a culvert with about three other guys, wondering if I'm gonna spend my life in there. As it gets darker, the command group very cleverly sets up on a high point and puts up all their two-niner-twos [antennas] up and there they are. Here we are! Here's the command post!

I'm thinkin', "This ain't a real good spot for me." So I found a hole down further from those guys. Maybe an eighth of a mile down on the other side of the perimeter. And I find a ready-made hole and I just had to clean out a few things. And there I stayed for the night. About three in the morning, we're gettin' probed . . . and there were gooks runnin' around and . . . it was a busy night. And all of a sudden I hear an airplane. And then he let loose with a couple of bombs and *zzzzzzzzz*. I says, "Goddam, that's *close* air support." *Baloom!* Right on the hill. It made hamburger meat out of a bunch of people. According to reports later, there was somebody flying a north mission and said, "Oh, there's some lights down there. This is the DMZ. I'll pickle my load here 'cause I can't land with it." Well, you couldn't tell that to the troops. For the next four days everybody's walking around lookin' up at the sky and lookin' at each other and sayin', "MIGs, MIGs, they're down here." [Four Marines died and six were wounded by this "friendly" bombing.]

PFC Tom Ryan

When we showed up to help 2/4, right in front of the bunkers that we got there was like eighteen dead gooks laying around all out in the front. We gathered up all these weapons and ammo and we had the job of burying all the dead NVA. We just buried them in the holes we were closing up and moved the perimeter in a little bit.

Corporal Bill Brocksieker

There was blood all over the area. There were pieces of equipment all over the area. I have a Gideon's New Testament Bible that I found, that had a person's name in it. I read it once in a while. I found that on that hill by a foxhole, but I don't know if the guy lived or died or whatever. There was equipment laying all over, strung all over.

Lance Corporal Tom Ryan

When we closed up the perimeter and took over these holes, there was a giant explosion which a plane coming by, they say accidentally, dropped a bomb. Which accidentally landed right in front of this perimeter. Killed some people. There was just feet left of one guy. He was sitting on top of a hole, with his feet in the hole. There was a guy laying on his back in the hole, talking to him who wasn't touched. The bomb just landed and zip, there was just two feet.

About three days later, you know, the sun was . . . there was hunks of meat all over the goddamn front of the perimeter there. Right in front of the trenchline. Larry Horne was picking them up with a stick with a nail in the end of it or something and singing "Bits and Pieces." It was the sense of humor . . . we used to laugh about anything.

It was just after that I got lance corporal, finally. Then we hit the shit again. And bingo, I was the squad leader again. This time they made me a corporal. And then we lost another lieutenant. We had this one for about three weeks. I think he was just there to try to win a medal and impress somebody.

Nice enough guy, but you don't go charging out of a goddamn treeline when you don't even know what you are doing. I remember him hollering "Charge" and everybody just looked like, "Did he say what we thought he said?" He got about three feet and got shot up. And then while he was laying there and we were dragging in other wounded and stuff all over the place, a chicom grenade came into the pile and he took one more splinter. Well, he died. That was the third lieutenant we lost. Talk about officers and luck . . . I don't think they had too much.

We were bouncing around a lot then, Cam Lo, C2, Alpha 3. 3/3 wasn't exactly sitting around anymore watching everything go by. We were being pulled in and out of different places as a blocking force here, a sweeping force there. Who ever knew? We never knew what the fuck was going on. Somebody knew. We were just always just humping around and I guess where we got our name "grunts," we were all gruntin' and moanin'. What you carried, you had. That was your possessions.

23

. . . .
IMPROVING THE SUPPLY SYSTEM

In his book, *First to Fight*, Lieutenant General Krulak devotes a chapter to "The Honorable Art of Institutional Theft," which arose from the poverty of the Corps in the 1920s and 1930s but developed into a skill. By contrast, the general recounts an incident in Vietnam in which a large quantity of plywood remained unguarded and intact for a week, whereas "thirty years earlier the plywood would not have survived a single night." The general should know that at least two Marines, Lance Corporal Jim Finn and Lieutenant Dan Ryan, kept the tradition of "the exhilaration of the chase" alive in Vietnam.

Lance Corporal Jim Finn

I was involved in an explosion in one of the mortar firing pits and lost the hearing in my ear. Every time they would fire the guns after that my eardrum would bleed, so they sent me back to the rear area, to Dong Ha to take over in supply.

This is probably where I came to the forefront . . . where I recognized what my true calling in life was . . . that I was one of the better scavengers that the battalion ever had. The first thing that I was able to do, again getting back to this no discipline, no regimentation, no control situation, was recognize that. 3/3's mortars were in dire need of some fundamental stuff for the guns . . . aiming sticks and sights and maps. In Dong Ha in those days 3/3 shared a supply area with a couple of other battalions and their supply huts were pretty close to each other. So, one day I just walked into one of their supply huts and I asked them for all the supplies that 81s needed, and they had them and they gave them to me. Then I went back out and I sent them out to the field to the guys. I think that they made me sign some sort of chit, and I signed it Lance Corporal Joe Smith or something.

Lieutenant Dan Ryan

At that time Sergeant Pope figured out that I would do better in the rear. He knew that I had a certain level of commercialism about me and that my mercantile aspect to the S-4 job was a little more, uh . . . acquisitive than his. So Pope went out to C2 Bridge and I back to the rear.

It was during my stay in the rear that I encountered Lance Corporal Finn. Basically, we hijacked the entire supply system of Dong Ha. We'd go out at night with a PC, those little trucks. I'd get about five, six guys out of the motor pool and we'd go out. There were a couple of warehouses around Dong Ha that had been hit by rocket fire or whatever, and people thought they were unsafe and they never used them. They were packed full of gear and we would go in there at night and just loot the place. Just truckloads and truckloads. And everybody was pleased, 'cause everybody had new stuff. We were pursued one night by the MPs. That was a . . . kind of reverse firefight. It's funny feeling like a gook . . . running away from your own.

Lance Corporal Jim Finn

Lieutenant Danny Ryan from New York City was more of a scavenger than I'll ever be in my life. Between the two of us we struck up a relationship with the U.S. Air Force over in Dong Ha. And what we also found out about the Air Force is that they had planes that would land usually every day at the airport at Dong Ha. And the Air Force pilots would be more than willing to fly things in for their brothers who were on the ground at the Air Force compound there.

We found out rather quickly that they had access to whiskey, beer, all the necessities of life. Along with the fact that they also had access to sandbags, vehicles . . . . You name it, they had it. One incident that springs to my mind was when the colonel was desperate, desperate. He was trying to hold down a position, but he did not have a sandbag that he could put his hands on. And he couldn't get sandbags from the Marines no matter who he asked or what regiment he asked. He told Danny Ryan to go back and get ahold of me. By that time my reputation had started to spread, that I was the guy who could get things. And Danny came back and he told me what the challenge was, that we were supposed to get some sandbags and get them quick. So, there came a time then that there were some *blue* sandbags that said "United States Air Force" that ended up on our bunkers in the forward area. Danny and I were able to come up with those. The point was that the colonel got them and that is all we really cared about.

Lieutenant Dan Ryan

During my stay in the rear . . . the kids out at Charlie-2 Bridge didn't have all the timbers . . . those 12 by 12s and all the other good stuff that you put in the overhead of the bunkers. They were just puttin' shit up there and the gooks would make chopped meat out of 'em. Well, I got wind that there was . . . some runway matting in Dong Ha. I knew one of the colonels up in division. I used to drink with him. And we got to bullshittin' one night and I had a requisition with me and we had more drinks and he signed this thing and I got a couple of pallets of runway matting. 'Cause I told him that we were building a helicopter pad and it was much too marshy and we needed this runway matting. Needless to say, all the runway matting went into the bunkers and the troops were happy. Colonel Smith, the CO of the 9th Marines, came out when I was out in the field. And he says, "Where's the fuckin' helicopter pad, Ryan?" I said, "What pad, sir?"

OCTOBER 1967

For a second time in October, 3/3 was called upon to help out 2/4. The action described below occurred on the twenty-sixth.

Lance Corporal Gary Conner

My first real combat came probably three or four days after I got to Vietnam, and it coincided with the first time that I had received mail in the field. It was around five o'clock in the afternoon. I was sitting out on top of this bunker with my first load of mail. I had ten or twelve letters from my wife, my mom, my grandma, everybody. All of a sudden I hear a bunch of machine guns shooting and blasting and bombs and airplanes coming in strafing. It was coming from an area probably three clicks from the Washout, due west towards Mutter's Ridge. What had happened was 2/4 was out there and they had run into the gooks.

They were being really pasted. I heard some Sky Hawks coming in dropping bombs. I looked out there and I'm sitting on top of the bunker and I thought, "For crying out loud, I've got a ringside seat to the war." It was just like the five o'clock news back home. I'm sitting there and I'm watching these jets come in. The next thing I know, here comes a 34. There were some gunships and a 34 comes in and all of a sudden it bursts into flames and drops straight out of the sky. Black smoke started billowing up and I thought, "Holy Christ! I'm right in the middle of this stuff." Another 34 comes in and that gets blown out of the sky. So I thought, "Holy Crap! What's going down?"

All of a sudden this guy comes running up through the area hitting all the bunkers. He says, "Saddle up. We're going to help 2/4." And I thought, "Saddle up? We're going to help 2/4?" I said, "What's 2/4?" I had no idea what 2/4 was. I knew 3/3. We were 3/3. He says, "We're going to help 2/4 out there, you dumb shit. Out there to the west. They're being waxed." I thought, "Holy shit! Here I am a spectator, now I'm going to be in the middle of this thing."

I was scared beyond description. We ran through the bush the entire distance out there. It was just getting dusk when we came to a series of rice paddies that we had to cross to get to Hill 48 where 2/4 was and all this commotion and shooting was coming from. The gooks had set up a .50-caliber and probably some 30s at our left flank, and of course they commenced to pick us off as we were running across the rice paddies trying to get to the hill.

I hit the deck three or four times in the mud and garbage and had it all over my face, in my ears. My radio handset was full of it and I'm thinking to myself, "What the hell did I get myself into?" I finally made it to the hill and hit the base of this little rise.

One of the fellows from 2/4 hollered that there were snipers in the position. So we got down and spent the whole night there and commenced to get hit by artillery and mortars and everything all night long. When morning finally came, I was praying just to see the sun come up. I remembered the traffic jams back home that I used to cuss and swear, and I was just wishing I could be back in the biggest traffic jam in Chicago that there ever was in history. I prayed and prayed and we called fire missions all night long. I just prayed that I wouldn't be hit. I prayed that we would see the sun come up.

The next morning we walked back to the Washout. 2/4 was straggling with us, the remnants, and they were carrying their dead bodies, dragging the Marines. They had them in ponchos and of course the bigger guys were being dropped often. These big, metallic-green blowflies with big red eyes were crawling all over the faces of the dead fellows, flies crawling in the mouths of these guys. I'm just thinking to myself that this cannot be real. I can't actually be enduring this.

I'm sure I'll be waking up soon. But in fact, it was reality. It was the beginning of some pretty hard times that the battalion faced.

NOVEMBER 1967

Lance Corporal Stan Kerlin

Then we moved out to a perimeter around Cam Lo bridge, on the northern side of the bridge for a while. Captain Ripley left Lima Company and we got a big redheaded guy. [Captain Roger Zensen, who had been the 3 and the 3 Alpha, took over Lima Company at this time.]

Captain Otto J. Lehrack (Brand New Guy)

When I joined 3/3 in November of '67, I had already been in Vietnam six months, with the Force Logistics Command in Danang. It took nearly half my tour and a request to see the commanding general before I could get to an infantry battalion. When I joined 3/3 they were at Cam Lo. To my disappointment, I was not given a rifle company right away but spent a few weeks as Dan Ryan's replacement in the S-4.

PFC John A. Mick (Brand New Guy)

I arrived in Danang the 7th of November of '67. We went from there on into Quang Tri Province to Dong Ha on November 10th, the Marine Corps birthday. The evening when we arrived, the northwest perimeter of Dong Ha was being attacked. We stood around and watched all the tracers flying for about the next two or three hours and flares being dropped and thinking, "Oh, this is really great." The next thing you know, a lieutenant colonel come out and told us all to get into the trenches, stay down, they expected artillery and mortar fire at any time.

Afterwards, they brought us in a birthday cake with a Marine Corps emblem on it. The Marine Corps will be the Marine Corps, I don't care if you're in a combat zone.

PFC Richard V. Sherwood (Brand New Guy)

You get in Vietnam and you spend the first day or couple of days being assigned, in this case, to the 3d Marine Division and then ultimately to the 3d Marine regiment. You don't have a flak jacket, you don't have a helmet, you don't have a rifle.

John Mick, at Camp Carroll in summer 1968, by this time a corporal. (Courtesy John Mick)

We got into Dong Ha and the interesting part to me was how hot and dirty and dusty everything was as opposed to what you see Stateside. I found my way over to the 3d Marine regimental area and was assigned to the 3d Battalion, 3d Marines, and went through the various administrative check-in, "dump your seabag, here's a cot, go get a meal" routine.

I was a PFC at this time. Off to some butler building to pick up some supplies, helmet, and a flak jacket, store your seabag, put your nametag on it, pick up your basic gear and a rifle and a couple of magazines. Eventually caught a truck and was told I was going to go to Lima Company, 3d Battalion, 3d Marines, which then were occupied at the Cam Lo bridge, slightly north and west of Dong Ha.

A sergeant pointed out a truck and we climbed aboard and we took a ride out to the countryside. Being the brand new guy and not used to the roads or the travel or what to expect, when the truck hit a great big bump, my helmet bounced off my head and dropped out in the middle of the road. I never did recover it and it was kind of embarrassing when I got to Cam Lo bridge and hopped off and they said, "Here we are."

I was told that I'd be assigned to the 2d Platoon, and I grabbed some corporal that I saw in there and I said, "Look, I've got a problem. I'm a brand new guy. I'm supposed to go over there and see the platoon commander and I've lost my helmet. It fell off my head on the way out here." The guy sort of raised his eyebrows and said I could borrow his to go in and see the platoon commander, which I did. I was assigned to a squad, 3d Squad, and told where I could find their little hooch and the squad leader. I went over and introduced myself and was given a place to bed down with the rest of the guys, and that was about it for the first day.

PFC Vito Lavacca (Brand New Guy)

We landed in Danang right around Thanksgiving of 1967. And after a couple of nights stay at the Danang Hilton, a big old wooden-framed, barnlike structure, we were shipped out to Cam Lo on some trucks. I was given an M16 and one magazine of rounds, both of which looked like they had been sitting in a rice paddy for months. We were given the rifles just as we got on the trucks. And all I kept hoping was that we wouldn't get ambushed on the way to Cam Lo.

We tried to clean our rifles on the truck as we went up there, about five or six of us in the truck. But as it turned out, Cam Lo was a fairly secured area at the time. Everything was pretty quiet. Routine patrols and very, very little contact with the enemy. The first thing that struck me was the cold attitude that everyone had toward one another. I later learned that that really wasn't the case. My first impression at Cam Lo was that everybody was kind of . . . just watching out for themselves. My impression changed after about . . . a month. I don't know whether I had that attitude because I was the new kid on the block or . . . whether it was the old philosophy of "don't make friends or get too close to anyone." I'm not sure.

I guess the one message that . . . that was ingrained in us throughout all of the training was that the only way you were going to survive in Vietnam is if you believe you can survive. But it didn't take long once I was over there to come to a realization that . . . there was no way that you could survive. . . . I guess that kind of made the tour a little bit easier. It takes a great load off your mind when you just kind of toss everything to fate and say that . . . you have no control over what's gonna happen.

PFC Kevin T. Sweeney (Brand New Guy)

I arrived in Danang, went there, was there for about two days and I got sent to Dong Ha to go with my unit, 3/3. As soon as I arrived at Dong Ha, there was a young gentleman in the rear there and he says, "Whatever you do, don't go out to the field because you'll never make it back." I didn't think nothing of it, but I went and left the rear area of Dong Ha and went to Cam Lo.

24

. . . .
CHRISTMAS AT CAM LO

Lieutenant Dan Ryan

December rolled around and we pulled back to Cam Lo. Just north of the town to the north side of the river and we were billeted right behind an eight-inch battery. Your body got to the point where you didn't hear an eight-inch goin' off at night. You could sleep through it. Well, I don't know if you slept through it, but part of your body did. We were just north of the vill there and the Vietnamese were always trying to steal stuff from us. Being the S-4 I had to enforce some anti-hijack programs against local indigenous personnel. That brought their unending wrath. I was named the "Number 10 Lieutenant." Unfortunately, no one would go to the vill with me to get a haircut or go shopping or anything else, 'cause they were afraid that if I was in a cross hair and if Chan was a bad shot, it would probably get him.

I remember the haircuts. I had a Greasegun [M3A1 submachine gun]. I'd sit in the barber chair and just put the greasegun in my lap and sit there and the guy would cut my hair. And then he'd try to snap your neck and do the razor, and

Men of the 3d Marines on board tanks of the 3d Tank Battalion sweep the Con Thien corridor on Operation KENTUCKY, *north of the Cam Lo district headquarters.*

I'd just grin at him with a cocked greasegun. The guy cut some great haircuts. A couple for free, I think.

Captain Otto Lehrack

Once I went with Dan Ryan to get a haircut in Cam Lo. We sat facing each other in barber chairs made out of old ammo boxes while two barbers cut our hair. He watched my barber and I watched his, with a loaded .45 in my hand.

We were walking back through Cam Lo vill when one of our company-sized patrols passed through. The CO, trying to look like one of his enlisted men, was wearing no rank insignia and had an M16, usually not carried by officers. He fooled no one, particularly a little Vietnamese girl of about six or seven. Standing by the roadside, she yelled in English when he passed, "Hey, Cap-i-tan. What's goin' on there, duuude?"

Lieutenant Dan Ryan

We spent Christmas at Cam Lo. 'Course we had smoke jumper. That's not a springer spaniel either, it's a drink.

Captain Otto Lehrack

A smoke jumper was a pot of tea, brewed as strong as possible, sweetened a bit, and mixed with about an equal amount of whatever booze Ryan could steal or scrounge.

As Christmas approached, someone in the CP group decided that we were going to get some ducks from the villagers at Cam Lo and have them for holiday dinner. Anyway, one day we found ourselves in possession of a wire cage containing about a dozen ducks. All of them were yellow except one who was very, very black.

In the motor transport section there was a black corporal named Leonard Fernander, Jr., from Atlanta, a *big* man. There were several stories floating around about him in the battalion when I joined. One was that he once picked the front end of a Mighty Mite [jeep] out of the mud and held it while someone changed a tire. Corporal Fernander took a shine to the little black duck which stood out among the yellow ones. He called him "Splib Duck," splib being a slang term in Vietnam for a black person. As Christmas got closer he would take Splib Duck out of his cage, caress him in his huge hands, and say things like, "Don't worry, Splib Duck, old Leonard isn't gonna let nobody hurt you." Sometime between Christmas Eve and Christmas Day old Leonard must have done just that, because Splib Duck was nowhere to be found. So I guess the story has a happy ending.

Lieutenant Dan Ryan

Christmas there was one of these alleged cease-fires throughout the DMZ, Peace on Earth Goodwill to Men. Meanwhile Chan is movin' his entire fuckin' army down the Ho Chi Minh Trail so he can have his Tet party. Lyndon Johnson is a good man and should still be alive . . . hangin' in my room.

PFC Michael Velasquez

One real emotional time that I had was during Christmas of '67. One of my friends, Gary Hite from Long Beach, California, sent my name into the local newspaper there, and somehow or other the wire line picked it up and they distributed my name all over the country. During that time morale was kind of low because a lot of the guys felt they didn't have the country behind them as far as support.

We were out on an operation and came back in. I was the type of guy who hardly ever got letters. I didn't write to too many people. One of the guys was distributing the mail, and they called me Vasquez in Vietnam (my real last name is Velasquez), and he called out "Vasquez" and then he started to unload all kinds of mail on me. I just couldn't believe I had bundles of mail from people all over the country. I said, "What is this?" I just couldn't believe it.

He said, "These are for you. I don't know, man, just take them. Get them out of here." So I went back to my bunker and I started to open these letters from people that were really grateful that we were there, telling me how great a job they thought we were doing, people that really cared. I just broke down and cried. It really got to me. We were so far away from home. I just didn't know what to make of it.

PFC Vito Lavacca

Cam Lo . . . We were there for about a month. I felt very left out. And, of course, lonely . . . It was the height of the holiday season and . . . it was very depressing.

Captain Roger Zensen

I had a girlfriend down in Saigon named Nancy, God bless her. After I got over in country, she had taken a job with the Navy and was working in Saigon. She sent us up a Christmas tree. For lack of decorations we took toilet paper and wrapped it around the tree and had a bow on top of it or something. It made it a little bit more pleasant.

Also my mother, one of her friends at church had a daughter that was going to college. She was in a sorority and so they all got together and sent us cookies and packages and sent them to me. I gave them all out to the troops and kept some for us in the CP. I wrote them thank-you letters and they asked what else they could do for us. So we asked for Kool Aid and some other things, pencils and writing paper and things like that. It really made me feel good that we had that kind of support from some people back home and was able to give things out to the troops.

25

WORKING WITH THE ARVN

Lance Corporal Gary Conner

Dave Ducow, myself, Marty Kennedy, and Doug Miracle [all artillery forward observers] were sent for the month of December to Gio Linh to operate out of that sixty-foot tower. We basically were attached to a battalion of the ARVN that was there, about 600 South Vietnamese army soldiers that had a rather good reputation.

Anyway, that month we shot [artillery] up into North Vietnam. We shot a lot of precision destruction missions at a radio relay station that they called Signal Mountain, which was located about fifteen miles into North Vietnam. Through the very large, high-powered binoculars we had inside the tower, we could see it very plainly, radio antennas and everything. We used to shoot fifty rounds a day of 155-mm gun.

One time Dave Ducow (my lieutenant) and I, along with an Australian army captain and a U.S. Army captain that was assigned to these South Vietnamese troops, were to make a two-day sweep up the old railroad tracks up to the Ben Hai River and back. We were to go all the way to the river into an area that hadn't been really worked for many years. We were also told that during this two-day period, if we were to take any casualties or take any fellows killed, that the only people that would be air-evacuated out of the DMZ would be myself, my lieutenant, the Army captain, or the Australian. The South Vietnamese, if they got wounded or killed, would have to carry their people out. I thought this was kind of a bum deal, but that was the way we operated.

It was early in the morning and dark, because you never left out of there at light because the 152s and 130s [NVA artillery pieces] from up north of the river used to follow you across the trace. So we went out in the dark. As we were standing there, the South Vietnamese troopers were marching past us. There were 600 of them. They had little transistor radios that they had glued to their ears and they were playing all these gook songs and jing-jang stuff. They were walking butt to belly, extremely close, and I thought, "Well, that's okay while it's dark and you can't see anything." But as it got light they continued to snake-dance all the way down the old railroad tracks north, and that was their method of operation. They were in physical contact with each other all the way. They had these transistor radios blaring gook tunes stuck underneath their helmets and they had these packs full of live chickens and cats. As they walked past, you could hear the cats meowing and scratching and try to get out. The Australian said that that was their lunch . . . that was what they were going to eat. When it came time they'd kill a cat and they'd cook him on a fire.

We got on the north side of the trace and hadn't gone too far when we hit some tremendous contact. We were getting artillery fire up north, a lot of grenades. You could hear mines going off. We eventually learned that they had DH-10 mines [directional antipersonnel mines, also called "gook claymores"] all over the area, command-detonated DH-10s all over the area.

We were taking a lot of casualties. We continued to advance and finally hit a point to where we couldn't go any further. The two army captains, my lieutenant, myself, we were in a big bomb crater, right in what would have been the old railroad bed, and we were just huddled in there. We were calling artillery. The fire was coming in so fast, you'd look up over the crown of the crater to adjust and duck back down again. We were shooting like mad. They were shooting like mad.

A little bit later we moved out of the bunker towards one of the flanks. It was lunchtime, apparently. We came across four South Vietnamese soldiers; they were sitting in a little opening in the brush. They had a fire going and stretched across one of the bushes was an ocelot kind of skin. They had that cat stuck on a spit. It was in the fire and they kept turning the stick. I remember thinking, "My

God, here I'm scared to death. I don't think I'm going to get back, and these boys are calm and business enough about this thing to stop and have lunch." The war wasn't going to interrupt them. They'd been in war for so many years, it was just a way of life and it was just like you and I going to work—come lunch-time, we sit down and have lunch and pick up doing our work when we're done. That's exactly what these fellows were doing. But it was extremely creepy to me to see in the middle of a heavy firefight and incoming period that these guys would actually sit down and cook this cat.

Before we broke contact we found these big DH-10s and this was another very gruesome situation. We found a dead Vietnamese civilian. He was in a little bunker and there was a DH-10 five or six yards from him at the most. He was in a shallow depression and he had a leg iron on his ankles and he was chained to a big post that was driven into the ground. His role was to fire the DH-10, obviously a suicide mission because those things blow 360 degrees and are very devastating.

We shot this man before he activated the mine, but we saw several situations where bodies were totally destroyed and indications of them having set off a command-detonated mine with no intentions of being under cover or coming out of that alive. What the NVA had done was take farmers . . . and chained them up and staked them to the ground and apparently ordered them to deto-nate those mines when we came through the area. This is something that defies description. If you read the accounts of Hue [the former Imperial City, which was seized and occupied by the NVA during the 1968 Tet offensive] and how they killed the civilians and buried them alive, some of them, thousands of them, you knew these people were not beyond anything. That was something that was very hard to realize—the degree of brutality to their own people.

After we broke contact we assembled our wounded and dead and we had a bunch of them. I walked around them as we were trying to determine how we were going to get them out of there. One South Vietnamese soldier was lying there and I thought he was dead and I kind of tripped on him. He looked up and smiled at me. His flak jacket was open and he had a bullet hole right through midsternum, which should have taken part of his heart out. But he was alive, just lying there, not moaning, crying, groaning, or anything. He just looked up and smiled at me. And I thought, "My God! Here's a guy that's going to be history soon and he can smile!" It was a very frightening experience.

We did get back. The dead fellows were strapped and tied in ponchos and tied to poles just like the Pilgrims used to carry their deer. Their severely wounded people were carried out the best they could. The walking wounded were helped out with other soldiers. On our way back we went through a tea plantation, and they took out time to pick tea leaves. These people started picking all this stuff and putting it in their helmets. I just thought that it was awesome. Here it is an unbelievable experience for me that these fellows were eating their lunch right in the height of a firefight and now were in the process of dragging their dead and wounded back a good mile or more and were stopping to pick tea leaves.

26

• • • • • • • • • • • • •

ALPHA THREE

Captain Otto Lehrack

A couple of days after Christmas we took our turn along the barrier. India, Kilo, and Lima companies went to Alpha 3, and Mike went temporarily to Gio Linh [Alpha 2]. I took over India Company a few days later.

Alpha 3 was on a small rise almost equidistant between Gio Linh and Con Thien. When 3/3 arrived after Christmas, the wooden frames of the Dye Marker bunkers had been completed by the Seabees and engineers, but they had not been sandbagged. It was a barren piece of real estate, perhaps a third of a mile across with all vegetation bulldozed away. It was surrounded by barbed wire and a strip filled with antipersonnel mines. To the north of Alpha 3 a few hundred meters was Hill 28, which the battalion held with two companies most of the time it was in residence. Forward of Hill 28 were the two closest outposts to the DMZ in all of South Vietnam, Observation Posts [OPs] Gold and Silver. Gold, my responsibility, was less than 150 meters from the edge of the zone. 3/3 would operate from these positions through May.

Lieutenant Colonel Jim Marsh, commanding officer of 3/3 for the first half of 1968, at Alpha-3. (Courtesy Otto Lehrack)

Lieutenant Robert Montgomery (Brand New Guy)

Alpha 3 . . . I don't think I'd seen such a barren piece of real estate in all my life. Bunkers half completed, cleared off . . . and this was gonna be our duty station for the next . . . seven months.

I was an artillery FO. And when I joined . . . 3d Battalion . . . I picked up a lance corporal radio operator. We'd been assigned an aboveground bunker . . . fairly close to a half-completed observation tower, and were told that we would rotate patrols with the various companies as they went out.

We spent . . . most of our days sandbagging . . . fortifying our bunker, fortifying our observation tower . . . and taking turns going out . . . with the infantry companies as they patrolled the area.

PFC Joe D. "Reb" Turner (Brand New Guy)

I got to India Company 3/3 early January of '68. I landed at Alpha 3, brought in by helicopter. When the helicopters came in there was incoming. They were trying to hit the helicopters. The first thing I did when I got out of the helicopter during this incoming was dive into a bunker. I hit the chaplain. That was my first religious experience.

Corporal Benjamin Corbett receiving a Purple Heart from Lieutenant Colonel James Marsh. (Courtesy Otto Lehrack)

PFC James K. Yost (Brand New Guy)

I hit Vietnam, it was December 25th, 1967, just in time for Christmas and, later, Tet New Year of '68. The Year of the Monkey. When I went to Danang at the Danang Hilton for a couple of days, got processed, and I started learning very seriously that this was a war.

At Dong Ha it was very muddy and they put us on the gunny's working party after we got our processing done. I went over to supply and was given a pot [helmet], three magazines, an M16 rifle, and one flak jacket with a .50-caliber bullet hole in the back and blood all over it. I refused it and threw it down and I told them that I wanted another flak jacket. I believe that it was an omen and I didn't want to take it. I got another flak jacket that was too large and I ended up takin' that one. I was five foot eight and had an extra-large flak jacket.

I was twenty-two . . . an old man. Most of the people were eighteen and nineteen. So I kind of was the old man to begin with. Well, in about five days, I was shipped out to a firebase called Alpha 3, was assigned to Lieutenant Douglas' platoon, the 3d Platoon, India Company. And my first night there, after filling sandbags all day and halfway into the night, about four o'clock in the morning we were rocketed by 122s. When the first round came in about 100 meters from our bunker, I thought it was a freight train coming in and the concussion really shook everything up. Sergeant Dicker, the platoon guide, tried to wake Lieutenant Douglas, who was in a sound sleep, and he kept shaking him and calling, "Lieutenant Douglas." Finally about the third round went off about twenty-five meters from our bunker and Lieutenant Douglas was awake. He said, "Put your flak jacket on and your helmet and lean against the wall." We took about five more rounds after that and that was my initiation under fire. From a 122-mm.

PFC Vito Lavacca

Alpha 3 was really a scary place. At Gio Linh and Cam Lo we would see civilians . . . young kids out moving their water buffalo along and harvesting rice and that kind of thing. Even though you realized that some of those civilians might be Viet Cong, it kind of relieved the tension when you'd hear the kids playing or screaming and . . . going about their routine business.

At Alpha 3, the civilians were moved back to make it a free fire range and it became very eerie. . . . There were no people talking. It seemed like even our Marines spoke in hushed tones. You really got the sense that Charlie was behind every tree and every bush.

And that's the thing that made Vietnam so bad . . . the day-to-day tension, not knowing when it was coming, when you were gonna get hit. I had come to feel that I was gonna get hit, that there was no way of stopping it. Day after day of, when is it gonna be? Is it gonna be from a . . . sniper round to the head? Is it gonna be from an incoming artillery round? Is it gonna be after a long day of a firefight? It's hard to try to explain to people that once the firing started . . . you felt much better. At least now you knew . . . you knew that you didn't get it in the first volley. You knew where they were. You knew what direction to look and to protect yourself from. And then it became another day at the office. At Alpha 3 and at Hill 28, which was right in front of Alpha 3 on the DMZ, we would make contact every few days.

PFC Robert L. "Lex" Payne

At Alpha 3 every evening just before dark, we'd get incoming from the gooks. Just to keep us honest, I guess. Every day they'd fire, and it seemed like the first round that come in hit the 3d Platoon shitter. They always had a real nice shitter, it even had a tin roof on it. You could count on it; one of the first rounds would hit the shitter and the next rounds would be scattered around the base. When we used to get the new guys in, we'd be explaining the artillery to them and we'd tell them, "See this little building right over here?" And we'd point to the 3d Platoon shitter and we'd say, "When you see that son of a bitch disintegrate, you'd better be jumping in a trench."

One day we were getting artillery in. We were in the trenches. We were kind of kidding around, me and a couple of other guys, Michael Ferrara and Howard Randolph; they were both later killed. But we were in the trench there. Artillery was coming in. It was landing out in the minefield and we were kind of brave; we drew our tombstones on the clay on the side of the trench wall. We put our names down there, when we were born, and we put like we died that day, you know, and all of a sudden the gooks dropped the rounds down. They were laying right on top of us and we had our heads down in the mud and our arms were up there scrubbing off those tombstones off the side of the trench walls.

PFC Craig Pyles

Incoming was something that frightened me more than bullets did because at least if somebody's shooting bullets at you, you can do something about it. You can shoot back. That incoming artillery was terrifying and there wasn't a thing you could do except wait for somebody else to get some counter–battery fire to get it to stop.

People talk about artillery whistling. That's bullshit. It doesn't whistle unless it's a long way off. When they're real close you hear that screaming sound, and then for a split second there's just silence and then instead of a *kaboom*, there's just a crack. The ground just seems to leap underneath of you. Then you can smell that cordite from the explosion. That whole experience can be so demoralizing when there's nothing you can do to stop it.

·

The North Vietnamese continued their preparation for the General Offensive, General Uprising. In early January they infiltrated two divisions into positions around Khe Sanh in order to fix American attention on that remote frontier. They were also busy on the diplomatic and propaganda fronts. At an embassy reception on the evening of 30 December, they indicated for the first time their willingness to hold peace talks if the United States stopped the bombing of North Vietnam. Their earlier position had rejected any possibility of talks until *after* an unconditional halt to the bombing. In support of the anticipated uprising, they also began urging the formation of a "popular front" government of "neutralists" in the south and tried to win over South Vietnamese officials and soldiers by offering them positions in a coalition government. None of this was known by the Marines who fought along the DMZ.

27

MIKE COMPANY AT GIO LINH

PFC Vito Lavacca

After the holidays it seemed like it was time to get back to work. From Cam Lo, Mike Company moved out to Gio Linh, a small perimeter . . . on the DMZ. We were at Gio Linh for about a month and that's where I think I came to the realization that . . . survival was going to be unlikely.

Lieutenant William D. Kenerly (Brand New Guy)

We flew out of Okinawa and we got to Vietnam on maybe January the 4th of 1968. I followed the procedure of catching helicopter rides up to Phu Bai, spent a night, got a chopper out the next day up to Dong Ha.

Somewhere along the line I was asked to pick a battalion. They gave me a list of eight or nine that needed officers. I knew that the 26th Marines were at Khe Sanh. I had run into a couple of lieutenants that had told me about it, and I knew that they were basically surrounded and cut off and being resupplied by air. I gave some serious thought to asking for the 26th Marines before my common sense got the better of me, and I decided that it was stupid to ask for assignment to a battalion that was surrounded. Whether that questions my honor and commitment or not, I don't know. I had heard all the stories about 1/9, about how they could get ambushed in downtown Jacksonville, North Carolina, so I didn't ask for 1/9. At any rate, I'd never heard anything about 3/3. Maybe being a little bit superstitious, I remember thinking that the 3d Battalion of the 3d Marine regiment of the 3d Marine Division—that perhaps that sequence of 3s was an indicator of good luck and I asked for assignment to 3/3.

I got this platoon which was the 2d Platoon of Company M of the 3d Battalion, 3d Marines. At that time Company M was at Gio Linh. The rest of the battalion was already over at A3.

·

PFC John Mick

In my first combat I lost three of my best buddies. There was four of us sleeping in a bunker there at Gio Linh. This happened January 9th, 1968. We went out on a search-and-destroy operation. Recon spotted some movement or something out there and they wanted Mike Company to go out and see if anything was out there.

My squad, the 3d Squad, went out first. Woppo, this guy named Grez, and I— we were all walking more or less up in front and all of a sudden Woppo told us to get down. He wants to look over the map, so he sat down and started looking over the map. Grez and I walked a little bit further up and we were at this little hedgerow and I saw three guys sitting in a bomb crater and they had a machine gun. This was the first time I've ever seen an assault machine gun. I knew it wasn't ours, but I didn't know if they were South Vietnamese. I'd never seen them before, this type of uniform.

The next thing I know I saw the haircuts. I'd seen a few dead gooks and I seen how they had their hair all straight up like these guys. I knew the South Vietnamese soldiers didn't have theirs like that. About that time I saw all three of the guys bend down real low and they grabbed that machine gun and jumped up. I just about opened up and Woppo pulled my rifle down. He said, "Don't open up on them. Wait until the rest of them gets here." Well, he got the radio operator, called him over to tell the other squads what we have up here. Lieutenant Miller came up with us and the next thing I know, he said, "What'd you see?" And I explained to him and he said, "Where? Don't just point to the hole, just go over there."

We got in there and we could see they had hot rice and everything still sitting there waiting. And there was a trail, you could see all kinds of tracks on it. He said, "Let's follow the trail." We all lined up and we started walking on a line, and the next thing I know I heard Bruce Thomas saying, "Hey, I hear voices and they don't sound like ours." Right in front of us laying in the grass was about five NVA soldiers laying down. They opened up and just hit Bruce Thomas when he was talking. They must have thought he was the officer in charge. They killed him right there on the spot. We jumped up, ran to the right, crossed this little trail, and set in. About this time there was another little trail to our right and we were taking the machine-gun fire from there.

Lieutenant Miller told Tim Hazzard to jump across that trail. He jumped up and caught a round in his right armpit and he fell down. They drug him into a hole—Doc Winslow, Lieutenant Miller, and Al Winters. A chicom was thrown into the hole with them and even though Tim knew . . . he rolled over on the grenade.

So Tim Hazzard was killed, Bruce Thomas was killed. The next thing I know I heard them say, "Smitty, bring your machine-gun team up." Well, Smitty stood up. When he did, he got two .50-cal rounds, one over his right boob and the other one almost square in the middle of his chest. Now this guy fell right next to me. This was the first time I've actually seen an American this close to me, dead. I've seen guys wounded and hit from shrapnel and from mortars and artillery. But it was the first time I actually looked down and seen somebody that was dead. All three of them that was killed were from the same bunker that I was in. It hit me kind of hard.

It was still raining that day pretty heavy and we couldn't get any air support. An AO [air observer] did come out and spot a lot of gooks moving on the ridgeline above us. They said they were setting up machine guns. But we couldn't get any jets in here to drop napalm or drop any bombs on them. We had to pull back and leave two of the dead out there. David Cutshall was hit and we had somebody else helping him coming back. When we got back to the position, I was crying my eyes out. Lieutenant Miller said, "I'm going back after my guys."

Lieutenant Bill Kenerly

My third day with the company, we were on standby. We were monitoring the radios and the 3d Platoon was ambushed along the railroad tracks up on the edge of the DMZ. We could hear the gunfire and could also pick up the radio traffic. I told Sergeant Veteto to call the platoon out. I ran up to the company headquarters. Lieutenant Cialone, the company commander, was there getting his gear on. He told me that I was to follow an azimuth of 115 degrees until I found the firefight. He said that he would be bringing the other platoon and the balance of the weapons platoon in a separate column on the other side of the railroad tracks. I was always an awful map reader, but we followed the azimuth.

We got to the fight after it was over and we had the responsibility of retrieving two bodies. We did that and we never made contact, though we did get sniped at a couple of times.

PFC Vito Lavacca

I was sitting out on an LP [listening post] at the front gate, right along the road that led into Gio Linh, with two other guys. I was awake on the radio and the other two guys were asleep, when I heard a firefight and then our radio crackled and somebody called up our position, LP1 or whatever, and told us they had . . . two Aces and two Kings. I was still unfamiliar with radio brevity code and I woke up one guy and asked him what that meant. And he told me that that meant that a couple of our guys had gotten killed. [Radio brevity codes were an attempt to confuse enemy listeners. For 3/3 at this time, an "Ace" was a friendly KIA, a "King" was a WIA, and a "Queen" meant someone was missing.]

I was just kind of stunned for a while and then out of the dark . . . the platoon that had been out on an ambush came in past the LP, dragging the bodies. And I looked at them and recognized them. I had played cards with them earlier that night. I didn't really know them that well, but it's really a . . . a chilling experience when you first encounter death that way.

PFC John Mick

They did recover the bodies. I wanted to see them really bad and they wouldn't let me. I even really hate admitting to this, but I cried my eyes out. I even threatened to shoot Lieutenant Miller because he went 550 yards further than we were told to go by our company commander.

I threatened him and Staff Sergeant Curtis come into me and told me, "John, don't be doing this. This is what can happen." And I was crying, crying my eyes out. I was only there for two months and they sent me on in-country R and R. So I went to China Beach, got drunk for those three days, lived it up, I guess, and came back and tried to forget everything. But it was kind of hard.

Well, things went on. Lieutenant Miller and I became closer than what I really thought we would. He started talking to me all the time. He told me about how his wife back in the States was killed in a car accident and how his life was changed. I really began to like the guy a lot.

PFC Vito Lavacca

When we were over at Gio Linh, we used to be able to walk up to the DMZ, up Highway 1 to where it dropped off a cliff. And way, way off in the distance in the Z, you could see a North Vietnamese fortresslike structure with a North

Vietnamese flag flyin' over it. And we would call in heavy artillery and some-times airstrikes, and I think on one occasion, we even called in a mission from the battleship *New Jersey*. And each time, after the dust would clear, the flag wasn't there. But out would come Charlie and put the flag back up.

It was like a game we played with him for a period of about a month. I re-member sitting there wondering if the North Vietnamese had a national anthem that talked about bombs bursting in air and . . . giving proof that their flag was still there. That little son of a bitch is probably the custodian of a public school in Hanoi someplace now. Puttin' the flag up every morning.

JANUARY 1968

Captain Roger Zensen

My company, Lima, we got assigned out on Hill 28, which was the outpost north of the strong point [north of Alpha 3] along the trace. Having learned and observed Ray Findlay putting in wire, we went to work on that place. We put in triple concertina and the aprons and the tanglefoot [configurations of barbed wire]. I made a fougasse [a 55-gallon drum filled with explosive and rocks, scrap iron, or napalm and buried in the enemy's possible path, where it could be deto-nated on command]. We figured if they ever came up on draw, we'd have that thing laying there in front of us to support our claymores and what not.

So we had a pretty good position there. In fact, we had it wired and we patrolled out of there. We felt pretty snug in there. Ray was the operations officer and Otto was there on the perimeter with India Company.

At two o'clock one morning the radio operator woke me up. He said, "Hey, Skipper. I've got somebody on the land line." So I get on there and Nancy down in Saigon, the girlfriend who had sent the Christmas tree, had gone through the operators—she must have been patched through by about four or five different radio operators. She went from Saigon to Danang, and Danang up to Quang Tri, Quang Tri to Dong Ha, Dong Ha up to the 3, and then on out to Hill 28. I could just barely hear her, but all the Marines were hanging on the line listening to our conversation at two o'clock in the morning.

She worked for a Navy captain and she got me a couple cases of beer. The Navy captain asked what she was doing with it and had it all wrapped up in brown paper, and she said, "Well, I'm going to mail it up to Zensen." He says, "Oh, that's a good idea. Let me give you a hand." So he helped her carry the beer over to the post office and of course the mail clerk there said, "What's this?" And the Navy captain butted right in and said, "It's tomato juice and it's going to a Marine in the DMZ and you'd better get it up there in a hurry." So she mailed up two cases of beer up in Hill 28.

I had just come in off of a patrol with one of my platoons. The radio operator said, "Hey, Skipper. You've got a package." I told the operator, I said, "Call all the platoon commanders and platoon sergeants and tell them we're going to have a meeting." Because as soon as he handed the package to me, I felt it and I knew it was beer. So I ripped the thing open and sure enough, there it was. And we had some salami and cheese. As the platoon commanders came on in, I'd hand them a beer and say, "Take a seat and have a little salami and cheese and a beer." Bob Funk was a big guy from Ohio State. He was a placekicker for Woody Hayes. He came in. He'd been in country for about two weeks. He comes walking down these little earth stairs and I hand him the beer and I said, "Here you go, Bob. Have a beer." And he says, "Thanks, Skipper." And he grabbed it and took a big drink of it and he said, "Oh, it's warm. Don't you have any cold beer?" We all laughed and I shook my head and I said, "Just give it another couple more weeks and you'll be happy to have any beer."

.

TAC (tactical air control) party was a team commanded by a Marine Corps officer/pilot. Their mission was to call in various types of air support for the infantry, although they remain on the ground with the troops, sharing hardship and danger. T.J. Kelly was a TAC party radio operator during his tour.

PFC Thomas J. "T. J." Kelly

I thought that TAC party was a real good job to have because I knew what was going on all the time. I was talking to anything that flew up in that whole area, it wasn't just 3/3 that I was listening to. In our network, we had the air support for all the friendly units up in the whole DMZ area. So when another company got into a firefight, I heard it and monitored the whole thing. Plus helicopters, you could hear where they were coming or going and you really did know what was going on. Even in a firefight, the AO would just skim over the treetops looking down and telling us when we were being flanked.

One time in particular, we had some of our guys kind of stuck out in front of us in a bomb crater. It was an area where there had been an Arc Light (a B-52 drop) and there were a bunch of bomb craters in the area. So we had these guys stuck in a bomb crater and the NVA were in another bomb crater creeping up on them, but the NVA didn't really know where they were and the guys didn't know where the NVA were, but the AO could see the whole thing and was telling me about it.

He spotted my individual person and he started me over to this area, and I got close enough to where I could yell instructions to some guys who could yell them to the guys in the bomb crater and they started throwing hand grenades. First they were throwing them too far and so the AO was adjusting hand grenade range to me, and then I was yelling it to another Marine and that Marine was yelling it to those guys in the crater. The problem was, they were throwing the hand grenades too far because the NVA were in the very next crater. So finally we got the word passed down to those guys and they threw them half as far and they killed the NVA.

·

PFC Vito Lavacca

The . . . feelings I had after I had been in country a couple of weeks at Cam Lo, of everyone being . . . kind of standoffish, pretty much dissolved after we left Cam Lo. I don't know whether it was the people that we had there or the holiday season or what it was. My whole perception of the relationship between everyone totally changed. And I started to realize that everyone was out to cover and protect one another.

You developed friendships. Not the kind of friendships where . . . you know, where you dated each other's sisters or anything. You developed relationships where you would do anything to protect the next guy, whether you knew him or not, whether you knew his name. Whether he was a southerner or northerner or a black or a white . . . you protected each other.

·

Tet is the Vietnamese New Year, whose January date is determined on a lunar basis. In 1789, in one of their greatest victories against Imperial China, the Vietnamese had surprised their enemy by attacking in the middle of the Tet holiday. Almost two centuries later, the North Vietnamese would attempt to repeat that success against a new enemy.

On the night of 29 January 1968, six cities in the middle of South Vietnam were attacked by the Viet Cong. This was the original date set by General Giap for the beginning of his General Offensive, General Uprising. A twenty-four-hour delay had been ordered by Giap, but apparently the modification did not reach all units. Because of the enemy's false start, the scheduled Tet truce was cancelled in I Corps and in other areas of the country. The 3/3 received word of the cancellation by message at 1815 local time but spent a peaceful night.

28

• • • • • • • • • • • • • •

KILO COMPANY AMBUSH

The Tet Offensive swung into high gear on the night of 30 January when the remainder of General Giap's units attacked. That same evening a Mike Company ambush engaged about twenty-five NVA who were moving south. However, 3/3's most desperate battle of the Tet Offensive took place when Kilo Company engaged at least a battalion of NVA near Gio Linh in February.

Gunnery Sergeant Jimmie C. Clark

Kilo was assigned to sweep the road between A3 and Gio Linh on February 7, 1968. This was normally done by each company taking turns. One company would do it one day and another company another day.* We would have to sweep the road and make sure that the road was secure for supply convoys to get through or to haul troops or whatever.

Well, February 7th was our day. It was a nice day, pretty and sunny. It wasn't

---

*The author swept the same area with India Company on 6 February, and there was no enemy contact whatsoever.

Gunnery Sergeant Jimmie Clark, who received the Bronze Star Medal for heroic action in the February 7, 1968, ambush. (Courtesy Jimmie Clark)

raining bad like it normally did with the monsoons or anything. It was a beautiful day and we started out to Gio Linh sometime early that morning.

Corporal Gary Conner

What happened was the standard patrol briefing early in the morning when it was still dark. The lieutenant and I went up there with the CO and the other platoon commanders and sergeants and he told us what we were going to be doing. He also gave us an intelligence report that day that was from the Popular Forces [PFs] that there was a reinforced battalion of North Vietnamese dug in along the road that we were going to be sweeping. The intelligence reports were common. We would get them quite frequently and they usually were bogus. We normally didn't find what they indicated we would find. So I think as a result, we had a tendency to become complacent about those reports.

After the briefing we went back to saddle up and called some artillery prep fires into the area the PFs indicated the North Vietnamese were dug in. We fired a couple of missions, getting a couple of Battery 2s, which would be the six guns firing two rounds apiece; maybe we shot twenty-five or thirty rounds into that area. Then we moved out. 1st Platoon went north of the trace. The 2d and 3d platoons then split up on line and were traveling on either side of that road.

PFC William W. Clough, Jr. (Brand New Guy)

I was being trained at the time as a forward observer. I'd been going out with two or three different FOs. I finally ended up in Kilo with Everisto Johnston, who was almost through his second tour. Everisto had previously told me that I would be going out as the FO from now on. But he decided to make one last patrol and check me out and make sure that I knew what I was doing.

Gunnery Sergeant Jimmie Clark

Sometime down the road, I am not sure how far out of A3, we had contact with the NVA. The 3d Platoon had contact first at the edge of the woodline. They got some sporadic fire. And at that time the headquarters group that I was travelin' with—Captain Frank, the company commander, and a couple of radio operators and maybe a runner and myself—was travelin' with the 2d Platoon.

Corporal Gary Conner

We had gone quite a ways. It was probably a click and a half anyway from Alpha 3 to the east. My platoon, 2d Platoon, was on line, approaching an old vill. There were some scrub trees, we were in scrub bushes but spread out in the open approaching a hedgerow.

Hospital Corpsman 3d Class Alan B. "Doc" Sams

I was assigned to 3d Squad, 2d Platoon, on that particular mission. It was the 3d Platoon which bumped into the bunker complex. They were supporting us with flank security to our right, heading east, and through an accidental discharge of a Vietnamese soldier's weapon, this firefight broke out.

PFC Bill Clough

It didn't seem like very much at the time. Really wasn't that much fire, just a few sporadic rounds. But they got pinned there and took quite a few casualties right away. We got on line at Captain Frank's direction and proceeded to cross an open field into a treeline, and once we got into the treeline we found out that there was quite a considerable force of NVA regulars. They later on estimated it to be a reinforced battalion. In the process, Everisto took my map from me. I guess he didn't have time to fool around with me under the circumstances. He and I and Daniel Kaplan, who was his radio operator, proceeded to get on line with everybody else, and we ran into some barbed wire right at about the center of where everything was going on.

Gunnery Sergeant Jimmie Clark

We left the road and was going to sweep behind where they were getting fire, to help the 3d Platoon out. We crossed by some huts and people working in their gardens or fields or whatever. Real friendly folks, it seemed at the time. Well, we moved on through those huts and the 2d Platoon moved on into the woodline, in behind where the 3d Platoon was getting their fire. Well, all hell broke loose.

Corporal Gary Conner

We got in to within probably twenty yards, maybe a little more, of the hedgerow and the higher vegetation and all hell broke loose on us.

Doc Allan Sams

We had small-arms fire coming from ahead when we hit the dirt. We got on line and proceeded through the treeline while running. I asked the sergeant next to me why we were running on line through a bunker complex which had not been checked out and we did not know for sure whether there were enemy soldiers in these bunkers. I was challenged by the sergeant not to continue questioning but just to continue running. We ran on through this bunker complex until we were near a hedgerow. Almost directly in front of me about twenty-five yards away, there was a soldier running towards us that apparently was a North Vietnamese soldier. He was about six feet two inches, the biggest thing I'd ever seen in Vietnam, and had a blue cap on his head with a red star in the center of it.

Members of our squad opened fire on this individual and he disappeared in a hail of bullets and fire from the M79 grenade launcher. At that point, we took refuge in this very small hedgerow in a depression in the ground, and every other Marine turned around facing rear for security, because we were going to then stay in this position as a defensive line of fire while the 3d Platoon pushed the enemy forces into our line of fire. However, we did not know at that time that this was a battalion-sized enemy force.

PFC Bill Clough

Part of the line swept on across the trail and about ten or twelve of us had to push over to the right to try to get around the wire. And in the process of doing that, we started taking a lot of fire from our right front. To the best of my knowledge, everybody who went across the trail to my left was killed later on. I never could figure out exactly where they were killed, but everybody that got across the trail there that didn't shove to the right was eventually killed, and that included Everisto Johnston and Daniel Kaplan. We ended up in about a twelve- or fourteen-man perimeter there and we were taking fire and mortar rounds and it was really the worst chaos I've ever been in, although in just about every firefight nobody seemed to know what was going on. This was the worst one. We were taking fire from two or three different directions and there was even some sniper fire coming from the area that we had just swept across. I ended up right on the trail and everybody else was circled around me, either lined up down the trail or back in a perimeter facing back in the field in a small 360 [degree perimeter]. Anyway, I was the person in the corner at the barbed wire and the trail. In the confusion and the haste, they forgot to pass the word and they ended up moving out with everybody else while I was looking down the trail.

Doc Allan Sams

I was sitting down in a hedgerow wondering what I was to do with myself, because at this point there had been no casualties on our part. There was some small-arms fire in our immediate vicinity, but things quieted down for a few moments. The next thing I remember, there were enemy soldiers sneaking up from our rear. As I turned around, someone hollered "corpsman" and I looked to my rear, which was the area that we had already run through, past the bunker complexes. Apparently the bunker complexes were occupied with North Vietnamese soldiers. They had come out of the bunkers and they were advancing on our rear position and we were totally exposed.

We knew that there were no friendly soldiers either to our front or our rear and we were a singular line of a squad in this hedgerow. So looking to our rear, we could see the North Vietnamese advancing on us. One of my Marines called "corpsman" even though no one had been hurt. I asked, "Who's hit?" and they indicated no one was hit at that point. I saw a grenade tossed into our hedgerow and it was picked up by one of the Marines in my squad. Quick, Charles Quick, picked up the grenade and tried to toss it clear. But that grenade left his hands and then exploded. I then made my way towards this area where two Marines on either side had been hit by shrapnel. One was a fellow by the name of Feliciano who was wounded and had lost an eye. He was also wounded in the shoulder. The fellow next to Quick on my side, Quarrels, had been hit in the shoulder and the arm with shrapnel but was otherwise intact. Quick, as I rushed over to him, was bleeding from the head and face. I tried to perform a tracheostomy because he was unable to breath and he was gurgling. As I created the tracheostomy he died. At that time his helmet fell off and I realized that the grenade had caused the top of his skull to be removed and there was no way to save him.

PFC Bill Clough

I turned around and nobody was there but me. One of those fluke things that happens in war. I laid there, probably for thirty or forty minutes, it seemed like a week. NVA soldiers kept walking up to me and jumping down on the trail and I killed . . . about five in that area. Shortly after that, I had decided that it would be a real good time for me to be moving somewhere else because I didn't have any security on either side. All I could see was what was in front of me and I didn't think that it was going to be a long time before the NVA figured where the fire was coming from. So I got up on one knee and was looking around to see if I could see any friendlies, and of course it was not real thick vegetation but there were a lot of treelines and I really couldn't see anybody.

During that process, I just glanced to my left and about the time I looked over there an NVA threw an chicom at me, from about twenty feet away. I don't know why he didn't shoot me, I never did see his rifle but . . . he almost hit me with the doggone thing. I knew it hit the ground close to me, but I couldn't find it and finally after looking for it for what seemed like an hour, I decided it was going to go off. And I got just as flat as I could and was about to give up on it when it finally went off and it put shrapnel in my rifle but fortunately didn't wound me other than some tiny fragments which came up about a week later. The concussion made my ears ring really bad and blood in my nose, but other than that it wasn't anything serious. But it did convince me that it was time for me to move. With all that I yelled "Friendlies!" at the top of my lungs, and some folks just happened to be about fifty or sixty yards away from me on my right flank. It was about the longest sixty yards I ever remember moving.

Finally I did hook back up with elements of the 2d Platoon. And there again were about fourteen or fifteen guys in a perimeter and almost all of them were wounded. At least half were wounded three or four times. We did manage to establish a perimeter there.

Gunnery Sergeant Jimmie Clark

Our headquarters group, we were cut off from the 2d Platoon or anyone else. We had NVA between them and us and behind us and all around us. We were receiving fire from every direction and were really in it in a bad way. Captain Frank, he kept jumping up and down just like a jack-in-the-box, you couldn't keep him down. We kept pulling him down and the limbs was cracking all around us and we couldn't get nothing, no info from the 2d Platoon radio. All we could get was screaming over the radio. But Captain Frank finally got to where he could talk to the radio operator and we found out that the platoon commander had already been killed. Lieutenant Deeter. And that they were in a hell of a mess. And there wasn't many of them left alive even then, from what we could get from the radio operator.

Doc Allan Sams

At that point I was to the far extreme of my squad and could not make my way back to where my position was closer to the main body of the platoon. I was trying to center myself near the platoon near the radioman and the lieutenant, but at that point I was pinned down. I tried to minister to one or two other people who received small-arms fire, but the fighting at this point had intensified greatly and we were in a full-fledged firefight, both to our rear and to our forward position. We were calling in artillery fire and airstrikes.

Lieutenant Bob Montgomery

My radio operator got ahold of the firing battery and . . . all the time I was trying to pinpoint exactly where we were and as luck would have it, the map was not good for that area . . . we found out later. But in any case, we started walkin' out 105 rounds and kept snappin' them in as close as we could get 'em. All this time my radio operator and I never moved. We had a good position behind a hedgerow and we could peek around it or lift up and see what was going on. I looked over a couple of times to my right flank and there was a rifleman over there and farther down the road, a little farther, was a . . . machine gunner. So I thought we were probably in as good a place as any.

However, after about two hours of that, I looked over and apparently that rifleman had been shot. Right away. Because all the time that I thought he was looking straight out at where the firing was coming from, he was . . . poised there . . . dead. That was my first time ever seeing anyone, a human being, shot . . . and killed. I didn't have much time to think much about it at that time. It was fast gettin' dark.

Corporal Gary Conner

I think our platoon was somewhere around thirty-five to forty men. Most of the fellows went down either killed or wounded in the initial few minutes. I was laying there. My lieutenant was on my left flank. I had a machine gunner and his A-gunner [assistant gunner] immediately on my right flank. We called for fire missions right away. It was standard procedure for us FOs to follow where we were on the map very closely because at any point in time we may be calling in an artillery mission, so it was common practice for us to be moving through the brush and picking out a spot up ahead of us and firing an orientation round. If we weren't sure where we were, we'd fire a white phosphorus, too, to make sure that we had a pretty good indication of where we were. And that was very difficult. The maps weren't really worth a damn. If you were lucky enough to kill a North Vietnamese who had a map, you took his map, because they were much more accurate than ours were, and just transposed our grids on there. Anyway, we called a fire mission right away. The fire was so heavy we couldn't even adjust with white phosphorus, because we couldn't pick our heads up high enough to look for the white smoke. We adjusted just by the impact of the high-explosive rounds, and we started dropping them on the North Vietnamese within a very short time and we were very accurate.

Doc Allan Sams

It was late in the afternoon. Fighting was still continuing and I was, at this point, the most extreme individual, that is . . . the most flanking of the individuals in my squad, having been pinned down next to Willie Adger, a black fellow who was facing rearward and was the most remote individual in the squad.

I had got myself pinned down beyond Willie Adger, trying to get to a fellow named . . . Robinson. But Robinson was dead when I got there. I did have an M16 at this point. We were under full fire. There was no one injured that needed further assistance, so I was going to try and lend support to the Marines. The M16s that I attempted to use all had shrapnel wounds that made them unserviceable, and the magazines for the ammunition, which I recovered, were in the same condition and wouldn't feed into the weapons I was able to find. I did, however, find grenades that were nearby. I pulled the pins on a couple of grenades and tossed them out of the hedgerow, both to my right and to my left, to sort of clear the field of any people that might have been in that area that were North Vietnamese.

This apparently proved fairly satisfactory and it gave us a breather until Willie Adger caught my attention and tapped me on my foot. I looked at him and he looked at me and in a very calm voice said, "Doc, I'm hit." As he said that, I looked and indeed he had a bullet hole immediately between his eyes. And then he very calmly and quietly slumped forward in death. The importance of this, I realized, was that even though Willie had been hit, he was alerting me, knowing that I was the most extreme individual down this line of friendlies. Being hit, he realized that he was going to no longer be able to provide security for me. He was letting me know that I was then on my own. I'll never forget what Willie did for me.

The squad . . . was pinned down and could not move; it was getting dark. I was trying to work my way back to the main body of the platoon and was checking pulses of those members of my squad. I remember checking the pulse of Willie Adger, of course, Feliciano, and fellows named MacPherson, Ripley, and Robinson, and these individuals had all been killed.

I did arrive at Manter, Ferguson, Granberry, and Shelton. These individuals were pinned down with me and ended up spending the night in this hedgerow. I was trying to maintain a sense of calmness. The fighting had died down in our immediate area. The artillery was ongoing. An artillery barrage had been called in on our position. Mortar fire was quite heavy during this period of time, and I distinctly heard 1st Platoon or the main party of our company being pulled back to regroup just outside of the treeline, and I knew where that was. But I also knew that there were enemy positioned between us and that clearing.

I also knew that when they pulled back, our company would then be calling in reinforcements and be sending mortar fire into the area. Indeed, the 60-mm mortars were sent in as fire and we were just very fortunate that none of these rounds hit us during the night. These rounds took some of our hedgerow out and it came very close, but we were spared. The spotter plane came by and I had a flight panel with me and I was trying to flash this flight panel. I was laying flat on my back trying to indicate to the spotter that indeed there were still some friendlies in this area after our main force had withdrawn to set up a perimeter.

Corporal Gary Conner

Word came somehow to pull back. I don't even know how it came. We did try to pull back. I crawled over to the machine gunner and the A-gunner. They weren't but five yards from me. I crawled over to try to get the word to them because they weren't moving. They were both dead. My lieutenant and I turned around, crawling, and managed to begin to withdraw back to the west. We didn't know what we were withdrawing into. But we did manage to get back some distance. I don't know how far we did go, but the relief forces from Alpha 3 came out and we linked up with them.

As soon as we got a reasonable degree of distance between us and what appeared to be the frontline NVA forces, I called to our counterparts, our 81 FOs that were with 3d Platoon. I called them initially to find out what their situation was. I never got any response from them, which wasn't unusual because our radios didn't work half the time. I ended up trying intermittently all night long, never once thinking that they could have been killed. In the morning we again attacked the treeline. We couldn't get in. We took more casualties. We were getting a lot of hand grenades, a lot of mines, command-detonated stuff. We just couldn't get in.

PFC Bill Clough

During that time, Ward and a guy named Eddy Lazata crawled out under some pretty intense fire in a wide open trail. There was an L-shaped treeline on the other side of about a ten-acre field there and a trail running straight out from us. There was a couple of guys laying down there hit, and Lazata and Ward crawled out. Of course, we were trying to suppress fire back across to the treeline, and as they were crawling out, some gook was in the trees, throwing chicoms out in front of them as they moved along the trail, and Ward was just crawling up to them and picking them up and throwing them back into the treeline . . . like he was on a Sunday stroll, except for the fact they were crawling. They did bring the two Marines back in. Both of them were dead.

Gunnery Sergeant Jimmie Clark

Finally, we got the 1st Platoon linked up with us quite late in the afternoon. And the 3d Platoon finally moved on down and we all got together, maybe five or six hours after the initial contact. The whole company, what was left of the whole company, got back into one outfit, and not separated into platoons as we were.

Then we started getting a little movement with some of our troops to get in and help out the 2d Platoon more. We got in and got some of our casualties drug back and we got some of our KIAs back inside of our lines. We tried to get helicopters to evacuate our wounded and we had quite a task in doing this. We tried to get back through the area of where we had come, back to the road, away from where all the firing was going on. And we had the NVA who had moved around to the huts and the places we had come through, and we couldn't get back in that direction to establish an LZ. We brought choppers in, when they could get in, and in most cases they came in on a hot LZ. Our KIAs remained on position, but our worst wounded we got on the choppers. And then, the battalion had Mike and Lima companies on the way to help us out.

Major Ray Findlay

We took off on a tank-infantry attack, the only one I saw while I was out there. It went as planned that night. We went in there and as I was running behind one of the companies, I looked in this little hedgerow and there was this NVA soldier standing there. I didn't know who it was. There was a lot of chaos, the way attacks are supposed to be. You just go straight ahead. The guy looked at me and I looked at him and I wasn't convinced it wasn't another Marine. I took my pistol out then, although I could never conceive of shooting anybody with that thing or hitting anybody anyways. I jumped in on him and we captured this guy and we kept him in the battalion for a couple of days.

PFC Bill Clough

When we did take the wounded back to the helicopters, the fire was so loud that I couldn't hear the helicopters running. I don't know to this day how the helicopters were able to get in and out.

Gunnery Sergeant Jimmie Clark

Mike Company came out from A3 and they joined up with us. Before they got there, numerous amounts of times we had tried with the remaining troops that we had to get through to the end of the 2d Platoon and get in with them and we could not penetrate to where they were at. We would find out later that they [the NVA] let the 2d Platoon walk into and beyond their position before they opened up and that was the reason we couldn't get in to them.

Before Mike got there, we called in jets and the jets came in and dropped 250-pounders [a bomb commonly used in close air support]. They came right over our position and we were so close to them that a time or two I thought that the 250s were going to land on us instead of them. We received shrapnel back from those into our position, and then we had Army rocket ships [Hueys fitted with rocket pods] come in and run down the lines right in front of us. It was fifteen to twenty feet to where they were firing their rockets. We were too close to call in artillery. At that time I wouldn't have given you a plugged nickel for my life 'cause I didn't think any of us were going to get out of it.

After all this, Mike Company arrived on the scene and set up a perimeter defense around, and then we pulled back into the perimeter to spend the night.

PFC Bill Clough

Strange coincidence. I was talking to a kid named Jimmy Rice. I think he was twelve months and twenty-six days in country. And while we were talking, lying flat on the ground almost, he was hit by a sniper round that really rung my ears. He was on my right-hand side and it rung my ear real big like a close round would do. I don't know how in the world it ever missed me, but it did miss me and hit him through the temple. Oddly enough, in '82, his dad sat down on a bus beside myself and three other friends up in Washington, D.C. I guess God sometimes does influence what we do to bring about good things.

Gunnery Sergeant Jimmie Clark

Along about dusk Captain Frank led an assault, one last assault to try to get through to the end of the 2d Platoon. We received such heavy stuff that there were two chicom grenades [that] bounced off Captain Frank's flak jacket, just bounced off it. It was so hot in there that we couldn't get through and we had a couple more KIAs in that little skirmish and some more wounded.

Doc Allan Sams

At that time I felt isolated and surrounded by the enemy. This later turned out to be the true case. The spotter plane apparently did see us . . . I didn't know whether he did at the time . . . and called in airstrikes, and the airstrikes were warned not to hit this hedgerow, if at all possible. I also remember an A-4 Skyhawk coming in with napalm and watching him do his dive and drop his napalm, and that napalm took out everything to our western side, behind the hedgerow, scalding the hedgerow and blackening everything in the area, but did not harm any of us. I also remember that this would use up all the oxygen when it exploded and warned everybody to hold their breath long enough so we could survive the explosion itself if we weren't burned with the napalm.

Corporal Gary Conner

We had napalm so close you could feel the air being sucked into the combustion of the jelly gasoline. It was just a horrible situation. There wasn't a lot of fire coming from our side because most of our fellows were either dead or incapacitated at that point.

Doc Allan Sams

The next morning the relief forces come in. They called in tank support and it was the tankers that found us. The wounded were all still alive in the morning. I stayed awake all night so I could hear if there was motion in the bushes, so if the enemy pulled out and left a suicide squad behind, that we might be best to stay put. I knew that the Marines would be back in in the morning to clear the area and that they would find us if we could just make it through the night.

Gunnery Sergeant Jimmie Clark

And we pulled back out and pulled into Mike Company's perimeter for the night. We didn't have any of Kilo's people on the perimeter that I remember. We were trying to regroup. We had men out there—and we didn't know if they was dead or alive—that we hadn't recovered or we couldn't account for. And what we did was try to figure out who we'd lost, who was killed, who was wounded. We were very mixed up. I was new as the company gunny and didn't know all the personnel, and we were up all night trying to figure out who was out there and who we had. It was a long night, I'll tell you that.

Sometime that night or early morning three tanks joined us. We took the three tanks and they pushed through the position where 2d Platoon had been. What NVA hadn't been killed had moved out of the area. They slipped out sometime in the night. And what we found was some wounded people who had laid in there all night. Doc Sams had laid in there all night and he crawled around and helped what wounded he could through the night.

Doc Allan Sams

I didn't count on the tanks. In the morning, they [the tanks] did come and they laid down a barrage of fire, which I knew they would, at this hedgerow—which was not a big hedgerow and the depression was just enough to sort of hide your body with a pack on it, but it wasn't deeper than that. I knew that if anything really got down toward the ground level, we'd be hit. And I said, "What a shame if we made it through the night only to be found warm but dead in the morning from our own friendly fire."

However, I was trying to think how to get the attention of these people coming through. I realized that if I fired back at them, they would call everything in on top of us and we'd be gone. I realized that if I tried to get their attention by just calling out to them that we'd be considered North Vietnamese and pulling a trick and we'd be eliminated that way. So I was in a quandary as to how to get the attention of our friendly troops and yet not be killed in the process. I also knew from this firefight that everybody's emotions would be extremely high and they weren't going to wait around and find out if this were friendly or not; they would eliminate it first and then check it later.

I heard the tanks and that alarmed me a great deal, because I figured they might do clearing fire with the tanks and we'd really be in a fix then. They didn't use the tanks, however, but tracer rounds came over our head. You could hear the people and when I thought that they were almost upon us, almost where they could see us, I blurted out every known expletive that I had ever come across in my experiences, and that includes everything that the Marines had taught me, which was quite extensive at that time. This enabled me to gain the attention of those people who were firing in our area. . . . I heard the comments, "Hey, guys, there must be Marines over here." And I said, "You're damn right there are Marines over here. Just don't fire." And I cautiously kneeled up and then stood up, fully expecting to get blown away when I did. Fortunately there was enough control with the Marines coming in that we did survive.

Corporal Carl E. "Tank" Elliott

When we were sweeping through there the next morning, we came across a dead Marine with two dead corpsmen draped across him. It looked like they were trying to protect this guy from the enemy fire.

Doc Alan Sams

They helped us evacuate that area and called in medevac choppers. We medevaced Granberry, Shelton, Ferguson, and Manter. Granberry was next to me when we first had the grenade thrown in to my right. Later that night when I was on my stomach and was going up and checking pulses and checking people to see who was alive and who would get out with us, I came across Granberry and he was the first individual with a pulse, besides Ferguson, and when I felt the pulse, I called his name. I said, "Granberry," very quietly, of course, because we were still surrounded. He looked over at me and told me, "Oh, Doc, I'm glad it's you." Apparently not long before me, a North Vietnamese soldier had come up to him and had been checking the bodies in that area. They were either looting or they were checking for life or what, I don't know. Granberry related that he was concerned that someone else had come up to kill him. He remembers a North Vietnamese soldier talking over him and then a bayonet being placed between his side and his arm, indicating that the North Vietnamese soldier knew that he was alive but chose not to kill him.

Aside from this, Granberry had been involved in a crap game or poker game the night before our February 7th firefight and had a lot of money on him—I think it was $1,000—and he was concerned that somebody was trying to steal it. I assured him that I was not interested in his $1,000. I was interested in his being able to survive. Indeed, he got medevaced with his money intact and I hope that he made it through the war okay. I don't know.

Gunnery Sergeant Jimmie Clark

We retrieved, I think, nineteen wounded and KIAs out of there. What NVA was left in the holes were chained to the guns in their holes so they couldn't get up and run. I think it was finally determined later that there had been approximately 100 or 111 NVA killed.

We lost twenty-nine KIAs and we had thirty-one wounded in action. The next morning when we pushed through to retrieve our people, Kilo didn't want nobody else to do it for us. We went in and retrieved our own and brought our own people out. We wouldn't let Mike nor nobody else do it. We were pretty beat and torn up, but we had to do it. And we went in and did it.

From there, once we finished pushing through and getting our people back, we were getting concerned about getting our KIAs out and we finally decided to take them to Gio Linh on the tanks. So what we did, we loaded all the KIAs on the three tanks and we took myself and a squad of Marines and we left from there with the three tanks. I was the only one from Kilo who went and I followed the tanks down the road with all our KIAs going to Gio Linh.

Corporal Gary Conner

It was a very horrible experience to be involved in. We put the bodies of our dead Marines on the tanks. The last body we loaded on the last tank was that of Jimmy Rice. Jimmy had, I believe, seven days left on his tour in country. As we loaded him on the tank, he was on the right side of the tank. He had been shot in the head and the blood was just dripping on the tank track as the tank drove up the trace. It's a sight that I just can't ever forget. But it was one of I'm sure thousands and thousands of similar experiences that other fellows had.

PFC Bill Clough

Colonel Marsh was standing there inside the perimeter when Kilo did make it back the next day. And . . . he shook hands with me and said, "You Marines did a good job," or something to that effect, and that made a lasting impression on me that a new CO would come out and do that. So I always thought he was a superb leader, and it seemed like every time one of the companies was in trouble, he or Major Findlay would come out and, when needed, provide leadership and direction. And I thought that was fairly important because a lot of the leadership we had in Vietnam was untested and untried.

Corporal Gary Conner

Everisto Johnston had twenty-three months in country and this was his last patrol. He volunteered to go on it because he had a brand new FO that he was going to show the ropes to. The radio operator, Dan Kaplan from Cedar Rapids, Iowa, was a very good friend of mine, a very good radio operator. He was killed. Johnston was killed. It was an extremely stressful, emotional situation.

PFC Bill Clough

Strange situation there. The first body I found was Kaplan's body. After going through all of them, I had hopes that Johnston had been medevaced but oddly enough, one of the last bodies loaded on the tanks, somebody was asking . . . was keeping a list of the KIAs . . . asked somebody who it was and I heard them say it was Johnston, the 81s FO. So I went over and looked at the tank and sure enough, that's who it was. So the first I found was Kaplan and the last one was Johnston. . . .

I remember a lot of confusion and I guess one of the good memories I have about Vietnam . . . . I was giving first aid to a guy name Teague who was about forty pounds heavier than me and I was having a devil of a time. I'm holding him on his side and he had a sucking chest wound. I don't know how long I did that but quite a while, and we were still taking fire and waiting on medevacs and . . . somewhere during the course of that time I kept this kid held on his side long enough for a medevac to get in, although he had turned blue and was barely breathing and was almost stiff when we put him on the helicopter. Somebody told me that he survived, so I've always felt pretty good about that.

Gunnery Sergeant Jimmie Clark

Now that's what I remember about the 7th of February. It's an experience I'd never want to go through again or have anyone else go through, but I'll never forget it as long as I live. I know one thing: through that whole episode, our company commander, Captain Frank, he was what you would call a *company commander*. He was cool, calm, and collected through the whole thing. I have thought about it many times and I know that I was sure scared and I think everyone was scared and I'm sure that he was too, but he sure kept his cool under fire and he was really a company commander. He cared for his troops, his men, and he did a hell of a fine job. And I know that all the men that was there that day will never forget what Captain Frank did and how he did it and how he operated and took care of his company. He is a mighty fine man.

Something to add to what has already been said. Doc Sams crawled around out there and gave water to the wounded and treated the wounded Marines all night out there, with the NVA all around them. The wounded Marines that was out there, they played dead while the NVA took ammunition and water and personal effects off the Marines. They played dead. In fact, the NVA shot some of them as they laid there on the ground. But they laid there and played dead. Doc Sams received a Bronze Star for that action. And also Gunnery Sergeant Zemsky received a Bronze Star. He was with the 3d Platoon that day. I received a

Bronze Star, and Captain Frank, I believe he received a Bronze Star. He should have been awarded a much higher award.

We regrouped pretty fast and re-formed the 2d Platoon. We only had, as I remember, four people left that was in the platoon. We took the rest of the company and new people that we had gotten and we re-formed the 2d Platoon back again, and I think within a week we were back out on patrol and doing what we normally did in our right rotation. They felt that if we sat in there too long and cried over our wounds and the people that we'd lost, well, we'd get down and never get back on track, so we were back out beating the bush soon after that. Which I think was a darned good idea.

PFC Edwin Seretti

I got to be my squad radioman and sometimes when the whole platoon went out, I was a platoon radioman. I remember trying to move up. I was trying to get better and better all the time on the radio. There was a guy who didn't have long to go, I think he was a company radioman, his name was Jenkins. I remember him getting killed and me feeling really bad about moving up. When my platoon went out to bring the bodies back, throwing them on top of tanks when they had rigor mortis in them, he was one of them.

Doc Allan Sams

Corporal Harris was the maverick of the platoon. He was a loner. He was experienced, he was wary, and he was very capable. He most often took point and did a remarkable job of doing that service. However, in the perimeter area he was generally considered to be a goof-off and not a very by-the-book individual, which led him into some problems with the administration while we were in the bunkers and the perimeters. However, there was nobody that one would rather be with in the bush and outside of the perimeter than Corporal Harris. I do remember telling Captain Frank about that and suggesting that he be placed for the Medal of Honor for his actions on that day of the 7th. Early that day before we got into the treeline, Corporal Harris had advanced toward the treeline . . . and slightly into it, retrieving two or three wounded Marines from the 1st Platoon . . . and dragging them to safety. Corporal Harris had been struck several times by enemy small-arms fire in the chest and had started IV [intravenous] fluids and patched up the Marines he had dragged back and was going back for more when we insisted that he be medevaced. This was against his nature. He wanted to go back and get more Marines out and go and engage the enemy again. That was Corporal Harris.

Corporal Gary Conner

When it was all said and done, I believe we killed in the neighborhood of 140 to 150 North Vietnamese there. Some of them were in uniform. Some of them were in civilian clothes. I think they were obviously heading down towards some of the southern battles, possibly to reinforce the activity that was going on down at Hue.

Major Ray Findlay

It was the joke around the battalion, the one prisoner I captured. And we got in trouble because we kept him for a few days. We liked him. First of all, he was a neat little guy. He could write with his right or left hand. And second of all, he was an infantryman, right? He's not going to hurt anybody too bad.

It was the most interesting thing that happened out there. After the war, one of the things that I was happy about, we didn't kill that guy. There wasn't any need to. He was behind what was going on. He was totally confused. The only reason I jumped on him and started pounding on him with my pistol was because he scared the daylights out of me. It was one of the times I can remember that my heart was racing when I saw that guy with a rifle.

I gave one of the guys in the command group my R and R for capturing the prisoner and then when he went to Bangkok on R and R, he brought back these pictures of all these lewd and lascivious things that he'd done when he was there. He's probably in my debt forever!

They finally took the NVA back to a POW camp. The thing that was funny, they sent him back to division and he got away. Jim Marsh, the CO, the 2, the XO, all these guys in high-level positions were being berated, beaten about the head and shoulders, because we kept this prisoner out there longer than we should have. Then when he got back to division, they let him escape.

Battalion records reported 139 NVA killed during the 7 February ambush. Three days later, elements of 3/3 discovered another 60 NVA graves. Expended and discarded enemy equipment and ammunition were found in the area for weeks. There were also reports that villagers in the region of Gio Linh treated large numbers of North Vietnamese wounded.

Giap's roll of the dice, the General Offensive, General Uprising, was a military failure. It was poorly coordinated and did not take into account American ability to rapidly deploy their forces from the frontiers back to the cities. Most communist units were routed within a few days, although fighting went on in Saigon for two weeks and in Hue for nearly a month. The enemy lost somewhere between 35,000 and 45,000 troops, most of them VC, in contrast to about 3,000 killed on the allied side. Manpower itself was not that difficult for the VC to replace. What hurt them most was that their professional officer and NCO corps was decimated by the event. Many U.S. units reported the poorer quality of VC soldiers after Tet.

Moreover, the population of South Vietnam failed to rise up against Americans or against the Saigon regime during the offensive. On the contrary, communist atrocities committed in Hue and elsewhere mobilized the civilian populace against the VC and NVA. Only 2 percent of several thousand communist POWs captured during Tet reported having received active assistance from civilians.

Tet was also a high point for ARVN performance. Fighting for their lives and families, they fought heroically. Desertions dropped dramatically, and a higher proportion of those drafted reported for duty.

However, the violence of Tet, coming on the heels of Westmoreland's predictions of victory, shocked the American public. Reports of initial VC and NVA gains gave the impression of smashing successes for the enemy while in fact U.S. and ARVN troops soon stabilized and recovered lost ground. Adding to the general dismay, Westmoreland's request for 200,000 more troops was misinterpreted. To the media, to the public, and to many influential Washington officials, it appeared that the additional forces were needed to forestall further disaster. From this point on, the Vietnam War became a political liability of the greatest magnitude. Meanwhile, the servicemen in Vietnam fought on.

29

A SWEET LITTLE AMBUSH

PFC Craig Pyles

In mid-February we had that ambush that 1st Platoon India sprung southeast of A3. We had gone over toward Gio Linh, turned south, and then we were working our way back toward A3 and were sort of following a little valley. As we got to one section of that valley my platoon, the 1st Platoon, was all the way in the rear.

Corporal Tom Ryan

That ambush was one of the best ones I was on. We set up, the whole company set up a big perimeter and we just lolly-bowed around and we dug in, our platoon, in the middle of it and we put out some bangalore torpedoes all along the trail that was right in front of us. We just sat in there and as it got dark, the rest of the company booked [departed].

PFC Craig Pyles

My machine gun was positioned right at the joint of an L in the trail. We sat there for maybe an hour or so when we heard 81 mortars. They were being fired from back at A3 and I could hear that hissing sound going way over our heads and they were coming down on the other side of that valley. They seemed to be getting closer and closer.

Finally I hollered over to one of the guys in my gun team, Kopp, and I said, "Look up there and see where those damned mortar rounds are hitting." Kopp sort of peeked his head up over the bushes, and then he popped back down and his eyes were just as big as silver dollars. He looked at me and he said, "Gooks! Holy shit!"

They were coming right at us. They were walking toward us, although I couldn't see them yet. So everybody sort of got themselves ready. I got up on the gun and was waiting. Then I could hear the gooks talking. They were just babbling to each other like it was nothing. Then I see one go by and then another one right behind him and . . . that trail was not more than maybe ten feet off to my right. I looked through the bushes and saw a third one.

He had one of those big NVA packs on and was walking the way the Vietnamese walked, with that funny lope. I looked right at the guy as he walked by. He looked in the bushes and I don't know whether he saw me or he saw the guy next to me that was drawing a bead on him with an M16, but suddenly his eyes got real big. He got about a word or two out of his mouth as he tried to grab the guy in front of him to dive for cover.

That's when everybody opened up. I just cut loose with that machine gun and held back on the trigger for all it was worth. The really crazy thing was I couldn't even see what I was shooting at. When we set that gun in, we had it set on the tripod and we had the T and E locked down [the traversing and elevating mechanism, which allows precision control of machine-gun fire]. We had good grazing fire all across that rice paddy. Joe Craig on the other machine gun was to my left about twenty-five yards away, up on a little rise. So I had the grazing fire and he had the plunging fire and I knew we had these son of a bitches cold.

I looked over at my A-gunner who was also my team leader, Milton Lee. Milt looked at me and he pointed up and he said, "Chicom, chicom." I looked and there was this little tree to our right front and there was a chicom hanging right up in the fork of a tree. He'd seen a guy throw it and it hung in the tree. This probably only took just seconds for this to happen. When you tell it, it seems to take so much longer. Then it exploded, *boom,* all this black smoke and stuff. For a second I was just sort of stunned, unbelieving that I didn't get hurt. I found out later that evening when I got back I had a nice hole in one of my canteens from it, but I didn't get a scratch.

Corporal Tom Ryan

It was nice to be on the other side for a change. Everybody just opened up, just blasted everything out there. We didn't receive too much back because that was a good ambush. Felt good that time. They pulled us back and kept artillery fire in the area, blowing up the area all night. The next morning we came out first.

I picked up a few souvenirs then. I took a helmet and pair of shoes, the pack. I got everything but the person. These were uniformed NVA soldiers. We had a half dozen at least . . . who knows how many they took away.

PFC Craig Pyles

The dog handler and the dog found an NVA who was still alive. The guy had crawled up under some bushes and had taken his pants off trying to administer himself first aid. His back, his buttocks, and legs were all peppered with shrapnel from one of those M26 frags.

When I got over to where they found him, the dog handler was trying to restrain the dog and the corpsman was holding up bandages talking to this guy trying to explain to him that he was going to bandage him up and take care of him. The dog was going kind of crazy and the little NVA soldier realized that the dog was there and sat up, turned pale, and started babbling. I guess he was terrified we were going to turn that dog loose on him. Then he just sort of fell back down on his back and then expired.

Captain Otto Lehrack

That was a sweet little ambush. I don't remember the exact body count. We found several on the scene and one of the other companies found some more that probably came from the same ambush a few days later in shallow graves. The guy who found the live NVA was ecstatic, because if you captured a prisoner, you got an extra R and R. The corpsman started working on this gook because he was in bad shape. He even started an IV on him. The Marine who captured him was standing by with a smile on his face and even gave him a cigarette, when the dog started in on him and the gook's eyes just glazed over and he died. The Marine was real upset and cursing and kicking him and all. He said things like, "You son of a bitch, you lay out here all night long alive and I find you and you have to fuckin' die." And, *pow*, he'd kick the gook again.

PFC Craig Pyles

That was my first experience with having to grab ahold of a dead body. The company gunny told me and another guy to grab ahold of this NVA soldier and take him over to one of the fighting holes that we had and throw him in there. It was a gruesome experience, to say the least. I can still remember how uncomfortable it was grabbing this guy by the ankles. I had one ankle and another guy had the other one. We just sort of dragged him over the ground. His head was bobbing, his eyes were open, it was like he was looking at me. We just sort of threw him in a hole.

It's one of those horrors of war that stick with you forever. You don't forget it. It's hard to reconcile that, less than twenty-four hours before, we were in a struggle of life and death trying to kill each other, and then when you watch the guy face-to-face die and then have to grab him like an animal and throw him in a hole, it's kind of disturbing.

Captain Otto Lehrack

We stuffed him in one of the fighting holes we had used, like we did the others, threw a little dirt on him, and left. The stench along that trail was enough to make us want to avoid it for a few weeks. Sometime later we took a patrol past there and here was this gook's skull poking up through the dirt. It was an odd feeling. Seeing him die, burying him, and then, sometime later, seeing his skull looking at you and remembering what it looked like when it had flesh on it.

PFC Craig Pyles

It was interesting—the excitement of all that when we got back and everybody was talking about what they saw. We knew we'd really kicked their butts. We really put a hurt on them and yet we got out of there without a scratch.

30

. . . .

INTO THE DMZ

Captain Otto Lehrack

Termed a "reconnaissance in force," the operation began on the 16th of February. We moved to the east, about halfway to Gio Linh, and then crossed into the DMZ parallel with an abandoned railway.

PFC Craig Pyles

The North Vietnamese had a loudspeaker up in the DMZ that used to play music all night long. The next thing I know, we're kicking off this operation like two o'clock in the morning and hiked all night long. Then we came to that railroad bed. It was the main railroad that ran all the way from Hanoi to Saigon. It had to be one of the spookiest things I've ever done in my life. We walked up on that railroad bed that crossed a long stretch of rice paddy. On the other side was where you actually got into the Demilitarized Zone. As we crossed that trestle, it kept getting more light. Here we were out in the open and the music kept getting louder and louder. It was really like something out of a movie. To

me it was really frightening, real spooky.

Corporal Tom Ryan

We left at midnight and we walked across along that crest of that abandoned railroad and I was walking the point. Point. I always liked point. I'd rather be up front anyway where I could know what was going on when it did happen.

Captain Otto Lehrack

India Company was in the lead. It was the first operation into the DMZ itself since Operation HICKORY the previous summer. The plan called for us to cross into the DMZ a few meters west of the railroad. Unfortunately, this was in the middle of the monsoon season, the paddies were flooded, and the water in our path was over our heads. We nearly drowned a couple of our heavily laden Marines and battalion was on my back about coming up with a solution to the problem. So I just took a deep breath and said, "We're gonna use the railroad." It was elevated at least ten feet above the surrounding terrain and to an alert enemy, we would have been just like ducks in a shooting gallery. We double-timed across that sucker and all got across before we made any contact.

PFC Reb Turner

The sun was coming up over the hill as we were coming across the rice paddy and up the hill. My platoon was in the lead going across, assholes to belly buttons. We went right into a bunker complex.

PFC Jim Yost

We start finding this long trenchline of mortar rounds, 82-mm Chinese variety. And we were checking that out when the scouts up front shouted, "NVA," and opened up. They were carrying a pig on a pole for a barbecue and they thought we were the other NVA joining them. Then when we opened up on them, all hell broke loose. And we were scattered.

PFC Reb Turner

Mansfield looked like John-fucking-Wayne crawling along. He was on his back and he was throwing grenades in bunkers. I was an ammo humper and I turned gunner about two seconds after that shit began.

PFC Jim Yost

And about fifteen minutes into the firefight, Sergeant Dicker got a AK round into his shoulder and he went down. I was the closest one to him. And I immediately rushed over and . . . put a combat bandage on him, on his shoulder . . . . He was bleedin' pretty bad.

Captain Otto Lehrack

We obtained some initial air support in the form of a couple of F-8 Crusaders whose only usable firepower against ground targets was a few 20-mm rounds. They managed to get the gooks to put their heads down for a few minutes and that was about it.

PFC Jim Yost

One of the killed was Harry. And Ski, from Pittsburgh. I finally broke away and rushed up and Harry had took a round in the throat and the stomach. By the time I got to him, he was dead and so was Ski. But there were six Marines in front of them in a bomb crater hole, about five meters from Harry and Ski. I jumped in and they were out of ammo and everybody was pretty well shot and tired with their nerves, and several of the men were wounded and they were out of ammo and they had a sniper shootin' and gettin' closer.

Captain Otto Lehrack

The bomb crater our guys were in was in an open area, completely exposed to enemy fire. Moreover, there was an AO report of a large enemy force approaching on the ground to reinforce the group that had them pinned. We finally got them out by using M79 tear-gas rounds. I had been given about a dozen of them to test on an experimental basis. I collected them all, passed the word to don gas masks, and had a couple of the gunners lay them in the treeline upwind of where the gooks were. That gave us enough of a break from the NVA fire to recover our casualties.

We lost four killed and seven wounded that day. One of them was Harry Matthew who was posthumously awarded the Silver Star for pulling Sergeant Dicker to cover under intense fire. We were credited with sixteen NVA KIAs and we blew a lot of their mortar ammunition and bunkers.

Corporal Tom Ryan

We took some casualties, but it felt like we kicked more ass that time than they did. We crossed that DMZ and went right into their base camp. They had food still cooking. There were ammo bunkers. We just started blowing things up and meanwhile we kept getting reports that they were lined up on line and coming back on us. I used to pride myself on saying there ain't nobody in my squad got hurt a couple of times when we hit shit. This was one of 'em. I got a week left in this god-forsaken country. But anyway, we came out of it pretty sweet. It felt like another win.

FEBRUARY 1968

Although General Westmoreland reports in his memoir that there were only two instances before 1972 when the NVA used tanks—at the Lang Vei Special Forces Camp near Khe Sanh and once in the central highlands—there was one other, when two NVA tanks crossed the trace near Alpha 3.

Sergeant Tank Elliott

The thing with the tanks was Tet 1968. We was set up in a night ambush, south of A3. I was the 3d Platoon sergeant of Mike Company at the time. John Aaron had a starlight scope with him. He spotted them at first. They were east of us, in between us and Gio Linh village. And they were heading south. The gooks were using loudspeakers and playing music to cover the sound of the tracks moving. We didn't have any LAAWs [light antitank assault weapon—a portable bazooka] with us, so what we did was call in eight-inch guns from Con Thien and they blasted the area.

Then we pulled back, went back into A3, and never saw these tanks. Sometime later, after I had left 3/3, some intelligence officers from division came over to where I was transferred to in Dong Ha, and they told us that they had found two heavily damaged T-76, Russian-made amphibious tanks. [Tank Elliott's account of this is very modest. Besides his nickname, he won a Silver Star that night.]

·

PFC T. J. Kelly

I just loved to call in napalm. One time in Leatherneck Square, I singed my eyebrows as I looked at it and I should have had my head down in a hole. Then we would call in those 250-pounders, snake-eyes, and nape and that was the preferred load. ["Snake-eye" bombs had a special tail fin that slowed their descent. This allowed the pilots to come in low, drop them accurately, and still leave enough time to get away and avoid being damanged by their own bombs.]

Helicopters were amazing things. We'd run night medevacs talking those guys into your zone with no lights on and we'd be surrounded, which was not unusual at night out in the bush. Guys would come in just by trusting your voice, and you'd carry the wounded guys and put them on the helicopters and it really felt good when you heard that they made it. I medevaced an awful lot of people, I would say close to a hundred, maybe more, maybe more, wounded and dead. I always liked to get the wounded out before they became dead.

·

Lance Corporal Ed Seretti

I got hit in the head and the rounds just kept coming. Doc Judd came out right in the middle of all that, and he dragged me in the trench and patched me up until the medevac came and got me. I thought my eye was gone. I was still delirious and I stuck my finger in a hole there above my eye. I thought for sure it was my eyeball socket. I remember feeling almost . . . relieved. I thought my eye was gone and then I said, "Well, at least I'm going home."

31

. . . .

MIKE COMPANY AMBUSH

PFC Lex Payne

On March the 6th, we left out of Alpha 3, headed into an area northwest of Alpha 3 and northeast of Con Thien. We moved until we made contact with the NVA and that's when we found out we had them right where they wanted us. They had artillery support and mortars set up, and they were waiting on us with an ambush. We walked into it.

Lance Corporal Vito Lavacca

Nothing was as bad as when Mike Company was ambushed on March 6th of 1968 . . .

PFC Thomas Evanoff (Brand New Guy)

My life basically changed March 6th, 1968. Just as daylight was breaking, we walked into a battalion ambush. From then on it got worse. Halfway through the day into the afternoon, we were taking so many casualties we couldn't get them out. I'd never seen a dead person before or even been to a funeral.

Corporal Vito Lavacca, who became a Mike Company squad leader after the March 6, 1968, ambush, with an unidentified Vietnamese man. (Courtesy Vito Lavacca)

PFC John Mick

I think we had fifteen KIA that day in my platoon when we walked into the *325th [Division's] 27th Regiment*. It was dark when we went out and we were all kind of scared because we didn't know what we were going to run into. Someone says, "Hey, the sun's going to be hitting us and you should carry plenty of water." I carried five canteens of water that day. I loaded up, like, nine grenades. I carried 752 rounds, I'll never forget that amount. I know I was weighed down, but I was never so thankful as I had that ammunition with me when we got out there.

Lieutenant Bill Kenerly

March 6th. By that time my platoon had sort of shaken out of the doldrums that we had been in and we had the point on that day. We knew that we were probably going to make contact in that area. Of course, the whole reason for the March 6th operation was that intelligence had reported that there was a road through the DMZ in that area and that the North Vietnamese were moving supplies down by truck. The objective on March 6th was a piece of high ground that we were supposed to use as an observation post, to sit up there and spend the day looking for this road and any movement along it. It was Company M's operation.

PFC John Mick

Our squad was walking on line. We stopped at the base of this one little hill and I saw these blades of grass with a lot of footprints all around them in the mud. Luce was next to me and Ronald Ellis. He stood straight up. The next thing I know, there was a gook up behind this great big tree on top of this hill and he opened up. When he did, one round hit Luce just below his rib cage close to his belly button.

I reached down and grabbed ahold of Luce when he was shot. I asked Doc Winslow if I could help, and he said, "Help me hold him down. Help me hold him down." He kept trying to get up. I sat there for what seemed like forever and watched this guy slowly die. The blood drained. What happened, the bullet went through him, which we didn't realize. Luce was a big man. You really couldn't see what went on on the back side. The doc was trying to stop the front and it was all running out the back of him. We just couldn't get an IV in him and his veins were collapsing. Luce died right there.

As we started advancing up the hill, Freddy Brookins ran to the right. There was a machine gun sitting on the ridgeline just a little bit above us. It had us just in its sights and opened up and hit right across Freddie Brookins. M79 grenades blew up and blew out a whole section of his right side and his fingers were blown off. He was a big black guy, a super nice guy from Philadelphia. He was killed there.

So I kept on advancing. If we'd waited another ten minutes I think they'd have killed a lot of us, because they were setting up a .30-caliber machine gun. Thank God we surprised them.

Lieutenant Bill Kenerly

When the fighting broke out, I tried to get my mortars in position. The hill that we were supposed to be on was entirely too overgrown with vegetation to shoot a mortar from the top of it, so I moved my platoon and the mortars down into a creek bed where the mortars could set up and didn't have the overhead cover that would keep them from firing. At that point in time we weren't involved in the firefight. It was going on 150 or 200 yards away. We hadn't been there long, maybe twenty minutes, when the captain radioed me that he needed one of my squads to reinforce 3d Platoon. I detached a squad and sent them over there. That happened three times.

By the time I got to where the firefight was, myself and my radio operator were all that was left. Everybody else had been assigned out somewhere to reinforce the line at different positions, so I didn't have a platoon to command. I was told by the captain to go up on the hill, where one of my squads had reinforced right in the middle on top of the objective. I was told to go up on top of the hill and to organize the evacuation of casualties from that point. There were . . . a couple of dead and some wounded up there.

So I went up and did what I could to get those people moved off of the top of the hill. Once they were cleared out, I stayed up there and attempted to move our people down the sides of the hill. We certainly, at that point, had not received any artillery or mortar fire but were expecting it . . . literally at any moment, and I was trying to get them spread out and down the slopes of the hill.

Each time we sent a stretcher-bearer back with dead or wounded, we sent back requests for hand grenades. My troops had thrown all of theirs. I had given the four that I carried to them and we were out. We sent back request after request. Nothing happened. Somewhere along in there Colonel Marsh, who was with us that day, came running across this little field. He had one of those flak jackets with the big bellows pockets on the front. He had both of those pockets full of hand grenades and had his two arms full of hand grenades. He came running up that little hill and he dumped what must have been twenty or twenty-five hand grenades at my feet. I was literally struck speechless at that and said, "Colonel, what the hell are you doing here?" And he said, "Well, you said you needed hand grenades." With that he went back to the CP. That, at the time, was probably the best thing that he could have done to keep my spirits up. It was a real morale boost on what was becoming a very crummy afternoon.

PFC John Mick

The firefight kept on going. Lieutenant Miller called me over and a guy by the name of Tiny. We went over towards him and Tiny fell. I looked down at him and I thought, "Oh God, he's dead." He carried a little pouch on his flak jacket, a little pocket we had, he used to keep a pouch of .45 rounds in there. By some luck of God the bullet hit that pouch, ricocheted off there, but was enough to hit him so hard it knocked him out and we thought he was dead. He came to and we were sitting there talking and he scared me to death. We opened up his flak jacket and all it was, was a great big bruise on him. This guy later on ended up getting six Purple Hearts out of Vietnam.

PFC Lex Payne

It was the only firefight that I was in, in the open, where the gooks actually massed up and attacked us, sweeping on line like our tactics. We were pulling the pins on the frags and letting the spoons go and counting to three and throwing them and getting an air burst just to keep them off of us.

PFC John Mick

We advanced around the side. We didn't attack that machine-gun bunker because after we got hit we forgot what we were doing because everything was happening around us so quick. A guy named Thatcher ran ahead. Well, we got up on the hill and we were looking over when Thatcher screamed a bloody scream. We called down, "Corpsman up. Corpsman up." A gook threw a chicom in there on him and it blew his left leg off just about six inches above his knee-cap. When I jumped down there with Doc Winslow, red, dirty-looking blood was pumping out of his leg. We put a tourniquet on and helped pick him up and carry him out of the hole.

Lieutenant Bill Kenerly

I moved off the top of the hill for a while toward our right flank. I had a squad engaged there. I crawled down to them and as I got there, they were beginning an assault into a bunkerline. My 3d Squad leader was a corporal named Charlie Lee. He said, "Hey, Lieutenant. We're going to check out this bunker." We could see a dead NVA laying in the door of it. So Charlie Lee, his 1st Fire Team leader, whose name was Hall, my right guide (a guy named Bobby Pigg), my platoon sergeant, who was a sergeant named Gonzales, and me moved in on that bunker. Lee and Hall were out front.

When we got to the edge of the trenchline, there was a .45 pistol laying in the trench that one of the M79 men who had been wounded earlier dropped. Pigg jumped down in the trench, grabbed the .45 and emptied it into this guy that was laying in the door of the bunker and into the contents of the bunker itself. We were just kind of watching him, obviously not doing what we should have been doing. I heard a burst of automatic-weapons fire and I could see the bullets strike Lee and Hall. I could see the stuffing flying out of their flak jackets as it hit them across the shoulders and neck and face. They both fell in the trench. An NVA came out of an adjacent bunker and was startled to see us standing there and wheeled an AK47, fired one long burst, and dove back into the bunker. It wasn't even a particularly aimed burst, but it killed Charlie Lee and B. R. Hall where they stood. We all hit the ground at that point trying to figure out where the hell the fire was coming from. I called to Lee and Hall. At that point I wasn't sure that they were dead. We didn't get any response, so one of the troops slid into the trench and pulled them out while we provided cover.

They were both nearly decapitated by the burst of fire. I'm sure they never knew what hit them. Charlie Lee had been my friend. He had had two years at the University of Maryland. We were the same age. He had gone to Cuba before he came to Vietnam. His dad was a career Marine officer. He had gone on that patrol to help me. He had had ringworm on his tail and the battalion medic told him he didn't need to go to the field. He only had forty days left in Vietnam. He had been in fact staying in the rear, but when he found out where we were going that day, he came back to me after I briefed the squad leaders and said, "Lieutenant, you're probably going to step in it over there, and I'm one of the few people that you've got that have been in a real firefight before and I want to go along so I can help."

PFC John Mick

Woppo, my squad leader, was getting short. I think he had a few days left. He went over and picked up a body, I think it was Corporal Lee. Six of them ran over and a mortar round came down right next to him and took almost all of them out. One other guy was killed, but Woppo had both of his arms, the muscles torn completely out of his arms and his face was just peppered with little teeny pieces of fragmentation all over his face. It took quite a few more people to medevac them out. Our mortar team fired just two or three rounds; it wasn't but a few seconds later that they fired their mortars and knocked our mortar team completely out. It was one hell of a scary day.

PFC Lex Payne

After about three hours when we were running out of grunts, the gook artillery had Lima Company at Alpha 3 pinned down where they couldn't leave the gates and they had the Marine battalion and Con Thien pinned down. They couldn't leave and assist us either.

Lieutenant Bill Kenerly

Things were so confused that as I looked around I had maybe twenty people, twenty-five people, in what the company commander was calling my platoon and about half of those were from other platoons. I had a gun squad that I knew. I had six or eight riflemen and my right guide and that was about it. But these guys hung tough and maybe twenty of us provided security for the company as it withdrew.

As the company withdrew through our lines the mortar fire started to come in. The North Vietnamese mortared the hell out of the top of the hill. That was the most frightened I hope I'll ever be in my life. When we pulled off the hill, the North Vietnamese seemed to come up it. We were taking direct rifle fire.

Every time we tried to move I was either taking wounded or we were getting near misses. The mortars were slamming into us and I lost one rifleman killed with a direct hit. My gun team was wiped out.

I had tried to do a little fire and maneuver in reverse—that is, a team cover, two teams pulled back, those two cover, one pull back—and that worked for a while, but we got eventually into a flat area where we were just getting chewed up. We had pretty much gotten all of the wounded out. There was one man dead that we couldn't get to. I finally gave the order that each man was to help the wounded man nearest him and we were to get up and just run like hell . . . and that's exactly what we did.

By some absolute miracle nobody got hurt when we ran that last forty yards or so to get out of the line of sight of the rifle fire. We realized at that point that we had left one of our dead, a man named Ronald Dobbs, a black man who was in my platoon. The operations major [Ray Findlay] was there. He asked for volunteers to go back and get that body. I didn't volunteer. The major, Staff Sergeant Veteto, and maybe two other men went back and got Dobbs' body. The ten or twelve of us that were left were sort of semicircular, providing some security at that point. They came back with Dobbs without taking any casualties and we were starting to pull back. By that time I was carrying my own radio and was armed with an M79.

Earlier in the withdrawal phase . . . a hand grenade had hit my radio operator's helmet and had fallen at our feet. We both ran four or five yards and hit the ground. The hand grenade did not go off. It was a dud. After that, he couldn't talk for forty-eight to seventy-two hours. His name is Kevin Sweeney. It'd be interesting to hear what he says about March 6th, but he has been in and out of VA hospitals and he thinks that part of it was March 6th and what happened on that day and specifically the damned hand grenade that didn't go off.

PFC Kevin Sweeney

March 6th. We were hit so bad . . . I can't talk about it.

PFC John Mick

David Cutshall had been wounded in January. He'd caught one through the leg and just got back on March 5th. He was getting ready to throw one of those new M33 grenades and a gook threw a chicom which landed real close to him. He dropped his grenade and went down for it. It blew his arms off up above his elbow, both arms. I couldn't even recognize him. The only thing I know is he had a tattoo on his arm and it was written in Vietnamese and it said, "A penny saved is a penny earned," or something like. Cutshall was one heck of a Marine.

He had a beautiful girlfriend back in California that used to send him gobs and gobs of goodies all the time. He'd pass them out to everybody and that girl wrote to him daily and really missed the guy.

Lance Corporal Vito Lavacca

The worst part was . . . carrying somebody back to . . . what we were trying to clear as an LZ . . . to get the bodies out. And goin' back there and seein' a whole pile of bodies. Just stacked on top of one another. A guy named Ron Ellis. They called him Moose. Moose was the epitome of what a Marine should look like. He was a big guy, about six-three, six-four [height], dark hair, big kind of lantern jaw. Good lookin' guy. Deep voice. Funny. Came from someplace around Chicago. And Moose was the kind of guy that you would think couldn't ever be killed. And I remember goin' back to where the LZ was . . . and seeing Moose laying on the top of the pile with a grin on his face. . . . And I remember just stopping in the middle of everything and . . . and . . . just hangin' my head and . . . just shocked . . . that Moose could be killed.

PFC Tom Evanoff

There was a brother sitting there. He had a hole in his left side. I'll never forget his face because everything was on his face—terror, shock, "it couldn't happen to me" kind of look. His mouth was wide open, his eyes wide open. It was all froze this way. He was dead. They told me to grab him and put him on the chopper. We started throwing them on the choppers. First I tried to be careful. It just seemed like the thing to do, but there was just too many of them. We just kept throwing them on the choppers. As the choppers were rising it looked like water, rain, was coming out of the choppers. It was the blood flowing out. Pretty soon it was late afternoon.

The CO, Captain McAdam, came up to us and said that we had to get out of here. He pointed back towards Alpha 3 and told us all to meet at the big tree. Everybody that could was packing the wounded and the dead that we couldn't get out on the choppers back to Alpha 3. I was packing a guy on a stretcher and I gave the corpsman my rifle because I figured it wasn't going to do me any good anyway . . . hell, we were down to almost no ammo. When we got back to Alpha 3 it was already dark. I almost dropped the stretcher and crawled down into the bunkers. We just picked a spot to fall down and sleep because there were so many empty spaces. The rest of the companies pulled watch for us. We were all in shock. The next morning we got a roll call on who got back and who didn't. We lost one-third of the company. All of the machine gunners and just

PFC. Tom Evanoff is shown guarding NVA POW in spring 1968. (Courtesy Tom Evanoff)

about all the A-gunners, the medics, a lot of people. A lot of good Marines were lost that day.

Lance Corporal Vito Lavacca

In the morning, somebody, a runner that I didn't recognize, came in, woke me up, and asked me if I was Lance Corporal Lavacca. And I said I was. He said the captain would like to see me. I went up to the CO's bunker and there were just a handful of us there. And the captain told us that we were the . . . squad leaders and platoon commanders. . . . And the five or six of us just looked around at each other and uh . . . we just couldn't believe it. I think there were only about thirty or forty of us left that hadn't sustained some kind of wound.

Lieutenant Bill Kenerly

This was my first real firefight. I talked with the company commander about needing to get back to the field before everybody got crazy on us.

PFC John Mick

As far as I can really sit down and relate back in Vietnam, I think March the 6th sticks in my mind more so than anything else. I mean, mortars and artillery scare me, but sitting there and seeing people to the right getting shot and people to the left and everybody around you getting hit—really, it shook me up so bad at that time that when I got back I didn't know whether I wanted to shoot myself in the leg or the arm and try to get out of this. I really had those thoughts, but I just kept saying to myself, "What would my mom and dad think if I shot myself in the leg or arm trying to get out of combat?" I just don't think I could live with myself if I did something like that, but I really had those thoughts. I couldn't believe that our platoon of forty-five guys, when I got back, there was like seven of us and everybody else was either killed or wounded. It really shook me up.

32

• • • • • • • • • • • • • •

GREEN JUST LIKE THE
REST OF US

Lance Corporal Vito Lavacca

Shortly after March 6th, Captain McAdam called me up to the company command post and asked me about a black guy named Woodward, with whom I had gone through training back in the States. Woody had apparently stolen a jeep from an officer down around Danang. And . . . in lieu of disciplinary action, they were lookin' for somebody who would accept him in their squad, and the captain asked me if I was willing to vouch for Woody. And . . . would I want him in the squad. I had no problem with Woody. He always struck me as bein' a good Marine and Woody and I had a fairly decent relationship. . . . But one day, I was given another black guy who'd just come from the States. This guy was a Black Panther, came from the South Side of Chicago. Real bad dude. I don't know what movement of the stars led him to the Marine Corps. Probably some judge. Anyway, this guy had a real bad attitude. And we were preparin' to go out on a patrol . . . and being the new guy in the squad, I asked him to carry the base plate for the mortar.

He refused and we got into a bit of a confrontation. This guy . . . pointed his rifle at me and told me that he wasn't carryin' any base plate for the mortar . . . when Woody came up beside him, put his arm around his shoulders and his .45 to the kid's head, and said that . . . suggested that he pick up the base plate and . . . also that we were going out on a patrol now and if anything happened to me, Woody was gonna hold this kid personally responsible.

Well, that didn't do anything to ease the tension, but it got the patrol under way. We headed out and we hadn't had water in a while and the first bomb crater that we came to, we stopped to fill our canteens. It was really nothing but just a big mudhole with a water buffalo floating around in it.

I suggested to this new kid that he fill his canteens, and he was real surly and told me about how he wasn't gonna drink this kind of water. I suggested that he fill his canteens anyway and if we found fresh water, he could always pour it out. But he wasn't gonna take any advice from me. The rest of us filled our canteens and we moved on and it was hot and about midday this kid just fell over from heat exhaustion.

I guess the base plate was a little too much for him. But we all passed our canteens up and we poured a lot of water over him and we gave him water to drink, which he didn't seem to have any aversion to under the circumstances.

From then on, without any other words being exchanged, his whole attitude seemed to have changed and he became just another one of the guys. He wasn't black anymore; he was green just like the rest of us. And brown from the dirt.

There wasn't very much racial tension at all. If there was, in a situation like this, in the beginning, it didn't last very long. After a firefight or some type of situation, it . . . like the one with the water . . . it kind of defused itself. And again, it came back to that . . . everybody watchin' out for each other. New guys coming over all seemed to come over with preconceived notions . . . dispositions . . . personality quirks . . . uh . . . maybe that's what I experienced when I landed at Cam Lo. But after a very short time in country . . . you suddenly seemed to all have been stamped from the same mold and suddenly your values were the same as the next guy's. Which is what the Corps is all about.

MARCH 1968

Sergeant Major Neal D. King

Sergeant Major King enlisted in the Marines in 1942 and served in the 21st Marines in World War II and the 5th Marines in Korea. He was in Vietnam first on advisory duty in 1962, returned as the sergeant major of the 4th Marine regiment in 1965, and then volunteered to come back to Vietnam, for a third time, in 1968.

Sergeant Major Neal King in Leatherneck Square in 1968 on his third tour in his third war.
(Courtesy Neal King)

I'd rotated back to Hawaii, to FMF Pac, and became the sergeant major back there. During this time from July '66 until I came back in country in March 1968, I did seven trips back into country. While you are there at FMF Pac, you're living the war but you're not in it. I said to them, "Well, I'm going to go back in now. Because I just don't feel right here. The American people aren't with it, but at least they're doing the right thing over there. I'd rather be with them." So I volunteered and set it up so I'd come with the 3d Battalion, 3d, and I was transferred and I arrived with 3/3 in March 1968.

When I first joined 3/3, I joined them at A3. It was sort of reminiscent of the French, living in a fort. I was impressed with the outfit, in that with Colonel Marsh, the fine leader that he was, and Major Findlay, we had two real cracker-jacks.

·

Lance Corporal Vito Lavacca

After March 6th I had a squad for the rest of my tour. And we managed to hold together pretty well. My feelings on patrols were that the most important thing was silence, irrespective of anything else. If we could move quietly on patrol, my feeling was that we could surprise the enemy or at least hear them before they heard us. We'd always take the trails . . . which was against the conventional wisdom at that time, and we'd always take the river beds. And we'd be absolutely silent. The men in my squad were pretty good at that.

·

Gunnery Sergeant Jimmie Clark

We got a first sergeant who joined us, 1st Sergeant I. V. Long. He flew into us from Stateside just before an operation and he was an old recon Marine. He had muscular dystrophy years ago and they gave up on him, but he told the doctors that he would outlive them and he did. He joined us and he was unacclimatized and we got started and he got too hot. He picked up a stick and told me to take that stick and he said, "Don't you let me fall behind. Don't you let me get behind or stop. You take that stick and you beat me until I get to the top of that hill. I'm not going to quit down here and nobody will have to carry me up that hill." We kept him watered down and we got him to the top of the hill and I've never seen a Marine like that in my life.

And later on he made sergeant major and transferred from us and went to Dong Ha. And someone threw a grenade in his bunk one night. They had to evacuate him out of country, but after that grenade hit him and he had shrapnel all in him, he got up and yelled for his jeep driver and walked to the jeep and got in the jeep and they drove him to the airstrip. That's the kind of Marine he was.

Lance Corporal Ed Seretti

Actually doing the fighting, I was not that scared. After it was all over and after every firefight or every incident, that was the worst time, for some reason. It was always the worst time when it was all over, thinking about what I should have did or what I could have did. Another bad time was getting off the choppers, getting into a hot LZ or something, that sickening feeling in your stomach. It was awful. And I'll tell you another thing that really, really got to me was the sound of those rockets . . . that incoming sound . . . it sounded to me like a woman screaming. It was an awful, awful sound; it just went right through you.

PFC Bobby Jefferson (Brand New Guy)

I got to Vietnam in '68. I knew that this was goin' to be a big change in my life. When I got off the big plane down in Danang, oohhh, the weather was so hot. I kinda just walked off the plane and the heat just took my breath. We stopped off in Danang overnight. They assigned me to the 3d Marine Division which I didn't know what the 3d Marine Division was. Next morning we got on a C-130 headin' up to Dong Ha.

They was taking bodies off the plane . . . the same plane that I was gettin' on, and that like to scared me to death. I didn't know what to think so I got on the plane. This guy on the plane asked me did I have a Bible. And I told him, "No, I didn't have one," and he said, "You can take mine, 'cause you gonna need one." And that almost scared me to death. When we got to Dong Ha, we was gettin' incomin' . . . on the airstrip, so . . . I didn't know what to do . . . I just followed everybody else and we went and jumped in these holes they had dug along the airstrip, 'cause I guess they was expectin' this. That like to scared me to death.

Sergeant Major Neal King

Colonel Marsh . . . he would sit down to eat a C-ration and he'd say, "A grateful republic has rewarded me once more."

Corporal Tom Ryan

When I left, I rotated around the beginning of March. I went to the rear, got my shit together, and I go down to Danang. I want to get outta here, so I'm waiting in this line you gotta wait in and here comes this friend of mine I went to school with. He was down from Khe Sanh with 3/26. Eddie Pendergras. He was down there on an in-country R and R and he had a case of beer and a friend of his, Perez, from New York City. So the three of us got the case of beer and went out to China Beach. I was done with my paperwork there and I gotta wait another day or so. Pendergras is supposed to fly out of there that afternoon. So we got time. We run over to China Beach. We got a case of hot beer. We got our shirts off and we're sittin' on the beach soppin' old times and stuff. We're talking about high school and this and that.

Things got carried away a little bit, and we were drinkin' all this beer and that wasn't enough. Now we went looking for more beer and we found a little beer slop. We were sloppin' down the beers and one thing led to another thing and we got pretty smashed. And we get back late and he is supposed to take off . . . . And now it is the next morning. I'm supposed to go late that afternoon or something. Anyway, our drinking went into the next morning. We just kept drinking and partying. There was no stoppin' us.

He ran into this friend of his from ITR and he was an officer now and he was gonna get us a jump out of an airplane into the Danang River. And we were all up for it. You know, the beer was doing our logic for us by now. We were all for it, drinking all night, and we were "yeah yeah yeah, we're going to jump into the Danang River there." Like parachuting practice. I had never parachuted and I wanted to try it. Well, anyway, it fizzled out the next day. Somebody wouldn't let us. Meanwhile, Eddie and his buddy, they missed the plane that was supposed to take him and Perez back to Phu Bai.

When I get home, I finds out that they got back to Phu Bai a day late and they manifested on the plane as numbers seventy-eight and seventy-nine. Well, the plane only took seventy-seven people from Phu Bai to Khe Sanh and they were left. And they knew they were in trouble now. They were AWOL and blah, blah, blah. To make a long story short, that plane never made it. It got shot down coming in at Khe Sanh and everybody aboard died.

And my buddy was in the newspaper back home. They couldn't tell them they was drunk and that was why they missed the plane, so they made up a big story how Perez went back to get this present he had bought for his mother and they missed their plane. Now we always talk about the time I saved his life. In fact, how he named his first kid Ryan. After me. He'd start telling somebody about how I saved his life in Vietnam and they're ready for a machine-gun story and then you tell them it was over a case of beer.

33

• • • • • • • • • • • • • • • • •

PAYBACK

Lieutenant Bill Kenerly

The 16th of March, the NVA were caught napping. We were moving along the crest of the hill and somebody in one of the other platoons spotted a machine gun that did not have anybody manning it, and the entire company went down on their bellies and faced uphill. And several NVA were walking around on top of that hill, walked into our ambush, and that's what started the fight.

The company did well that day. We had a couple of men killed and some wounded, but we fought our way into that trenchline and I think the company got credit for forty or fifty KIAs, but the NVA shot down a jet that day and shot up a spotter plane pretty badly.

PFC Lex Payne

March the 16th we went out and we left before daylight. The point man had a compass and we all followed him holding on to canteen belts. Just as day was breaking we came up on the NVA and they were taking a crap and they were cooking rice and there were several of them still sleeping in their hammocks. So naturally we went wild. We had a field day with kicking their ass.

When the day was over, when we collected their weapons and stuff they'd dropped when they ran and everything, we found the mortars they'd left and their RPG and B40 rocket rounds all had marked on them "3d Battalion, 3d Marines," you know, the regular slash 3/3. We were pretty well impressed with ourselves because we were proud because here we had an NVA unit that had decided they were going to hit us, but it turned out that we paid them back and we did it in good fashion.

Lance Corporal Vito Lavacca

After March 6, Mike Company started to rebuild. And suddenly, you're in country for months and you're an old salt. And . . . you start to feel very old when the replacements come in, and their dark green utilities that haven't been faded by the sun and the mud. Well, March 16th, 10 days later, we went out on another patrol and . . . this time we fared a lot better. There was a saying at the time that "Payback is a motherfucker." And that's really the way we felt on March 16th. Charlie had been set to ambush us, but we spotted 'em. And this time we were ready. We were about twenty-five yards away and there was a bomb crater between our line and their line. A little black guy named Thrasher . . . got up to the bomb crater . . . and he started hurling grenades. We couldn't reach them from where we were. But we would toss our grenades up to him . . . and he'd pull the pin and toss them over to Charlie. And Thrasher alone must have wiped out half of their line.

I've been trying to think of the most heroic act that I witnessed while I was there. But . . . hell, I think . . . there was so much of that no one incident stands out. . . . Shit . . . it was an act of bravery just to get on the plane to go over there. Uh . . . maybe Darrel Thrasher. It was like a bucket brigade. Everybody tossin' his grenades up to each other and getting them up to him . . .

I heard from the radioman that one of the pilots . . . who could see the back of the ridge said that it looked like there were hundreds of them, just running from the airstrikes. It's a sad thing to say . . . but . . . it made us feel like we had atoned a little bit for the guys who didn't make it a couple of weeks earlier.

Captain Otto Lehrack

March 16th stands out as the best day I had in the entire war. When Mike Company became engaged with the NVA, I went out to OP Gold to take a look. OP Gold was forward of Hill 28, which was forward of Alpha 3 and was the closest position to the DMZ in all of South Vietnam—about 150 meters across a rice paddy from the Z itself. It also afforded a good view of Mike Company's firefight.

We kept a 106 recoilless rifle, a .50-caliber machine gun, and a squad of Marines with an FO out there all the time. Sometimes we even had a tank. OP Gold belonged to India Company and the NCOIC [noncommissioned officer in charge] out there was a Staff Sergeant Reidel. Reidel had built some lawn-type chairs out of ammo boxes and would lie on one of these things in the trench below ground level and sun himself. Mike Company was pushing the gooks off Hill 31 to the northwest, and the only way off the hill was on a rice paddy dike that was in full view of OP Gold. Some of them would, from time to time, try to cross the paddies, but apparently the water was too deep because they always returned to the dike.

Anyway, I had an 81 FO out there with me and every time they would try to get across the paddy dike, we would call in a mission and just blow the hell out of them, bodies flying everywhere. The 106 was anxious to get into the act, especially when the 81s had to stop firing for us from time to time to fire direct support missions for Mike. So, during those times I had the 106 load beehive rounds, which were antipersonnel rounds containing about a jillion little steel darts that just filled its target full of lots of little holes. They wouldn't penetrate the skull, however, and we'd find dead gooks with a couple of dozen of them just sticking out of their heads. We fired beehive up the gazops until we expended all we had. From that point on, we fired antitank rounds at groups of them as they'd cross the dike.

Late in the afternoon as the traffic was thinning out, we saw a lone gook stick his head out to peer at us from the back of Hill 31, to see if it was clear. He was almost like a cartoon character. When no one shot at him, he picked up a little steam and started tippy-toeing across the dike. Well, the 81s were shooting for Mike and we were out of beehive, so the 106 gunner says, "Come on, Skipper, let me have just one more antitank round." So I says, "Fire the 106."

Well, the gunner pinged out a couple of .50-caliber tracer rounds from the spotter rifle mounted on the 106 to get the range. With that, the gook really picked up speed and took off for the only shelter in sight, a large tree about half-way across the dike. I yelled to the 106 gunner, "Shoot for the tree." The gunner had already figured it out and fired the antitank round at the tree. The gook reached the tree about a tenth of a second before the round. *Blam!* The round, which could penetrate something like eleven inches of steel, hit this tree about three feet off the deck, shit flew everywhere, and the tree wobbled and then toppled. If the gook survived, which I doubt, I'm sure he's told this story a million times, too.

The reason that I thought that it was such a good day is that I had dragged Sergeant Reidel's "lawn" chair out of that trench and spent the afternoon relaxing in it with my binoculars, adjusting fire and killing NVA. Not a one of them thought to shoot back at us on OP Gold.

·

Although a variety of factors drove Lyndon Johnson from the White House, the strong showing of peace candidate Eugene McCarthy in the New Hampshire primary was confirmation of the president's weak political position. In a speech to the American public on 31 March 1968, Johnson announced that he would not seek reelection. At the same time, he further limited the bombing of North Vietnam and called for negotiations.

The process of limited bombing in an attempt to encourage the North Vietnamese to open negotiations was folly and was easily manipulated by them. The enemy quickly learned that when the United States applied unbearable pressure they could relieve it with a few vague promises that it was not necessary to keep. When things were going their way, they could ignore American pleas for negotiation.

PFC Jim Yost

We were listening to the radio and the news came on that LBJ was not rerunning for president of the United States, and the whole damned perimeter, you could see Marines throwing their helmets up and cheering. We had felt we had lost support from our Commander in Chief because he had stopped the bombing and was trying to negotiate as we were still fighting a war with an enemy that used deceit and lies as tactics. We were beginning to understand some of the demonstrations back in the States. They were turning against the American soldier in the field, so our morale was down and we were disgruntled. We were making contact and getting high body counts all the time.

34

• • • • • • • • • • • • • •

THE DAY
MARTIN LUTHER KING, JR.,
WAS SHOT

Lieutenant Bill Kenerly

I went through a period of about two months where we were just never called on to be the point platoon when the company was out. In spite of my hope that we could do our job and avoid a fight, I was still depressed by the fact that the company commander didn't trust me enough to give us the point position. My squad leaders shared that and we worked toward doing better. On the operation where I was wounded, which was a battalion sweep from A3 down to Cam Lo bridge, we were the first platoon in the battalion out of the wire. We went out the day before to set up some ambushes along the battalion's route of march the next morning and also to secure a hill that was the company objective the first day.

India Company officers at Dong Ha, April 1968. From left: Captain Otto Lehrack, Lieutenant Dave Brown, Lieutenant Paul Carr, Lieutenant Bill Douglas, Lieutenant Corky Schron. (Courtesy Otto Lehrack)

PFC T. J. Kelly

On this operation in Leatherneck Square, I was assigned to India Company as their one-four [tactical air control] operator. After about three days of this operation, we set up in the afternoon on this ridge and Mike Company and Lima were on the far end and India and Kilo were on the north end of the ridge, and no sooner had we gotten there than we started taking mortars, 82-mm. The battalion command group with all the radio antennas were by Mike Company CP.

Captain Otto Lehrack

When the mortars started coming in, Corporal Mike Picreaux, one of my radio operators, and I were up near the battalion CP. We figured we had nothing important enough to keep us around the impact area, so after the first rounds exploded around us, we got up and ran back to the other end of the perimeter where India Company was, rapidly picked out a spot, and started digging. We got several volleys of rounds and between them we'd dig like hell. After several months of digging holes every day, my hands were really calloused, but this ground was so rocky that I tore off all the callouses and ended up with bloody hands. So much for the motivating power of incoming.

PFC T. J. Kelly

We set in that night and we took a probe [enemy activity around one's defensive position] and a lot of chicoms. They were throwing these chicoms over the lines and all the way over up into the India CP. The suckers were going off all over the place. I found out later that they were putting these things on bamboo poles and using the spring and flexing action of the pole and just whipping these things a country mile.

Captain Otto Lehrack

That night as we finally finished our hole, sent out the night activities, and got the frag order for the next day, Corporal Picreaux and I settled into our rocky little hole. After some shuffling around trying to get comfy, I said, "Hey, Pic, this gas mask makes a pretty good pillow." Corporal Picreaux's reply, delivered with the salty tone that only an old timer in country can use: "No shit, Skipper. Maybe you're not such a boot after all."

PFC T. J. Kelly

The next day India went on a patrol. We went over to the east trying to find where that mortar was. We were climbing up kind of a ridgeline and all of a sudden the point held up, and way, way, way down the end of this valley were two gooks sitting on the side of a hill eating chow. A sniper team came up and these guys took their time; it took them a good five minutes to set up the shot. It was a black guy, the sniper, and he had one of those bolt-action Remington 700s [sniper rifle] with a big scope and he fired and the round hit this NVA right in the chest and the guy just laid back into the hill. He ejected the shell and put another one in there and fired again at the second guy. The second guy didn't move when the first one was hit because I guess he didn't hear the sound and the guy just laid back into the hill. When he fired at the second NVA, we saw the dirt right beside him just puff up and blossom up into a puff of dust, and he scrambled up the hill and we all laughed, we all got a big charge out of that. We thought that was real funny. That was some real fine shooting by that sniper. He got one of the two and it looked like it was a half mile if it was an inch.

Captain Otto Lehrack

While the snipers were setting up their shots, I was fascinated just watching through binoculars the gooks eat their lunch. I had never seen a live, *relaxed* NVA before.

Lieutenant Bill Kenerly

I was wounded on this operation, on April 4th. It was the same day that we heard that Martin Luther King, Jr., was killed. We had been out already two nights and were getting ready to set in for the third night in a two-company perimeter. Along about 5:30 or 6:00 P.M., just as we had finished digging in, one of my squad leaders told me that he saw movement in front of the lines. There was a water point outside of our lines and there had been Marines going back and forth to the water point for thirty minutes or so, and my first thought was that it was Marines out there.

I said as much and the squad leader told me that in fact they were wearing Marine uniforms. I had never seen any drugs, but it did occur to me that somebody might be out there smoking a joint and acting strangely for that reason. At any rate I duly reported it to the company commander. He told me to take a squad and go out and see what it was. Now we're not talking about these people being far away. I mean they were 100, 125 yards at the most outside the perimeter. I looked. I walked back and forth. I just couldn't see them.

The squad leader *could* see them and he told me that they were hunkered down in some high grass. I took one squad and a gun team along. We got on line and we moved out maybe 50 yards. The same squad leader was with me. And he said again, "Lieutenant, they are in front of us, they are hunkered down in the high grass." Like a damned fool I was shouting back and forth to Captain McAdam, the company commander, and I told him, "They're in the grass. They're dressed like Marines. What were we to do?" The captain said to kill them. I still thought they were Marines. I gave the order to shoot but to shoot over their heads. That's what we did.

As soon as the first rounds were fired, they fired into us. A rocket went by me just two feet from my left side. I hit the ground screaming for my men to get back to their fighting holes because we were on a flat piece of ground with some knee-high grass growing. I was armed with an M16. I was firing it, screaming for them to get back to their holes. At that point, I heard a round crack by my head, close. I slipped my rifle to full automatic and fired a burst. Another round came by. Insofar as I know, the third round is the one that hit me.

I thought the sensation was a huge amount of noise, plus it rocked me over. I was up on my elbows but I was laying down, and it rolled me over onto my right side. I didn't have any sense of pain. I just didn't have any feeling. It was like my left arm was gone and in fact I thought I'd been hit by a hand grenade and that my left arm had been blown off. I looked around for it and saw my left hand with my watch and my wedding band on it but I couldn't feel any of that. I rolled over onto my right side and my hand came with me, so I knew that it was attached.

I crawled a few yards and a corpsman came out and got me. His name was Vitorek. I don't know what happened to him. I've always needed to thank him. But Doc Vitorek kind of dragged me and I pulled myself and I got back to the lines like that. It wasn't a hand grenade, it was a bullet. It went through my left arm just above the shoulder and went into my chest, where it remains today.

I was very disappointed that I came home before my tour was over. I was glad to be out of Vietnam and to be alive, of course, but we were just sort of getting organized in my platoon when I was wounded.

APRIL 1968

PFC T. J. Kelly

After that [the April 4 action] we walked down to Cam Lo and the trucks met us there and they took us by truck convoy into Dong Ha where we had a couple of days off and hot showers and all that stuff. I walked back to the comm [communications] platoon rear area, and boy, everybody treated me so nice and this sergeant ran up and helped take my radio off and offered me a cold beer and everything.

Come to find out that somehow or other my medevac number showed up as being a KIA. They kept going down to the hospital looking to pick up my body. Obviously, I wasn't dead but they really treated me good and I enjoyed walking around; my trousers were torn and I was all dusty and dirty and hadn't shaved in a couple of days and looked like a real combat Marine and I really enjoyed walking around there.

I was still pretty new at the time, and in my head, this was the kind of thing that I really wanted to be . . . a hardened combat veteran Marine. That lasted about five months. About five months of that before all of a sudden my eyes opened up and I realized that hey, this isn't a movie, this is for real. I came to be thinking that an awful lot of guys were very naive like me and went over to get themselves involved in a war not really for very honorable or patriotic reasons but because they maybe saw too many John Wayne movies and wanted to see themselves as heroes, this sort of thing. I sort of smartened up after a while, especially when I saw so many young men die.

You didn't change what you did. You fought hard in the beginning because you wanted to be a hero and then you fought even harder after that silliness wore off because you wanted to live, you wanted to survive, and there was only one way to make it in the DMZ and that was to kill the enemy and to beat them in battle. The only way to beat them was to fight them aggressively.

That's the one thing about the Marine Corps; the tactics were pretty simple. It seemed to me like we would walk all day through jungle or through the hills or through the flat area over by the coast. We would constantly be moving, trying to find them, and when we found them, we attacked them. It didn't get much more sophisticated than that. I guess it was, but it just seemed to me that basically we found them and killed them.

Corporal Ed Seretti

One time I was walking flank security. I found a couple of dead NVA. I was going through their pockets and stuff and I remember really getting mad because I was finding all our stuff on them, like insect repellent made in the USA, our cigarettes, finding Winstons and stuff like that. I was really mad about that, saying, "What are they doing with our stuff?" I remember having some of their ammo and breaking the projectiles and the casing and looking at their gunpowder. Their gunpowder was like little tiny squares, instead of . . . like, ours was round, you know. Thinking about what was going through their minds. Did they hate us this bad? That kind of stuff. I remember thinking about what they were thinking . . . a lot. Thinking about . . . they don't even get to look forward to an R and R and stuff like that. Wondering if they had families. I guess, trying to read their minds.

PFC Jim Yost

The stress and strain from the combat, it's taken its toll on a lot of people. People that were nineteen and twenty looked fifty. The captain and the lieutenant kept the morale up, kept making sure we knew what we were doing, constantly reviewing us in squad tactics, keeping a sharp eye on the radio so we could call in artillery or medevacs in case the officers and the radiomen were taken out of action. They always stressed that.

Several times in the firebase we took incoming and it was quite colorful. One time we had a tanker that just came back from R and R from Australia, and he had put on his tank aerial all the escapades of his R and R with the girls. He had like fifteen different colored panties, red, blue, green, yellow, and he just finished tying the last one up at the base of the antenna when incoming started. But we scattered and jumped in a bunker. It was about thirty minutes, maybe thirty-five, when it was all over. And we came out and there was the tanker just in despair because shrapnel had ripped the panties on his aerial to shreds. And he said, "Ain't nothing sacred to these damn heathen gooks?"

35

· · · · · · · · · · · · · · ·

BLOODY MAY

More Americans died in the first week of May 1968 than any other week in the war, and the month was one of the bloodiest for 3/3 as well as many other units in Vietnam. The North Vietnamese did not yet understand the psychological victory they had scored at Tet. They, like the U.S. military, judged their General Offensive, General Uprising, a failure, and in desperation they tried to repeat Tet in May. However, the losses sustained earlier in the year had affected their training and readiness. Nearly 50 percent of the NVA soldiers who participated in the May offensive had less than three months of service. It was another disaster for the communist forces and a costly victory for the Americans.

Captain Otto Lehrack

On 8 May the battalion uncovered and overran an NVA regimental command post near the center of Leatherneck Square. The position was not relinquished without a fight. Supported by heavy artillery and mortars, the NVA inflicted 102 casualties on 3/3 before being driven from the hill. If March 16th was my favorite day in the war, May 8 was the one I hated the most.

We were on this sweep down through Leatherneck Square and on the morning of the 8th, at about ten o'clock in the morning, we heard a couple of artillery tubes pop and the rounds came in fairly close to where India Company was. I yelled at Corporal Ray Dasilva, my two-four operator [the forward observer or radio operator on the artillery radio net], to get on the arty net and tell those bastards that that was just a little too close. I had had too many experiences of close calls with our own artillery. Well, after some checking on his radio, Dasilva comes back to me and said, "That wasn't ours, it was gook." *Boom, boom,* a couple of more rounds leave the tube and this time they were even closer. They obviously had an FO somewhere around us and he was skillfully adjusting fire right onto our position. That was the start of an extremely long day. The shelling started in the morning and it didn't let up until six-thirty that night. Before the day ended, the battalion estimated that it received "in excess of 500 artillery rounds and approximately the same number of mortars on friendly units" from the NVA [quoted from 3/3 after-action report].

PFC Craig Pyles

May the 8th was a typical hot, muggy day. We started moving in a company tactical column. Then the NVA started slinging artillery at us. Every once in a while they'd throw a few rounds and everybody'd bite the dirt. Then we'd get up and keep moving.

PFC Jim Yost

Several from our company . . . they were cut to ribbons. We got the choppers in, put them in the body bags . . . they were mutilated pretty bad. During the artillery barrage we were ordered to take the hill.

Captain Otto Lehrack

We were approaching what turned out to be an NVA regimental command post. As we got closer and closer to them, their fire became more and more intense. There were two 152s, the biggest guns they had, up north of the DMZ and two more out west, somewhere around Mutter's Ridge. The guns were probably well hidden in caves, because we sent air after them and they couldn't find them. They'd look for the two in the north and the ones in the west would shoot and vice versa. As we got closer to where the gooks were, we began getting both 60 and 82 mortar, and then small-arms fire.

Once we figured out where the gooks were, we lined up with Mike Company on the left and India on the right and started down this one flat hill to cross a large stream and assault up another, steeper hill.

PFC Jim Yost

This was on the plateau and across it we had to jump a ravine. We had a lot of casualties and what was left of us was pretty tired. Just as we started out, they opened up with light machine guns and AKs. I come to the edge of the plateau and there was a drop into a small stream about four feet wide and I didn't know how deep the water was and I figured, well, better jump in, maybe it won't be over my head. That was my constant fear when it come to water because I was shorter than anybody else. I jumped and the water came up to about chest level and the rest of the platoon stopped and laughed for a second and said, "It must be all right. Yost survived and it's not over his head," so they all jumped in.

PFC Craig Pyles

The whole world went crazy. It was one of the most terrifying experiences I ever had. You'd hear the rounds come in and you'd hear people screaming "Corpsman." I heard a round coming and I was sort of down in a little gully and I knew it was going to be a close one by the sound. I hid up against the side of that gully. A round came from behind me and landed twenty feet in front of me. I saw it explode. For an instant I could feel the concussion off of it. I saw the dirt fly and that was terrifying enough, but I looked down and I was carrying a can of machine-gun ammo and I had that can of machine-gun ammo laying up against the side of my leg and I looked down and that can of gun ammo had a huge gash in it and was nearly cut in two. I realized instantly had it not been for that can of machine-gun ammo, I'd have lost my leg right below the knee. That scared me.

Captain Otto Lehrack

India Company stalled, for two reasons. One was that the gook artillery was registered heaviest in the ravine we were attacking up. It was thick brush, almost impossible to move through, and we were getting almost constant artillery from the north and west and mortars from the south. I had wounded lying in the grass and brush, which was burning furiously, and more casualties every minute.

The other reason was that one of my platoons, which was leading the right front of my assault, just fell apart. The platoon commander went to pieces and crawled into a hole. I had heard a few rumors about him being a coward and had dismissed them as mutterings of troops who didn't like him for other reasons. I wish I'd listened. His leadership failure, and therefore mine, was responsible for many of my casualties, although I didn't know it at the time.

Mike Company did an outstanding job of carrying the assault across the hill while we kind of straggled up to the top.

PFC Craig Pyles

Mike Company got into heavy contact. As we moved across this hill I could hear this heavy machine-gun shooting and bullets whizzing through the grass and, at the same time, NVA artillery coming in. We'd get up and we'd run about twenty or thirty feet and hit the dirt again. I was laying face down in the dirt and it was hot and it was frightening and I looked back behind me at my gun team leader, Jerry Mehan. His eyes were as big as silver dollars and I thought to myself at that very moment, "If he's this scared, I wonder how in the hell I'm supposed to feel."

PFC T. J. Kelly

It was a heck of a day, just an incredible day of combat. We had 152-mm artillery being fired at us from North Vietnam and I ran through barrages of that stuff, the rounds exploding around me. And then we crossed the river and a sniper took a shot at me and he would have got me in the chest except that his bullet hit my rifle and bounced off and knocked my hand guard, screwed my rifle up.

PFC Jim Yost

We finally took the hill by crawling up belly button to asshole, and shell casings from AK47s and SKSs [Soviet-made carbines] just littered that hill and it was just like trying to climb up a hill that had marbles rolling down.

PFC T. J. Kelly

A few minutes after that, the gooks started running. First Platoon was firing and the gooks started running away and they got out into the open and we were all shooting like crazy, and it's the first time I ever shot at a gook because most of the time I was talking on the radio in a firefight. I was so thirsty and tired I just let the whole magazine go, just pointed it in that general direction, and I was so tired, I didn't really care if I hit anything. The whole company was shooting at about thirty gooks running up the side of this hill, and there was no cover there. You'd see dust flying off their backs as the bullets hit them.

PFC Jim Yost

When we got up there, they had boogied and we had a small clearing into the hill. We were setting up the gun position and setting our 360 [degree perimeter] when the gunner opened up. He had set his gun right on top of a spider trap and the spider trap come open. There was two NVA getting ready to rock and roll into our 360 and he blew those guys away.

PFC Craig Pyles

I had a rookie, a new guy down there on watch, and I told him to get back up there and start digging and I'd stand guard. So I'm down there and I'm looking around and I look in this clump of brush and I see a fighting hole in the middle of this clump of brush and there's a magazine for an AK47 laying right on the lip of this fighting hole. And I thought to myself, "Ah, souvenir." So I start to work my way over to the hole. It wasn't more than ten feet away from me. As I started to go over there, a little voice in the back of my head says, "Be careful." So I flicked my rifle on "fire," and as I peered over the edge of that hole and looked down in there, there's an NVA laying down in the bottom of this thing and he's got his rifle between his legs and he's got his helmet sort of pulled over his head. I looked at the guy and I thought, "Is he dead or what?" I couldn't tell. I just said, "Well, better safe than sorry." So I put a bullet right through the side of him. Well, this guy was very much alive and he was probably the one that had just thrown a grenade at us. He starts squirming around the bottom of the hole. I just went bananas. I'm jumping around saying, "I got one. I got one. I got one." I didn't have enough sense to shoot him again. Some guy named Burns, a redheaded guy, runs over from his position and he looks down in the hole and he goes, "Oh, well." *Boom, boom, boom, boom.* He plants about six rounds in the head of this guy.

Captain Otto Lehrack

Just when I thought things were secure, we found several gooks among us in holes and spider traps. We killed them all before it got dark. Then I finally found out about the platoon commander's cowardice. I was so pissed that I pulled my .45 out and went looking for him. I was determined to kill the son of a bitch. Luckily for both of us, Dave Brown, my XO, had strapped him to a stretcher and had him medevaced. A day or so later, Colonel Marsh talked to me over the radio and asked what I wanted to do with him. I said that I didn't care as long as they didn't send him back to me. The colonel said, "Okay, I'll just tell division that we'll trade him for a bucket of sand." I never saw him again.

PFC T. J. Kelly

The NVA pulled back to the next ridge. So we were going to get ready to go up on the next ridge and an AO came up and our 60 mortars fired willie peter over there, and the AO swooped in right on top of the mortar and he whistled and he said, "You just hit twenty-five gooks with that willie peter. You've got boocoo [Marine version of *beaucoup*] gooks down there." And he was saying numbers like 400, 600 gooks and things like that; he said they looked like an ant pile. Major Findlay came up and they brought Lima Company up and they were preparing to assault that ridge and then we had our medevac, so Captain Mac [McAdam] told Findlay, he says, "I want to get these medevacs out." So anyhow, I got sent to do the medevacs while Lieutenant Myers, the air liaison officer, ran the airstrike.

While Lieutenant Myers was running F-4s so close that by the time the medevac bird . . . the CH-34 came in, shrapnel just showered the aircraft and the pilot was chewing my ass on the radio. He sounded like an older man, like he might have been a colonel. He didn't like any part of this and was really giving me holy hell for bringing him into a zone that wasn't properly secure and too close to an active airstrike. Just as we were getting ready to put the wounded on, another 250-pounder goes off. Doc Devette, my chief corpsman, the guy who knows which wounded go on the plane, *bang*, he got hit in the back with shrapnel and he's down rolling around on the ground and I'm standing there with all these wounded guys. I didn't know who was worse off or anything so . . . I think the CH-34 held seven and we put seven guys with the bloodiest bandages on there and let it go and the second bird came in and we got most everybody but minor wounds out. That was a bad medevac. And it was dark by the time he set down and I was real happy when we got out of that one.

Sergeant Major Neal King

I was going across the LZ and First Sergeant Johnson was on the zone. I said, "What are you doing here?" He said, "I'm getting evaced, I got hit." Anyway, the helicopters came and went and the fight went on for the rest of the day. Then I got hit and I went out with the first chopper in the morning.

We had a lieutenant in L Company. He had been an All-American lacrosse player. He was killed that day. I'd been shot in the left thigh. I got in a chopper but I was real lame and I tried to step over him and I hit him in the face with my foot. I never felt so bad about anything in my life. It wasn't intentional, I couldn't help myself, I couldn't lift that leg. To this day I still feel bad about it.

I got to D Med at Dong Ha and I'm laying on a table and I looked across the aisle and there is a Marine laying on a table right across from me. We're both on our stomachs. They're pulling shrapnel out of our butts, of course. It's Johnson. I said, "You got wounded yesterday. Did they just get around to you?" He said, "No, I got in last night. The club was open."

PFC Jim Yost

We got up in the morning and the NVA had left and it was one of the mysterious phantom-type things they would pull, where they were in close and tried to make contact and then disappeared like smoke into the wind. That psychologically wiped out some people . . . the younger ones.

Sergeant Major Neal King

One of the big problems that I noticed . . . As soon as we got replacements there was always somebody with a big mouth that got in among the replacements and told them how rough it was on the last operation and everything else and scared them half to death.

There was a kid by the name of Campbell. Good kid but somebody had got next to him and scared him to death and then we got into the firefight on 8 May. Well, Campbell made it out. He evacuated himself [without authority, thereby committing an act of deserting the battlefield]. He was in the rear and we had him up for a general court-martial and he passed the word that he wasn't coming back to the company. So I told First Sergeant Johnson and the gunny, I said, "Go get him." And he had said that if they came after him to come shooting. So they went and got him and they brought him back hanging on a pole like a tiger. They brought him down and I ran down to the LZ and I cut him loose. Campbell got back to the outfit and I explained to him that you have to do your job here. We all get scared but you've got to live with fear. And [later] they'd have firefights and he'd say, "How am I doing, Top?" General court-martial was still moving forward but then Campbell got hit, and as you well know, you can't court-martial a wounded war hero, so everything worked out happily ever after.

·

On 22 May, India Company discovered an occupied enemy harbor site southwest of Alpha 3. As the scope of the action broadened, Lima Company and a 3/3 command group were committed, and then elements of 1/9, 3/9, and 1/4 moved in to seal off the area. Two Marines were killed and forty-nine wounded. Most of the casualties resulted from enemy artillery and mortars.

PFC Jim Yost

Well, I can't think of much more to tell you except the day I was wounded. I've been dreading to tell you that, but I'm going to let you know anyway. It was May 22d.

They had arc-lighted [B-52 strike] an NVA bunker complex in Leatherneck Square. They must have been droppin' 10-tonners, because the people inside the bunkers were buried, were pulverized. Nothing but bloody masses and there must have been about a hell of a lot of casualties. We got four or five Chinese .51-calibers [machine guns] and a whole bunch of chemical rubber suits that the Chinese had made and gave to the Vietnamese. They must have anticipated chemical warfare next. We stayed in the area and took all the C4 out of Dong Ha and we had to stay there for another day to blow the bunkers and the weapons. And we got ice cream, beer, and steaks because we did that.

We were going back in that area three days later and I knew it was a bad omen. We came to this treeline . . . I was just taking a smoke break when I hear mortar tubes pop. I yelled, "Incoming," ran fifty meters, and jumped into a hole. And they walked 'em right in on my previous position. First and 2d platoons started into the treeline and they got mauled bad.

PFC Craig Pyles

My squad was the rear squad in the whole column and we had no idea what was going on up there. Sometimes these firefights would begin and you'd hear a few shots, and then the pace of the fire would pick up and build to this big crescendo of shooting and grenades and M79s going off.

They kept moving us up until we were laying behind this little dike as low as we could get and I could see Captain McTiernan over there behind another dike, trying to figure out what was going on and maneuver people. About this time I looked up and I saw four guys carrying the company gunny [Gunnery Sergeant Bill Brooks] and I could see that his foot was dangling where it was almost completely off, right about the ankle. I thought, "Holy shit! This is really getting bad."

At this point they sent one squad of our platoon around to one flank and we were sent around to the other, trying to pull a flanking movement on them. We maneuvered into this little wooded area and then we came to another little open area where there was a big shell crater and there's a dead Marine in there. A couple of our guys crawled out there, got ahold of him and drug him back. I had the machine gun and I thought we were supposed to assault through at that point. I did. I stepped out there with that machine gun on the hip and I went for it. I was assaulting through. I looked down and saw I only had about 10 rounds left of the 100-round belt, so I had to stop and grab another 100 rounds. I dropped down on one knee and I was about to clip them together and *wham*, I went down. I thought the whole squad was in the assault. Joe Turner tells me that everybody looked up and there I was taking off into the middle of these guys banging away with the machine gun. And then they saw me go down. I had taken a bullet right through my right hip, just below the pelvic bone. So I was laying there and I hollered for somebody. I said, "Corpsman," and there's all this shooting going on and I thought, "No, there's no corpsman that would come up here and get me." So I said, "Turner. Come get me." And he says, "What?" And I said, "I'm hit."

I hear him yell over to Metters and say, "Metters, Pyles is hit." And Metters says, "I'll go get him." And Turner says, "No, I'll go." And then Metters says, "No, I'll go." So I'm laying there thinking, "Jesus, these guys are having an argument about who's going to come get me and I'm laying here shot." Finally they both came. Before they could get to me I started to panic a little bit. I thought, "Oh, my God. I'm so close to these NVA." During this fight you could hear the NVA yelling and shouting orders at each other.

I was in a lot of pain. Metters got me up on my feet and we started hobbling along. About that time a burst from an AK went right over our heads and I saw limbs falling in front of us from the bullets. All of a sudden I wasn't hurt anymore. I could do the 100-yard dash. We started boogying through that woods. We finally got on the other side where they had set up an evacuation point.

The corpsman got to bandaging me and they give me a shot of morphine and another guy comes over from one of the other platoons. His nose was gone. He'd taken a bullet right across the bridge of his nose. I could hear Lieutenant Corky Schron [the weapons platoon commander] screaming and throwing his helmet because his platoon sergeant or somebody had just gotten killed. He'd taken a bullet right between the running lights.

PFC Jim Yost

The Vietnamese were yelling, "Today you die, Marine," and "Fuck LBJ." They were only about fifteen to twenty meters in and we were shooting like crazy. And I was given orders by . . . Corporal Monsheen to take my fire team, cover the left flank, and . . . I didn't like the order, I was in a well-dug trench, and I thought I'd be safe there, but I followed my orders and took my fire team out.

And I was about fifteen meters out when I got hit and Paul Herring got hit and some other people got hit right behind me. I went down and I was surprised and bitter. I laid there for two-and-a-half hours. My legs were bent behind me and I was layin' on them and I was in terrible, terrible pain, it got worse and worse. I laid there. The next thing that I knew, Lance Corporal Talbert run up and said, "Are you okay?" He rolled me over and he said, "Oh, my God." And they picked me up and put me on a stretcher and carried me back. Lieutenant Douglas was there and saying, "Hold on." A corpsman was working on me. Doc Owens was telling me he couldn't give me morphine, I'd go into shock and die. I was so surprised it hurt. They put me on a medevac and I went to Phu Bai. They laid me down and didn't attend me for about twenty minutes. They took care of the other casualties and I finally said, "Fuck you, the hell with you, I'm gettin' up and going to another field hospital. You're going to let me lay here and die." That's when they started to attend me. I talked to a couple of corpsmen later and they said that if I hadn't done that they would've let me die. They figured I was going to die anyway. I woke up five days later. Had both my legs then. They was telling me that they was trying to put artery gaps in. They took about seven AK rounds out of me and shrapnel. Enough to sink a battleship. Said they'd send me to the USS *Repose* for more intensive care. They flew me out there. They told me they had to amputate my left leg above the knee.

PFC Craig Pyles

I got back to D Med at Dong Ha and there's all these Marines in there shot to pieces. It was sad and depressing. So they load us up on a C-130 and flew us down to near Phu Bai to a hospital. When I got to that hospital I was being wheeled in there and I was starting to feel some pain at this point, more than I had before. These doctors got me in there and got to probing around. I'm laying there in quite a bit of pain and this chaplain comes over and I thought, "Oh God, I know it's not this bad." The chaplain comes over there. He looks at me and he kind of shakes his head and he said, "Son, don't feel bad if people start calling you 'half ass' from now on."

PFC Jim Yost

I was in Japan, General Army Hospital, and I woke up to this inhuman sound . . . "*Ooooh*," like that. So I asked the Army medic what had happened and he said that this Marine had been captured by the North Vietnamese. They cut his ears off, they poked out his eyes, they cut his nose off, they cut his hands off at the wrist and they stuck a bamboo shoot up through his rectum and punched it out through his stomach and left him to die. And he made it through and he couldn't talk and was blind. Was mute. And he was mutilated. And that's what the North Vietnamese soldiers did to Marines if they caught 'em.

36

. . . .

DAI DO

In May 1968 the NVA made several moves to seize Dong Ha, the dusty little town at the junction of Routes 1 and 9 that had become the headquarters for the 3d Marine Division. To counter these attempts, the Marines fought several battles around the village of Dai Do, near the mouth of the Cua Viet River. The capture of Dai Do by the NVA would have cut off one of the major supply lines to the Marines in Northern I Corps and would have endangered the Dong Ha Combat Base and the other positions along Route 9. 3/3 participated in the last of these battles. On 26 May, in response to a verbal order from the 9th Marines, the battalion was helilifted out of Leatherneck Square and taken to the east to the rolling sand dunes of Dai Do. They remained there for the rest of the month as part of Operation NAPOLEON-SALINE, a large operation that also involved units from 1/3, 1/9, and 3/9 and a battalion of the 2d ARVN Regiment.

Lance Corporal Richard V. Sherwood

We were able to trap a large number of NVA in a small oasis of trees with their backs to the river and us out in the sand dunes surrounding them and do a pretty good job on those guys.

PFC William Frantz

We had what we called a "turkey shoot" where the NVA was in the treeline. We called in artillery and napalm. They had no choice but to come towards us in about knee-high grass. They was crawling through there and we says, "Pluck them off."

Lance Corporal Rich Sherwood

And then the next day, we moved across the sand dunes to another area in Dai Do area and got ambushed very badly.

PFC Bill Frantz

We was sweeping past the treeline. I looked down because I seen something moving. There was elbows with greens on. There was enemy down to my left. I heard gooks and I told the fellas to throw a grenade in there. What happened, they was underground in all around the bushes all around us. It wasn't but seconds later that everything started. It turned out they was all around us. It was sandy down there. None of the M16s was working. They jammed up because of the sand. The 60s [machine guns] were working somewhat. It got crazy. You've got the enemy all around you and behind you. I started to fire at them and ended up just tossing grenades at them because the 16s wasn't working.

By now this action went on down the line to where it started to affect Mike and other companies. A number of tanks come in and they was doing mutual splits. That's where they grind back and forth, grind the hole down trying to collapse the hole on top of the NVA. The enemy come up out of the holes and they got caught under the tracks, the tanks just grinding away at them. The action kept going on down the line and shortly after this I started to pass out from my wounds.

I went down to Phu Bai for a while and they sent me back with one arm bandaged. I was back in the field with just the use of one arm. I guess that's how much we needed to have been there. That's the firefight I have nightmares about the most.

Corporal Ed Seretti

I got shot. My squad walked right through an ambush and right in the middle of it I got blasted and got my second Purple Heart. That was an awful day. A kid named Davino, he must have got hit twenty-five times. I mean he was a mess laying there.

I was laying there for a long time after I got shot, pulling a chunk of meat out of my back and then somehow thinking that shoving that meat back in the hole there was going to do any good. I was bleeding and had bugs inside my wound and everything else. As I was laying there the squad leader was still hollering out orders and directing fire. This kid was great. That was Hemstreet. Never batted an eyelash giving out orders and that.

Guys were screaming and moaning and crying, those sounds you never forget the rest of your life . . . guys calling for their mothers. I was laying there bleeding, thinking for sure I was going to die. When I went down, I somehow put a gash in my cheek. My face was bleeding and I was thinking all kinds of crazy thoughts, like "If I do get out of here, what girl's going to ever go out with me with the scar that's going to be on my face now."

These Marine Corps jet pilots is the reason we got out of there. They came down and dropped napalm and every time right after they'd drop, we got up and ran like maybe fifteen or twenty yards or so. They just kept coming and we just kept getting up and getting out of there. Finally we got back to the river where we got medevaced out. I would love to know who those jet fighter pilots were. They were Marines. I remember seeing "Marines" on the jets. I'd love to shake their hands.

Lance Corporal Bill Clough

One of the most selfless acts that I've been familiar with was a kid named Swain. He was in guns section and he was about twelve and twenty-three or twelve and twenty-four [months and days in country on a thirteen-month tour], which is the thing everybody lives for in Vietnam. We were pinned down by three 50s [machine guns] in an L-shaped treeline and every time somebody either moved up to assist someone else or tried to move back or raised their head up they got hit. We were trying to get some wounded back and he took the gun and stood up and ran up and down the treeline while the others managed to pull some of the wounded back for better cover. I think he was subsequently awarded a Silver Star for that effort, but I'm not sure that was a high enough award if all the factors were considered.

Marty Grace, who was a machine gunner and a good friend of mine, was wounded five different times that day. They had a lot of snipers in trees and Marty was on the gun and the first time he was wounded he was shot through his left shoulder. Then through his left arm and then through his chest and then through his neck. Each time they tried to get him to get off the gun and give it to the A-gunner, he just kept shooting. The last time he was wounded he was shot between his eyes. When they pulled him off the gun, he was still firing.

I knew Marty Grace quite well. He was just a little ol' redneck boy from Topeka, Kansas, but he had a lot of heart and he believed in the Marine Corps and he believed in God and he believed in his country. Probably got a Purple Heart. I doubt if he even got five of them. But to my knowledge nobody ever recommended him for anything and I thought that took a little bit of courage, suppressing fire and refusing to give up the gun to somebody else because I'm sure he was convinced that he was going to die. I think that probably Marty decided that he was going to sacrifice himself regardless of the consequences to his family, so somebody wouldn't have to die in his place.

Corporal William W. Sessions

We were pinned down all night. When daylight came I crawled over closer to my platoon. I was to spot the enemy targets for aircraft to conduct airstrikes. I learned that Corporal Crawford was shot in the head and killed. Sergeant Garcia, one of our platoon leaders, had been shot in the throat. He was still alive and coughing blood. They told him to stay still but he wouldn't stay still. He later died. I crawled over many yards from my position, shot my 3.5 rocket launcher into the enemy position. While I was in the prone position with my rocket launcher, an enemy sniper shot at me. The rifle round went right by my face and head. The bullet traveled inside my helmet and went through the side and through the back of my helmet. I thought something hit my head, maybe a grenade. When I had crawled back to my outfit, I took my helmet off and found out what really had happened. A bullet went through the side of my helmet and caused a small wound on the top of my ear. The wound wasn't bad. It was only a scratch. [Will Session's helmet was pierced by bullets five times on that day. He received the Bronze Star for his actions during the firefight.]

PFC Anthony Stanisci

I was hit in the neck. It went in my neck, the base of my neck, it traveled through my chest and collapsed my lung and came out the upper right-hand side of my back. I didn't realize what happened at first but I got whammed pretty good. I lost control of my right arm and shoulder and had a sucking chest wound. I laid there for a while until I took some inventory of myself and kind of realized where I was at. When I realized I was hit, I kind of got scared and called for a corpsman. There was no corpsman because I was too far out for a corpsman to hear me. Rod was in the area and called out and sure in hell, he showed up and tried to get us out of there, but I couldn't move too good. He tried to pick me up and run with me but I told him, "You've got to lay me down, Rod, because my lung collapsed," and I was hurting and I couldn't get anywhere fast. He settled me down a little bit and went and got some help, and two guys in my squad came out and they put me on a poncho and they tried to double-time and they had to hit the ground a few times and return fire. By the time I got back there to the perimeter, they called for a chopper.

Lance Corporal Rich Sherwood

I lost my two guys. Funny, I'm a kid from New York, New Jersey area, and my two best friends were Fred Thrift and Ronny Smith. These two guys had gone to high school together; they were both from Huntsville, Alabama, and they were my best friends in the squad. The three of us were sort of like the Three Musketeers and both Freddy and Ronny both took a hit and both died in that ambush. It was a real bad day for us and the low point of my tour. These were my two best friends, and living here in Washington, I go to the Vietnam Veterans Memorial a lot to talk to my guys.

All told, 53 members of the battalion died in May 1968, and another 319 were wounded badly enough to require medical evacuation. The numbers are especially significant because the casualties came from only three companies; Kilo Company was attached to 1/9 for most of the month. Nearly one out of every two grunts in the field were killed or wounded badly enough to require medical evacuation. This caused severe shortages of experienced personnel in the battalion.

In return for their sacrifices, the Marines killed 206 NVA (by body count), captured 31 prisoners, overran a regimental command post, and probably destroyed the effectiveness of two NVA battalions. Equipment captured during the month required several single-spaced, typewritten pages to report.

Captain Otto Lehrack

India Company had 141 of the battalion's casualties during May. When I turned over the company in midmonth to rotate back to the States, two-thirds of these were yet to come. My guilt over having left the company during such a time remains undiminished to this day and resulted in my volunteering for, and receiving, a second Vietnam tour less than two years later.

37

· · · · · · · · · · · · · ·

BROTHERHOOD

Lance Corporal T. J. Kelly

There was a young lieutenant, an artillery FO, named Fred Dyer attached to Mike 3/3 and his radio operator was named T. J. McManus. Those guys and I were real good friends because we got to working with each other in firefights, and he'd have to lift his arty when I brought my air in and as soon as my air was over, he'd go right back to his arty.

I always felt good going into combat with them because Fred was so good at arty, he could just put that stuff anywhere. T. J.—we also called him "the Kid," because I personally believe he got in the Marine Corps on a fraudulent enlistment. The guy didn't look more than fifteen years old. But he was a very interesting character. He could play the harmonica really well and he used to play "Dixie" for the guys from the South and he'd play all kinds of other songs. He'd just say things, like he claimed he could speak Japanese. Yeah, sure. But I had some sergeant who was stationed in Japan, I asked him, I said, "Hey, speak to this guy in Japanese." Sure enough, he did know some Japanese, quite a bit in fact.

Well, anyhow, he bought it after we went down to Dai Do in that area down by the Cua Viet River. Mike boats picked us up and we steamed downriver to a village and came ashore in the village and made a real combat amphibious assault. We were all thinking it was going to be a real Marine traditional assault and as we were coming up to the beach, the squad leaders are saying, "Lock and load" [a command given in preparation for firing], and they're pumping their people up saying, "All right, kick ass, motherfuckers," and we were getting all ready to charge out of there and go into combat.

As soon as the ramp went down, we came charging out of there and here they had little stands set up and kids were already waiting on us, and they were going to sell cokes and marijuana and the whores were calling us over to the little hooches and saying, "Hey boys, want to fuck." They knew well, well in advance where we were coming.

They said there had only been about ten NVA in the village and they had taken off the night before. We had to walk back and I was off to the flank and T. J. McManus was sort of walking behind me. The next thing I know, I was flat on the ground, knocked down by a blast. I thought it was incoming and then I saw Lieutenant Dyer was up and he was running around yelling, "T. J., T. J., where are you?" So I said, "I'm right here." He said, "Not you—my T. J., my radio operator." There was some confusion, we both had the same nickname, T. J.

The next thing you know, he went running out into the water and he picked up a piece of flak jacket, with a little piece of meat, red meat on it . . . that slipped into the water . . . and Fred Dyer just went numb. It had been a command-detonated mine which left a huge crater . . . maybe five feet across and three or four feet deep. The engineers figured the NVA gathered up some old dud 105 shells and put them together and fused them and set that sucker off when we came along.

There was nothing left to medevac. We found T. J.'s helmet and it was flattened out like one of those World War I doughboy helmets, and we found his radio and the antenna base and the handset were all burned right off. And we found nothing else and we looked pretty thoroughly.

After that Lieutenant Dyer kind of went to pieces. His brother was a CH-34 driver. A number of times I would get a call from the brother asking the two-four actual [artillery FO] to come up on the one-four [air] net. They would come up and he would say, "How are you doing?" and say a few words to his brother. The brother came out and spent a couple of days and helped Lieutenant Dyer get over his grief and he seemed okay except that he became exceedingly reckless in a firefight. He'd stand up to watch his arty rounds. He'd be like Major Findlay standing up in a firefight and watching. Really exposing himself bad. I talked to him about it. I said, "Hey, what are you doing?" and [he would] laugh at me and grin sheepishly.

The day he got killed, it was the same deal. We were in Leatherneck Square and we walked up one side of a hill as the NVA were coming up the other side, but we happened to get there first and set up real quick and we started shooting. I ran up there to get on line when somebody came up to me and said, "T. J., they need you to run a medevac." One of the guys from the squad had got shot through the arm. He was really lucky because the round went through his arm, through bandoliers of magazines that were hung across his chest and wedged into his flak jacket. And I had some other wounded from the morning's action where we took some mortars and they were real minor. So I go to get those guys out.

I went out to the east side of the hill and ran a medevac and got them out and when I came back, they said they had another guy who was wounded and this time it was Spaceman. His name was Spaceman because he had a pair of NVA goggles on his helmet and looked kind of weird and we all called him Spaceman. He was shot through the throat and his lungs were filling up with blood. There were no medevac choppers and I was begging and pleading to our control station in the regiment, but they said there was nothing they could do. A 53 happened to be flying overhead and he monitored what I was saying. He said, "Don't worry, Mike. I'll call DASC [Direct Air Support Center]." He called them and came back and said, "Ten minutes." I said, "No ten minutes! Ten minutes is no good! This guy is going to die!" There was silence on the radio for a minute and he said, "Pop smoke, I'm coming in." And he brought that big sucker down and took Spaceman out.

After this we were taking all kinds of mortars on the LZ and I'm really starting to get kind of gun-shy from the LZ because the LZ was definitely hot, and we were starting to take small arms as well as mortars and they chased me and the corpsman off the thing. No sooner do I get back up the hill than I hear some more gunfire and then I've got another medevac and I'm thinking, "Oh, no. God, not again. I don't want to go back to that LZ." Well, this isn't too easy for me to talk about. This dark thought crossed my mind, where I was thinking . . . pure selfishness on my part, I didn't know who was hit, but I kind of said to myself, "Let them be a routine." In other words, let them be dead [which meant a low priority medevac, instead of the higher priority given to wounded]. That way I won't have to go back down there. Not now, anyhow.

It was routine, permanent routine and it was Lieutenant Dyer. When I found that out, I really felt like shit. The corpsman had Lieutenant Dyer really wrapped up good in a poncho, and I tried to take one last look at him and the doc said, "Don't do it. Remember him the way he was."

The way he got killed was, some of the gooks were sneaking out of the ambush, so he went out there with nothing but a stupid .45, him and the 3d Platoon commander. Then the platoon commander came back to his troops, but Lieutenant Dyer stupidly stayed out there. A gook snuck up on him and shot him. Lieutenant Dyer drowned to death in his own blood because he was shot in the throat, too.

So the chopper comes in, it's a 34 and it's his brother's, and he's asking me when he can talk to Fred. Shit, I didn't want to tell him he was going to haul his brother's body out. He didn't know, obviously, so I just told him he was on patrol and I couldn't reach him.

A couple of days later, I'm on patrol and the helicopter-pilot brother calls me again and wants to speak to his brother, Lieutenant Dyer. So I went to Lieutenant Logan who was our 6 and asked him, "What do I do?" He said, "Wait a minute." And he got on the battalion net and the next thing I knew, Colonel Marsh is on the TAC party net and he asked the helicopter pilot, "Are you in control of the aircraft?" And the brother said, "Not now." Colonel Marsh said, "The worst thing that could possibly happen has happened." The brother just said, "When?" And he said, "Two days ago." Colonel Marsh said he could check with Fighting Mad 5 [the executive officer of 3/3, whose radio call sign at this time was Fighting Mad 5] in Dong Ha for more details on the thing. Colonel Marsh was very nice. He extended his sympathies and he said we shared in his grief and things like that, but it was pretty bad. I was listening on my radio with Lieutenant Logan; our helmets were touching as we listened.

38

· · · · · · · · · · · · · · ·

BEYOND ALPHA THREE

After nearly five months of operating out of Alpha 3, the 3d Battalion, 3d Marines, was on the move. They spent most of June 1968 at Camp Big John on a tributary of the Cua Viet River. During that month they saw little action and, consequently, had an unprecedented low casualty rate.

PFC Jack W. "Pops" Wandell (Brand New Guy)

When I went over there I was twenty-six years old, so I was older than the others. I became a fire team leader, a squad leader. I moved up quickly that way, but as far as rank I never moved too fast because the officers always thought I was overly cautious. I was very cautious.

I was there a month and a half, two months, and I never saw a gook, so I got a feeling they weren't around. Until you see them you get an idea they're not around. People tell you they're there. We'd have incoming every so often, but when we'd walk down the trails you just didn't think they were there.

·

Lance Corporal "Pops" Wandell, the old man of 26 years. (Courtesy Ken George)

Lance Corporal Vito Lavacca

From Alpha 3, we moved on to a series of operations . . . we were part of Operation SPARROWHAWK that provided reinforcement for any other unit that made contact. We shuttled around from area to area: Cua Viet and Camp Carroll, the Rockpile, Khe Sanh, Mutter's Ridge, Dong Ha Mountain. And the contact, again, was fairly often.

The Sparrowhawk concept had been operational since 1966 and would remain in use as long as Marines were in Vietnam. A ready response force that had helicopters standing by would be lifted into action when the enemy had been engaged by another unit or spotted by reconnaissance. At first generally of squad size, the idea had been to close with the elusive Viet Cong guerrillas before they had a chance to melt back into the population. Now battling NVA regulars, this reaction force was rarely smaller than a platoon.

·

PFC Tom Evanoff

When we were at Camp Carroll we were down inside the bunker one night. We had some rotgut booze we got from the gooks, some kind of rum, I believe it was. It tasted like tiger piss. We were drinking that and we even had a little light fixed up where we stole the generator from the Army. We had a big poster on one of the beams, a full-length Playboy girl. We were dancing with that, dancing with each other, singing, just having a good time for a night. We were closer than brothers. It's hard to explain it to other people. There was a bondness and a closeness that you'll never have ever in your life again.

There was a guy named Ropie. I think he was from the Ozarks. He wasn't too good on reading and writing, but goddamn, he was a good mortarman. His mom used to send him cassette tapes. A mom was a mom, it didn't matter whose mother. When you could hear a mother saying, "Ropie, this is your ma speaking. We love you. We miss you," it was like she was talking to us, like all of our mothers were speaking through her. It made us feel good.

.

PFC Ken George (Brand New Guy)

I was assigned to Mike Company. From the training I received in the States, I was under the impression that when you got to Vietnam you went out in the field and you fought all day long every day and at night you pulled back and you were in a secure environment. It never dawned on me that we were going to spend so many nights sleeping in the mud. And that really threw me a curve. I expected an occasional bivouac as we did in the States, but I never expected it to be like it was. The amount of gear that you lugged around also was something new and totally caught me off guard.

.

Lance Corporal Rich Sherwood

I was extremely angry at one exercise we ran south of Con Thien in the Quang Tri Province, where we had a CBS news reporter and television crew came with us, and intelligence apparently said there was a large NVA group. That we were going in on one side and another regiment was on another side to trap them. The CBS crew was with us, but there wasn't any firefights or any action going on. So the CBS crew actually staged a firefight with us throwing grenades and shooting off the M6o machine gun and firing the M79, just so they could get good stuff on tape. I had a very bitter, bitter feeling about that, and I still am to this day. They weren't really reporting what was really happening, they were building something up to look good on television to show back to the people in the United States when in fact it wasn't true and had never happened.

.

Lance Corporal Ken George, loaded up and ready to go. (Courtesy Ken George)

Lance Corporal Vito Lavacca

We went out on a squad-sized ambush one night, out of Camp Carroll, and set up by a river bed. When we saddled up at dawn to move back to the perimeter, we were just covered with leeches. And everybody started droppin' their pants to burn the leeches off each other.

We had a guy in the platoon named Charlie Hatfield. Hatfield reached down to scratch his balls and there was a leech on the head of his dick that he broke. And the blood just saturated his pants, right at the crotch. Hatfield was a big strapping guy, but he just screamed for the corpsman to come up. And all the corpsman had were three-by-five-inch battle dressings with two long strips of gauze. Charlie tied this thing around his dick and buttoned his pants up. But he left his dick hangin' out. And we saddled up and started walking back to the perimeter.

Colonel Marsh always met the ambush team at the gate as they came in and had a few kind words for everybody. You know, he'd pat you on the shoulder. "How'd everything go out there last night, Wilson?" "Fine, sir, no problems." "Anderson, when are we gonna get some cookies from your sister?" "Real soon, sir." And he sees Hatfield comin' up with his pants soaked with blood and this big battle dressing hangin' out of his pants. And he says, "Jeez, Hatfield, if I knew you were on the rag, I wouldn't have sent you out last night."

•

By July, 3/3's rest was at an end, and battalion operations during the remaining summer months ranged the length and breadth of Northern I Corps.

39

ANOTHER MARINE'S CHAPLAIN

Lieutenant Commander (Chaplain) Bob Bedingfield (Brand New Guy)

I put in a priority message to Washington to the chief of chaplains saying that I had volunteered to go into Vietnam and if it was not proper for me to go in, then I wanted him to consider my message to him to be my resignation.

As you might imagine, there were not a whole lot of chaplains volunteering to go into Vietnam in those days, so almost by return message, there was a "you asked for it, you got it" kind of thing. I was ordered into the 3d Marine Division. Fortunately the division chaplain and I were friends from a previous tour and I said to him, "I'd like the battalion that you think is probably being the least served." That happened to be the 3d Battalion, 3d Marines. They had a young chaplain there who, for a variety of reasons, did not relate well. Chose to not go into the bush or into the field. And so I was given a set of orders that day. Reported that afternoon to 3/3 Rear. Next day went out by jeep and joined the battalion at Camp Carroll.

Sergeant Major Neal King

While we were at A3 when I first joined there, we had a chaplain and a doctor. Both these people were a couple of sheep, just terrified of everything. Well, as a result, anytime anybody had a little lack of courage, they went to the chaplain or the doctor and one of these guys would come to me and say, "You've got to get this man out of here." Well, if we'd continued with these two people, there'd have only been you and I and the colonel up there. Thank God the colonel made a move and got rid of those two guys and we got Doc Ashford and Chaplain Bedingfield.

Corporal Gary Conner

We were at Camp Carroll. I was sitting in a bunker and a helicopter landed and some replacements got off, and I noticed one fellow that got off had gold parachute wings on his utility jacket and I could see a gold cross on his collar. Being in a parachute outfit back Stateside, 2d ANGLICO, we had at that time the only parachute-qualified chaplain in the Navy, Lieutenant Commander Bedingfield. And as he approached, I recognized him and he recognized me. We had a nice reacquaintance.

ANGLICO stands for Air and Naval Gunfire Liaison Company, a unit of Marine and Navy personnel who provide support to U.S. Army and allied units during joint operations. Because they might see action with airborne units, ANGLICO personnel are parachute qualified.

Chaplain Bob Bedingfield

[Lieutenant Colonel] Jim Marsh then had the battalion. He was in his very final stage. He was going to make one more grand sweep. I joined the battalion on one day and the next day we walked out the gates of Camp Carroll and down the road and the mission was to claim Dong Ha Mountain. So out we went, the entire battalion up the mountain. In the process, Mike Company got a 75 [mm] pack howitzer that was continually harassing Camp Carroll. And we claimed the top of the mountain in short order. My second day with the battalion I had six services, moving from place to place, and a wonderful introduction.

From that point on, for almost ten months, I stayed with 3/3. Covered a lot of territory and did a lot of things. Moved from Camp Carroll west as far as Khe Sanh and, on one particular occasion, moved across the Laotian border. We operated at the southern end of and well into the Demilitarized Zone. We operated out of the Cua Viet.

Sergeant Major Neal King

Bedingfield was a stud. He got two Bronze Stars while he was in country and one would have been a Silver Star but they had to delete the part in the citation where he was throwing hand grenades. They didn't think that was appropriate for a man of the cloth.

We were up on the first hill south of Mutter's Ridge. While we were on that hill, 130s got in on K Company on the other side of the valley and caused them quite a few casualties. Chaplain Bedingfield had just joined the battalion and these 130s are zipping over the top of the hill, and after about the sixteenth of them got over he said, "Sergeant Major, have I lost my virginity?" And I said, "Yes, you sure have."

They made a concentrated attack and they fired on us with 60 and 81 mortars, I'd say 400 to 500 rounds. But we were on a real skinny ridge and every one of them went right over the top of us. Then they followed it with an attack. They hit right in L Company. L Company repulsed them with forty confirmed [enemy KIA] and we just had two people that had wounds similar to when you cut yourself shaving.

During this same time was when I and K Company got down into the valley and really run into the mortar fire and got casualties . . . fifty-some wounded. They couldn't get any of those helicopter pilots to do anything about it because of the fire, until finally some major said, "Ah, hell, I'll take them." That chopper went up and there were people hanging out the windows and off the ramps and he got the whole damn crowd out of there in one load. The load was supposed to be twenty-six people but he had forty or fifty hanging out of that helicopter. I thought that was quite a heroic thing.

During this whole time, we didn't get resupplied with clothes. I wore the same clothes for thirty-one days straight.

Chaplain Bob Bedingfield

As I scan back over the whole experience, there are a couple of people that certainly stand out. Neal King. Neal King, is for me, without peer, a Marine's Marine. Probably the best that I have ever seen. Tough, hard, crude. I'll remember him humping, remember him moving, remember him cajoling and encouraging. Neal King brought to the battalion a sense of urgency and a sense of direction. He had an uncanny ability to gather people around him in a fashion of absolute loyalty to him and to the people that he focused on, believing more in them than they sometimes did themselves. He was tough and he was hard and he was crude. He was a man's man. And he had an unbelievable ability to make things work.

40

. . . .

UNFAMILIAR TERRITORY

Movement from July to September was nearly nonstop. The battalion command post reported eight different locations in July alone, compared to four in June and two in August. Among other consequences, this constant patrolling further hampered resupply and exacerbated sanitation problems. In particular, hundreds of Marines were plagued by cellulitis, developing sores from even the smallest breaks in the skin that oozed pus and wore deep into muscle tissue until arrested.

PFC James D. Howe (Brand New Guy)

My first impression of Vietnam is getting off the Continental Airlines in Danang and going from the culture that I was familiar with . . . the western, white middle-class culture, to a culture that was thousands of years older. It was as if I had stepped into a time warp. We had been trained that once you landed in country, that there was no longer any time where you could feel safe. You were in a combat zone, and unlike World War II there was no behind-the-lines. I think that possibly it is one of the key factors of stress in Vietnam veterans, especially the delayed stress syndrome . . .

When I got off the plane there was a paradox. Here I was in a combat zone, yet the people that met me seemed relaxed. It wasn't until a few weeks later that I realized that you had to relax and you had to get "constantly looking for the enemy" out of your system. The human body requires that you have some time to regenerate your juices and to relax.

PFC Peter A. Tramonte (Brand New Guy)

One of the first impressions that hit me when I landed in Dong Ha was the place was really in a shambles. The first night they had like an enlisted men's bar. It was a bombed-out bar area. There was no roof on it. There was just some sandbags there. I didn't know anybody. I was in a state of shock, total shock. I went to the mess hall. There was just a dirt floor with some benches and I got some chow. There was about sixty thousand flies on it. It was really a shock for me to come from the world all the way to this place in Vietnam and I didn't really know what it was about.

PFC Jim Howe

My first day in the bush . . . we had taken off from Quang Tri and we were going out to a place around the area of Mutter's Ridge. There was myself and Pete Tramonte . . . and several other fellows. Luckily, we had a sergeant that was starting his second tour of duty in Vietnam and knew some of the ropes. 'Cause we went out by helicopter to a landing zone and we were supposed to meet our unit there. We exited the helicopter in a quick and fashionable manner, the same way we trained, and we met our first great surprise. The helicopters took off and there was no one around. They had dropped us off at a point where the company had been the day before but had moved out from already.

So there was six of us on top of this hill in Vietnam, first day in the bush and nobody around us. I don't know what I would have done had I been alone or had I been in charge of the group I was in. Luckily, this sergeant who was on a second tour of duty picked up a trail and in three or four hours we met up with the tail end of the company.

Lance Corporal Rich Sherwood

We left Camp Carroll for an exercise in August up into an area called Mutter's Ridge and we went on patrol up there and we stayed out for about thirty-five days. Thirty-five days patrolling that area before we returned to Camp Carroll, and it was the most difficult and arduous time of my entire tour, without exception.

We stayed up on one hill for three . . . probably closer to four weeks. And by that time we were pretty well wiped out, tired. Those of us who had been through this entire operation had been out for better than thirty days. We were so disgusted with the whole thing that when a Marine general flew out to check the morale and see how we were doing—in a protest of having been left out there so long with no relief, very few replacements for the wounded that we'd lost or the dead we'd lost, and the company getting smaller and smaller, and the conditions getting worse and worse—that quite a few of the guys shaved our heads sort of as a protest. That turned out to be a pretty poor decision on our part because you've got a shaved head in the hot sun and you put your helmet back on and you start getting blisters and problems, so we all regretted our protest movement.

Sergeant Major Neal King

One real interesting character was the one-four [tactical air control] representative that I met. A corporal in L Company. He was a very competent NCO. He could control airstrikes or helicopter evacs at night or anything else. But he used to make me nervous every time I got around him because he had a slogan on his helmet that said "Fuck God, I make my own luck."

Chaplain Bob Bedingfield

I remember sitting on top of a hill one day. We had claimed that hill the first day; the second day we were still there and we had our positions. It was a very hot, quiet afternoon. A patrol was out; the rest of us were in and I hunkered down to take a nap and had no sooner closed my eyes about midafternoon than there was this terrible roar and explosion at the top of the hill, just a couple of meters above me. A rocket had been fired at us and had hit a tree at the very top of the hill and exploded. The explosion took away four NCOs who were playing cards and two that were watching. Instant death. And I went up and gave them last rites. Chaplains do all things for all men. I looked down at my hand and my hand was just . . . covered with blood. Shrapnel continued to impact and the rockets kept coming. I was standing out there in the wide open with the rockets still coming at us, doing nothing more than being angry. Angry! Cursing God! Cursing the North Vietnamese! Cursing everything around because so little of it made sense.

Corporal Vito Lavacca

The news of . . . Robert Kennedy's assassination and Martin Luther King's assassination and the riots at the Democratic National Convention were just kind of ho-hum events. Just seems like that was takin' place so far, far away, it didn't have anything to do with us.

.

SEPTEMBER 1968

Lance Corporal Rich Sherwood

They finally decided to bring another company out, I guess to keep the firebase going with the 105 [artillery] crew, and we were flown finally, after about thirty-five days, back to Camp Carroll. We had been out so long and we just looked as bad as you can get. Filthy dirty. I'm not sure in the entire company you could get one uniform that was an entire piece if you took everybody's. We were ragged, we were filthy, we were extremely tired.

We'd taken a lot of hits and we had a lot of walking wounded. We got off the 46s at Carroll and had a lot of new guys that were waiting there to join the company. There was a hot chow line not too far from the LZ, so as we came off, the first thing we could do was get a decent meal. Guys were dragging their packs, dragging their rifles in the dust at Camp Carroll, which was just ever-present at that time of the year. And here were these new guys in their bright spanking-new green jungle utilities and fresh boots that hadn't turned that gross reddish yellow color yet. They were nice and crisp and they had hats and they all looked like Marines look in the picture books. And here we come, probably about a hundred strong—bandaged, bloody, filthy, smelly, bearded Marines that had been out for some thirty-five days. And these guys had paper plates and ladles to serve us food and we just looked at the food and reached in with our bare hands that were filthy and awful and just grabbed handfuls of steak, and the hell with the knife and fork. One of the new guys looked at me and I said, "Where are you guys from?" and they said, "We're new guys, we're going to join Lima Company. Do you know when Lima Company is coming back in?" And I looked at him and said, "We are Lima Company." And these brand new guys just looked absolutely aghast at us and said, "You guys are Lima Company? You guys are Marines?" I said, "Don't worry, son,"—by then I was the old man of twenty-two—"in a week or two weeks, you'll look just like us and nobody will be able to tell whether you've been here two months or two years. You'll all look like garbage like we do."

.

Chaplain Bob Bedingfield

One day we were operating out of the back side of Camp Carroll . . . to the south just a bit. There was a village that was populated by both South Vietnamese refugees and Montagnards [one of the many non-Vietnamese ethnic groups that inhabit the mountainous border regions of Vietnam]. There was not much of a relationship between Montagnards and the South Vietnamese. The South Vietnamese had been their oppressors for a very, very long time. The Montagnards had been put on very high ground, away from the water, and yet had been expected to maintain themselves and grow their own crops. But all their crops were water-dependent. The issue was, how could we get water to them? So I went out to the battalion and said, "Okay, who knows anything about windmills?" The most absurd request in the world. Two guys from Kilo Company came forward, from Iowa, who knew a whole lot about windmills. And between what we could get and what we could steal, we probably built the finest low-level windmill that has ever been seen in Vietnam, that was able to pump a minimal but required amount of water a distance of some hundred meters, into the fields that were being cultivated by the Montagnards.

.

Gunnery Sergeant Jimmie Clark

We had spent a little time at Carroll and we was in one of the tents . . . myself and 1st Sergeant Long and a few more staff NCOs. We commandeered some rat traps somewhere and there was rats everywhere. I may have been half drunk or something, but I decided that I was gonna have me a rat killin' that night. I baited traps all on the inside of the tent, under bunks, and all night long them damn traps would go off and 1st sergeant would holler, "Clark! You got another one!" Hell, I got up and stabbed one or two. I think I ended up getting thirty-some rats that night. They wasn't likin' cheese too much. The best bait was that Dawson, Georgia, peanut butter. Out of C-rations.

.

Lance Corporal Vincent C. Morrison

Sometimes we ran out of chow. When we had been getting our Cs, we used to throw the peanut butter and crackers over the side of the hill. Nobody wanted to eat them. We'd had enough chow. Now we had to go back on the side of the hill to pick this stuff up. There was this guy, a Swede, and he says, "I've got to show you how to eat this stuff." He caught a salamander. And he put the little salamander in between the peanut butter and crackers. I said, "How can you eat that?" And he says, "Wait till the eyes blink."

.

PFC Jim Howe

One day during the day we were sitting in our position and I was talking to a fellow that had over a year in country. He was very short and was ready to get out. And he was taking me under his wing and telling me what I should and shouldn't do. As I was talking to him, some sort of noise sounded far off on one of the adjoining mountains. This guy's eyes seemed to dilate, his chin tightened, and the next thing I knew he was making a move toward the hole. And finally he turned around and said, "Get into the hole." I did what he told me to do and I said, "What's going on?" And he said, "That report, that sound that you heard, was a recoilless rifle." And he went on to explain what a recoilless rifle could do. But I noticed that first he took the opportunity to use his knowledge to obtain cover and safety. And then he told me to get in the hole. So the first lesson that I learned was that you have to obtain knowledge and you have to use that knowledge if you are going to survive the Vietnam experience. I don't think it was cowardly for him to do that. You have to react immediately. If you fail to react, you fail to come back.

.

PFC Pops Wandell

We landed on this hill, the whole company. We're in the middle of nowhere. It was a big forest and they dropped us in there. There's nothing around. James [Howe] and I were in the same hole just laying in the woods.

PFC Pete Tramonte

He used to say, "James, pick something soft that you can dig in for the fox-hole."

PFC Pops Wandell

By this time it's about six or seven o'clock. It's getting dark. I had first watch that night. Then the second watch comes up and I wake Jim up and say, "Watch." I didn't even get to sleep and I hear, "Pops, Pops, stop that. What are you doing?" I wasn't doing anything. James said, "You grabbed my leg." I said, "No, I'm not grabbing your leg." So I went back to sleep and then we changed watch again.

PFC Jim Howe

You used to set the watch ahead, right? You'd stand ten minutes of watch and set the [wrist] watch ahead. I had a half year of college at the time and it took me thirteen months to figure that out.

PFC Pops Wandell

So James gets the watch and we're laying there and all of a sudden he says, "Pop." "Jim, I'm not doing anything." He looks around and this monkey is sitting right there looking eyeball to eyeball.

PFC Jim Howe

He tried to get my rifle!

Chaplain Bob Bedingfield

It's amazing how the Commandments are so easily broken. "Thou shall not steal" really was rationalized by all of us, because the issue was that those that had, had just so the rest of us who hadn't could get.

The Army, of course, was always fair game for us and every so often we would be assigned to a particularly cushy job of protecting a battalion-size or company-size artillery unit that the United States Army would roll in on wheels. It just amazed me that we were fighting for the same country but fighting with such very different equipment. And the revelation would continue to show that the Army had to maintain itself with hot chow and soft mattresses when we were living out of our backpacks, carrying everything that we possibly could or would ever want.

And so, as we got into situations that would make life a bit more habitable for us, the Army was always fair game. It was invariable that Marines could supply the kinds of things that were needed. Let me give you a for instance . . . We pulled into a little village just south of the Rockpile. And there were a lot of refugees who had come down from Khe Sanh. With them was a South Vietnamese priest, a Father Ho. I went to meet Father Ho and to pay my respects to him. He had some 3,000 refugees with him. He was much more than a priest. He was not the head man but certainly the counselor, the prime minister; he was the physician; he was the chief of police. He was the guy that gave order to disorder. And I said to him, "Father, what do you need? What are the kinds of things that you need?" And he said, "I have antibiotics and I need to keep antibiotics cool, and in order to keep antibiotics cool, I have to have a refrigerator. In order to run a refrigerator, I have to have a generator."

So, with all the innocence I could muster, I went to Mike Company and said, "Gentlemen, I have a problem. And the problem is, I need one generator and one refrigerator." Now the setting for this is at least 150 miles from any kind of reasonableness for the fulfillment of that request in the midst of a combat zone.

Well, Marines tend to do the impossible well, don't they? Within one day I had a refrigerator and within two days I had three generators. I woke up one morning, being shaken awake by a sergeant who said to me, "Padre, I want you to see something." So I rolled out and went down a little kind of draw outside the village and there sat three generators, each of them with the tac marks [unit tactical markings] still on them. And he said, "Which one do you want?" And I said, "Eeney, meeney, miney, mo" and picked the one I wanted and said, "What are you going to do with the other two?" He said, "Don't ask, you needn't know." Within a very short period of time, that generator was rigged, that refrigerator was going, and I thought that was the end of the story.

I went back to Father Ho and said, "Is everything alright?" Now you have to understand that being able to provide the impossible makes you a miracle man. But the wonderful thing about Vietnamese with miracle men is not only did they give you their thanks but they also gave you their shopping list. The next thing he needed was a jeep. So I went to Lima Company, not wanting to overstay or overwork my interest in Mike Company, and said, "I need a jeep." And lo and behold, within twenty-four hours I had two jeeps, both of whom had Army tac marks on, one of whom I took, painted off the tac marks, and gave to Father Ho, and the other one had to go back to its home.

Invariably, that kind of attitude, of taking care of those who were in need, taking care of one another, is what remains probably best in my mind. The idea is that Marines were able to make a difference for Marines and for those people that Marines cared for.

·

PFC Lex Payne

I've seen several acts of individual heroism in Vietnam, but I guess the most heroic person or persons I met when I was over there were the old-salt corporals, the squad leaders, who had to go out at night with an ambush. A lot of times half of his guys were new guys and they were usually about four people under strength. He had to make sure everybody stayed awake. He had to know when to set the ambush off. He had to know whether to stay or to run and pop a green flare and go in. He had to be able to call in artillery. He had to be able to call in airstrikes or even naval gunfire from the USS *New Jersey*. He had to be able to call in a medevac chopper. He had to be able to read a map and a compass.

Corporal Vito Lavacca

Concerning the drugs over there. There really wasn't very much of it that I saw. . . . Maybe down around Saigon or someplace, or maybe after I got out of there. The worst, the most drug use I ever saw was guys smokin' a joint now and then, and it was generally five or six people on one joint.

Stories of people being high on watch or durin' patrols . . . I never experienced any of that over there. I never saw it or even heard of it. Most of the guys, I think, were too scared . . . to do anything that would alter their senses. Everyone was like a coiled spring and they . . . pretty much had to be that way or wanted to be that way to be sure that they were prepared. I remember guys wouldn't take their boots off at night. They'd sleep with their boots on. They'd be afraid that if they took their boots off and . . . and we were hit during the night, they wouldn't be ready. So the use of drugs . . . very, very little from what I could see.

PFC Kevin Sweeney

November 1st, Lyndon Johnson stopped the bombing. We were on the northernmost point of Con Thien watching the NVA come down with their lights on in their trucks because they knew they weren't going to get artillery or anything. We watched them. That was it. A couple of days later they say, "Okay, you guys go out. You guys go kill them." Well, that's what we did. We went out, we tried to kill them, but the problem was they killed us.

· · · · · · · · · · · · · · · ·

PART THREE

AFTER THE BOMBING HALT

WAR WITH ONE HAND TIED,

1968–1969

41

• • • • • • • • • • • • • • •

THE BOMBING HALT

The war had changed dramatically since 3/3 came ashore in May of 1965. The halt to the bombing of the DMZ called on 1 November 1968 by President Johnson added a new dimension, which took on a personal character to the men of the battalion. A bombing halt was one thing to diplomats and to Americans safe at home. To the embattled Marines along the northern frontiers of South Vietnam, it was quite another. Marines were forced to watch helplessly as large convoys of men and munitions, instruments of war designed for their own destruction, came toward them from north of the Ben Hai River. It was like fighting with one hand tied, a phrase Westmoreland used in his memoirs to describe the entire war.

Corporal Vito Lavacca

It was about this time during my tour that . . . they stopped the bombing of North Vietnam. Everyone's hopes had really skyrocketed when the peace talks became public. And then it just seemed like they went on and on, negotiating over the shape of the table they should meet at in Paris. Here we all were in Vietnam, people getting blown away, day by day, and all these statesmen in Paris are discussing whether or not they should sit around an oval table or a square table or a round table.

I had a squad out on a night listening post. Up on the DMZ, someplace outside of Con Thien. We were way up on a hill, overlooking the DMZ and a part of the Ho Chi Minh Trail in the mountains. And we saw a truck convoy coming down. We could follow it with a night scope . . . coming down through the DMZ, from the Ben Hai River on our side of the DMZ. And we counted about fifty vehicles. Trucks and jeeps. And we estimated probably two to five individuals with each vehicle. We called for an airstrike. I only had a squad and I hadda call back to the platoon, which called to the company and the company had to check with the battalion and the battalion had to check with the regiment and the regiment had to check with division and division had to check with the commander of I Corps who had to check with Saigon who had to check with Washington. And three days later, word came back to us that we could go ahead with the airstrike.

Everybody in the squad just looked at each other. And the joke was, "Did we remember to tell them that this was a convoy and that it was moving or did we leave that out?" I mean, three days! By now, Charlie was down havin' lunch with Westmoreland in Saigon!

PFC Kenneth K. George

This definitely hurt morale. It only got worse as time went on. I really pity the guys that were over there in the early seventies.

Corporal T. J. Kelly

This was supposedly going to bring the gooks to the peace table or something. Sitting up there at Con Thien, it was pretty hairy because we felt the bombing was necessary to keep the gooks off our backs. I counted as many as fifty trucks in one convoy just coming right at us, coming down south.

This went on for a few days and then we started taking all kinds of rockets. They were being fired from the DMZ or just south of the DMZ. In the towers the spotters were looking for flashes and they decided there was one area in particular where a lot of rockets were originating from. It was to the west of Con Thien where the DMZ jutted off to the southwest. The NVA were coming out of the DMZ, setting up rockets, firing them, and scooting back across the line again.

They decided there would be an operation down that way. And we were all sitting there waiting to go and all of a sudden we started taking rockets and mortars like crazy at Con Thien and we canceled the lift for that day. We went the next day. We got in the 53s and it was just a little short ride out there to the area about a mile or two away.

When that bird came in, I had that tightening in your gut you get every time you come into an LZ, when you expect to get reamed out by bullet fire coming up through the floor of the airplane. The bird came in and we scrambled out of it. All quiet. So far so good. They waited until we got about half of the battalion in and they timed their rockets to try and catch the birds as they hit. It was a mess. As a 46 landed, the rear door opened, the guys came running out, and a rocket hit right behind them. Half of them got blown right back into the airplane. The bird picked up and this brown smoke just poured out of the side of it like burning oil, and I said, "Oh, God. Get that thing out of here," because I didn't want a crippled bird in the zone and then we're really stuck. He did, he picked it up, and he limped back to C2.

We got about half the battalion in and we were taking KIAs like crazy. This friend of mine named Greenspan was a grunt in Lima Company and he was a real funny guy. He was from New York and he was always making comments about the lifers, not nasty but humorous. Lifers even laughed at it too, but they didn't like him because he was a kind of anti-establishment type guy. So he had like ten days to go in his tour and as punishment for all the ball-breaking he had done to them, they made him go on this operation. But not as a grunt, as a medical supplies humper for the battalion surgeon. It was a pretty safe job, but he got killed on the LZ with rockets. Ten days to go in country.

I got a flight of Phantoms circling over us and we had already spotted the flashes where the rockets were coming from. The jets tallyhoed that they saw the target and I said, "Okay, you're cleared and hot," and they said, "Negative, DASC won't give us clearance to run on the target." I said, "Why? Why? What's the matter?" They said, "The target is over the red line," meaning inside the DMZ. They had to wait on clearance from a higher authority. I said, "I'm clearing you in. I'll take full responsibility," and all this kind of thing and they wouldn't buy it. In the meantime, the rockets were coming in.

Finally one of our leaders decided, "Well, screw this," and they canceled the rest of the lift. All of a sudden the choppers stopped coming in, the jets were circling overhead but not attacking, and the rockets were just coming in one after another. Somebody says, "Okay, move off the LZ, everybody move into the trees." We were running, just a-shittin' and a-gittin' to get away from the rockets. We moved into the trees and a sergeant said, "Don't shake the trees. Don't shake the trees. If they see the tree shaking, then they'll know where we're at. Then they'll send rockets into the woods."

Tanks came down from Con Thien and we boarded the tanks and they were

going to give us a lift back up so we didn't have to walk it. We were all standing around the tanks and this guy carrying a machine gun from Mike Company
recognized me and said, "Way to go with the air," or something like that because he was very unhappy that we had the jets there but they wouldn't attack
the target. I was very bitter. I wanted to assassinate Lyndon Johnson and all this
sort of thing.

The regiment called, it was like five hours later when we were back on the
road, and they said that they had received clearance to fire on the target. Well,
five hours later, there are no rockets there. The gooks are gone. They're back
inside the safety of the DMZ. I said, "Negative, cancel the request." They said,
"No, we're going to go do it anyhow." I thought to myself that it sounded like a
cover-your-ass type thing where they would just go through the motions of an
airstrike at a piece of real estate and say, "Well, yes, we did return fire, just a
little late." Five hours is totally useless. I was very bitter about the whole experience. I thought if you've got to commit troops to something like that, you don't
just leave them hanging out there to dry. If you're going to go into a war, you've
got to go to win. You can't be playing by some kind of weird rules that you make
up as you go along. It was pretty lousy. I lost a good friend. I lost Greenspan.
There were a lot of Marines killed on that LZ.

NOVEMBER 1968

PFC Mike Velasquez

When we got into some hot spots I prayed. I wasn't overly religious. I never
have been. When we got into these tight spots I always told God, "I don't prom-
ise anything, God. A lot of guys out here are promising you things they're not
going to keep. I want to be realistic." I guess I've always been that way. I said,
"God, pull me out of this. I'm not promising anything but if you'll pull me out
of this, we'll work something out."

·

PFC Lex Payne

On November the 10th we were on a patrol in about the same area that we
had been in the firefight on March the 6th. It was hot and we were all sweating
and we were tired and we were kind of keyed up and looking around and this
prop job comes flying over us. It was pretty low and we were wondering what the
hell he was doing. All of a sudden he starts dropping these leaflets. So we picked

them up and they read, "Happy Birthday, Marines." And then they played the Marine Corps hymn as they flew around. Nobody said anything for ten or fifteen minutes. We just milled around. We were all kind of choked up but we wouldn't admit it. And of course after the aircraft flew off there was the usual jokes, like "It grabs me right here" and people grabbed their crotch, and guys yelled, "Eat the apple, fuck the Corps," that kind of stuff. But it took about ten or fifteen minutes for everybody to get their composure back.

.

Lance Corporal Jim Howe

Out of all my Vietnam experiences, Con Thien stands primary in my memory. I really loved that place. It afforded me a sense of security, although where it was positioned was probably one of the most advanced and dangerous compounds that American forces ever had. However, I liked the layout of it and also it gave me a sense of tradition and history and I knew that Con Thien at one time was a French position. From the bunkers you could look out and see the flat lands off to the east going towards Cua Viet. You could see the sand and you knew that somewhere over that sand was the ocean, and that always meant a lot to me since I was from Rockaway Beach in New York City, which is adjacent to the ocean. You'd look off the north and you'd see the hills in the Demilitarized Zone.

At Con Thien we had a bunker that afforded us protection. We got our back mail, and it was very nice. We had strung up some electric wire and had light in the bunker which afforded us the opportunity to sit around at night and to socialize with the other guys in the squad.

One time at Con Thien we received packages from home and Pete Tramonte got a package containing Ronzoni spaghetti and Ragu spaghetti sauce. We took the exterior of my helmet, the metal portion, to a curve of the road that ran around the interior minefield. It was quite rutty. These ruts were made by tanks and when it rained the water would collect. Pete went into the puddle and took the exterior of this helmet and filled it up with water from the puddle. We brought it back to our bunker and we started to boil it. We were going to make spaghetti. All we had to do with the sauce was just heat it up with that plastic explosive, C4.

I had to do something, possibly check and make sure people were in their holes, so I left the bunker. Upon returning I started down the stairs and the smell of the tomato sauce made me immediately think of being back home and walking into my house where my mother would be cooking spaghetti and sauce. It was outstanding. It was a smell that was unusual to Vietnam. It was a smell that I think would make any American that walked into the hooch immediately think of their home.

Pete was in charge of the situation and, being Italian, knew what he was doing as far as cooking. Finally we had maybe ten guys in the hooch and we all sat down and we had a spaghetti dinner. It was delicious. The mood made all of us bright. The sense of family that we all have, even today, this sense of family was compounded again, reinforced, because now we were sitting down for a family meal. We had the smells and the taste of home and we were all together and that basically gave us this camaraderie, this family type of feeling.

I remember this very well because at the time they had asked me if I would be interested in transferring to recon. And I said, "Sure." This is one of the experiences that made me rethink the situation. I was together with them now for maybe four or five months, but I knew at that point that these guys had become my family, my friends. I could count on them. I knew their weak points. I knew their strong points. I knew who was good at doing what and in what situation somebody would rise to the occasion, someone's expertise would become important and they would take command of the situation.

For instance, we've had guys that were terrific point men that could see things that nobody else could see. And you had guys that when we hit a firefight would know exactly what to do without being told by their squad leader or their fire team leader. They would instinctively do what they were supposed to do, make decisions on where they should locate themselves, where the gun should be located. And they were right. So everybody had their little niche. And I said to myself, "There's no way in the world that I can leave these guys to go to recon."

·

Lance Corporal Pops Wandell

They [another unit] used to have these big recoilless rifles near us, so one night Jim snuck up and borrowed a big can of their fruit cocktail.

Lance Corporal Jim Howe

It was a gallon can and it was just myself and Pops on hole watch. We had opened it up shortly before darkness and when we had our fill, we put the can down, both of us relying on each other that there would be some saved in the morning. While I was on hole watch the first time, I didn't bother to take any and naturally it was Pops' turn for two hours and he in turn awakened me again. And this time I was a little bit hungry and I knew that it had gotten cooler and that the fruit cocktail would really taste good. I didn't have a spoon and without light or anything else I picked the can up to take a mouthful of fruit cocktail, and although it went down rather easily, it felt that it was a little more chunky than I had remembered it earlier that night.

Lance Corporal Pops Wandell

So all of a sudden I hear Jim make spitting sounds. I said, "What's the matter, James?" And he said, "Oh, there's all lumps in here." I said, "It must be the seeds." He said, "You want some, Pops?" I said, "No, I'll wait until morning."

Lance Corporal Jim Howe

In the morning when I looked down and I saw that the whole thing was infested with insects, I suddenly realized what the extraordinary lumpiness was caused by. I had taken the can trying to be a wise guy in the dead of night so that Pops wouldn't know that I was cheating and because of that I inhaled a good portion of the insects from the area. That in turn gave me dysentery and I spent quite a few days getting over the experience. It was Thanksgiving of 1987 before I ventured having my first bowl of fruit cocktail from that time, 1968 . . . almost a nineteen-year period.

Lance Corporal Pops Wandell

Now it's the big thing. They take the ants and they put chocolate on them.

Lance Corporal Jim Howe

I was ahead of my time.

.

Lance Corporal Jim Howe

Christmas Day. By this time I was settled in and I was in a position of authority in the squad. Christmas for any eighteen- or nineteen-year-old, especially from a Catholic Irish background, is a very special time. It's time spent with your family. It's a time of giving and receiving. It's a time of renewed worship, a renewed sense of your religion. This was the first time that I would be celebrating without my family and all of the support groups that I have known growing up.

My parents had sent me sheet music with traditional Christmas songs. A kid from the South by the name of Saint had a real good singing voice and he was of Baptist background, knew all the traditional songs, and we had an enjoyable time. We sang a few of the carols and everybody participated. So as bad as it might be being away from home for Christmas, these people had become as close, if not closer, than your normal family members. I think what made Christmas bearable was that you were with family and with anything that you could

Lieutenant Joe Thompson, who would survive a gunshot wound to the head, is shown at
Christmastime, 1968, at Quang Tri. (Courtesy Joe Thompson)

borrow from the home front, such as singing of songs or carols, people receiving
packages for Christmas. It could have been a lot worse.

Christmas Eve—we spent that on an ambush. Thank God there was no contact on Christmas Eve. I can remember thinking how paradoxical it was. The
Son of Man was born on this day to save the world and here the people we were
saving couldn't take the time out to put down their arms.

42

. . . .

OPERATION TAYLOR COMMON

Among the goals assigned the Marines in 1968 was to locate and destroy several enemy base areas. Of particular concern was Base Area 112, which sat in the hilly, dense jungle region west of Danang and posed a threat to that population center. In response to this threat, III MAF formed Task Force Yankee under Brigadier General Ross Dwyer. Originally composed of 1st Marine Division units, this force was augmented in late December by the 1st and 3d Battalions, 3d Marines. For the first time in over two years, the battalion would operate outside the DMZ area.

Chaplain Bob Bedingfield

Taylor Common is the place where a lot of my memories reside. We operated out of An Hoa [Combat Base, a major Marine position south and west of Danang], that rather dusty, dirty place that sat—and one had to wonder why it ever did sit where it did—surrounded by hill lines. Of all the places for Marines to be. Flown down on 130s, evacuated very quickly into a muddy field alongside the airstrip because the belief was that we were going to move out rather rapidly when in fact we didn't. We sat there for three days. At least there was hot chow. **315**

Midway through TAYLOR COMMON, on 15 January 1969, the 3d Marines suffered a severe loss. A helicopter carrying regimental commander Colonel Michael M. Spark, Sergeant Major Ted McClintock, Lieutenant Colonel Ermil Whisman (the CO of 1/12), and others was shot out of the sky. All aboard were killed.

Chaplain Bob Bedingfield

On Taylor Common we were heloed out into the back . . . really into the back country. So far back that we ran into areas, early on, where the North Vietnamese hadn't bothered to pick up their gear and run because they had no sense that we were there. We would wander into places and positions, into hooches and rest camps that either the North Vietnamese would fight for or would have evacuated so that the rice was still in pots. That was always eerie, always frightening.

The whole battalion moved out again into various directions. I was with India Company and India Company took off and went deep, deep into the terrain west of Taylor Common. We humped for two days and at the end of two days we took the high ground one night and it was eerie. Because as we sat on the top of that hill, there was a general feeling among all of us in the company, and the company was then commanded by a man named John Trott . . . that we were not by ourselves. Odd.

That was reinforced the next morning when we awoke to the sound of a rooster down in the valley below us. For whatever reason, we didn't go down and investigate the rooster, but we moved off to make the great circle to finish up the patrol that day to get back to a base camp. We came down to a valley that had a very large river moving through it.

As we got to the river edge where we were to cross and pick up a trail, the scout and the point man picked up movement on a hillock on the other side of the river. We dropped and paused and then there was no more movement. We crossed the river fairly rapidly in column. I was about number twelve . . . number thirteen, in the column of roughly fifty men. In front was the dog and the lead fire team and then the platoon leader (a guy named Joe Thompson) and then a radioman and then the rest of us, single file.

Hospital Corpsman 3d Class Douglas D. "Doc" Stone

An NVA was spotted in the grass to the right of a stream next to the trail that we were walking. Actually, all he was was a decoy. We fired a few rounds at him but missed. What this did was to let the NVA ambush that was ahead of us know that we were coming.

Doc Doug Stone, recipient of the Silver Star Medal on Operation TAYLOR COMMON *for "conspicuous gallantry and intrepidity," is shown here with a Vietnamese child. (Courtesy Doug Stone)*

Chaplain Bob Bedingfield

We moved out from that hillock and down the trail and couldn't have gone more than 300 meters when suddenly there was a burst of machine-gun fire, picked up by at least two more machine guns. We had walked into an ambush. The entire column dropped and I moved forward as quickly as I could to find out what the story was. We were pinned down. Absolutely pinned down.

John Trott moved forward and brought up a machine gunner, a youngster from Texas. The call came from the front of the column that they needed more ammunition. I collected more ammunition, in my helmet, my pockets, my flak jacket, and ran forward and dropped it and looked out to see in front of me that the platoon leader was down.

Doc Doug Stone

That's when we got the call for "one-six up." One-six was the radio code name for corpsmen. So off I go, heading toward the ambush site. By the time I got there, I had already expended five or six magazines from my M16. I'm not really sure why I didn't get it. The rounds were flying all around me and the adrenaline rush was really something else. So I get to Joe and see what a mess he is. I start patching him up and giving him an IV and also firing back at the NVA trying to protect Joe. Finally everything settled down and the NVA ran toward the west and we called in the medevac helicopter to get Joe out of there.

Chaplain Bob Bedingfield

The corpsman and I had wrapped Joe Thompson's head as best we could. He was bleeding from the head, having taken a round through the top of it. And the last I saw of him was when we brought in the medevac helicopter and Joe Thompson was lifted into the air in a harness in a sling, and as he was lifted the bandage began to unwind from the top of his head. The chopper took rounds, so it turned very quickly before Thompson got into the chopper and started down the valley. The bird with a man dangling underneath . . . swinging like a pendulum . . . with the bandage slowly coming unwrapped from his head.

Trott, meanwhile, got an M79 grenade launcher going, and an M60 machine gunner rushed into the machine-gun nest and broke it up. And in breaking it up was killed himself. Written up, eventually, for a Medal of Honor which was given to him.

Doc Doug Stone

After Joe was medevaced, we started heading out again, on the trail. I don't believe we got but about fifty feet when a sniper in a hole shot Cumbie, who was the dog handler. Shot Cumbie right through the forehead. The scout dog was unable to warn anybody of the NVA in the hole. The next person to get it was Lance Corporal Prom [the Marine who was awarded the Medal of Honor— see Appendix B]. He had a fair idea of where the gook was shooting from and started returning fire, but he took a round in the chest. At this time, I'm going pretty crazy again. I used up all my M16 rounds and called up from the back for some more. Someone threw me up another bandolier and I used up all those rounds. And at that point the M60 machine gunner to my right froze up, so I grabbed the M60 machine gun and started firing in the direction of the NVA. Finally, I'm not sure which one, one of the grunts nailed the NVA.

Lot of the guys in my platoon were emotionally upset after the firefight. Lot of them were crying and a lot of them were confused. And I did the best that I

Lance Corporal William R. Prom, who posthumously received the Medal of Honor.
(Courtesy Department of Defense)

could to try and calm them down. Finally, later that day we made it back to the LZ without any further contact. I got a Silver Star out of my craziness.

Chaplain Bob Bedingfield

Months and months and months later, when I was back in this country, I got a note from Joe Thompson. He'd seen my name somewhere and wrote me a note from the VA hospital in Michigan saying to me that he was much on the mend and things were getting better. 'Bout a year and a half later I got two T-shirts from him inscribed "Southeast Asian War Games, 2d Place," which I thought was an absolutely wonderful bit of humor and commentary on the event.

Gunnery Sergeant Jimmie Clark

We were out on a hill somewhere and we got holed up and couldn't be re-supplied (because of the weather) by choppers, and we were held up and lost strength and had eaten about all our food. We were making three meals out of one and were held up because we was so weak waiting for the weather to break.

Chaplain Bob Bedingfield

I was with Kilo Company and we were rained into the top of the hill and there was no food at all. We went eight days without food. I'd never gone eight days in my whole life without food. It is just an amazing experience. We stopped talk-ing about sex the second day and the stories about food got greater and greater and greater. Even the fruitcake went. [C-ration fruitcake was almost universally despised.] We couldn't move because of the monsoons and because we didn't have food; we just stayed in position and I can remember time after time just wondering, wondering to myself how long we were going to last.

Gunnery Sergeant Jimmie Clark

It was a Sunday and Chaplain Bedingfield was holding services on the hill. At the time he was praying and asking for food, this Marine spotted this wild pig coming down the trail and he called in on the radio and asked permission if it would be alright to shoot that pig. He definitely received permission.

Chaplain Bob Bedingfield

The pig got blown away on the "Amen." And I suppose from that point on, at least with Kilo Company, there was nothing I could ever do wrong.

Gunnery Sergeant Jimmie Clark

The next day the weather lifted and the choppers come in and we got resup-plied.

Chaplain Bob Bedingfield

About the first of the year, he [Lieutenant Colonel Bob Bates] had been re-lieved by a man named Dutch Schulze. I was close to all the battalion com-manders but, I think, particularly to Schulze. Schulze had a pragmatism, a style

Major General Richard C. Schulze, who, as a lieutenant colonel, commanded 3/3 for much of 1969. (Courtesy Department of Defense)

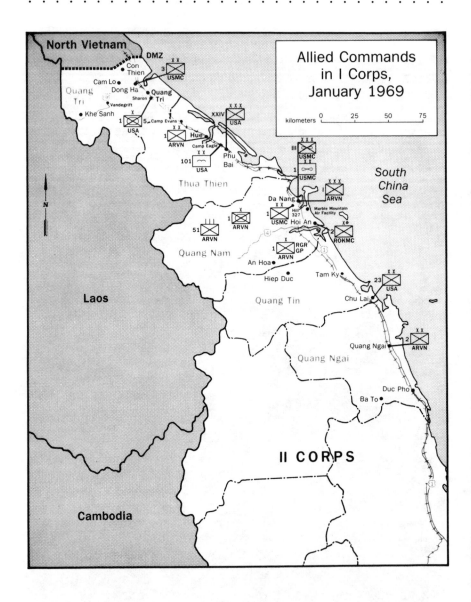

Allied Commands in I Corps, January 1969

and a manner that allowed the actual company commander and then platoon leader to very much take charge and do the things that had to be done. Dutch was in the field constantly. He was a grand leader for us because he could conceptualize what we had to do to carry out the mission but he allowed a free hand in the field. So what he really did was to grow Marines. He grew Marines in responsibility and leadership.

Dutch Schulze is dead. Dutch Schulze was always, for me, a paragon of what a leader should be about. He made major general, was director of personnel at

Headquarters, a guy who really took care of his own. His name has appeared in the newspapers as one who assisted Ollie North, in terms of his medical records in 1978. [During the Iran-Contra investigations it was alleged that someone had tampered with Oliver North's medical record to conceal the fact that he may have had emotional problems.] Some criticism [was] directed toward Schulze because of that, but those who directed the criticism just never knew what the bond was, how we forged the bond, those of us who served together.

TAYLOR COMMON ended for 3/3 on 16 February when the battalion was withdrawn. After spending a few days in the Danang area, 3/3 returned to the DMZ.

43

AN EROSION OF DISCIPLINE

By the late 1960s and early 1970s, the Corps itself began to experience the impact of the countercultural and Black Power movements, of growing drug use, and of widespread antiwar sentiment. Many Marines believed their toughest enemy was not the NVA but rather these societal changes that seemed to assault the very foundations of the Corps. In June 1971, the worsening state of affairs was summarized in a *Detroit News* article by Colonel Robert Debs Heinl, USMC (Retired), one of the Corps' most distinguished writers and historians: "By every conceivable indicator, our army that now remains in Vietnam is in a state of approaching collapse, with individual units avoiding or having refused combat, murdering their officers and noncommissioned officers, drug-ridden and dispirited where not near-mutinous." *

For 3/3 in 1969, the changes in the Corps were confined primarily to the rear areas. However, not even front-line units were immune, and the battalion was faced with breaches of discipline that would have been unthinkable several years before. One type of unauthorized activity was the bullshit band, an illegal form of entertainment by which

324 *Quoted in Phillip B. Davidson, *Vietnam at War* (Novato, Calif.: Presidio, 1988), p. 663.

some radio operators amused themselves during long night watches. It could also provide a potential source of intelligence for an alert and listening enemy. Obviously, the worst expression of a breakdown in discipline was fragging—the murder or attempted murder of a disliked officer or NCO by rolling a fragmentation grenade into their sleeping quarters.

Hospital Corpsman 2d Class "Doc" Jeffrey B. Bussiere (Brand New Guy)

I was assigned to 60 mortars of Mike Company. There was a lieutenant in charge who was from the Virginia area. On the radio at night . . . on the bullshit band . . . he'd get on the air and his nickname was "Grey Ghost" and he was supposedly a relative of the Swamp Fox; Marion, I think his name was. He was a very nice guy. About my age at the time and seemed to be pretty tight with the men in the unit. They seemed to look up to him and respect him. At the time I had heard rumors of things like fraggings. And people were always putting down boot lieutenants as, you know, worse than a boot enlisted man. He wasn't that way. He didn't give a lot of orders. He'd say things and make suggestions and occasionally tell you to do things. But for the most part, people did things because what he said made the most sense. I was pretty impressed with his quiet type of leadership.

.

PFC Ken George

We wanted to do the job, but the whole thing about that war which was a drawback from the getgo was the fact that in other wars you were sent there to do a job and you stayed there until the war was over and that was it. In Vietnam, you went there for thirteen months. Thirteen months seems like thirteen years when you first get there. But then all of a sudden before you know it, six months are gone by, and then seven and eight and nine, and then you start getting down to two or three months left and you just don't want to do a lot of the stuff that you did earlier in your tour. That had to hurt performance.

Granted, you had a lot more expertise and knowledge that you could relay on to the newer guys, but you lost the hungriness and desire that you had to do the job that you were sent there to do. That was compounded by the fact that the way the damn government handled the war. Giving days off. No war today because of Ho Chi Minh's death . . . no war for this reason, that reason . . . all these asinine things. We can go to this point, but we have to stop here because there is no bombing in this section.

Leadership. I always felt that in a battle situation that people turned to leaders and expect a quick decision. At those times there was little, if any, insubordination . . . where there might have been if we were at Con Thien or the Rockpile or when I'd have to get someone to burn the shitters or . . . mess duty. In the rear you get a lot of flak from the guys because they think that you are picking on them. When you are in the field and the second there is any kind of problem . . . the minute you open your mouth, they react and they react very quickly.

·

Doc Jeff Bussiere

We had a fragging of the battalion aid station. The doctor, Walter "Pepper" Ashford, was from Mississippi and he didn't get along too well with some of the colored soldiers in our unit. They would break their glasses or whatever and say that they'd have to stay in the rear. They were always finding some excuse to stay in the rear and trying to get some medical reason. He'd send them back to the field. He got to be very unpopular. They thought he was quite prejudiced, I think, just because he was from Mississippi. They wanted to get rid of him.

So when we settled back in up there, having come back from Taylor Common, all the corpsmen from the different units got together. There was a big tent out in back of the battalion aid station in 3/3. We were settled in there for the night and there was a first-class corpsman who outranked me and who was sort of second in charge of the battalion aid station there and he fell asleep on my bunk. I went over to the supply tent and stretched out on an air mattress on the floor.

In the middle of the night there were a couple of good-sized blasts and I thought we had incoming or something like that and went charging out and into the bunker. When I jumped in the bunker, I could hear all this screaming and moaning from the tent in back of the station, so I hopped out to see what was going on. Somebody had thrown two frags, one on either side of the tent in back of the battalion aid station, and a bunch of the corpsmen had been wounded. The first-class was sleeping with his head down at the foot of my bunk and he took a piece of shrapnel through his left arm and into his left chest that collapsed his left lung. So we hauled the three of them out and patched them up as best we could. If I'd been sleeping on that bunk I would have been dead, because I would have slept with my head up on the pillow and the whole top of the bunk was just shredded . . . hundreds of holes through everything.

·

Corporal Vito Lavacca

I never really experienced any cowardice over there. There was certainly fear on everyone's face, the whole time. It's like fear was issued to you with your rifle when you first got in country . . . and wasn't taken away from you until you landed safely back at El Toro, California. There were instances where guys would try to get out of patrols, fake an injury or an illness. But it really didn't come down to cowardice.

Very, very late in my tour, we were at Con Thien and Mike Company was preparing for an operation someplace. I only had a few days left in country so I wasn't going on the operation. But we had a platoon radioman who had a few months left and he just had a bad feeling about this operation. He was certain that he wasn't gonna make it. It was the night before and we weren't manning the lines that night and we had managed to get ahold of a bottle of bourbon and a couple of joints. And . . . we were in his bunker, just kind of relaxing and gettin' a little high. And he asked me if I'd break his arm to avoid his havin' to go on the operation.

We argued back and forth and first I thought he was just jokin'. But he was serious. And we went so far as to set up two ammo boxes and he put his arm across and he asked me to hit it with the butt of my rifle. It's a simple thing, I guess, but when it comes right down to it, I just didn't know how hard to hit his arm . . . I just couldn't bring myself to do it. I liked the guy and I would have done anything to get him out of going on the operation but . . . if there was an easy way of breakin' his arm, I think I woulda done it. But all I had visions of is that I would hit his arm too hard causing a compound fracture that would get infected and he'd lose his arm or somethin'. The next morning it was gonna be the last time I saw a lot of these people . . . and we just laughed about it and they took off. I promised him that on my way back through California—he lived around Anaheim—I would stop in and see his folks and let them know that he was okay.

By the time I got back to the States, I heard that he had been hit on the operation. It turned out that he was okay. It turned into a million-dollar wound and he came back to the States shortly after I did. But I often wonder how I could have faced his family if he had been killed on that operation and would I ever be able to . . . tell them the story of how he had wanted me to . . . break his arm.

·

Chaplain Bob Bedingfield

Never have I ever seen the Marine Corps better than I saw it in Vietnam. The level of leadership that we saw, from lance corporals and corporals and sergeants and . . . staff sergeants and gunnies and first sergeants and officers, was something that was exceptional. Rare, really rare, was the aberrant behavior.

Rare was the person who didn't fit, the person who didn't march, the person who didn't make it.

As chaplain, it was my theory that my job was to support both the mission and the men. Once in Camp Carroll a young fellow came to me and professed to be a pacifist. He was the duty pain-in-the-ass for the battalion, a guy who obviously didn't want to serve, didn't want to fight, only wanted one thing . . . to go to the rear with his gear. My take with him was a very simple one. If you were a pacifist, we would allow you to be a pacifist. And what that meant was that you gave me your M16 and I dropped the magazine out and took all the rest of the rounds you had and all your hand grenades, and now you were a pacifist and you went back to your unit. Because that was the way we had to operate.

Fortunately, those who allowed their feet to be bitten by rats, those who nicked themselves with K-Bars, those who occasionally shot themselves in the foot, were very, very few. 3/3 had absolutely outstanding leadership in the time I was with it.

Richard M. Nixon took the oath of office as president of the United States in January. His electoral victory was due, in part, to the public perception that he had a plan for ending the war in Vietnam; that policy became known as Vietnamization. This strategy, adopted without consulting the South Vietnamese leadership, represented not so much U.S. confidence in the progress of their Vietnamese allies as a determination to extract the United States from the war.

FEBRUARY–MARCH 1969

PFC Ray K. Wilmer

A lot of the guys would get newspapers from home and we had the *Stars and Stripes* to read and a lot of time we'd read about all the protesting and rioting back home about the war. We just couldn't understand it. Here we was, over there humping ourselves to death and we were worried about what was going to happen next, and here these bunch of long-haired hippies back home protested on the street and lived and did what they wanted to do. We swore when we got back home that we were going to lock and load on them. Of course, it never did happen, but it sure did give us a lot of comfort to think that when we did get back there we'd be able to talk to them and tell them what we had to say.

Captain Paul B. Goodwin

I arrived in Vietnam in March 1969 for my second tour and I ended up going to 3d Battalion, 3d Marines. At the time it was commanded by R. C. Schulze. When I reported in, the XO was a major named Skipper and he assigned me to Kilo Company. Kilo Company was in My Loc which was south of Con Thien and was an airstrip, and at one end of the airstrip was a Special Forces camp. The end that my company was on was a camp that was shared with some Army advisors and some ARVN troops.

I was there for about two days with a fellow I relieved. He wore a red bandana and everybody called him the Organ Grinder. Even the troops and his radio operator called him the Organ Grinder. The troops were reasonably dirty and long-haired . . . not the most disciplined that I had ever seen. But times had changed from 1965–66 till '69. My lieutenants . . . were a fairly independent group and didn't appear to be much better disciplined than the troops. One was named Bill Haskell who had the 1st Platoon. 2d Platoon was a guy named Ollie North, who has since had a lot of notoriety. The 3d Platoon was commanded by a fellow named Rich O'Neill. Bill Haskell was from Maryland, probably had two years of college. Went through Parris Island and was commissioned because he was very bright. Ollie of course was a Naval Academy graduate and Rich O'Neill was a college graduate and a little older.

I was a couple of days with this fellow called the Organ Grinder and the morning he left I got my 1st Sergeant, Gonzales, and I got my officers together and I told the officers . . . it was about eight o'clock in the morning . . . I said, "At ten o'clock I want you back in this CP and I want you clean shaven. . . ." They all had mustaches. "And I want your hair cut." They looked at me like I was insane, but they came back at ten o'clock with haircuts and their big old mustaches shaved. Then I said, "I want to tour the perimeter with each of you." And we did. In turn. Nobody was, in my opinion, paying much attention to the troops. They'd been there for about ten days and no effort had been made to set up a shower. Most of the time the officers hung around the CP.

I moved physically off the property of My Loc . . . and moved south and west to a river and set up and did some patrolling out of there for a few days.

·

In 1969, during a time of upheaval for the Corps, fifteen Marines posthumously won the Medal of Honor; two of them were in 3/3. One, as already recounted, was Lance Corporal William R. Prom. The other was PFC Ronald L. Coker.

PFC Ronald L. Coker, who posthumously received the Medal of Honor.
(Courtesy Department of Defense)

Lance Corporal Ken George

On the 25th or 26th of March 1969, we were at Fire Support Base Alpine out in western Vietnam, really out in the sticks. We were getting mortar fire on top of Alpine around dinner time every day, so we were out there finding out where these mortar tubes were. We came across where they had set up. Naturally, there were no gooks to be found, just some old rounds and stuff.

On the second night, we set up on top of this mountain and in the morning, we came around and again nothing happened. The next morning at about 6:00 A.M. we were getting ready to move out when a plane overhead spots gooks down in the valley, gets ahold of us through our company radio frequency, and tells us to stand put, he's going to call in an airstrike. So a couple of Phantoms come in there and they rock the ground with some 500-pounders for an hour or so. I mean there was shrapnel all over the place. It was a wicked, wicked airstrike. When it's over we got to go down there and check out the damage. It turns out there's a few gooks down there hiding under some rocks. One of them shoots our point man and kills him. The guy's name was Playford, a short-timer that was taking over point for a guy named Coker. Coker was supposed to be on point, but he acted like he didn't have the feel of the bush that day, and Playford was getting pissed off at him for not walking point properly.

Playford takes over point and gets shot and killed. Minutes later Coker has this guilt trip and goes out to try to save him and gets shot, doesn't die. The gook throws out a chicom and when he picks it up and tries to whip it away from Playford, it explodes and blows both of his hands off, shatters just about every bone in his body. He must have been shot about six or seven times. He had shrapnel all over every inch of his body and was still alive, still trying to drag Playford out of this hot spot. Finally, we flanked these gooks and we get a machine gun pumping belt after belt of rounds into this hole and killed all three of the gooks, but not before Playford and Coker both died and Coker subsequently received the Medal of Honor [see Appendix B].

44

• • • • • • • • • • • • • • • • •

SCHOOL SOLUTION

Captain Paul Goodwin

The first major contact that I was in occurred in My Loc. It was early one morning and Bill Haskell's platoon had been on an all-night ambush. Fortunately for us, and unfortunately for the North Vietnamese, a North Vietnamese company was apparently lost, about sixty or seventy people, I guess. Was on a trail right where the platoon was set up. As light broke, a couple of NVA officers moved up to the head of a column and apparently were discussin' a map, and Bill Haskell had the presence of mind . . . he was getting ready to break his ambush, and stopped everything and waited until they walked into the killing zone. And a big firefight ensued. Bill started running low on ammunition . . . called me . . . I got another platoon, some tanks, a little bit of the headquarters element, and went out and reinforced him. There was a firefight still goin' on. I put the 2d Platoon on line with Bill's 1st Platoon. Put the tanks on line with the two platoons and . . . it's the only time I think I've ever seen an assault that really developed similar to a Basic School solution. We fired the tanks, put in a lot of firepower, and assaulted through what was left of the company. We killed twenty, twenty-four NVA. We captured one, possibly two, and had thirty to thirty-five weapons and forty or fifty packs.

Bill Haskell, the platoon commander, was awarded the Silver Star for that action, and we only had one or two wounded. We killed at least one NVA officer and a great deal of intelligence information was gathered. Dutch Schulze, the battalion commander, flew out to meet me for the first time at the end of that engagement. And later the CG of XXIV Corps came up [a U.S. Army unit subordinate to III MAF but in control of all U.S. divisions in Northern I Corps], landed the helicopter, got out, and looked at the . . . weapons and packs and all that stuff. 'Cause it was a fairly large contact.

APRIL 1969

PFC Ray Wilmer

One of the things that sticks out in my mind is kids. We weren't around them too often. Most of the time we were on an operation; after we had been on an op for a month or six weeks, they'd take us back to a secured area, maybe a bridge or somewhere around a village. The smaller kids, they looked like they appreciated us. But they were hungry, they wanted food. And the older kids, the teenagers, they resented us. They were always cussing us, "Your mama does boom-boom with a water buffalo," and stuff like that. Mamasan and papasan, they didn't care. They were friendly because they had to be. Some of the guys in the unit would be around by a village on a truck or something, and they would light heat tabs [chemical briquettes] and throw them to them or give them a heat tab like it was candy or stuff like that. It would really hurt me. Some of the guys just hated them and thought everybody over there was Communist.

·

Doc Doug Stone

About my eighth month in the bush, I finally got my R and R to Sydney, Australia. I was ready for that. After I had taken about a two-hour shower and had couple of glasses of J&B scotch, a buddy and I decided to go out and check out the town. We're all dressed up and walking downtown Sydney and we get to the corner of one of the street walks. And around the corner they were doing some construction. Well, the street workers opened with a jackhammer and both my buddy and I dove into a store, into the door of a store, flat on our backs and then rolled over onto our stomachs in a crouched position. And the lady that owned the store really cracked up laughing saying, "I know where you guys are from."

Sydney was great. I ran into a beautiful girl down there. Her name was Maureen. And we fell in love pretty quick. Or at least I did. This was really a hard time for me . . . She said that she would hide me, help me change my name, and find a job if I would just stay down in Australia. That was a real tough decision. The night before I went back to Vietnam, I made sure I packed my suitcase and had everything ready to go. Because when I woke up to catch my taxi back to the airport, she was still sleeping. I'm not sure what I would have done if she would have woken up and said, "Hey, stay here."

·

Chaplain Bob Bedingfield

Divine service was always intriguing . . . You know, I suppose we always had awfully splendid attendance because in the field I was always the best show in town. I learned early on that the best service was a service that went no more than twenty minutes. Because, first of all, you didn't want to group people and, secondly, our attention spans ran awfully short. So the words were always words that were very simple and plain and the words were always words that ended with Communion. I carried a chalice and by the end of my ten months with 3/3, I had been on my third chalice. The first chalice was lost as a pack was lost. The second one took a round through the back and was split in two. And the third one was pretty bent and bruised by the time we finished.

I was out of Communion wine one day. I said to Dutch Schulze, "How 'bout some of yours?" Dutch always managed to carry a bottle of scotch with him. And so, understanding that it was for a good better than his good, for a real ecclesiastical requirement, he gave me his scotch. Put it in the chalice, watered it down, of course, and began to pass the common cup as I always did. And the first Marine took a drink and looked up at me and took a very long second drink and I had to take the chalice away from him. I think back and laugh and think that that was probably the best Communion that he ever had and also the greatest surprise.

·

Captain Paul Goodwin

You know, one of the things that I discovered about the company when I went to My Loc . . . is that not only did I make 'em clean themselves up, I made 'em build a shower and take showers and clean themselves up and shave, which they thought was terrible.

The other thing was that, Christ . . . my kids were carryin' 800 to 1,000 rounds of ammunition apiece. Goddamnit, they couldn't hardly move. I cut their basic allowance to about 400 rounds 'cause I felt that too often they were on automatic fire and just wastin' rounds. That held us in good stead over the months I was there. I don't think there was any question that aimed rounds count. That's what hits.

I insisted, routinely, that everybody get haircuts in the company. Even when we were on hills I made 'em cut their hair. We just carried those hand clippers and just wouldn't let 'em get so shaggy. Because I felt that all that was a break-down of discipline. It didn't make any difference how long a guy's hair was, but just the fact that you made him get a haircut was adhering to a discipline that they needed.

·

PFC Ray Wilmer

One time we had been out on a two-month operation and they brought us back to the rear somewhere and they gave us hot chow and said they had a flick for us. We gathered all around and got ready to watch the flick and believe it or not it was *The Green Berets* with John Wayne. Oh, guys went crazy! They was throwing everything at the screen, rocks and going crazy laughing at this stuff.

·

Corporal Pops Wandell

There was a guy named Henry who was in Pete Tramonte's fire team. We were in a real rough area—LZ Chance. We had a heck of a time getting this hill and had pushed the gooks off it. Jim and I are in our foxhole and Pete's sitting in another foxhole with this guy Henry. He had thick glasses and he looked a little Oriental.

Lance Corporal Pete Tramonte

He was part Filipino.

Corporal Pops Wandell

Jim and I are talking and having a good time and somebody yells, "Gooks in the line." And Jim says, "I'm going to check, Pops. You stay here." I said, "Oh, that sounds good." The gook came into the line. He'd left the hill that day when we took the hill. He came up the hill and Henry was sleeping against the tree and he opens his eyes and this gook comes up and thinks Henry's a gook and goes "Oi, oi, oi, oi" to Henry.

Lance Corporal Pete Tramonte

I had had the watch before Henry and we had had a sniper in our platoon who had bushy hair. I had woke Henry up to take the watch and I had laid down. I had seen this bushy-head fellow come up, but it was in the early morning, it was maybe five o'clock in the morning and I had thought to myself, "Well, it's the sniper coming down from the CP to take a whiz."

And the figure got closer and he put his hands on this tree I was sleeping against and he saw Henry and he started talking Vietnamese. And Henry says, "It's a gook." I looked up and I says, "Holy Christ, a goddamn gook!" But the kid, and he was a kid, didn't run back down the hill, he ran across the hill and Jim was in the next hole over and we were yelling, "It's a gook, it's a gook!" Jim threw a body block at him. I wanted a souvenir, but by the time I got to him he was nude. They took his pants, they took everything. I didn't get any spoils at all.

45

· · · · · · · · · · · · · · · · ·

THE BEGINNING OF THE END:
TROOP WITHDRAWALS

After the Nixon administration took office, rumors abounded about the future of U.S. forces in Vietnam. In May 1969 the president publicly stated that a reduction of troop levels in country was being studied. Then, after conferring with South Vietnam's President Nguyen Van Thieu at Midway in June, Nixon announced the immediate withdrawal of 25,000 troops. Before long the withdrawals became reality, and General Abrams's overall campaign plan for 1969 reflected the U.S. political situation: The American public did not see the war as worthwhile.

Lance Corporal Ken George

A turning point was when President Nixon announced in 1969 that there were going to be troop withdrawals. What that meant is that the war is now winding down and supposedly going to end in the near future, so why get killed now? So the first thought is, "Is our unit going to get pulled out? Are we going home next week, next month, or whatever?" The first unit removed from Vietnam, as far as the Marine Corps was concerned, was the 9th Marines because they had got kicked around more than anyone else. [The official reason was that the 9th Marines were "sort of Division reserve . . . not occupying a fire support base."]

Attitudes changed drastically. From that point on, if the shit hit the fan everybody reacted pretty much the same, but you didn't have that "let's go out and find them" attitude anymore. You'd have it with the newer guys coming in country but not with the guys that had been there for a while, and that included all types of people in all ranks.

·

Although withdrawals had been announced, it would be nearly two years before all Marine ground units left Vietnam. For those who remained, it was business as usual.

Captain Paul Goodwin

The next engagement of any size was 25 May. We had been operating a click or two from the DMZ for about a week to ten days and had had a series of successful ambushes on small groups of NVA. We were given the mission to move up into the DMZ with the purpose of trying to get a prisoner. We moved forward with my 1st Platoon on the point, which was Bill Haskell. As we got up onto the hill which brought us right into the DMZ, the company was ambushed. I was moving behind the 1st Platoon and the ambush extended back as far as me because I came under fire, although they were doin' a poor job. . . . Once we went to ground they were well above our head.

Bill was hit during this engagement. I was talkin' to him on the radio when he was hit. . . . He lost an eye and most of his 1st Squad was knocked down. Because of the lieutenant being hit and the 1st Squad being hit and the squad leader, I passed Oliver North's platoon through and told Ollie to move up. Said, "Just pass through him and continue the attack." So we did. We just rolled right on through and continued the attack, and it was a long day because they had this machine gun that kept tying us down, but eventually we kicked them off the hill.

During the next couple of days we had a series of meeting engagements and successful ambushes. And one of these was where we did shoot an NVA and captured him. Oliver's patrol did that when he moved down into the DMZ. We were so close on the heels of someone that they attempted to ambush us and were not successful. We killed two or three of them and moved into an area where their packs were left and there was hot chow.

For some reason we could only move a hundred people into the DMZ. So we left Oliver there that night and I moved back up with the rest of the company. There was another lieutenant with Oliver named Art Vandeveer, my artillery

FO. Art and Oliver spent the evening in an ambush site and Oliver was callin' back and saying that there was a lot of heavy movement around him. The next day the prisoner that we got reported that they had been shooting for Kilo Company and were prepared to conduct a night attack against us the following evening, if we were still in the DMZ area. I thought that it would be a good idea for me to get the hell out of there, but Schulze or somebody thought that it would be a good idea for me to stay.

They flew in all kinds of extra ammunition to me and I brought in the two patrols I had out. I had sent a couple of patrols out to my front and to my side and we killed three or four people. We weren't attacked and I'm convinced the reason we weren't attacked—although we stayed up all night anticipating it and had been mortared and thought we were getting prepped—is that the people we had killed to our front that day were guides that were in place to bring in the rest of this battalion.

I wrote Oliver up for the Silver Star for passing through Bill's platoon after the platoon commander had been hit and the subsequent continuous actions that he did over the next two or three days. This is the celebrated incident that Oliver North participated in. And where there were rumors that he went to the Ben Hai and General Krulak said this incident didn't happen. [The Ben Hai River flowed through the eastern part of the DMZ and separated North and South Vietnam. The proscription against military action in the zone was still in effect except for very carefully controlled, limited events. To go to the banks of the Ben Hai would take one as far as one could go without crossing into North Vietnam.]

The biggest . . . most impressive . . . devastating . . . firefight . . . started with the contacts that I just described and ended with the action that follows.

One day Oliver was wearing long sleeves and I grabbed him on the arm and almost took him to his knees. I made him take his shirt off and let me look at it . . . and he had blood poisoning going up his arm from some shrapnel that he'd taken. Not a lot, just a couple of small slivers, but he was startin' to get blood poisoning. So he was medevaced out from being wounded. Bill Haskell had been wounded and had already gone. My other platoon commander was Ross Peterson . . . and Ross had been wounded previously but was back with me.

We were moving away from the DMZ and came up near a landing zone named Sierra. It was early one morning and I had two platoons out, one patrolling north and one patrolling south. A platoon led by a staff sergeant named Arnold, who took over the platoon when Bill Haskell was wounded, came across a fairly large bunker complex and said he could see soldiers and so forth.

I told him to hold on. I picked up part of my headquarters group and whatever platoon was left and I left a small group of people at the headquarters and closed on Arnold to give him some support. When we got to where Arnold was, we took a look at the complex and I sent a platoon under another staff NCO around to flank this area, and I initiated an assault into the bunker complex. We hadn't gone very far when we were engaged in a fight. And my platoon commander went down.

When he went down the fight bogged down. I moved up to him and saw that he'd been shot through the chest. The unit I'd sent around on the flank had gotten involved in a firefight, and the sergeant that was leading that outfit was a Puerto Rican fellow. And he'd gotten shot in the head and was in bad shape.

This thing started in the morning and it was startin' to get into the early afternoon. . . . Art Vandeveer, who was the artillery lieutenant . . . I had him come up and told him, "Well, you're a frustrated grunt and you always wanted the opportunity to do somethin'. Now, lieutenant, you get up there and take charge of this outfit and clean out the rest of this bunker complex." He was the only guy I had left besides me, the only officer. And old Art moved up and took charge of the remnants of those two platoons and did a hell of a job. Cleared it out. Killed a bunch of the gooners and got all kinds of weapons and ammunition and shit. But we didn't get 'em all because a bunch of 'em just scooted out the far end. We hadn't done it by ourselves. I'd used our 60 mortars until we didn't have any ammunition left. I'd used 81s. I'd used some artillery and had used some gunships. And I called in for some medevacs to get . . . I had two or three dead and I had a bunch of wounded.

I think that the group that was defending the place was bigger than we were, and had they fought a little harder, they would have kicked our ass. But they didn't, they elected to pull out. And then when they did . . . they didn't pull out far enough that we didn't have a runnin' little fight with them. When the helicopters came in, they got three straight. Now, none of them just crashed and burned, but they all got hit severely enough that two of 'em limped back into the Rockpile and the other one limped in to Vandergrift. They had to take the casualties out on the slings . . . and they had to sit there so long . . . the NVA started mortarin' the zones that we were in and RPGin' the helicopters. The Marine pilots did a hell of a job. I wrote a note saying, "I don't know who in the hell they were, but they certainly deserved all the credit in the world." They hovered those damn birds when the zones were under fire and they were getting shot at. I had a couple of really bad head wounds and sucking chest wounds and they had to get these people out of there and they did.

When the last bird went out and got hit, around midnight, I felt like we were probably in deep shit. My company had been down to the lowest it had ever been. We were under a hundred people. I didn't have but one platoon with me and part of the headquarters element, and I was down to about fifty people. I took this group and we moved up to Landing Zone Sierra and set in for that night, and I called the boss and said, "I've got to have some help in the morning." And at first light they flew helicopters in to get the eight wounded still with me . . . and to bring us in some reinforcements. The problem with carrying eight wounded people, as you can imagine, for about three hours in the middle of the night, and you've only got about fifty people, is damn near everybody has got to tote wounded. So it became a hell of a problem for us. The next morning they came back in and fortunately they brought my XO, a guy named Harry Chermalinsky, and a new lieutenant. Also, Oliver North came back to me that morning.

Ross Peterson had closed on me as rapidly as he could, knowing that I was with not too many people, picked up the elements of my headquarters, closed on me on Landing Zone Sierra. About nine o'clock in the morning we were prepared to saddle up and move out. As we moved out of there . . . we'd only been gone about an hour and, shit, it was slow. Harry Chermalinsky calls me and tells me that I've got somebody down from heat exhaustion. I said, "I can't believe I've got anybody down from heat exhaustion. Just drag the fucker, 'cause we got to get the hell out of here." I felt like if we hung around there too long, that this group was gonna find out that they were a lot bigger than we were and go smack the hell out of us.

I had probably twenty BNGs with me and I needed to pull back and get things kind of squared away. And the guy that goes down is this dipshit lieutenant. And Chermalinsky comes back up and says, "Six, be advised it's the new 3 Actual [lieutenant commanding the 3d Platoon] that's down." And I said, "What do you mean, he's down?" Chermalinsky says, "Well, I think he's got too much gear." So we took this sweetpea's gear and handed it out to the troops.

46

. . . .

OPERATION VIRGINIA RIDGE

In mid-June, intelligence reports indicated that a large enemy force had infiltrated through the DMZ into positions near Gio Linh. 3/3 was chosen to counter them and, breaking with the usual policy of avoiding motor marches through uncertain territory at night, boldly loaded the battalion on trucks and drove toward Gio Linh. They found and engaged elements of the *27th NVA Regiment* and the *33d Sapper Battalion*.

Corporal Jim Howe
On the 16th of June we started getting some very special treatment. We were told that there was going to be a battalion-size operation and that we were going to some sort of checkpoint and there the big-time guys would receive the orders of where we were going. They had set up chaplain services for us and they had set up armorer services. There were steaks; it was almost like an R and R.

Corporal Ken George
I looked at Howe and the other squad leaders and said, "Uh oh." Everybody had the same feeling . . . you know. Beer, cold beer and cold soda. All day long

we had a party. But I couldn't enjoy myself because I knew that we were up the fuckin' creek. So about four o'clock in the afternoon they called for "squad leaders up." We go up there and the platoon commander, Hoffman, was saying, "Okay, here is the scoop." And he hands us all camouflage grease and he says, "Here, this is for you guys."

What the hell do we do with this? I've been in country eleven months now and we never once used camouflage on our face. He said, "Okay, we're moving out at night, tonight." This was another first. We never moved at night as a company, never. I said, "You're kidding." He said, "No, we're going out tonight. We're going into Leatherneck Square. We're moving out tonight and our platoon has point for the company. And George," meaning me, "your squad has point for everybody. We're taking trucks up Route 1 and we're going to stop about a half a mile from Gio Linh and we're gettin' off and we are taking this old tank trail heading west through Leatherneck Square working our way right across to Con Thien."

There was no moonlight that night. So we get off the trucks and I saw a light at Gio Linh which was no longer an American outpost. It was an ARVN outpost. We moved out along this tank trail until we came to this knoll and we set up for the night. And since we had point the night before, I had the rear squad for the company the next day, when we moved out in the morning on the 17th of June.

Corporal Jim Howe

As we moved out, the 2d Platoon started taking fire but it was really nothing to talk about. The captain ordered that we go on line. I had had problems before with this kid by the name of Woody. As we would advance on line, Woody wouldn't keep abreast of the people to his left or right. I would go up to him and say, "Woody, this isn't hard. All you have to do is dress right and just keep abreast of that man so if something happens, you don't end up shooting him by mistake."

Lance Corporal Pete Tramonte

As we started to march on line, we started to take fire and I said to myself, "This is it." Jim was on the left with me. He had stopped the column. I looked over the hedgerow and there was a freshly dug enemy trench. The word was "Come on up, come on up," and we got to a crossroad in a hedgerow and we started really taking fire. I jumped into the hedgerow and rounds danced around me. I hit the ground. A machine gunner came up. His gun jammed. He was cursing like a son of a gun. One of the guys in Jimmy's squad, Woody, he got hit. Eli Colon, a Spanish fellow from New York City, was hit. And there was a third person hit. They were the last three guys on my left side. As those three went down, we turned towards the fire and there was maybe a two- or three-foot embankment of dirt which was perfect for us because we could all get down and take some sort of cover.

Corporal Jim Howe

Woody was out too far. I don't want to talk bad about the dead, but Woody had a hard time following orders. When I had asked him to pull back, either he misunderstood what I said or he disregarded my orders. My last words to him weren't the kindest words in the world. And now he was out. I very honestly thought to myself, "He's probably dead and he probably did this on purpose and now I have to go out and I have to get him." We were under *extreme* fire at that point and the next thing I know somebody to my right started to throw up, a kid from 1st Platoon.

I had this other guy, Terrell. At that time, as we all know, we had a black militant move on here in the States and naturally anything that happens in society filters down into the military also. And he was quite outspoken on the fact that he felt blacks were not getting their fair shot. He was a professional boxer and I had had run-ins with him before. Terrell was in another squad at the time and he came running over to me and anything I asked that guy to do, he did. He had the 79 and I'd say, "Okay, I want you over here. Then, I want you over there." "Okay, Jim." And boom, he went and he did it. I guess we put all that black/white issue to bed right then and there. It was just now all "let's help out." If I had to describe or characterize his actions that day, I would say they were heroic. He and this guy Chuck Wright, who was also an M79 man, stayed with me and we were directing fire at different positions.

We had a couple of brand new guys. As I ran back and forth along the line doing what I had to do as a squad leader, I noticed this one kid was really petrified and made the mistake of instead of hugging this mud wall, he leaned back against the tree that was in back of him. With this, a round came and implanted itself about six inches from the top of his head. The kid just looked at me. I grabbed him and I threw him down towards the mud wall. And as he looked up he said, "Does this happen every day?" Because this was his first firefight and I think maybe he was in the bush two or three days. And I started to laugh and I said, "I hope not, because neither of us is going to survive."

Hoffman, my lieutenant, I think he was an All-American from Chico State football and the guy was excellent. He had a very big personality, a very big ego. You either liked him or you disliked him. I happened to like him very much. And when he saw us really getting hurt, he ran over and he must have thrown about forty grenades. The guy was a quarterback. He was putting them right where he wanted them.

Anyway, this kid crawls over and he grabs my lieutenant, and he says that his lieutenant was dead and he said that he needed help, that his squad was just about wiped out. And that he couldn't get his wounded out. At this point, I had had it. I had seen my men go down. I had a tough time holding my position and I really wasn't concerned . . . selfishly, I wasn't really concerned with this other guy's plight.

Hoffman's response was firm and immediate. "Son, you take us back to where your squad is and we'll get them out." And as it turned out, Hoffman went back and what had been happening was—when we called in incoming, we were so close that as the Marines would put their heads down for the incoming, our own artillery was coming in so close that the gooks would advance from their positions and fire on the Marines. All they needed was four or five steps and they were right on top of them. And they were killing them. Hoffman went over with one other guy, a fellow by the name of Frank Jerome. They went over and they took care of the situation and they ended up getting the dead out, and whatever wounded were still alive were brought back to a position of relative safety.

By this time we had called in airstrikes and we could hear the pilots over the radio, and they were yelling and screaming that there was gooks all over and they had gooks running in open fields and the whole bit. And we called for napalm and the napalm was so close that it was staggering, the lack of oxygen and the tremendous heat. Now we could see another Marine was still out in the open. I ran out to get him and as I grabbed him, I noticed that he was . . . although he was shot by enemy fire, that he had experienced the napalm to a greater degree than anyone else and he was dead . . . and he was partially burned. And I tried to grab him and bring him back and for some reason he was stuck and I didn't have the physical strength to pull him back. I was aided by Frank Jerome, who I mentioned before. Frank and myself grabbed this guy and dragged him back. As I crossed into that muddy walled area, I put the body down and I turned it over and it was this kid Woody that I had been complaining to regarding his lack of military procedure and on-line advancements.

We looked up and over the ridge we saw this tremendous sight. Boocoo people all on line, coming down at us. And our first reaction was "Holy shit, this is it. They got us." The 1st Platoon, which was our backup force, had been contacted about our plight and were on their way. This is who's on line coming down to help us out. But that first thought, we just saw that . . . felt that it was NVA and they were coming down to finish us off. By this time now, we had taken the dead and were puttin' them in body bags or ponchos. And I know that Lieutenant

Hoffman felt very bad because the lieutenant from the 3d Platoon was dead and they were very friendly. It was just a bad scene.

After it was done, I went up to several guys and the first thing they would do was shake my hand. It was almost like playing a real tough game of football and now that the game was over, everybody on the team was shaking hands with each other and the day was done. I really thought that odd, because that would have been the reaction a year earlier when I was playing football and baseball. It just seemed so American and the reaction was like, well, this is a great football field and we did our best and we did a good job and we held them off.

Lance Corporal Pete Tramonte
We lost about thirteen men that day, KIA.

Corporal Jim Howe
There were some funny parts to this day, too. Pops, who was due to rotate back to the United States, was taken out of the squad. His job was to take Chieu Hoi leaflets [propaganda that encouraged NVA or VC to defect] and to throw them along the trails as we went about our mission. Pops didn't want to get captured or caught by the NVA with this bunch of Chieu Hoi leaflets.

Corporal Pops Wandell
They gave me all these Chieu Hoi things, little leaflets. So I had my rifle around my back and I was dropping these leaflets. All the guys were in front of me in line and I'm back there having a good time for myself because there's no weight in my pack and I'm dropping all these things. All of a sudden the shit hits the fan. I've got these Chieu Hoi things and the gook bastards are going to think I'm some kind of spy. I'm stopped and trying to get these things out of my pack, but everyone else kept going. I'm behind the lines and all of a sudden I hear, "Pop, Pop, what are you doing back here?" Ken George was coming back trying to find the lieutenant. He says, "Pops, you're behind the line. There's all snipers around here."

Lance Corporal Pete Tramonte
Ken George that day, he tells it to me and he starts to laugh and said, "You had to see Pops. He was all alone and there was gooks running back and forth across his position. By the time I got to him, he had all the Chieu Hoi leaflets and he was scratching at the ground with his fingers trying to bury these things so he wouldn't get caught with them."

Corporal Ken George

After the operation they choppered us out of the field to an in-country beach resort where the Cua Viet River emptied into the ocean. They sent us there for about two or three days R and R.

The battalion lost 19 killed and 28 wounded on the operation. Enemy losses totaled 193 KIA, 9 prisoners, and 77 weapons captured.

JULY–AUGUST 1969

Corporal Jim Howe

The feelings that I had seeing Pops go home were unique, because I felt that I was very glad for him to leave and yet I felt that he was abandoning me and that why should he be the lucky one to go and not I? And also that I knew that I was more exposed because I didn't have him around to act as a second opinion or use his judgment. It was something I would experience again when my mother died. Basically, I was glad for her that her suffering was over but that it would certainly be an individual loss to me to not have her there for her guidance and good fortune. And yet I know that Pops felt bad leaving us, because I was with him when he got on the chopper.

·

Chaplain Bob Bedingfield

Just before coming home . . . I had known the commanding general of the 3d Marine Division in a previous life. He invited me for dinner with him in his hooch in Quang Tri before we left. It was the night before I headed back to the United States. We were sitting on the veranda, having a drink, and I looked out with him and he pointed to the north and he said, "Bob, we're really in the wrong place." And I said, "Yeah, I suppose, but where would you suggest that we might be?" And he said to me, "We should be at Vinh." And Vinh, of course, was that wonderful airbase that just sat wide open on the other side of the Demilitarized Zone. That's where we should have been. We should have been on their territory, in their day, on their time.

·

Lieutenant Richmond D. O'Neill

August 1st the battalion was located at Cam Lo. It was about this time that we started hearing rumors that the 3d Marines would be pulled out of Vietnam. Some people were saying we would be out by Thanksgiving.

·

Captain Paul Goodwin

Early August we were out near the DMZ and we were just gettin' pounded by mortars. We got our wounded out and then we get the hell off that hill, 'cause it's zeroed in. We pulled back two or three clicks and end up on Hill 162, to the west and north of Charlie 2, and put out a couple of ambushes that night. We start getting movement around ten-thirty or eleven o'clock. And at twelve o'clock that night one of my night acts triggers ambush and we knock down about eight or ten of these little gooners and captured all their weapons. An hour later we have some trip flares that go off and we fire on these things. I've got most of a company of tanks with me and a fellow named Mike Wunsch, a captain, who is the tank company commander. He's been with me on and off for about six months and was due to leave country in two days. About two-thirty in the morning Mike tells me he has some movement in front of him. I go up and get on his tank and I said, "What I think that we ought to do is fire a couple of canisters of beehive out there." And he said, "But I've only got a few left, Paul. I carry an M79, let me fire this thing." So he fires a couple of M79 rounds and we get nothing. No movement, nobody's reportin' anything. My listening posts are not reportin' anything. So I said, "Okay, Mike, I think that by being successful on two ambushes that night we probably don't have any problems." Unfortunately, I was wrong. About three-thirty, shit hits the fan. Man, the lights go out. Mortars just drop all over us. RPGs come flying in from everywhere. And . . . they assault our position.

Obviously what Mike had picked up is their movin' into position and I should have insisted that he fire. But I didn't and Mike was killed . . . in his tank. An RPG caught him in the chest . . . and he just . . . he was blown right off the tank commander's hatch. This is the action that a kid named Herrod was decorated for. He was on a machine gun and really kept us from being overrun on that side of the perimeter. Ollie North was with me then. I remember movin' around the perimeter and seein' the Vietnamese on top of Mike's tank. And Ollie had a shotgun and . . . blew one of them off the tank. Anyway, we were able to hold that part of the perimeter without it gettin' penetrated, but they certainly got up to the line and up to the tank. We got a listenin' post overrun on the other side and a couple of kids killed. Other than that, we held throughout the rest of the morning and at first light we evacuated our dead and wounded.

I always have felt bad about Mike. He was a Naval Academy graduate and a bright guy. We had become friends. I had the company that had a good reputation. It had been aggressive and Mike wanted to go out with us one time and have his tanks with us. Probably, like most tank commanders, as a company commander, he never really got to see a lot of action. I guess I just felt that if I'd been . . . more insistent with Mike, I might have kept him alive.

That night was the first time I ever had to fire my night defensive fires so closely. And it was the first time that I ever used the "Whisperin' Death" . . . the Gatling guns that were on those slow-flying Air Force planes . . . that came up and just ringed the perimeter for us. [These gunships could put a round into every square inch of an area the size of a football field in one minute.] Because we were really under a lot of heat. And when I called for the night defensive fires on my company net, some guy comes up and says, "Do you realize that they're danger close." And I told him, "I don't give a damn if they're danger close. [The enemy is] so close now, I want everything I can get to get them off my ass." But anyway, the night defensive fires were fired and they worked.

47

• • • • • • • • • • • • • • •

THE LAST OPERATION

The battalion's last major operation was IDAHO CANYON, which they began in late August in an area near Mutter's Ridge. Contact was light until early September when India Company captured three wounded prisoners—teenagers who had had minimal training in North Vietnam before being sent south. They divulged that India Company had been targeted for attack by the North Vietnamese. The next few days were quiet, primarily because of a cease-fire in observance of Ho Chi Minh's death. During this so-called truce India Company walked into an NVA ambush. In the type of incident that hurt morale more than any other, when the company commander called for artillery support, he was told that he would be limited to two rounds per gun after adjustment because of the ceasefire agreement.

Lieutenant Rich O'Neill

It was about this time that Colonel Schulze started talking about me being a company commander. I had been in the field my entire tour to this point and staying was not exactly what I had in mind. However, once the colonel started

Swollen by heavy monsoon rains, one of the many streams near Mutter's Ridge is forded by the Marines of 3/3 during Operation IDAHO CANYON.

talking, there wasn't much of a chance that I wouldn't do whatever he asked. By the 23rd of August I was the company commander of Kilo Company.

We were at the Rockpile. Colonel Schulze rotated, Paul Goodwin, who I replaced, became a general's aide, and Ollie North, who was my XO for about twelve hours, became a junior aide for the 3d Division commander. There was not a captain in command of any of the companies in the field.

Around the 3d of September we started another operation back on Mutter's Ridge. It was a three-company operation with Mike on the left flank with a new captain who had just taken over as CO. Lima was on the right flank and Kilo was in the middle. It took six-and-a-half hours to make the climb up the ridge. Ollie came out [by helicopter] with seven cases of ice-cold sodas and three cases of ice-cold beer, the compliments of the division commander. Never has anything tasted better than the drinks that day.

Mike Company wasn't so lucky. They ran into an ambush on the way up. Every officer but one was hit. Both the CO and the XO, who the captain had just replaced, were killed. The only uninjured officer had been in country only a couple of days.

Kilo had 203 men in the field when we started up the ridge attempting to go to the aid of Mike. They were only three or four clicks away. Normally you could make that in a matter of hours. Eight days later we were approaching 100 men in strength and were still a click away from where Mike had first been hit. We hardly fired a rifle or had a rifle fire at us but, man, did it rain mortars.

We had some special visitors with us on the last trip up the ridge and, as it turned out, the last field operation for the battalion in Vietnam. The Army had some success with the Chieu Hoi program. There was an Army lieutenant, two enlisted men, and two former NVA soldiers. The idea was to have the Vietnamese speak through a radio that was relayed to a DC-3 that would circle above us and tell the NVA to give up because we were going to kick their butts. All of this was as the three-day cease-fire when "Uncle Ho" died was ending.

None of the Army people had ever been in the field overnight. I was able to convince them to dig in the first night and they had a fairly decent foxhole. The next night they sort of scraped a hole. When I discussed the situation with the lieutenant, he told me that he was responsible for his people and they didn't see the need. Before ten o'clock the next morning they were all medevaced. It seems that Charlie really didn't care to hear that crap so close to North Vietnam and so soon after Ho Chi Minh died. I hated to see anyone hit, but I don't think any of my Marines were unhappy to see the DC-3 leave. It was like the North Vietnamese knew where we were when the plane was circling.

The troops of Kilo Company never carried personal transistor radios into the field. But the Army didn't understand field security, and it was through them that we learned that President Nixon was pulling out the 3d Marines after the 9th Marines.

IDAHO CANYON cost the Marines twenty-four dead and seventy-four wounded. A few days later the battalion wrapped up its last operation and withdrew to rear areas in preparation for leaving Vietnam. The last Marine from 3/3 killed in Vietnam was Private Roland Nathaniel Agard, age nineteen. He had been in country just a few days, and he was walking down a street in Dong Ha when he was shot by an unknown assailant at 11:45 P.M. on 23 September 1969.

The battalion's four-and-a-half year saga sputtered to an end on 1 October 1969 when the 3d Battalion, 3d Marines, sailed for Camp Pendleton, California. Actually, few Marines who had fought with the battalion went to the United States at that time. Using a "mixmaster" concept, the Corps transferred those with most of their tours remaining to other units in Vietnam. Others went to Okinawa, and some of those who returned to the United States with the battalion had never seen combat with it. There were to be no parades for the men of 3/3, or for any others who served in Vietnam. Those who survived returned a few at a time to a population that seemed indifferent or hostile to their sacrifices.

The allies were winning the war militarily when 3/3 left Vietnam in the fall of 1969. But the enemy's leadership correctly foresaw victory for their cause in the U.S. withdrawal. The NVA cautioned their forces in the field to limit their activity to guerrilla warfare while America withdrew. Victory for the NVA was slow but, in the face of America's absence, sure. Five-and-a-half years after 3/3's departure, NVA tanks rumbled onto the grounds of the presidential palace in Saigon to signal the Republic of Vietnam's and America's defeat.

48

• • • • • • • • • • • • • • •

PARTING SHOTS

For better or worse the Vietnam War was, with few exceptions, the biggest event in the lives of the men whose words adorn these pages. But, in contrast to the media portrayal of the crestfallen, maladjusted Vietnam veteran, most of these men were strengthened by the experience. The Marines who fought in Vietnam, and their brothers from the other services, were second to none in professional conduct and sacrifice. Their casualties were not in vain but were a monument to their heritage and their brotherhood. During the siege of Khe Sanh in early 1968, a reporter found scrawled on a wall, "For those who fight for it, freedom has a flavor the protected will never know." As they have testified, the scars of their sacrifices and a generation of indifference or hostility by their fellow countrymen have not dimmed their spirit. The following comments summarize their feelings about the war in Vietnam.

Lieutenant Colonel Robert C. Needham

I was responsible to my boss for carrying out all assigned missions, and I was responsible to the Marines of 3/3 for doing this in a manner that caused as few casualties as possible. I will tell you that the weight of the latter responsibility was, for me, far heavier than that of the former and caused much more internal stress and self-doubt.

Lieutenant Bill Kenerly

I liked my people. I still feel a lot of attachment to them even though I only knew them a very short period of time. That was for me a unique situation. I was never in it again after I left Vietnam and now the future doesn't hold that for me. It was something I had looked forward to and anticipated for twenty years and it only lasted three months. I did not want to lose any men. I can remember telling some of them once that if we could just do our job and not make any contact that that would suit me fine. Now I know that that is not the spirit of the bayonet. I think the key to what I said is doing our job. If we could do our patrols, run our ambushes, not avoid anything, not shirk any duty, but get through it without anybody being hurt or being killed, then that was all that I wanted to do. If that is an attitude on my part that needs to be faulted, I think I can at least partially attribute it to the nature of the fighting.

There weren't any objectives. You ran a patrol route. If you found them, you fought them. At the end of the fight you came back and maybe a week later, you fought them again at the same place. There was never anything like an island in World War II or even like a territory in Korea where we were on a peninsula and therefore could literally push north and push them out of the country. That was never the case. There was no place to push them in Vietnam. There weren't any objectives to seize. And I think that that type of war tends to sap some of the aggressive spirit from the troops. The frank thing is, there just wasn't a hell of a lot worth dying for.

Captain Roger Zensen

I want to conclude with the feelings we had while we were serving in Vietnam and the camaraderie, the togetherness, the working together, and how it really was one of the most rewarding times of my life. It was the ultimate in terms of what you were working for. You were dealing with people's lives, getting wounded, getting killed. War certainly wasn't pleasant, it wasn't amusing, but from an aspect of teamwork and success and doing what you had to do, it was one of the most satisfying times I've ever experienced.

PFC Jim Yost

This tape is one of the hardest things that I ever did because of things I realized later on had happened that I didn't realize at the time. I had post-traumatic stress disorder [PTSD] very, very bad. I almost committed suicide a couple times. Nineteen seventy-eight, seventy-nine, I was really into it. Several times I got drunk and crawled around on the floor with my .357 Magnum in my house looking for North Vietnamese soldiers with my wife and kids terrorized, till I passed out and they'd take the guns, and finally they just hid 'em for a year.

I'm a lot better and I don't have that problem any more. Now I've got my degree and I work with veterans and it took me a long time to understand what had happened to me. That's another story.

Lance Corporal Vince Morrison

Vietnam gave me a sense of dealing with situations in life where maybe if I didn't have that experience, I wouldn't have had the drive to continue on. Or I might say, "Oh, well, to hell with it all," and just give up on life or whatever. But here I said, "You know, you've been through so much hell, there ain't nothing else can be any more worse than 'Nam." It gave me a lot of leadership authority on dealing with people from all walks of life, a better understanding of the human mind. We had a good time and we had some bad times, but all in all, I wouldn't trade that experience.

Hospital Corpsman 3d Class John A. "Doc" Combs

It was the most singularly spectacular event of my life at this point. I lived in a contrast, a paradox, over there. I was the only person rooting for survival. Everybody else was out trying to kill each other. That weighed on my mind constantly. I worked my way through college. In college you had these high ideals. I was in the College of Agriculture and the goal was someday we're going to feed the world. There'll be no hunger and starvation.

But to go from that perspective to a negative one two years later, where "let's get rid of everything that moves." It was such a dramatic twist and shock that it's taken me a long, long time to really develop a worthwhile sense of values over the thing. For better or for worse, it's contributed to my understanding of life and how I deal with it. I'm better for it now.

Corporal Jim Howe

One of the things that I think is important is that you learned how you should act in the different roles that you played. When you were just a member of a fire team, member of a squad, you acted one way. And then when you assumed responsibility of fire team leader or squad leader, you learned that there was another way to act.

One time in October [1968], we were in a firefight and were being shelled. We took casualties, KIAs. They were exposed in a position where we would have to go out into a hostile area, an area that was being machine-gunned or had enemy small-arms fire plus 82s [mortars], to bring the bodies back. My squad leader, when we were ready to move to another position, had to make a decision on what we were going to do about the bodies. It was a very easy decision because he said, "Hey, they're from my squad. They're my responsibility. I'll go and get them."

Captain Paul Goodwin

My first tour in Vietnam was with a reconnaissance unit in Chu Lai and it was almost cops and robbers compared to the second tour. We worked in small units and we ran against the Viet Cong. Often in our first tour, we just found guerrillas and South Vietnamese carryin' weapons. But they were never armed and equipped as well as the North Vietnamese Army that I saw in my second tour.

The war wasn't unpopular in 1965. When I went back in '69, it was really unpopular. The biggest problem we had, I don't think was drugs. . . . The drugs weren't that kind of an issue because the troops were policing themselves too well. It was "A day on and stay on," you were in the bush forever and they just didn't . . . allow it. I do think we had people that drank more than they should sometimes.

The biggest problem I had was with some of our blacks. We had a couple of these guys that were just real problem children. You know, very sensitive. Felt oppressed by the white man. Race relations were really touchy at times in the companies. I had my share of those problems. Including one guy that, when we were on a Sparrowhawk out of Vandergrift, shot himself in the ankle rather than go with us.

I had some great lieutenants who probably carried me . . . who always showed remarkable leadership ability because they constantly set the example. They were great under fire. They always moved to the point of the heaviest contact and directed their men, and you can't ask people to do more than that.

I think if you had to say one thing about the war it would be the American Marine. The guy was probably eleventh grade, high school dropout, who had no earthly idea of why he was fighting a war so far away and yet . . . never once failed . . . to respond. Day in and day out they humped this huge pack that was breakin' their back under terrible conditions, but they fought with skill and bravery. When well led, the American Marine will march down the barrel of an enemy rifle for you. It just continually has amazed me over the years . . . just how good the individual Marine could be. And that is something that our country can certainly be proud of . . .

PFC James W. "Birdman" Byrd III

We really weren't supported by the country as far as an all-out effort. If only they'd just said one day, "Okay, today's the day. Let's go over there and let's take it." It wasn't like World War I or II or something like that. It wasn't where you were going to fight for a military objective where you'd go in there, kick ass and take the place and raise the flag. It was like always fighting the thing with one hand tied behind your back. There were a whole set of rules. You can't do this and you can't do that.

There were a lot of times when we'd seen action and some of our members had been killed that we would have our own private funeral. We'd get together quietly and reflect upon it. We'd be sitting laughing with them one day, one minute, and the next day we'd know they'll never be with us again. It saddens you a bit. But as a group we consoled one another. We shared a lot. We shared the hurt. I most certainly felt a brotherly feeling towards the guys I served with, more so than if they'd been people in my immediate family. It was that kind of love. It couldn't be duplicated. It's a thing that lasts for life. I figure my Vietnam experience is invaluable. It's priceless. It's something no one can take from you.

Corporal Rod Consalvo

One of the hardest things to cope with in Vietnam was your 395-day tour. When that was up, you rotated back. I think that's why the Vietnam veteran had such a hard time coping, because you would always go over an individual and come back as an individual. When your time was up you were history, you were gone. Guys were there one day and gone the next.

When my time was up, I got my orders and got my stuff together and got my pack and I was heading back. I'll never see those guys again. That's always been hard to deal with. I've felt a little bit lonely all these years never seeing these guys that you put your life on the line with day after day after day, did so many things with. You always wonder how they turned out and how everything's going for them and whether they all adjusted well and were able to cope with what we went through in Vietnam.

But I got my orders to head back. I hit Dong Ha and . . . forty-eight hours later was in Main Street USA. And I came from a small town in Indiana. I knocked on my door at two o'clock in the morning. My parents had an idea I'd be home sometime in September but they didn't know. They had a big banner on there—"Welcome home, Rod"—and when I knocked on the door, I heard my Dad scream, "It's Rod!" They opened the door and we hugged and sat down and the first thing I asked for was a glass of milk and a cheese sandwich. God, that sure tasted good. But just forty-eight hours before, I was sitting in a hole eating C-rations wondering what in the hell is going to happen to us next.

And the first morning I got home, I just went out to the front porch and sat and just looked out at everything. I think what bothered me the most was knowing that all my buddies were still there along with 500,000 other servicemen and everything was just going on normal back home. It didn't seem to me that nobody knew there was a war going on. The guys were getting killed. Guys were living in holes and walking streambeds and having leeches eat on 'em and having that thousand-yard stare and always worrying what was going to happen the next minute and always listening for sounds.

Captain Dave Ramsey

I've said often that I think that the greatest challenge and the greatest reward is leading men in combat. Especially if you are successful. And I think that there is nothing quite like it than to say, "Up and at 'em," and everybody gets up, no matter how heavy the fire. Of course, you've got to get up first.

But in any event, I can't say enough about the American Marine. The individual fighting man. And the staff NCOs and the NCOs and the young officers. They're just a great group of guys and I'm privileged to have served with them.

PFC Craig Pyles

I look back on it now and say, "Well, that was the beginning of a new me right there." We all have influences in life that make us turn out the way we turn out. There's no doubt in my mind that that experience at India 3/3 had as much to do with making me the person I am today as anything that ever happened to me.

Corporal Bill Clough

There were several firefights I was involved with with Kilo that I was reasonably certain I wasn't going to live much longer. But after about two or three of those and you realize the amount of devastation that you can live through. I think it tends to give you strength. In fact, I think a lot of people felt like they were invincible and I'm not too sure that a lot of times I didn't feel that way. Then again, something would happen to bring me back to reality. Most of the time I stayed somewhere in between those two ends, but oddly enough, I think the further along I went, the less concerned I was with dying. It seemed up near the end of my tour that it didn't really matter to me anymore.

A lot of the people my age, which was almost everybody, had trouble after the war, learning to deal with the emotional changes. I think probably I felt like I had lost my soul, lost my relationship with God. But I did definitely learn how to hate, and hate with a vengeance, and learn how to kill and enjoy it. All of those things that aren't exactly unified to my beliefs. The worst effect the war itself had on me was the fact that I had become so disunified with my beliefs that I couldn't even incorporate my life into any semblance of religious conviction. With the background I've always had, that was very difficult to overcome. Finally I did so, but it took a long time.

PFC Bill Frantz

Vietnam . . . It was the biggest event of my life. I've lived with it emotionally, physically, emotionally . . . I have my resentments. I know we could have won the war but wasn't allowed to. It's like brothers. It's actually closer than family. Nobody else could understand unless he was there. I found out through research that in no other war in American history was men put in this kind of situation for thirteen months. World War II, you went in on an operation for a couple of weeks or a month and you was pulled to the rear, to Australia, a ship or something. And another unit come in. And I feel that's why myself and other vets have PTSD and problems with life. I know for a lot of years I struggled with alcoholism and violence. At this time I haven't drank for like almost seven years. I can't, but it would be an easy way out for me.

But I'd do it all again. Yeah. I would do it for a couple of reasons. To find the soul I lost. And to be allowed to win. Because . . . I lost my soul. It would be kinda like going for broke. To get a piece of my soul back . . . or to just get taken out. Because I feel like I died twenty years ago. I really do. You was taken out of youth and you'd go beyond manhood.

Captain John Ripley

The Marine asks for nothing. He asks only that someone be responsible for what the hell he's doing and look after him. "If you're telling me to do this, I'm going to do it. Just be damned sure what you're telling me to do is worthy of doing." That alone is incredible. And every time somebody's in a crack you don't even ask for volunteers. They show up. Everybody wants to go help. What makes them do it is they are so concerned about their buddy next to them, their fellow Marine. And this accountability: "I want the people who I'm here with, regardless of how I feel about them, I want them to know that I'm up to the task and I'm not going to abandon them." The worst that can be said about a Marine is that he wasn't around when we needed him, that we couldn't count on him. That was absolutely unthinkable to him.

I want the general public to know that everything they've seen in print or in picture is radically, overwhelming inaccurate. Overwhelmingly! That's not too strong a term. In a year's time, this is in all 1967, I never saw any marijuana. I never saw any drugs. Our sensibilities and our associations were so tight that there wasn't even a thought of antagonism between those being led and those leading.

I don't think the public knows how dirty and devastating the war was, how tough the grunt's job was. What extraordinary deprivation our Marines dealt with on a daily basis! Every single day. Learning how to look after your personal hygiene . . . with a half canteen cup of water. First you'd brush your teeth, then you'd shave in the same water, then you'd take your socks off and squeeze them out in the same water.

The supply system was screwed up. I can remember evacuating my dead from the field and always taking their boots off and seeing these bare feet sticking out from under a poncho and thinking, "My God. We're the richest country on earth and I've got to steal boots off the dead to make sure my men have boots." And seeing one case which tore my heart out. One of my men had gotten (for Christmas) socks, argyle socks from his parents. Here he is, his feet sticking out under a poncho with these argyle socks on because the Marine Corps couldn't get us adequate supplies.

You'd have dysentery and you'd get this, like a mailed fist would grab your gut and just go "crunch" and it would double you over, *wham*! You'd just fall to your knees and double over and evacuate your bowels. You couldn't stop. When your head quit swimming, you got back to your feet, you'd keep driving on.

Lying in an ambush, lying in a puddle, freezing, indescribable. You can't move. You've got to make a head call, you make a head call, but you can't move. You can't dare do anything. Squeezing your eyelids so the sweat will run down over your eyes and you can open your eyes and still get a sight picture on the enemy as he's approaching you because you can't afford to wipe the sweat out of your eyes.

Nobody knows about the enemy atrocities. This fellow I was telling you about that got skinned. When we went up to aid Bravo 1/9, we found their radio operators for some reason had been nailed to trees by their shoulders, just the radio operators. They'd taken these big engineering nails and nailed them to the trees. Nobody's ever heard about those atrocities. It never appeared in *Time* magazine, it didn't in the official history.

With the exception of Guadalcanal, which was a long-term operation, no Marines had ever done this before Vietnam. In our case we went there and we lived through this monsoon, the first people to do this. Nobody'd done that before in Vietnam. They didn't know how cold it was up there. And yet we just went day after day like this. It's amazing how few people even know that that went on. So if you can somehow portray that fact . . . that the written word can't deal with . . . It's almost impossible.

Major Ray Findlay

I'm eternally grateful I didn't miss Vietnam because I've always held in suspect people who did, even though I also held in suspect the people who sent us there. I was glad I didn't miss it. I came home with my mind at ease and said, "You know, it probably wasn't conducted the way it should have been conducted but, hell, if there was a perfect war, you wouldn't need a Marine Corps."

I think when you really register on what a man does who's an American, a man who goes where his president sends him, then the guy that would die in vain is in my mind the guy that didn't go. The point is that if a guy didn't go, then I think that he'd have to worry about where he was instead of where he should have been.

The best company you're ever going to find in combat is in the worst living conditions. All the assholes live around the flagpole. When you get into country, you'd go to Danang or you'd go to Dong Ha, wherever the hell you were, and then out to report to battalion. I thought that was a pretty humble place when I first reported in. Then you'd get down to report into the company, in some *really* humble surroundings.

A guy could get killed out there but if you're going to die, you want to die around those kind of people, around Marines of that quality. I think the thing that really made the rest of my career in the Marine Corps easy was I found if you supported him and lived with him and did what he did and led him right, that that Marine private and lance corporal could do herculean things.

Lance Corporal Ray Wilmer

I've never seen a bond between such a bunch of guys. We very seldom ever argued among ourselves. We complained a lot, but we knew that we needed each other and we had to depend on each other. We would always talk about home, about our families. Very seldom did we talk about dying. It just never came up. We were all young . . . over there if you were twenty-two years old you were considered old. Most of us were eighteen or nineteen years old and we just never did talk about dying.

Corporal Rich Sherwood

I have no regrets and I wouldn't trade a day of it, not a given day in Vietnam for the experience, the friendships, the camaraderie, the incredible esprit de corps that exists within the Marine Corps that I think is so unusually unique to us and so important to what makes us go and continues to this day to keep us going.

Corporal Vito Lavacca

I don't think we were lookin' for a hero's welcome. I just think that we were lookin' to be accepted . . . But I know that I felt very, very different from everyone. Much the same as I would expect a handicapped person or a . . . black person to feel. Just different.

So it was very lonely when I got back. Lonely . . . in 'Nam, lonely back in the States. And I think it's not the thirteen-month tour of duty in Vietnam that's left all the scars. It's the loneliness and hostility that a lot of us felt when we got back to the States. And that lasted for more than thirteen months.

Corporal Ed Seretti

There were a whole lot of bad times. There were some good times, too. There was the closeness. Not growing up with them and knowing them all your life for years and years, you can't believe how close you can get to somebody you hardly know for any length of time. We had a lot of laughs over there, a whole lot of laughs. I guess a bunch of young guys, you put them somewhere, sooner or later they're going to laugh. I'll tell you, I joined the Marine Corps, and I'm certainly glad I did. If I had it to do all over again, I certainly would go again.

Corporal John Mick

These guys died for a reason. They believed in it. If I had to do these years over again, I would with no regrets. I just wish we could do it the way we wanted to do it. We have to live with that right now.

Corporal Kevin Sweeney

I talked to a friend of mine at work. He was in 1/3 and he says every day that we've been alive since we made it back from there is just like an extra day. So you live like that. I more or less believe in that.

PFC Mike Velasquez

As corny as it may sound, I'm proud I was a Marine. It's like the old slogan goes, "Once a Marine, always a Marine." That just speaks for itself.

Chaplain Bob Bedingfield

That's . . . kind of my story. It's . . . kind of my memory. I have no idea what you are going to make out of it. Absolutely none. This has been a series of memories that flowed from the top of my head. I'm grateful. I'm extremely grateful that you allowed me to share these with you.

I was hesitant about doing it. Almost frightened. And not much in this world frightens me. I thank you for the opportunity . . . to talk about people I have not talked about for a long time. But people I really love. Because for those twelve months together, I lived with them, and they were family . . . my kith and my kin.

Yet I suppose that is what the Corps is all about. Once a Marine, always a Marine. I guess in many ways those things I have shared with you . . . prove that to some degree, don't they? There is something about the Corps and there is something about the people in the Corps that isn't like anything else, anywhere.

Thanks for the opportunity . . .

APPENDIX A

• • • • • • • • • • • • • • •

Passing in Review

Ashburn, Lee. (Vietnam Service 1967–68)
  One of Ripley's Raiders and a platoon commander, Lee is the president of
  two lumber companies in North Carolina.
Austin, James. (Vietnam Service 1966–67)
  An early contributor to this work, James was a flamethrower squad leader in
  Vietnam. He now lives in Warren, Ohio.
Bedingfield, Robert W. (Vietnam Service 1968–69)
  A retired Navy captain and holder of two Bronze Star medals for action with
  3/3, Bob is pastor of a church in Michigan.
Belanger, H. Tyrone. (Vietnam Service 1965–66)
  Tyrone works for the U.S. Postal Service in a small town in Massachusetts.
Breeze, Eugene. (Vietnam Service 1965–66)
  Gene received a commission during the Vietnam War and retired a captain.
  He works in security at a North Carolina hospital and is active in veterans'
  groups.

Brocksieker, William H. (Vietnam Service 1965, 1967–68)
Living in a small town in Ohio, Bill works with an appliance company. He may have been the only Marine to serve two tours with 3/3 in Vietnam.

Bussiere, Jeffrey B. (Vietnam Service 1968–69)
One of our corpsmen, Jeff lives on Cape Cod, Massachusetts, where he is a respiratory therapist.

Byrd, James W., III. (Vietnam Service 1969)
Wounded and a veteran of several major operations near the end of 3/3's time in Vietnam, James is a civil engineer draftsman in St. Louis.

Clark, Jimmie C. (Vietnam Service 1965, 1968–69)
A career Marine, Jimmie retired as a master sergeant. He is now with the U.S. Forest Service in Kentucky. He won a Bronze Star medal for heroic action.

Clough, William W., Jr. (Vietnam Service 1967–68)
A mortar forward observer and a survivor of one of the worst ambushes suffered by the battalion, Bill has since earned a degree in social work and is a veterans' counselor for the state of Alabama.

Combs, John A. (Vietnam Service 1968–69)
Another of our corpsmen, Doc Combs spent his tour with the battalion's artillery support where he won a Bronze Star medal. He is a configuration specialist with Ford Aerospace in Florida.

Conner, Gary D. (Vietnam Service 1967–68)
Gary lives in Illinois where he is a deputy fire chief and helps run a family-owned business.

Consalvo, Rod W. (Vietnam Service 1967–68)
Wounded in action in Vietnam, Rod Consalvo is now a supervisor with GTE in California and is still in the Marine Corps Reserve.

Davis, Joseph J. (Vietnam Service 1967)
A squad leader and another of Ripley's Raiders, Joseph is a CPA with an MBA and president of his own business in San Diego.

Elliott, Carl E. (Vietnam Service 1967–68)
Severely wounded in an ambush on his way to join the unit, "Tank" later won a Silver Star medal for the action where he earned his nickname. He is a mechanic in New Jersey.

Evanoff, Thomas. (Vietnam Service 1968–69)
Wounded in action and the holder of three personal decorations, Tom lives in Olympia, Washington.

Findlay, Raymond F. (Vietnam Service 1967–68, 1972–73)
Ray retired from the Corps as a colonel and works in real estate and

development in California. Among his numerous awards is the Legion of
Merit medal, presented for service with 3/3.

Fink, Charles. (Vietnam Service 1965–66)

Wounded in action in Operation STARLITE, Chuck now lives in Florida.

Finn, James P. (Vietnam Service 1967–68)

An insurance investigator, Jim lives in Framingham, Massachusetts, with his
family. He is a veteran of the Boston Marathon as well as Vietnam's "Von
Ryan's Express."

Finton, Patrick. (Vietnam Service 1965–66)

Now a highway engineer in Arizona, Pat received a battlefield commission in
Vietnam and retired as a captain.

Frantz, William. (Vietnam Service 1967–68)

When last heard from, Bill was living and working in Virginia where he was
still struggling with the effects of Vietnam. We have lost touch with him.

George, Kenneth K. (Vietnam Service 1968–69)

A former squad leader and one of the earliest contributors to this work, Ken
is now in the nursery business in New Jersey.

Goodwin, Paul B. (Vietnam Service 1965, 1969)

Paul retired from the Marine Corps as a colonel and is now director of
administration for a law firm. In Vietnam he won numerous awards
including the Silver and Bronze Star medals and Legion of Merit medal.

Hammett, Gary W. (Vietnam Service 1965–66)

Still very active in veterans' affairs, Gary works for the U.S. Postal Service
in Maryland.

Harrington, Michael H. (Vietnam Service 1967)

A retired colonel in the Marine Corps Reserve, Mike is an attorney in
Houston.

Horne, David L. (Vietnam Service 1965–66)

One of the original members of the battalion to land in Vietnam, Dave
retired as a major and now lives in Santa Claus, Indiana.

Howe, James D. (Vietnam Service 1968–69)

A highly decorated policeman since leaving the Corps, Jim won two
personal decorations in Vietnam including the Bronze Star medal.

Jefferson, Bobby. (Vietnam Service 1968–69)

Bobby now lives in Huntsville, Alabama, where he works for a tire company.

Kelly, Thomas J. (Vietnam Service 1967–68)

T. J. lives in Florida where he works for a major airline and runs a small
business. He is also writing a memoir of Vietnam.

Kenerly, William D. (Vietnam Service 1968)

Shot on his ninetieth day in country, Bill was medevaced from Vietnam. He is now an attorney practicing in North Carolina.

Kerlin, Stanley E. (Vietnam Service 1967–68)

A ranger with the Bureau of Land Management, Stan lives in the desert lowlands of California.

Kidwell, Richard G. (Vietnam Service 1965–66)

One of the original members of the battalion, Richard retired from the Marines as a sergeant major. He now works in Florida as a facility supervisor for an adult retirement park.

King, Neal D. (Vietnam Service 1962, 1965–66, 1968–69)

An Iroquois Indian from New York State, Neal was already a veteran of World War II and Korea when he came to 3/3, serving his third tour in his third war. He is retired from the Corps and lives in Virginia.

Lavacca, Vito J. (Vietnam Service 1967–68)

Wounded in action and the holder of four personal decorations, Vito works as a construction manager in Connecticut.

Lehrack, Otto J. (Vietnam Service 1967–68, 1970–71)

A mustang and veteran of two Vietnam tours, Otto retired from the Corps and now lives and works on the Big Island of Hawaii.

McPartland, Guy I. (Vietnam Service 1966–67)

Holder of the Bronze Star medal and Vietnamese Cross of Gallantry, Father Guy is the chaplain for a hospital in New Jersey where he has been for over fifteen years.

Masciangelo, William R. (Vietnam Service 1967–68)

Retired from the Marines as a lieutenant colonel, Bill is an executive with a hotel chain in the Washington, D.C., area.

Mick, John A. (Vietnam Service 1967–68)

Wounded in action and holder of two personal decorations, John is the engineering director for a hospital in Florida.

Miller, Howard G. (Vietnam Service 1965–66)

Now a retired police lieutenant in Kentucky, Howard was another STARLITE veteran.

Montgomery, Robert. (Vietnam Service 1967–68)

An artillery forward observer with 3/3, Bob now lives in California.

Morrison, Vincent C. (Vietnam Service 1968–69)

Vince works in Houston as a national service officer with Paralyzed Veterans of America. In Vietnam he was an artilleryman who provided hundreds of fire missions to 3/3.

Mosher, Thomas C. (Vietnam Service 1966–67)
A San Diego resident for over twelve years, Tom works for a copier company.

Needham, Robert C. (Vietnam Service 1967–68)
A Naval Academy graduate and commanding officer of 3/3 from July 1967 to January 1968, Robert retired as a colonel and now lives in Florida.

Norman, John W., Jr. (Vietnam Service 1966–67)
Living near Pittsburgh, John is employed by the U.S. Postal Service.

O'Neill, Richmond D. (Vietnam Service 1968–69)
Currently a production manager for a national homebuilder, Richmond served as the company commander of Kilo Company in the closing months of 3/3's time in Vietnam. He lives in San Diego.

Payne, Robert L. (Vietnam Service 1967–68)
A rifleman in Mike Company during all of 1968, Lex now lives and works in Florida.

Petty, Arthur. (Vietnam Service 1965–66)
Art was the 1st sergeant of India Company during STARLITE. He is retired from the Corps and lives in Seattle.

Pyles, Craig. (Vietnam Service 1968)
Wounded in action in Vietnam, Craig now lives in Kentucky.

Ramsey, David A. (Vietnam Service 1965–66)
A veteran of Korea and Vietnam, Dave retired as a lieutenant colonel. Twice wounded in action and holder of the Legion of Merit medal and Bronze Star medal, he lives in Virginia.

Ransbottom, Kenneth G. (Vietnam Service 1965–68)
Ken went to Vietnam in 1965 and stayed, voluntarily, for twenty-seven months. He probably spent as much time in the bush as any Marine in the entire war. He now lives in Ohio.

Ripley, John W. (Vietnam Service 1966–67, 1972)
A career Marine who has held numerous prestigious assignments, including that of regimental commander of the 2d Marines at Camp Lejeune, North Carolina, the colonel's list of personal decorations includes the Navy Cross medal, Silver Star medal, Legion of Merit medal, Bronze Star medal, Purple Heart medal, and almost everything else. John G. Miller's *The Bridge at Dong Ha* (Annapolis, Md.: U.S. Naval Institute Press, 1989) is about his heroism on his second Vietnam tour in 1972.

Ryan, Daniel F. (Vietnam Service 1967)
Wounded in action, Dan was a special agent for the FBI after leaving the Corps and is now a private investigator living in Scottsdale, Arizona.

Ryan, Thomas F. (Vietnam Service 1967–68)

A native of Philadelphia, Tom works for a construction company and owns a small business.

Sams, Alan B. (Vietnam Service 1967–68)

A survivor of the 7 February ambush where he won the Bronze Star medal attending the wounded, Doc Sams is a physician's assistant in Georgia.

Seretti, Edwin. (Vietnam Service 1968)

Recipient of two Purple Heart medals, Ed lives in a suburb of Pittsburgh.

Sessions, William W. (Vietnam Service 1967–68)

Holder of the Bronze Star and Purple Heart medals, Will works for a paper company in Georgia.

Sherwood, Richard V. (Vietnam Service 1967–68)

Commissioned after his Vietnam tour, Rich is now a lieutenant colonel and lives in Washington, D.C.

Stanisci, Anthony. (Vietnam Service 1968)

His Vietnam tour shortened by a severe wound, Tony now lives in Arizona.

Stone, Douglas D. (Vietnam Service 1968–69)

Living in Colorado where he makes custom furniture, Doc Stone won a Silver Star medal for gallantry in action and received a Purple Heart medal.

Sweeney, Kevin T. (Vietnam Service 1967–68)

Twice wounded and holder of the Navy Achievement medal, Kevin works as a lineman for a power company in Cleveland.

Tramonte, Peter A. (Vietnam Service 1968–69)

Living in Long Island with his family, Pete is a manager with an electronics company.

Turner, Joe D. (Vietnam Service 1968–69)

Reb is still in the Corps after a career change into the air controller field.

Velasquez, Michael. (Vietnam Service 1967–68)

Wounded in Vietnam, Mike now lives and works in Houston.

Wandell, Jack W. (Vietnam Service 1968–69)

Jack is a businessman who divides his time between Florida and Massachusetts running five different businesses.

Wilmer, Ray K. (Vietnam Service 1969)

Twice wounded in action with 3/3, Ray now works for the U.S. Postal Service near the Blue Ridge Mountains in Virginia.

Wright, Jack. (Vietnam Service 1968)

A platoon commander in John Ripley's company, Jack is now a business executive who lives in Oregon.

Yost, James K. (Vietnam Service 1967–68)

Badly wounded in 1968, Jim lost a leg. As he related, his life after Vietnam has been a struggle. He has since earned a Master's degree and is employed as a veterans' counselor in Pennsylvania.

Zensen, Roger. (Vietnam Service 1967–69)

Roger extended his tour in Vietnam by six months to serve as an air observer after he left 3/3. He retired from the Marines as a lieutenant colonel and now works with Ray Findlay in real estate development in southern California.

APPENDIX B

• • • • • • • • • • • • • • •

Medals of Honor

Three members of the battalion won the nation's highest military decoration—
the Medal of Honor—for service in Vietnam. Their citations follow.

CORPORAL ROBERT E. O'MALLEY'S CITATION:
For conspicuous gallantry and intrepidity in action against the communist (Viet
Cong) forces at the risk of his own life above and beyond the call of duty while
serving as Squad Leader in Company "I," Third Battalion, Third Marines,
Third Marine Division (Reinforced), near An Cu'ong 2, South Vietnam, on
18 August 1965. While leading his squad in the assault against a strongly en-
trenched enemy force, his unit came under intense small arms fire. With complete disregard for his personal safety, Corporal O'Malley raced across an open
rice paddy to a trench line where the enemy forces were located. Jumping into
the trench, he attacked the Viet Cong with his rifle and grenades, and singly
killed eight of the enemy. He then led his squad to the assistance of an adjacent
Marine unit which was suffering heavy casualties. Continuing to press forward,
he reloaded his weapon and fired with telling effect into the enemy emplace-

ment. He personally assisted in the evacuation of several wounded Marines, and again regrouping the remnants of his squad, he returned to the point of the heaviest fighting. Ordered to an evacuation point by an officer, Corporal O'Malley gathered his besieged and badly wounded squad and boldly led them under fire to a helicopter for withdrawal. Although three times wounded in this encounter, and facing imminent death from a fanatic and determined enemy, he steadfastly refused evacuation and continued to cover his squad's boarding of the helicopters while, from an exposed position, he delivered fire against the enemy until his wounded men were evacuated. Only then, with his last mission accomplished, did he permit himself to be removed from the battlefield. By his valor, leadership, and courageous efforts in behalf of his comrades, he served as an inspiration to all who observed him, and reflected the highest credit upon the Marine Corps and the United States Naval Service.

LANCE CORPORAL WILLIAM R. PROM'S CITATION:
For conspicuous gallantry and intrepidity at the risk of his life above and beyond the call of duty while serving as a Machine Gun Squad leader with Company I, Third Battalion, Third Marines, Third Marine Division, in action against the enemy in the Republic of Vietnam. While returning from a reconnaissance operation on 9 February 1969 during Operation TAYLOR COMMON, two platoons of Company I came under an intense automatic weapons fire and grenade attack from a well-concealed North Vietnamese Army force in fortified positions. The leading element of the platoon was isolated and several Marines were wounded. Lance Corporal Prom immediately assumed control of one of his machine guns and began to deliver return fire. Disregarding his own safety he advanced to a position from which he could more effectively deliver covering fire while first aid was administered to the wounded men. Realizing that the enemy would have to be destroyed before the injured Marines could be evacuated, Lance Corporal Prom again moved forward and delivered a heavy volume of fire with such accuracy that he was instrumental in routing the enemy, thus permitting his men to regroup and resume their march. Shortly thereafter the platoon again came under heavy fire in which one man was critically wounded. Reacting instantly, Lance Corporal Prom moved forward to protect his injured comrade. Unable to continue his own fire because of severe wounds, he continued to advance to within a few yards of the enemy positions. There, standing in full view of the enemy, he accurately directed the fire of his support elements until he was mortally wounded. Inspired by his heroic actions, the Marines launched an assault that destroyed the enemy. Lance Corporal Prom's indomitable courage, inspiring initiative and selfless devotion to duty, upheld the highest traditions

of the Marine Corps and the United States Naval Service. He gallantly gave his life for his country.

PRIVATE FIRST CLASS RONALD L. COKER'S CITATION:
For conspicuous gallantry and intrepidity at the risk of his life above and beyond the call of duty while serving as a Rifleman with Company M, Third Battalion, Third Marines, Third Marine Division, in action against enemy forces in the Republic of Vietnam. On 24 March 1969, while serving as Point Man for the Second Platoon, Private First Class Coker was leading his patrol when he encountered five enemy soldiers on a narrow jungle trail. Private First Class Coker's squad aggressively pursued them to a cave. As the squad neared the cave, it came under intense hostile fire, seriously wounding one Marine and forcing the others to take cover. Observing the wounded man lying exposed to continuous enemy fire, Private First Class Coker disregarded his own safety and moved across the fire-swept terrain toward his companion. Although wounded by enemy small-arms fire, he continued to crawl across the hazardous area and skillfully threw a hand grenade into the enemy positions, suppressing the hostile fire sufficiently to enable him to reach the wounded man. As he began to drag his injured comrade toward safety, a grenade landed on the wounded Marine. Unhesitatingly, Private First Class Coker grasped it with both hands and turned away from his wounded companion, but before he could dispose of the grenade it exploded. Severely wounded, but undaunted, he refused to abandon his comrade. As he moved toward friendly lines, two more enemy grenades exploded near him, inflicting still further injuries. Concerned only for the safety of his comrade, Private First Class Coker, with supreme effort, continued to crawl and pull the wounded Marine with him. His heroic deeds inspired his fellow Marines to such aggressive action that the enemy fire was suppressed sufficiently to enable others to reach him and carry him to a relatively safe area where he succumbed to his extensive wounds. Private First Class Coker's indomitable courage, inspiring initiative, and selfless devotion to duty upheld the highest traditions of the Marine Corps and of the United States Naval Service. He gallantly gave his life for his country.

APPENDIX C

. . . .

Organization of Marine Infantry Units in Vietnam

The ranks and numbers of personnel are those called for by organizational tables. In practice, because of casualties and other reasons, the ranks were sometimes a grade or two below those specified, and the unit had fewer members. Since this book concentrates on war at the small unit level, greater detail is provided for the smaller units than for the larger.

Fire Team. The smallest maneuver element in any Marine Corps infantry unit is a fire team.
   Fire Team Leader—Corporal
   Automatic Rifleman (AR)—Lance Corporal
   Assistant Automatic Rifleman—PFC
   Rifleman—PFC

Squad. Made up of three fire teams and
   Squad Leader—Sergeant

Platoon. Made up of three squads and
  Platoon Commander—Lieutenant
  Platoon Sergeant—Staff Sergeant
  Platoon Guide—Sergeant

Weapons Platoon. During Vietnam, the weapons platoon consisted of the crews necessary to man six M60 machine guns, six 3.5-inch rocket launchers, and three 60-mm mortars. The 3.5-inch rocket launcher was gradually phased out during the war, in favor of the Light Antitank Assault Weapon (LAAW). This weapon was a portable, one-shot rocket launcher. The LAAW gunners would usually carry several of these on a packboard.
  Weapons Platoon Commander—Lieutenant
  Weapons Platoon Sergeant—Gunnery Sergeant

Company. Made up of three platoons, as outlined above, a weapons platoon, and
  Company Commander—Captain
  Executive Officer (XO)—Lieutenant
  First Sergeant—First Sergeant
  Gunnery Sergeant—Gunnery Sergeant

Battalion. Made up of four infantry companies, as outlined above, and a Headquarters and Service Company (H and S). In addition to administrative functions, H and S Company supported the rifle companies with an 81-mm mortar platoon (eight guns and their crews), a 106-mm recoilless rifle section (eight guns and their crews), and a flame section (eight flamethrowers and their crews). In addition to the command element the battalion has a staff as indicated.

  Command element:
  Battalion Commander—Lieutenant Colonel
  Battalion Executive Officer (XO)—Major
  Battalion Sergeant Major—Sergeant Major

  Staff:
  S-1 (Administration)—Captain
  S-2 (Intelligence)—Captain
  S-3 (Operations)—Major
  S-4 (Logistics)—Captain

  Adjutant—Lieutenant
  Chaplain—Lieutenant, U.S. Navy
  Communications Officer—Lieutenant
  Motor Transport Officer—Lieutenant

Supply Officer—Lieutenant
Surgeon—Lieutenant, U.S. Navy

Regiment. Consists of three infantry battalions, as outlined above, and

Command element:
Regimental Commander—Colonel
Regimental Executive Officer (XO)—Lieutenant Colonel
Regimental Sergeant Major—Sergeant Major

Staff: Generally the same staff as that on the battalion level except that each position calls for one rank higher at the regiment.

Division. Consists of three infantry regiments, as outlined above, plus an artillery regiment. It is commanded by a major general, whose assistant is a brigadier general. The staff organization is generally the same as for regiment and battalion. The differences are that staff officers here are a grade higher than at the lower levels and are designated by "G," e.g. G-1, rather than "S." Often, the S or G is dropped in conversation and a Marine might refer to the "1," etc.

Miscellaneous.

Attachments. In addition to the formal organization, any size unit may have various persons or weapons systems attached to them for a specific operation. Some of those mentioned in this book are:

Dusters
Engineers
Forward Air Controller (FAC)
Forward Observers (FO) for either artillery, mortars, or both
Ontos
Quad-50s
Scout Dogs and their handlers
Snipers
Tactical Air Control Party (TACP) consisting of the FAC and his radio operators
Tanks

Medical battalions. The medical battalions, those who most often treat combat casualties, are made up of lettered companies, e.g., Company D, 3d Medical Battalion. They are usually referred to by their alphabetical designator and the word "med." In the case here, this company would commonly be called "Delta med."

Command relationships. At best, these were confusing during the Vietnam War. Not only were chains of command frequently ignored but there was the delicate task of dealing with the Vietnamese military command and the commands of our third-party allies. What follows is a very general outline.

The Commander, United States Military Assistance Command (COMUSMACV), had operational control over all U.S. forces in Vietnam. He reported nominally to the Commander in Chief Pacific (CINPAC), an admiral based at Pearl Harbor. His real bosses were the National Command Authority—the President of the United States and the Secretary of Defense.

Vietnam was divided into four major military regions. The northernmost of these was I (eye) Corps. During the period that is covered in this book, the senior officer was a Marine lieutenant general, commander of the 3d Marine Amphibious Force (III MAF). Although the CG of III MAF was bound by the instructions of COMUSMACV for operational matters, he also reported to the Commanding General Fleet Marine Force Pacific (CG FMFPAC) for administrative matters. CG FMFPAC was another Marine lieutenant general, headquartered in Honolulu, who reported directly to CINCPAC in operational matters but to the Commandant of the Marine Corps in Washington, D.C., for administrative requirements.

XXIV Corps was a U.S. Army command, created during the Tet Offensive of 1968. Commanded by an Army lieutenant general, XXIV Corps reported to CG III MAF during the crisis. When the Marines finally began withdrawing from Vietnam in large numbers, XXIV Corps assumed command of all U.S. forces in I Corps.

GLOSSARY

• • • • • • • • • • • • • • •

Weapons. Reference to weaponry, as used in Vietnam, was by no means standard. For example, a 155-mm artillery piece may have been referred to as a 155, a 155 mike mike, or a 155 millimeter. An M79 was often called a 79 and an M16 a 16. A 60 may have been an M60 machine gun or a 60-mm mortar, depending on context.

3.5-inch rocket launcher. U.S. anti-armor weapon which was gradually phased out in favor of the LAAW.

5.56 millimeter. Ammunition used by U.S. M16 rifle.

7.62 millimeter. The standard NATO size cartridge adopted by the U.S. in the early 1960s to be fired in the M14 rifle and the M60 machine gun. Also the size projectile used by Soviet- and Chinesemade AK47s.

8-inch. Large U.S. artillery piece.

12.7 millimeter. Soviet or Chinese heavy machine gun. The equivalent of the U.S. .50 caliber.

20 millimeter. The size round fired by many aircraft cannon.

.38 caliber. A revolver.

.45 caliber. The U.S. standard automatic pistol in Vietnam.

.50 caliber. The standard U.S. heavy machine gun.

57 millimeter. Recoilless rifle used by NVA.

60 millimeter. Mortar used by both NVA and U.S.

75 millimeter. Pack howitzer, probably French made, used by NVA.

81 millimeter. Standard infantry mortar of U.S. forces. The NVA often had some 81s that had been captured from U.S. or ARVN units.

82 millimeter. Standard infantry mortar of the Soviets and Chinese. Much used by the NVA.

90 millimeter. Size of the main gun on U.S. tanks.

105 millimeter. The most common U.S. artillery piece.

106 millimeter. Recoilless rifle used by U.S.

122 millimeter. Soviet or Chinese rocket used by the NVA.

130 millimeter. Artillery piece used by NVA.

152 millimeter. The largest artillery piece in the NVA arsenal.

155 millimeter. U.S. artillery piece.

AK47. Standard assault rifle of NVA.

B40. A shoulder-fired antitank rocket used by NVA.

Bangalore torpedo. Used to breach barbed wire, it consisted of five-foot lengths of metal tubing filled with explosive.

C4. Plastic explosive.

Claymore. Directional, command-detonated, antipersonnel mine.

LAAW. U.S. Light Antitank Assault Weapon. A one-shot, throw away weapon used mostly in Vietnam against bunkers.

M1. Standard U.S. rifle in World War II and Korea. Found among VC and NVA in small numbers.

M14. The standard Marine rifle in Vietnam until early 1967 when it was replaced by the M16.

M16. The standard rifle in Vietnam from early 1967.

M26. The most common type of U.S. fragmentation grenade used in Vietnam.

M60 machine gun. Standard U.S. 7.62-mm machine gun.

M79 U.S. shoulder-fired 40-mm grenade launcher.

RPG. Rocket-propelled grenade. Anti-armor weapon used by NVA.

Thompson submachine gun. A .45-caliber automatic weapon made in U.S.

Other terms and abbreviations.

A-4. Attack aircraft. Skyhawk.

AO. Air observer. One who rode in a light spotter aircraft to perform reconnaissance and fire-control missions.

Apron. A configuration of defensive barbed wire.

Arc-light. A B-52 strike conducted in South Vietnam. Similar missions conducted in the north were called Rolling Thunder.

Arresting gear. The equipment that arrests aircraft landing on aircraft carrier decks or small runways.

ARVN. Army of the Republic of Vietnam (South Vietnam). The term was commonly used to refer to both the individual soldiers and the South Vietnamese army itself. It was pronounced to rhyme with "Marvin."

AWOL. Absent without leave.

Basic School. The school attended by all Marine officers once they are commissioned.

Battery. A U.S. artillery battery consists of six guns. To shoot a Battery one is to have all the guns in the battery fire one round.

BNG. Brand new guy or new arrival to Vietnam. In some units called FNG (fucking new guy).

Booked. Slang for departed.

Bronze Star. Fourth highest U.S. combat award.

C-130. A cargo aircraft. Hercules.

CH-34. The smallest of the troop and cargo carrying helicopters used by the Marines. Sea Horse.

CH-46. Medium-lift helicopter. Sea Knight.

CH-53. Heavy-lift helicopter. Sea Stallion.

Click. Slang for kilometer.

COC. Combat Operations Center.

Comm. Slang for communications.

COMUSMACV. Commander, U.S. Military Assistance Command, Vietnam. Often condensed to MACV and pronounced "Mack-vee."

Concertina. Large rolls of barbed wire used in this configuration.

Corpsman. A medical corpsman is an enlisted sailor who serves with Marines and takes care of their medical needs. *See also* Docs.

County Fair. A keystone of the U.S. attempt to pacify the population of South Vietnam, County Fairs were cordon and search operations designed to separate the VC from their population bases.

CP. Command post.

Crew-served. A weapon that requires more than one person to effectively operate, e.g., the M60 machine gun.

DC-3. Called the "gooney bird" in World War II, this aircraft found some limited application in Vietnam.

DMZ. Demilitarized Zone. The zone centered on the Ben Hai River and separated North and South Vietnam during the war.

Docs. Enlisted medical corpsmen are almost always affectionately called this by Marines. The medical officers, who are physicians, are always called "doctor."

Duster. A light armored vehicle with two 40-mm guns. In Vietnam they were generally used for convoy security.

E-tool. Entrenching tool. A small folding shovel used for digging fighting holes and the like.

Embark. To load aboard.

Exec. Executive officer. *See also* XO.

F-4. Fighter-attack aircraft. Phantom.

F-8. Fighter aircraft. Crusader.

FAC. Forward air controller. A Marine pilot who directs combat aircraft in support of ground units. He may do this from on the ground, with those he is supporting, or from the air.

Fighting Mad. The radio call sign for the 3d Battalion, 3d Marines for much of the war.

Fire for effect. Command given supporting arms when the forward observer is satisfied that they are registered on the target. Usually preceded by the firing of spotter rounds to ascertain this fact.

Flak jacket. Properly known as "body armor, upper torso," these were the armored vests worn by U.S. troops.

FM. Frequency modulated. Refers to several types of tactical radios.

FO. Forward observer. A spotter for mortars and artillery who adjusts rounds onto the target.

Four holer. Field toilet facility.

FPL. Final protective line. Defensive fires around one's position, preregistered if possible, which are generally used only when under heavy attack. Sometimes called final protective fire.

Frag. 1. (n) A fragmentation grenade. 2. (v) To use a fragmentation grenade in the murder or attempted murder of a disliked officer or NCO. 3. (n) A fragmentary, or informal, combat order.

Free fire zone. In Vietnam, an area from which noncombatants were removed. Anyone remaining in the designated area could be regarded as enemy and could be fired upon.

Grenadier. A Marine who carried the M79 grenade launcher as his primary weapon.

Gunnery sergeant. This is both a rank, pay grade E-7, and a position, that of the operations NCO of a rifle company. Commonly called "gunny."

Hand whizzer. Hand-operated pyrotechnic device.

HAWK. Antiaircraft missile fired by the LAAM units.

Heat tab. A small chemical briquette that, when lighted, provided intense heat for a short period of time. Used to heat rations.

Hell box. Firing mechanism used to detonate explosives, e.g., C4, or dynamite.

High port gallop. Moving out rapidly with weapons at the ready.

Ho Chi Minh. The leader of North Vietnam for much of the war.

Ho Chi Minh sandals. Footware made from discarded tires and inner tubes.

Huey. Popular name for HU1E helicopter, which was used both as command aircraft and as a gunship.

ITR. Infantry training regiment. Where all enlisted Marines received advanced infantry skills after they finished recruit training or boot camp.

JATO bottle. Jet-assisted take off. A small booster rocket that assisted aircraft in getting off the ground from short runways.

K-bar. A sheath knife.

KIA. Killed in action.

LAAM. Light Antiaircraft Missile units. One of these was the first U.S. combat unit deployed to Vietnam. *See also* HAWK.

Line charge. A high-explosive charge shaped like a large line, or rope, which is first propelled ahead of the vehicle into a minefield or other target and then detonated.

LP. Listening post. A small group of men stationed outside the lines or along trails at night who listened for and warned of enemy approach.

LST. Landing ship tank. Flat-bottomed naval vessel that could land tanks and other equipment directly across a beach.

LVT. Landing vehicle tracked. Amphibious, lightly armored vehicle that could bring Marines ashore and also carry them on land. The "E" model could clear minefields and the "C" could host a small command post.

LZ. Landing zone. Any place where helicopters were called upon to land.

MACV. *See* COMUSMACV.

Mechanical mule. A small four-wheeled vehicle that could haul cargo or weapons over mildly rough terrain.

Medal of Honor. Highest U.S. military decoration. Often erroneously called the Congressional Medal of Honor.

Medevac. Medical evacuation. Often, but not always, in Vietnam by helicopter.

MiG. Soviet made fighter aircraft.

Mighty Mite. A mini jeep that did not enjoy a particularly good reputation.

Mike mike. Phonetic pronunciation of mm, i.e., millimeter.

Montagnards. One of several hill tribes who occupy the border regions of Vietnam but are not ethnically Vietnamese.

Mount out. To pack up and leave.

Navy Cross. The nation's second highest military award.

NCOIC. Noncommissioned officer in charge.

Nguyen Cao Ky. One of the leaders of South Vietnam during the war.

Number 10. Slang for poor quality, or last, Number 1 being the best.

NVA. North Vietnamese Army. More properly called the Peoples Army of Vietnam. NVA, like ARVN, its counterpart in the south, was popularly used to refer to individual soldiers as well as the army itself.

OCS. Officer Candidate School. The commissioning school for Marine officers located at Quantico, Virginia.

One-four. The radio call number of the tactical air control party. Often used to refer to members of that party.

One-six. The radio call number of medical personnel.

OP. Observation post. A post manned by small groups of men to observe and report on enemy activity. *See also* LP.

Payable. One of the radio call signs for the 3d Battalion, 3d Marines during the war.

PC. Personnel carrier. A small truck.

Probe. An attempt by an attacking force to learn something about the defending force by sending small reconnaissance forces, or launching exploratory attacks, against the enemy line.

Punji pit. Pit filled with sharpened stakes, placed in camouflaged position on or near trails.

Purple Heart. Medal awarded for wounds received from the enemy. Since 1985 it has ranked immediately behind the Bronze Star in importance.

PX. Post exchange. Place where sundry items, tobacco, soap, and the like can be purchased.

Quantico, Virginia. Training ground for nearly all Marine officers.

R and R. Rest and recuperation. During Vietnam, it was the only escape from the war afforded the field troops. It lasted five days.

Razorback. A steep hill northeast of the Rockpile in Quang Tri Province.

Recon. Abbreviation for reconnaissance. Can refer to both the act of reconnaissance or to a reconnaissance unit.

Rough Riders. The name given the Marine vehicular supply convoys in Vietnam.

Route column. A formation whose main consideration is rapid advance rather than military security.

Sappers. Enemy engineer troops who are trained and equipped to breach a fortification.

Satchel charge. A quantity of explosive in a bag, or satchel, which, with its detonating mechanism, is placed or thrown against a fortification or other object with the goal of destroying it.

Seabees. Nickname for U.S. Navy construction battalions.

Short. One whose tour in Vietnam is almost over.

Silver Star. The nation's third highest combat decoration.

Six-by. Two-and-a-half ton or five-ton truck that has six drive wheels.

Skyhawk. *See* A-4.

Soft cover. Cloth cap.

Sortie. One combat flight by one aircraft.

Spider trap. A small, well-camouflaged hole that can be used by a soldier to conceal himself from the enemy. Called thus because of a species of spider that does the same thing.

Starlight scope. A passive light gathering device that permits one to see with remarkable clarity at night.

Tanglefoot. A way of configuring barbed wire at ankle deep height.

TAOR. Tactical area of responsibility.

Tet. The Vietnamese lunar new year. Commonly used to refer to the offensive launched by North Vietnam during that holiday in 1968.

Top. Informal form of address used for enlisted Marines above the rank of gunnery sergeant.

Two-four. Radio call number for the artillery forward observer.

Utilities. The Marine field uniform. In the army, the same uniform is called "fatigues."

VC. Viet Cong. Communist guerrillas.

Wet-net training. To practice climbing down nets of amphibious transports into landing craft.

White phosphorus. A very hot incendirary round fired by several types of weapons.

Willie peter. Slang for both white phosphorus and waterproof.

XO. Executive officer. Second in command of a unit.

BIBLIOGRAPHY

. . . .

The bulk of the material for this book came from several thousand pages of audiotape transcripts, recorded at my request by the Marines and sailors of the 3d Battalion, 3d Marines. The following works were also consulted.

Bendell, Lee R. "Marine Patrol." *Marine Corps Gazette*, November 1968, 99–102.
Davidson, Phillip B. *Vietnam at War*. Novato, Calif.: Presidio, 1988.
Findlay, Raymond F. "Behind the Hedgerow." *Marine Corps Gazette*, April 1969, 22–26.
Halberstam, David. *The Best and the Brightest*. New York: Random House, 1972.
Hammond, J. W., Jr. "Combat Journal." Parts 1, 2. *Marine Corps Gazette*, July 1968, 22–29; August 1968, 20–32.
Harrison, James P. *The Endless War*. New York: Macmillan, 1982.
Herr, Michael. *Dispatches*. New York: Alfred A. Knopf, 1977.
Herring, George C. *America's Longest War*. New York: John Wiley and Sons, 1979.
Karnow, Stanley. *Vietnam: A History*. New York: Viking, 1983.
Krulak, Victor H. *First to Fight: An Inside View of the U.S. Marine Corps*. Annapolis, Md.: Naval Institute Press, 1984.
Lewy, Guenter. *America in Vietnam*. New York: Oxford, 1978.
McAllister, John T., Jr. *Vietnam: The Origins of Revolution*. New York: Doubleday, 1971.
The Marines in Vietnam, 1954–1973: An Anthology and Annotated Bibliography. Washington, D.C.: U.S. Marine Corps, History and Museums Division, 1985.

Peatross, Oscar F. "Victory at Van Tuong Village." In *Naval Review 1968*. Annapolis, Md.: Naval Institute Press, 1968.

The Pentagon Papers. New York: Beacon Press, 1971.

Ripley, John W. "Tiger Tale." *Marine Corps Gazette*, June 1977, 39–44.

Schulze, Richard C. *Leatherneck Square*. Incline Valley, Nev.: Huckleberry Press of Lake Tahoe, 1989.

Shulimson, Jack. *U.S. Marines in Vietnam: An Expanding War, 1966*. Washington, D.C.: U.S. Marine Corps, History and Museums Division, 1982.

Shulimson, Jack, and Major Charles M. Johnson. *U.S. Marines in Vietnam: The Landing and the Buildup, 1965*. Washington, D.C.: U.S. Marine Corps, History and Museums Division, 1978.

Smith, Charles R. *U.S. Marines in Vietnam: High Mobility and Standdown, 1969*. Washington, D.C.: U.S. Marine Corps, History and Museums Division, 1988.

Smith, Richard B. "Leatherneck Square." *Marine Corps Gazette*, August 1968, 34–42.

Telfer, Gary L., Lane Rogers, and Keith Fleming. *U.S. Marines in Vietnam: Fighting the North Vietnamese, 1967*. Washington, D.C.: U.S. Marine Corps, History and Museums Division, 1984.

3d Battalion, 3d Marines, 3d Marine Division (Reinforced), Fleet Marine Force. *Command Chronology*, 1 June 1965 to 31 December 1969 (published monthly; declassified in 1988). Fleet Post Office, San Francisco, Calif.

Thompson, W. Scott, and Donaldson D. Frizzell, eds. *The Lessons of Vietnam*. New York: Crane, Russak, 1977.

Westmoreland, William C. *A Soldier Reports*. New York: Doubleday, 1971.

INDEX

• • • • • • • • • • • • • •